Economic Development Strategies and the Evolution of Violence in Latin America

POLITICS, ECONOMICS, AND INCLUSIVE DEVELOPMENT

Series Editors
William Ascher, Claremont McKenna College
John M. Heffron, Soka University of America
Natalia Mirovitskaya, Duke University

The Politics, Economics, and Inclusive Development series examines the challenges and progress in promoting humanistic development. The complex tasks of simultaneously pursuing economic growth, broad participation and equity, democratic peace, and sustainability require scholarship that merges in-depth analysis of the many factors that influence development outcomes with contextually rich experiences. The single- or multiauthored monographs use an interdisciplinary methodology to explore diverse experiences of individual nations, world regions, or the entire global system in their quest for more democratic, technically sound, and sustainable development. The publications from the *Politics, Economics, and Inclusive Development* series will be valuable to students, scholars, policymakers, and international development practitioners.

Economic Development Strategies and the Evolution of Violence in Latin America

Edited by
William Ascher and Natalia Mirovitskaya

Prepared under the auspices of the
Pacific Basin Research Center.
Soka University of America

ECONOMIC DEVELOPMENT STRATEGIES AND THE EVOLUTION OF VIOLENCE IN LATIN AMERICA
Copyright © William Ascher and Natalia Mirovitskaya, 2012.

All rights reserved.

First published in 2012 by
PALGRAVE MACMILLAN®
in the United States—a division of St. Martin's Press LLC,
175 Fifth Avenue, New York, NY 10010.

Where this book is distributed in the UK, Europe and the rest of the world, this is by Palgrave Macmillan, a division of Macmillan Publishers Limited, registered in England, company number 785998, of Houndmills, Basingstoke, Hampshire RG21 6XS.

Palgrave Macmillan is the global academic imprint of the above companies and has companies and representatives throughout the world.

Palgrave® and Macmillan® are registered trademarks in the United States, the United Kingdom, Europe and other countries.

ISBN: 978–1–137–27268–3

Library of Congress Cataloging-in-Publication Data

    Economic development strategies and the evolution of violence in Latin America / edited by William Ascher and Natalia Mirovitskaya.
      p. cm.—(Prepared under the auspices of the Pacific Basin Research Center, Soka University of America)
      ISBN 978–1–137–27268–3 (hardback : alk. paper)
      1. Latin America—Economic policy. 2. Economic development—Latin America. 3. Violence—Latin America. I. Ascher, William.
    II. Mirovitskaya, N. S. (Natalia Sergeevna)

HC125.E3733 2012
338.98—dc23   2012017258

A catalogue record of the book is available from the British Library.

Design by Newgen Imaging Systems (P) Ltd., Chennai, India.

First edition: November 2012

10 9 8 7 6 5 4 3 2 1

Transferred to Digital Printing in 2013

To Lisa Hirschfelder, the beloved Matriarch—WA

To Raisa Anatolievna Mirovitskaya, whose wisdom and grace in the face of adversity have guided me for many years—NM

Contents

List of Illustrations ix

Preface and Acknowledgments xi

List of Contributors xv

Chapter 1 Economic Development Patterns and the Evolution of Violence in Latin America 1
William Ascher and Natalia Mirovitskaya

Chapter 2 Violent Conflict and Unequal Development: The Case of Mexico 41
Judith Teichman

Chapter 3 The Evolution of Violence: Economic Development and Intergroup Conflict in Guatemala, El Salvador, and Costa Rica 71
Gustavo Arcia

Chapter 4 Violence and Sectoral Development in Colombia 95
Jennifer S. Holmes and Sheila Amin Gutiérrez de Piñeres

Chapter 5 On the Brink of Violence: Work, Fear, and the State in the Bolivian Regions 125
William T. Barndt

Chapter 6 Sowing Conflict in Venezuela: Political Violence and Economic Policy 153
Deborah L. Norden

Chapter 7	Education Policy and Conflict in Latin America: Lessons from Chile and Venezuela *Emily K. Penner*	181
Chapter 8	Economic Exclusion and the Shifting Patterns of Violence in Argentina and Brazil *Peter Kingstone*	213

Index   251

Illustrations

Figures

1.1 Income distribution and perceptions of income fairness, major Latin American countries — 26
3.1 Homicide rates per 100,000 people, 2011 — 73
4.1 Oil as a proportion of departmental GDP, 1990–2007 — 101
4.2 Human rights violations with attributions of responsibility in Arauca — 103
4.3 Human rights violations with attributions of responsibility in Casanare — 103
4.4 Coffee, as a proportion of departmental GDP — 105
4.5 Human rights violations with attributions of responsibility in Caldas — 106
4.6 Human rights violations with attributions of responsibility in Tolima — 107
4.7 Human rights violations with attributions of responsibility in Quindio — 107
4.8 Proportion of departmental GDP that is ranching and plantation agriculture — 111
4.9 Human rights violations with attributions of responsibility in Caquetá — 112
4.10 Human rights violations with attributions of responsibility in Chocó — 114
4.11 Human rights violations with attributions of responsibility in Meta — 115
4.12 Human rights violations with attributions of responsibility in Cesar — 115
4.13 Coca cultivation in hectares — 117

4.14	Human rights violations with attributions of responsibility in Putumayo	117
4.15	Human rights violations with attributions of responsibility in Nariño	119
4.16	Human rights violations with attributions of responsibility in Guaviare	120
5.1	Political violence in Bolivia, 1985–2008	126
5.2	Political violence in the central valleys, 1985–2008	128
5.3	Political violence in the eastern lowlands, 1985–2008	129
5.4	Political violence in the western highlands, 1985–2008	130
6.1	Inequality and poverty in Venezuela	162
6.2	Oil and GDP/PC in Venezuela, 1969–2008	173

Tables

1.1	Homicide rates of Latin American countries	4
1.2	Gini index of inequality, Venezuela, 1985–2007	27
3.1	Economic value of violence and crime in Central America per year	74
3.2	A conceptual framework for analyzing the links between the risk factors and economic variables affecting social welfare	75
3.3	Comparison of selected social and economic indicators in three Central American countries, 2009	80
3.4	Indicators of the rule of law in the three countries in Central America, 2010 and 2011	81
3.5	Rate of homicides per 100,000 people and estimated number of gang members by country	87
3.6	Percent of Costa Rican households reporting a crime committed against a household member	88
4.1	Select indicators for Arauca and Casanare	101
4.2	Select indicators for Caldas, Tolima, and Quindio	108
4.3	Select indicators for Caquetá, Chocó, Meta, and Cesar	113
4.4	Select indicators for Putumayo, Nariño, and Guaviare	118
7.1	Historical comparison of constructive and obstructive education policies and policy environments in Chile and Venezuela	183

Preface and Acknowledgments

The roots of this book come from a major multicountry research project on Economic Development Strategies to Avert Collective Violence, which started in 2009 with the support of the Pacific Basic Research Center of Soka University of America.

Development and conflict, though seemingly two sides of any major societal change, historically have been studied by different disciplines. More recently, however, they have become linked both in discourse and in much policy. The so-called conflict-security-development nexus has pervaded today's discussions in national planning agencies and economic ministries of many countries as well as in international development institutions. In today's world, where boundaries are blurred, authorities are fragmented and often powerless against nonstate actors, and new security threats emerge and metastasize unpredictably, the very existence of this nexus demands a well-informed and carefully crafted response from policymakers and development practitioners. A *global conflict syndrome*—the sum of factors that work in parallel to undermine the stability, prosperity, and security of many nation-states and their citizens—requires rigorous analysis of multiple linkages between development patterns and conflict as well as innovative ideas on how to effectively incorporate conflict prevention into the development interventions.

However, there is much less understanding, or at least consensus, about the mechanisms behind these linkages. And there is even less understanding of the economic development patterns that can create conditions of the peaceful coexistence and cooperation of different elements of the population and encourage their cooperation. The goal of the project is to determine which development strategies and specific policies create conditions that reduce the likelihood of intergroup violence, especially in developing and transitional countries.

Drawing extensively on the combination of multiple-case-study approaches, this project provides an in-depth analysis of how particular choices of development strategies may create (or magnify) the deep fault lines among collective actors, whether defined by social characteristics (shared ethnicity, language, religion, or regional identity), socioeconomic class, or political identity and role (i.e., government, opposition, or parties to patron-client relationships). In times of stresses (external shocks, economic crises, or internal political uncertainty), these fault lines may be used by conflict entrepreneurs to radicalize and mobilize groups into violence of different types and varying degree and duration. In some cases, the choice of development policies has heightened perceptions of a group's economic, political, social, and cultural disadvantages; in others it contributed to an overlap of various group cleavages; in both cases increasing their salience and inflammatory potential.

The project contributors were able to demonstrate not only how development per se (as measured by various economic indicators) is linked to the likelihood of large-scale societal violence, but most importantly they identify the multiple pathways connecting particular strategies and subsequent development patterns to large-scale violence. Until now these questions have not been addressed in depth in literature and this research project provides a unique contribution to the study of "development-violence" nexus.

This volume presents project findings for Latin America—a region that thus far has seen a unique combination of all forms of intergroup violence. The authors of the chapters were able to trace various pathways between development strategies adopted by Latin American governments of different orientations and the propensity of these societies to experience different forms of collective violence. We hope that these findings will be helpful for policymakers, development practitioners, and civil society leaders.

Various parts of this volume have been presented at workshops at Soka University (May 2010 and November 2011) and at Duke (October 2010). We are grateful for insights and comments from all the participants of these workshops. We are indebted to Soka University of America for the financial and administrative support, and for the fine work of Dr. John M. Heffron, Professor of History at Soka and Associate Director of the PBRC, ably assisted by Jason Tran, Jacqueline Mills, and Dawn Minette, in organizing workshops and overseeing the administration required to put together a collected volume such as this. We are also appreciative of the efforts of the Duke Center for International Development, especially Jonathan Abels, for arranging talks and workshop sessions that contributed to shaping the chapters in this volume. Valuable research assistance was provided by Claremont McKenna College students—Heather Beck, Nathan Bengtsson, Molly

Doyle, Jennifer Good, Isabel Harbaugh, Shanna Hoversten, Catherine Raney, Carlton Rueb, Laura Spann, and Jennifer Zavaleta, as well as Ariana Ascher and Kaitlyn Tsai.

At various stages of this project, the editors received helpful suggestions and insightful comments from Jaan Valsiner, Phyllis Pomerantz, Jenny Taw, Aseema Sinha, Michael Lofchie, Sebastian Lopez Azumendi, and Bautista Logioco.

Contributors

Gustavo Arcia is a Senior Economist at Analítica, where he specializes in education finance, social safety nets, poverty measurement, and fiscal policy in the social sectors. Previously he was a Senior Economist at RTI International and an Adjunct Associate Professor of Public Policy at Duke University. He has done extensive field work in Central and South America, Central and East Asia, and West Africa. He is currently working on issues of school autonomy and school accountability in Thailand.

William Ascher is the Donald C. McKenna Professor of Government and Economics at Claremont McKenna College. In addition to his earlier book specifically on Latin American politics and economics, *Scheming for the Poor: The Politics of Redistribution in Latin America*, he has written six books on the political economy or development covering multiple regions, including Latin America.

William T. Barndt joined the Department of Political Science at the University of California, Riverside, after receiving his doctorate from Princeton University in 2008. He is currently completing a book titled *Democracy for Sale: Business Parties and the New Conservative Politics in the Americas*, which identifies and explains the rise of a new family of corporation-based political parties in the Western hemisphere. In addition, he has published articles on the social foundations of democracy, business politics, and economic policy in *Latin American Politics & Society*, *World Politics*, and edited volumes.

Sheila Amin Gutiérrez de Piñeres, Professor of Economics, Dean of Undergraduate Education, and Mary McDermott Cook Distinguished Chair at the University of Texas at Dallas, specializes in the interdisciplinary study of economic development in developing countries as it relates to violence, illegal drugs and actors, and political instability with an emphasis in Colombia. She has written two books and twenty-five articles/book chapters in the area of Latin American growth and development.

Jennifer S. Holmes is an Associate Professor of Political Economy and Political Science at the University of Texas at Dallas. Her major area of research is political violence, terrorism, and political development with an emphasis on Latin America. She is the author of three and editor of two books on related topics, in addition to numerous other publications.

Peter Kingstone is Professor and Coordinator of the Program on High Growth-Emerging Markets at King's College London. His research focuses on political economy and Latin American politics. He is the author of *Crafting Coalitions for Reform* and *The Political Economy of Latin America: Reflections on Neoliberalism and Development*, as well as the coeditor of three books: *Democratic Brazil, Democratic Brazil Revisited*, and most recently *The Handbook of Latin American Politics*.

Natalia Mirovitskaya is a Senior Researcher & Lecturing Fellow, Duke Center for International Development. She published extensively on sustainable development, environmental security, and peacebuilding. She has led and participated in numerous national and international research projects and has taught in several countries.

Deborah L. Norden is Professor and Chair of the Political Science Department at Whittier College. Her research focuses on Latin American politics, especially civil-military relations and democratization in Argentina and Venezuela, as well as irregular transfers of power and international democracy promotion. Her publications include *Military Rebellion in Argentina: Between Coups and Consolidation* and *Argentina and the United States: Changing Relations in a Changing World*, as well articles in several journals and edited volumes.

Emily K. Penner is a doctoral student in the Department of Education at the University of California, Irvine. She studies US and international education policy and educational inequality. Her work is situated at the intersection of public policy, economics, and sociology. She is currently working on projects examining the ways in which parents, peers, and the social organization of schools influence student achievement.

Judith Teichman, Professor of Political Science at the University of Toronto, specializes in the study of poverty and inequality and welfare regimes in the global south, with particular reference to South Korea, Mexico, and Chile. She has authored or coauthored five books dealing with Latin American politics, with a focus on Mexico and Chile.

CHAPTER 1

Economic Development Patterns and the Evolution of Violence in Latin America

William Ascher and Natalia Mirovitskaya

Latin America is a region with a long history of intergroup violence. Consistent with Tolstoy's famous observation that "every unhappy family is unhappy in its own way," Latin America stands out in several ways. No other world region has thus far seen such a variety of forms of violence. Through most of the twentieth century, the continent was plagued with civil wars and large-scale guerrilla warfare, social uprisings and violent revolutions; its inhabitants endured many coups d'état and military interventions and brutal military dictatorships coupled with state and nonstate terrorism. Though at the turn of the millennium, many of these "traditional" forms of violent confrontation have ceased or have been greatly attenuated, they have been topped by the upsurge of urban crime ("slum wars"), proliferation of violent youth gangs, and intensification of domestic violence as well as "drug wars" and state-led "wars on drugs." Latin America has a dubious distinction of leading the world in most global indices of violence.

The high incidence and diverse patterns of violence in Latin America are linked to another record it holds. The region is defined by a significant, pervasive, and persistent inequality tied in with low social mobility. By many indicators of inequality, Latin America is still ranked first in the world (UNDP 2010, 16). Despite economic stabilization and the resurgence of growth, in the second decade of the twenty-first century Latin America remains beset by severe poverty and social exclusion. Inequalities among groups (of different racial or ethnic origin, gender, or geographical location) are observed in income, education, life expectancy, and other indicators of human development, and they persist from one generation to the next (UNDP 2010; de Ferranti et al. 2004).

There is an uncomfortable sense that some of these problems are self-inflicted, brought by a series of development policy choices. Like elsewhere, development strategies adopted by the Latin American countries in the last few decades have created "winners" and "losers," generating problems of social conflict and social control. Governments that embarked on a particular path of economic development (i.e., import-substitution industrialization [ISI], or market liberalization) often found themselves unprepared to manage the resultant conflict. This connection between development strategies and policies and intergroup conflict is the thrust of our inquiry.

This chapter provides the broad context of Latin American development and conflict since WWII and an overview of the following chapters that chronicle and explain the economic bases of Latin American violence. Thus this chapter offers a quick sketch of the economic strategies and patterns in Latin America, the political consequences of Latin American economic development, and some of the consequences for intergroup relations. We offer several complementary interpretations of the transformation of Latin American conflict and violence. Finally, we speculate on the future of development and conflict in Latin America.

Of course, several caveats apply to our general line of inquiry. First, it is important to recognize that the economic, political, and social conditions vary substantially among states and nations in all the Latin American subregions. Yet some degree of common history, more contemporary challenges, and especially convergence of many development strategies justify the regional focus, as long as the differences are recognized. In addition, our focus on economic strategies and policies does not mean that an economic determinist position makes sense. In fact, this volume demonstrates that similar development strategies and policies pursued in the region produced rather different economic and sociopolitical results, provoking or reducing intergroup conflict in different policy contexts. We recognize the importance of political institutions as foundations of societal instability as well the complexity of linkages between the economic and the sociopolitical patterns. No one can deny that causal links go both ways, but because our principal audience is policymakers and activists, we emphasize the need to anticipate how economic policy choices shape the sociopolitical patterns of development.

Changing Interface of Violence and Development in Latin America

The motivations for continued concern over development-related violence in Latin America are manifold. First, the state of stable democracy is still a relatively recent phenomenon in the region. Democratic institutions prevail all over the continent and, despite occasional setbacks,[1] seem to be more sustainable than ever; over the last decades, democratic regimes were able to eliminate or at least reduce armed conflicts by offering political and economic concessions to those in particular distress. However, democratic traditions are still weak in the region and some regimes are in fact "hybrid" political orders. Experience shows that weakly institutionalized democracies are particularly prone to social violence, and that it is during the period of sociopolitical transformation that various forms of violence rise dramatically and regime reversals are possible. Mass survey data from the Latinobarometro demonstrate that increased violence in the region erodes social support for democratic political institutions not only because of perceptions of increased insecurity and victimization, but most importantly, because many groups increasingly believe that the government cannot protect them (Cruz 2008). Observers of Latin American politics (Rodgers 2006; 2009;; Cruz 2008) report the various ways that democratic governments in the region have come to be perceived as the "enemy." This phenomenon not only makes democratic reversals possible (though far from inevitable) but also evokes social legitimacy of alternative forms of justice (self-justice, social cleansing, and privatized security) targeting migrants and other marginal groups.

Second, the scale of violence in the region is indeed unprecedented. Despite the fact that the civil wars that have plagued many Latin American nations have ceased or have been greatly attenuated and other forms of political violence receded significantly, different modes of violence have emerged and/or were brought to the forefront of public discourse and concern. The redemocratization of Latin America has arguably led to democratization of violence itself; the use of force is no longer the primary preserve of state and nonstate militant actors in political opposition to each other. The region has been confronted with the ubiquitous proliferation of gangs, often comprising former guerrilla and paramilitary, and often connected to a mushrooming drug industry. Other types of urban criminal violence, an explosion of social violence, and a precipitous rise in impersonal, anomic violence followed. As displayed in Table 1.1, no other region of the world has higher homicide rates.[2] Aside from the question of data reliability, the number of homicides per 100,000 people is a reasonable measure of these forms of violence, although it does not encompass killings by police, armed forces, or

Table 1.1 Homicide rates of Latin American countries

	1996–2000a	2001–2005b	2006–2010c
Argentina	5.0	6.6	4.6
Bolivia	Unreliable data		
Brazil	29.1	31.4	30.4
Chile	3.3	5.4	5.0
Colombia	79.4	72.7	54.6
Costa Rica	5.8	6.7	7.9
Ecuador	15.7	16.5	21.2
El Salvador	45.8	49.6	64.6
Guatemala	22.7	26.7	35.9
Honduras	42.1	42.3	61.4
Mexico	15.1	11.1	14.2
Nicaragua	11.5	16.2	13.2
Panama	11.2	13.5	17.4
Paraguay	18.8	20.3	16.3
Peru	Unreliable data		
Uruguay	5.2	4.5	
Venezuela	20.1	33.2	34.7
Canada	1.6	1.5	
United States	6.6	6.1	6

Note: a. Honduras: 1999–2000 only; Nicaragua: 1996 only.
 b. Canada: 2001–2004 only.
 c. Argentina, Brazil, Ecuador, Paraguay: 2006–2010 only;
Chile, Colombia, Panama, Peru, United States: 2006–2007 only;
Nicaragua, Venezuela: 2006 only.
Sources: Pan American Health Organization, *Health Conditions in the Americas*; *Health in the Americas*, various years.

other security forces, or deaths that are not specifically identified as homicides (United Nations Office on Drugs and Crime 2011, 21).

Of greatest current concern among governments and the public is "criminal" violence: street violence, gang violence, clashes among narcotics traffickers, and so on. In World Bank Enterprise Surveys, crime appears as one of the major constraints to productivity and macro- and microeconomic growth in all Central American and many Andean countries. An upsurge in urban violence, dubbed by the Pan American Health Organization as "social pandemic" is usually considered an apolitical phenomenon, distinct from the class-based violence of the past. However, an in-depth analysis of this phenomenon reveals its strong connection with social exclusion of some groups intensified by economic modernization and an "adverse" formation of collective identity within the boundaries of spreading informal economy. Some scholars in fact regard gangs as a potential vanguard of social mobilization of the new "informal proletariat"—those expelled from the "formal economy" through a combined effect of various development strategies (Davis 2006; Rodgers 2009).

Urban violence is not the only concern in the region. Another form of violence persists in remote areas, over control of land, forests, and areas subject to subsoil resource extraction. Clashes between forest residents from Mexico to Brazil continue to flare up, and often go underreported. Yet even without full reportage, Latin America stands as one of the most violent regions in the world.

Third, the possibility of renewed ideological and interethnic confrontations is by no means extinguished. It is true that armed conflicts between insurgents and Latin American governments have dwindled to the FARC (The Revolutionary Armed Forces of Colombia) and ELN (National Liberation Army) in Colombia and a modestly resurgent Sendero Luminoso in Peru, but the Uppsala Conflict Data Program deems them all as "minor" (Themnér and Wallensteen 2011, 535); and the SEHLAC Group (2010, 2) asserts that "Colombia could be considered as the sole example of an ongoing internal armed conflict still present in the region." Yet the polarization among classes and ethnicities seems to be on the rise in the Andean countries, especially in Venezuela and Bolivia, with Peru and Nicaragua likely to follow suit. Brazil, where violence, poverty, and discrimination all have strong racial characteristics but the level of race consciousness in politics and racial mobilization until recently remained quite low, may be experiencing the growing salience of ethnic identification, brought on by the surprising decision of the government in 2000 to launch an affirmative action program for Afro-Brazilians.

Fourth, the region's future depends upon young generations. However, it is mostly young people (predominantly male) who are both perpetrators and victims of violence in Latin America. Many young people (including those with high educational levels) have been relegated to long-term job informality and severely limited social mobility (ECLAC 2011), with indigenous and Afro-descent groups being particularly disadvantaged. It is difficult to miss the connection between high unemployment rates,[3] limited economic opportunities, social exclusion of the youth, and proliferation of violence.

Six puzzles make the analysis of development and conflict in Latin America anything but straightforward. First, while Latin America as a whole has become much less riven by organized political violence—at least for now—other types of violence at the community, family, and interpersonal levels have risen to distressing levels. Second, just as it seemed that most of Latin America had reached the "end state" of stable centrist democratic governments, with moderate pro-market economic policies, a largely unanticipated resurgence of leftist and populist alternatives has seemingly signaled the continuing cyclical nature of polarizing ideology and conflict, though the spread and degree of radicalism remain to be seen. In many countries, new governments came into power with a promise of promoting a more active state economic role and more ambitions redistributive policies. The wave of electoral victories by leftist presidential candidates began in 1998 with Hugo Chávez (Venezuela)[4]; by 2009, nearly two-thirds of Latin Americans lived under some form of left-leaning government (Levitsky and Roberts 2011, 1), which placed redistribution and social equality (as opposed to simply "helping poor") at the top of their programmatic agendas. In some countries, the political phenomenon linked to the economic agenda of the "New Left" is the resurgence of populism.[5] Populist leaders do not necessarily belong to the Left of the political center. Making unmediated mass appeals in opposition to the political establishment (presented as corrupt and exclusionary), some of them chose not to attack economic oligarchies. In fact, populists whose appeals focus on nationalism, public order, and achieving economic stability, rather than wealth redistribution, are closer to the ideological Right. Alvaro Uribe in Colombia is an example of populist right-wing leader, while Ollanta Humala (Peru) has been drawing his support from both ends of the ideological spectrum. Listening to the political rhetoric in the first decade of this century, one might assume that economic reforms of the 1990s were abandoned or reversed. Paradoxically, except for a few countries (Argentina, Bolivia, and Venezuela), the political "left turn" was not accompanied by populist macroeconomic policies (Kaufman 2011; Stallings and Peres 2011)—leftist criticism of neoliberal reforms remained largely rhetoric without the actual reversal of the reforms. Nevertheless, both leftism and populism still have substantial political consequences and policy ramifications for the region.

Third, yet another paradox revealed in the new political context is that the "New Left" and populists who came to power on the wave of public discontent with neoliberal reforms found themselves unprepared or unwilling to address the main underlying issues of this societal discontent: violence as an increasing threat to public security (a traditional issue for the ideological Right) and challenges of multicultural citizenship. While in the 1990s leftist and indigenous movements often converged in opposition to neoliberalism, once in power they were confronted with the challenges of balancing class, ethnic, and racial demands.[6]

Fourth, as a racially and ethnically diverse region, Latin America has traditionally been plagued with major group-based inequalities. Substantial gaps in poverty levels and economic opportunities exist between groups of European descent, indigenous peoples, and Afro-descendants. Levels of income and access to services differ markedly within different regions within the same country (UNDP 2011, 27). However, historic policies of assimilation, along with sustained myths of "racial democracy" have kept these discrepancies hidden. More recently, despite the ethnic homogenization that has been occurring in Latin America for centuries, the policies and the discourse in several Latin American countries, particularly in the Andean subregion and perhaps in Brazil, have elevated ethnic and racial differences as pivots of politics and contestation over economic policy.

Fifth, poverty alleviation has proceeded even as inequality over the past several decades has been little changed. It is possible that income inequality also slightly declined in the first decade of this century—recent studies report that 12 of 17 Latin American countries with adequate data showed less income inequality in that period, following a worsening of distribution in the 1990s (López-Calva and Lustig 2010; ECLAC 2011); this is consistent with estimates generated by the United Nations University World Institute for Development Economics Research (2008) and refined by Solt (2011). This decrease is ascribed to economic growth, increases in public spending, and especially to an improvement in the impact of social spending, in particular public transfers to the most vulnerable sectors (UNDP 2011, 7, 25). In the last decade, many countries also reported significant gains in terms of human development.[7] However, these aggregate numbers hide significant differences, including geographical inequality, inequality among different ethnic or racial groups, and gender inequality. In fact, data demonstrate that gender inequality in many countries of Latin America has increased during the last decade, both in terms of income generation and accessing social security (UNDP 2011, 27, 32). Many dimensions of inequality in Latin America seem to have survived not only very different political systems but also development strategies and public policy interventions specifically focused on poverty reduction and more inclusive development.

Insofar as a market economy permits those with greater initial endowments to prosper more than others, the income gaps must be offset by government transfers. Such measures do not have to be as provocative as land takeovers or confiscation of factories; they can entail devoting more budgetary resources to the health, education, and income support of low-income families, to improving rural infrastructure, and to generating employment. During the 1980s and the 1990s, Latin American governments did little in this regard; as a consequence, the distribution of income became more skewed (Mahon 2009; Solt 2010; UNU-WIDER 2008). The paradox is that while in the last decade, the gradual improvements in infrastructure, education, health, and sounder economic policies elevated the average incomes of the poor, and the development of more targeted social policies (including conditional cash-transfer programs) contributed to the decline in inequality, the resentment toward the wealthy has not abated, as the reality and perception of inequality certainly persists. Apparently, the impact of improvements was neither sufficient[8] nor equal.[9]

Sixth, in many countries the perceptions of the fairness of income distribution, economic opportunities, societal stability, and human security sometimes run counter to the reality. For instance, Latin American nations with greater overall inequality tend to have larger percentages of their citizens believing that the income distribution is fair (Graham 2002a; 2002b). At the individual level, very poor and destitute respondents report high levels of wellbeing, while wealthier ones report lower degrees of life satisfaction ("happy peasant and frustrated achiever" phenomenon). Describing this phenomenon, Carol Graham and Eduardo Lora (2009) also report the "paradox of unhappy growth"—a negative correlation between economic growth rates and citizen's happiness levels at the country level. Yet another paradox is the gap between reality and public perceptions of violence and insecurity. Many Latin Americans seem to feel less secure than they actually are while the threat perceptions in societies where rates of violence are relatively low (Argentina, Chile, and Uruguay) have risen steeply (Imbusch et al. 2011, 102). There are different explanations for these multiple "perceptional paradoxes." Nevertheless, it is difficult to overlook the importance of public discourse and media reporting. The mass media play an increasingly central role in constructing the "virtual reality" of people's lives and in their political mobilization. It often produces and amplifies societal fear, a sense of injustice, and intergroup animosity. Given that politicians (especially of the populist kind) often respond to public perceptions rather than economic reality, this phenomenon raises concerns about the future of development strategies and social stability in the region.

The Long Sweep of Economic Changes

Latin America began the post-WWII period as a largely agricultural region, despite the high levels of urbanization in Argentina, Chile, and Uruguay, depending on agricultural and raw-material exports to earn hard currencies for imports.[10] It also had a highly unequal and exclusionary agrarian system, which emerged from Iberian colonization dating back four centuries and was dominated by the large-landed estates (hacienda and latifundia systems). In most countries, landownership was established through expropriation of indigenous community lands (Bolivia, Ecuador, Guatemala, Honduras, Mexico, and Peru)[11] and was based on the extraction of economic surplus from the peasantry. Historically, unequal distribution of land in Latin America was a major source of high levels of economic inequality, unequal political influence, and resultant conflict. The overwhelming dependence on agriculture, along with population growth, heightened the imperative to control farmland, resulting in strong pressures for redistributive land reform by the landless and farmers with tiny plots.

Land Reform and Conflict

Much of the conflict during the first three decades of the post-WWII era was over land reforms, the demands for which were expressed through peasant struggles in such diverse countries as Mexico, Bolivia, Guatemala, Brazil, Cuba, Chile, Colombia, Peru, and Nicaragua. Consequently, almost all Latin American countries used the power of the state to grant access to land for specific categories of landless households and to redefine land rights for those who had access. Many of the reforms were initiated in the region after the Cuban Revolution of 1959 to preempt widespread peasant insurrections and guerrilla movements. In some countries, extensive land reforms were part of the outcome of revolutions (Bolivia 1952; Nicaragua 1979), in others they were imposed by authoritarian governments (1969–1975 land reform in Peru and 1964 reform in Ecuador). Land reforms in Chile (1964–1973), Colombia (1961), Guatemala (1952–1954), Honduras (1973), El Salvador (1980s), and the Dominican Republic (1961–) were pursued by democratically elected governments (de Janvry, Sadoulet, and Wolford 2001). Despite different political circumstances, the results were quite similar: extreme violence and low degree of success.

Land reforms largely failed through both the defeat of radical groups, especially in the Andean countries and Central America, and the land consolidations by large-scale farming and ranching operations that acquired land from small-scale farmers disadvantaged by the bias against agriculture embedded in economic policies (Bautista and Valdés 1993; Pinstrup-Andersen 1988; Timmer 1991). As de Ferranti et al. (2004) report, some efforts succeeded in breaking up haciendas, but almost all failed to transform the position of rural poor by making them efficient producers, sometimes due to the political context and most often due to shortcomings in reform design. For instance, the newly reformed areas were not supported by the infrastructure and other economic services needed to generate viable small-scale sector. In addition, landed elites, when faced with the reform of property rights, were able to preserve their economic position by other means, that is, securing subsidies on capital or outputs. For all the violence engendered by the clashes over land, the distribution of land has become even more skewed. Ironically, when the bias against agriculture was partially reversed through the promotion of agro-exports in the 1980s, the consolidation proceeded, harming the small landowners, tenants, and rural workers.[12] Lastarria-Cornhiel (2006, 17) concludes that these trends led to "increasing land concentration in Latin America." In many instances, the process of land reform had positioned different groups of rural actors against each other, or in opposition to the state, exacerbating violence in the region.

The clearest link between land-distribution reform, land consolidation, and violence, exacerbated by the neglect of social services, is seen in Colombia, until very recently the most violent country in Latin America. Holmes and Gutiérrez de Piñeres argue in this volume that much of the Colombian violence grew out of land conflicts. After the 1992 international coffee-market collapse, violence emerged in former coffee-producing areas, as small landowners' holdings were consolidated in favor of large landowners, and coca cultivation penetrated the region. Tensions worsened as commercial agriculture spread and rural agricultural workers were restricted from organizing. The government had largely neglected rural areas, providing few poverty-reduction programs or government services, even as income inequalities grew out of the lower labor demand of commercial agriculture. Guerrillas entered the region and upped their recruitment there since the early 1990s.

Colombian government efforts to rectify the land issues have been largely unsuccessful; many policies have benefited wealthy landowners. Plantation-based agriculture and ranching are both capital-intensive sectors dominated by large landowners. These industries receive considerable government support, despite being associated with the forced displacement of the rural poor. Large landowners within these industries are known to fund or affiliate with paramilitary groups to further displace protesting workers. Colombian laws also discourage sharecropping, which has further reduced opportunities for small landowners. Although the Colombian Land Reform Law intended to redistribute a million hectares of land, subsidies were generally captured by wealthy segments of the population.

Colombia is definitely not the only example of the links between access to the critical rural assets and class-based violence. Peruvian land-reform history illustrates challenges that even well-meaning governments face in balancing the interests of various actors. While President Belaunde's 1964 agrarian reform had very limited scale and did not alter the agrarian structure in Peru, it succeeded in buying the government social peace at least for a while. However, when the new government of General Velasco Alvarado attempted radical and sweeping agrarian reform aiming to attain mass support of the peasantry and destroy traditional rural oligarchy (Sloan 1984), many peasants—reform beneficiaries—resisted its statist and collectivist character. The most powerful opposition was launched by the indigenous communities that protested their exclusion from the land-distribution process and began to invade the newly created state or collective farms. In this case, the agrarian reform inadvertently brought out the deep-seated resentments of the marginalized indigenous communities. Many members of these communities in fact benefited from other policy initiatives of Velasco's government. However, their frustration with Peru's climate of entrenched racism and lack of upward social mobility were skillfully exploited by the Shining Path guerilla movement, unleashing one of the most violent chapters in the history of Peru (Kay 2000).

In Brazil, which has one of the world's most skewed land distributions, the last 30 years have been marked by conflict among the government, landowners, and the Landless Rural Workers Movement (MST). The original objectives of the movement were to redistribute land of unproductive "latifundios" and reallocate it to a growing rural population. The MST gained public support after two massacres in Corumbiara and Carajas—and is currently by far the largest peasant movement in Latin America. Often touted as the most dynamic, creative, inspiring, and influential movement in Brazil (Hammond 1999), the MST engages in both legal land reform and in illegal activities such as land invasions.

The land issue has been central to many other conflicts in rural Latin America, being famously dubbed as "Peasant Wars of the Twentieth Century" (Wolf 1999). When resident populations of rural areas lack access to land and other basic production factors as well as employment opportunities, they have low "opportunity cost" to choose violence as means of earning income and are easily exploited by conflict entrepreneurs, or, as more recently in Colombia, Mexico, Peru, and Bolivia, by drug lords acting as conflict entrepreneurs. Many families and individuals (especially young males) flow toward the outskirts of large towns and cities, joining the ranks of "informal proletariat" most prone to crime and violence. Thus the revolutionary rural violence of the past is being transformed into seemingly apolitical, but in fact deeply rooted in major social cleavages, urban violence—"slum wars of the twenty-first century" (Moser and McIlwaine 2006; Beall 2006; Rodgers 2009).

At the end of the Cold War, redistributive land reforms resurfaced in many Latin American countries following the renewed mobilization of landless peasants and indigenous peoples for land and other rights as well as increasing public concern about poverty and inequality. In Brazil, where until the 1990s the true land reform was substituted by colonization of frontier lands, strong political and social pressures, coming from different corners—from the left-leaning coalition commanded by the MST to the World

Bank—have finally resulted in new initiatives taken to promote redistribution (Navarro 2009). The Brazilian experience with negotiated agrarian reform, which started in 1997, has been touted as the most comprehensive, long-standing, and diverse program in the world (Sparovek and Maule 2009). Similar experiments in community and market-based land reform have been ongoing in Colombia, Guatemala, and Honduras (Binswanger-Mkhize, Bourguignon, and van den Brink 2009). Whether these reforms will be successful in addressing rural inequality in these countries and transforming their agricultural sector into the basis for social peace remains to be seen.[13] But the difference between land reforms of the twentieth century and current attempts of land redistribution lies in the fact that most of today's governments have been elected democratically and have been searching for the ways to redistribute land peacefully and at sufficient scale.

As experience of many Latin American countries demonstrates, social peace is still closely connected to agricultural development. Although large-scale urbanization and industrialization have shifted some of the political contention from agriculture to other economic sectors, land distribution remains an important concern for large groups in the region's poorer countries as well as for important, and relatively poor, minorities in middle-income countries (de Ferranti et al. 2004).

Sectoral Bias toward Industry

In emulation of developed countries, under the questionable premise that industrialization is equivalent to development, the governments of many Latin American nations attempted to industrialize. A confluence of theories and premises led to draining wealth out of the agricultural sector: the assumption that industry did not face the same physical land constraint limiting the expansion of agriculture; the belief that the terms of trade for raw materials would deteriorate; the hope that industrial expansion would absorb agricultural labor; and the belief that temporary support for new industries, through subsidies or protection from imports, would eventually lead to competitive industry. The initial protections of "infant" manufacturing industries would dictate a focus on the domestic market; hence the strategy of "import-substitution industrialization" (ISI). The major resource-extractive nations, such as Venezuela and eventually Mexico, saw combinations of ISI and resource-based industrialization focused on the expansion of the downstream processing of the materials and, if the resource was oil, greatly underpriced fuels for domestic industry.

The inward-looking development approach held little attraction for external investors; so many governments embraced the doctrine that inflation was a necessary evil to stimulate their economies. Once inflation became endemic, some governments found that the way to avoid open clashes between owners and organized workers was to permit the reciprocal elevation of wages and prices; validating price increases through increases in the money supply inevitably added to the inflation momentum.[14] This vicious cycle led to hyperinflation in many Latin American countries, and contributed to class animosity.

The ambitious industrialization strategy extended into the 1970s, but required capital beyond what could be mobilized by draining the agricultural sector or promoting domestic savings. Because of the leap in oil prices, oil-exporting countries accumulated huge dollar surpluses and deposited much of this wealth in private international banks. The need for these banks to recycle "petro dollars" led to very cheap capital available at negligible real interest rates. Therefore the 1970s saw many Latin American nations engaging in enormous international borrowing, most of which was supposed to be channeled to industrial projects, though in some countries the funds were devoted to current expenditures or were siphoned off through corruption. The continuation of the ISI strategy received ample financial backing, even though generally the competitiveness of the protected industries was never realized. With such an infusion of capital at negligible real interest rates, many public projects with low rates of return were undertaken. Yet such projects were financially unsound under the scenario of high interest rates.

The sequencing of industrialization and agrarian reform in Latin America was different from many other developing regions of the world. While in East Asia agrarian reform came before industrialization and was key to ensuring its success, in Latin America most agrarian reforms happened after industrialization and were sometimes seen as a way to counteract what has been termed the "exhaustion of the easy phase of import-substitution industrialization" (Kay 2006, 24). In comparison to other regions, agrarian reforms in Latin America happened too late, were restricted in scale, and were often thwarted by the landlord class or government mismanagement. As a result, in most of the region agriculture increasingly failed to provide the capital to fuel industrialization; the structure of the agrarian sector became an obstacle to further economic development, reproducing inequality, poverty, social exclusion, and resultant conflict.

Structural Adjustment

The "lost decade" of the 1980s came under this scenario. After the bankruptcy of ISI, Latin American countries had to face the reality of debt crisis as the United States and other developed-country governments ratcheted up real interest rates that almost immediately translated into far greater debt service requirements for indebted Latin American nations.[15] While economic conditions in the 1980s were dismal, the debt crisis did force many Latin American governments to face up to the dead weight of wasteful spending, protectionism of inefficient industries, overvalued exchange rates, tax loopholes, licensing favoritism, and other "illiberal" aspects of economic policies (Crisp and Kelly 1999; Edwards 1995; 2010). Under pressure from private lenders, developed-country governments, the International Monetary Fund, the World Bank, and the Inter-American Development Bank, most Latin American governments launched structural adjustment initiatives along with the austerity measures. Growth-promising reforms, undertaken (or at least proclaimed) by both left-wing and right-wing governments in the region, included fiscal and monetary measures to guarantee solvency of the state, control inflation, liberalize the financial system, and open economies to trade, as well as to privatize state enterprises. The reforms sought to eliminate the distortions caused by excessive state intervention and to make the economies of Latin America more competitive.

Despite the severity of crisis, governments had to contend with resistance of the entrenched interests in the protected sectors, as well as the risk of disruptions from low-income people reeling from the cutbacks in government social services. Therefore while structural adjustment was the most prominent element of the 1980s policy agenda, true reforms were much more modest[16] and produced varying results. Based on the evaluations by Edwards (1995, 41, 60–64), Crisp and Kelly (1999, 538) scored the extent of structural adjustment in sixteen Latin American governments, finding that across five aspects of macroeconomic policy reform (fiscal, labor-market, financial, trade, and privatization), five countries had no significant reform, four had significant or thorough reforms in only one aspect, and three others had such reforms in only two aspects. Only Chile had reached significant reform on all five dimensions (two—trade and financial reforms—having been accomplished earlier). Bolivia had enacted significant or thorough reforms in all but privatization; Mexico in all but labor-market reform; and Colombia in all but labor-market and privatization.[17]

The prior neglect of the agricultural and social-service sectors, especially in the rural areas, was compounded by the 1980s budget contractions. The shift from a state-centered inward-directed development to a market-based export-oriented model had dramatic results for the countryside. It contributed to the drastic fall in permanent rural employment and rise of temporary forms of employment, thereby weakening the power of traditional peasant organizations. Though new movements have emerged like the MST (Landless Workers' Movement) in Brazil and the EZLN (The Zapatista Army of National Liberation) in Mexico, liberalization has largely sapped organizational capacities of low-income groups as labor markets become more competitive, dispersed, and fragile. This in turn reinforced the preexisting attraction for young men from failing farms and stagnant small towns to go to the hills or jungles for the dual allures of leftist ideology and the possibility of prospering from banditry and drug trafficking (Colombia, Guatemala, and Peru) or move to larger cities, or more precisely into their slums (Brazil and most countries of Central America).

Much more thorough structural adjustment occurred in the 1990s when "second-generation reforms" were implemented. These reforms came in "waves" (Lora 2007): fiscal reforms of the early 1990s were followed by pension reforms in the mid-1990s, and by fiscal responsibility reforms in the early 2000s. In contrast to the Washington Consensus reforms (traditionally defined as structural adjustment, or "first-generation" reforms), these policy interventions were more complex, oriented toward addressing context-specific market and government failures, and involved a higher diversity of actors in their implementation (Lora 2007). Lora (2001) developed indicators of structural reforms in trade, finance, taxation, privatization, and labor-market regulation for 19 Latin American countries from 1985 to 1999, and found that the bulk of the progress was made in the 1990s.[18] This point is not well understood in the literature on Latin American economic reform—the sound and fury of reactions to the initiatives led to many assessments, and public perceptions, that the reforms were more thorough than they really were.[19] The implication is that the hostile reactions to structural adjustment in the 1980s were due more to budget austerity and the perceptions of threat than to the actual impacts of liberalization.

Small-scale agriculture bore the brunt of the redistributions effected through the promotion of industry, because by the 1980s, the turn to export promotion encompassed not only export-oriented manufacturing, but also agro-export promotion through favorable access to credit and lower agricultural tariffs. Lastarria-Cornhiel (2006, 17) notes:

> These policies, particularly trade liberalization policies together with agricultural policies that favor export products, stoked the growth of agribusiness, particularly in the production of high-value horticultural crops.
>
> At the same time, liberalization policies have resulted in higher input costs, lower farmgate prices, and significant cuts in access to credit and extension services for the smallholder sector that produces mostly food for local and regional markets.

In the case of Mexico, trade liberalization also meant the influx of agricultural products against which small producers could not compete (see Teichman in this volume).

In most countries of the region, liberalization has also extended to the streamlining or elimination of state enterprises. Because state enterprises tend to employ excess labor, this aspect of liberalization can have a major impact on employment and the dislocation of populations. William Barndt in this volume notes that labor shedding by the Bolivian state mining enterprise COMIBOL in the 1980s led to a flood of highland ex-miners and their families into La Paz and lowland areas.[20]

Trade Liberalization and Drug Trafficking

Because the United States is clearly the most lucrative market for the liberalized, export orientation of Latin American countries, cooperation with the US government has been a priority for governments seeking trade preference or even more ambitious free-trade pacts. For those countries with significant production of illicit drugs destined for the insatiable US market, this has often meant compliance with competing drug cartels and engaging in drug-eradication programs. This compliance has had several troubling consequences. As Jennifer Holmes and Sheila Gutiérrez de Piñeres note in this volume, the Colombian government's success in the 1980s and the 1990s to dismantle the existing drug cartels left a vacuum that was filled by the FARC (The Revolutionary Armed Forces of Colombia) guerrilla movement. In addition, the 1991 US Andean Trade Preference Act and the 2002 Andean Trade Promotion and Drug Eradication Act (for Bolivia, Colombia, Ecuador, and Peru) explicitly linked the eradication programs with tariff reductions. By reducing the supply, and heightening the illegality and risks of production and trafficking, this compliance increased the risk premium for successful producers and traffickers and provided greater incentive for them to use violence to force out competitors.

Poverty, drug trafficking, and the nexus between crime and violence are also tied together by the migration of low-income youth, especially from Central America, to the United States, exposing them to pressures to join gangs. The combination of deportations and voluntary return to home countries has propagated US gangs within home-country cities. Gustavo Arcia's chapter in this volume examines these dynamics in greater detail.

The "Silent Revolution"

Most recently, the region has undergone yet another partial wave of policy reforms, the essence of which is consistent with the so-called Beijing Consensus.[21] Along with the dramatic change in the composition of the governing elite, the role of the state has been once again redefined to include balancing social interests in addition to generating and providing services. One of the most significant changes has been the increasing role of the state in promoting economic development. As Stallings and Peres (2011) report, this still involves "horizontal" policies aimed at the correction of market failures as well as so-called vertical strategies of sectoral promotion, a departure from the development strategy of the 1990s. Colombia and other Andean countries (and more recently some Central American and Caribbean countries) resumed sectoral promotion strategies in the guise of cluster development or competitiveness policies. In 2008, the Brazilian government launched a rather comprehensive industrial policy with a strong sectoral focus; Argentina, Costa Rica, Peru, and Uruguay have been targeting development by supporting selective production chains or specific firms (Stallings and Peres 2011, 780).

Following this new developmental paradigm, many governments seek to achieve productive upgrading to enhance competitiveness along with social inclusion to address the problem of income concentration and economic opportunities (Kirby 2009). Such policies are highly context-dependent and are based on economic pragmatism: the performance of the Lagos, Bachelet, Lula, and Vázquez governments exemplify this approach.

Nevertheless, despite the prevailing leftist rhetoric and subsequent perception that the liberalization reforms have been reversed, in most Latin American countries the basic features of the market model—private ownership, free trade, openness to foreign investment—have not been challenged. Macroeconomic policies of almost all countries in the region remain conservative, while trade- and financial-liberalization reforms have not been reversed by even the most leftist governments. Significant backsliding from the policy reforms of 1990s has been limited to very few countries (mainly Venezuela and Bolivia) and concentrated on privatization alone. Thus, in 2006–2009 the scale of the region's nationalization was estimated at $39 billion (or about one-fifth of the proceeds from region's privatizations in the 1990s); the bulk of this amount came from one source: nationalization of the oil fields in Venezuela's Orinoco Belt (Stallings and Peres 2011, 782). At this time, the assets of companies nationalized by the government of Venezuela equaled 16 percent of its GDP, while in Bolivia nationalizations exceeded 5 percent of GDP (Stallings and Peres 2011, 784); in 2010–2011, both nations continued the takeover of private businesses. However, although the Morales government heavily taxed and regulated foreign businesses in key extractive sectors and launched yet another agrarian reform, it stayed away from nationalizing the gas industry or expropriating large amounts of private land (Madrid 2011). The scale of nationalization in Argentina[22] and Ecuador was much smaller. Almost all nationalized companies were producers of natural resources or public utilities—the targets of every liberalization in Latin America.

In sum, under the "Silent Revolution" the market model was not reversed but it has been supplemented with some significant social democratic features. Brazil, Chile, Uruguay, and few other countries actively used public policy, including minimum wage increases, expanded pension coverage, and large-scale transfer programs to boost the income of poor, which inspired some authors to refer to "Creole social democracy" (Lanzaro 2011). All were able to achieve substantial reduction in poverty and many reported some reduction in inequality of labor income and nonlabor income. Whether the "Silent Revolution" may indeed result in sustained economic development coupled with social democratization (the least violent form of societal organization) remains to be seen. Such an outcome is most likely in stable democracies, reinforced by strong and supportive labor movement and a strong state. While Brazil, Chile, and Uruguay appear closest to meet these conditions, Bolivia, Ecuador, and Venezuela are facing substantial political polarization, have tense or convoluted relations with labor, indigenous, and other social movements. At least in Venezuela, the politicization of state agencies has weakened state capacity. All these factors may undermine long-term prospects of these governments (Levitsky and Roberts 2011, 474–475), and eventually result in the resurgence of ideologically based violence.

Natural Resource Policies

For many Latin American countries, the continued reliance on subsoil raw materials (basically hydrocarbons and hard minerals) resulted in a cycle of nationalizations and privatizations vis-à-vis international companies, as governments tried to cope with the need for investment capital to gear up production versus the need to maintain exploration and extraction when world prices are low. State oil and mining companies have played crucial, highly controversial roles: sometimes directly exploring, extracting, and processing resources; taking over the operations of international companies or partnering with them; providing "off budget" funds for government leaders to engage in a host of controversial activities; monopolizing domestic sales, often pricing fuels far below market levels. The pricing problems have often led to disruptions, as unsustainable budget transfers to state companies to cover their subsidies forced governments to raise energy prices.

Where subsoil resources are extracted, the dissatisfaction of local residents, due to a combination of environmental degradation and resentment of being denied their "fair share" of the revenues, have recently prompted direct transfers of oil and mining revenues to subnational governments. Conflicts between the residents of these extractive areas and the national government may decline as increased revenues flow into the communities. However, the contention becomes more localized. Arellano-Yanguas (2011, 632–633) found more acute conflicts in Peruvian areas receiving allocations from the *canon petrolero* and *canon minero* formulae[23] between local people and resource-extraction companies over the magnitude of transfers; among local leaders pressing for greater shares; between local and higher-level authorities; and between local people and local authorities over inefficient allocations.

Forest-resource policies have been even more contentious as governments have wrested control from local people with customary rights, established forest reserves off-limits to those who had depended on extraction from these areas, granted logging concessions to outsiders, financed infrastructure that provided access to previously inaccessible forest areas, and other acts that have pitted rural people against outsiders and governments. However, many Latin American governments have responded to the opposition to these trends, as well as the widespread failures to conserve forests, by decentralizing forestry management, either to local governments or to local user groups. The recognition of traditional user rights has helped to restore the livelihoods and dignity of many people living in or near forests, but in some cases this has not prevented clashes with encroaching actors, as the recent bloody conflicts in Honduras demonstrate. The motivations of local governments given authority over forest regulation have not always been oriented to sustainability. Therefore this decentralization effort has also localized the conflicts.

In the Amazon region, the forestry sector has also been impacted by the efforts of various actors to control land: low-income migrants aspiring to small farms, wealthy aspirants to large-scale ranching operations, miners, and indigenous people. Deforestation should be understood as an outcome of forest clearing as part of the scramble for land. The sectoral emphasis on extending physical infrastructure into the Amazon—particularly roads— has increased the economic viability of farming, ranching, and mineral extraction, attracting growing numbers of newcomers. The clashes among these groups may become the major remaining ethnic and ideological source of violent conflict, as the guerrilla movements in Colombia and Peru shrink or become pretexts for straightforward narcotics trafficking. For example, Brazil's MST continued to engage in confrontations with large landowners and with agro-business companies even during Luiz Inácio Lula da Silva's presidency and became increasingly disenchanted with the government's reluctance to redistribute land.

From a political perspective, a key question has been whether the revenues from resource extraction would be allocated in ways that enhance or undermine perceptions of fairness. Venezuela prior to Chávez represents the greatest failure. The assessments in this volume by Deborah Norden and Emily Penner highlight, respectively, the general disillusionment with the fruits of what many thought ought to be prosperity through the oil bonanza, the high level of inequality, and the relative neglect of education for lower-income families even as university students, largely from higher-income families, were heavily subsidized. In contrast, the governments of other Latin American countries have employed various mechanisms, including Brazil's cash transfers to low-income families, Chile's strong emphasis on education (also reviewed in Penner's chapter), and the decentralization of control over mining and oil revenues in Bolivia and Peru, to convey that resource wealth can be shared.

The Broad Sociopolitical Consequences of Economic Development

While hardly any Latin American countries have escaped economic hardships over the past several decades, economic development has proceeded, albeit in fits and starts, with important consequences for the context of intergroup conflict. Real per capita income throughout Latin America has increased more than 2.3 times since 1960.[24] Middle classes have expanded. The capacity (though not necessarily the will) to make transfers to the poorest segments of the population without impoverishing the rest has increased, even without the most direct means of redistributing from the wealthiest to the poorest.

Expansion of the State

Development has meant that Latin American governments in general were able to develop better reach and administrative capacity; the state has been able to heighten its presence in areas that were previously only minimally governed. This has been a countervailing tendency to the reduction of state economic involvement through regulatory liberalization and privatization. Historically, most Latin American states have been weak (Centeno 2002), which undermined the effective implementation of previous state-based development strategies, while some areas remained virtually "ungoverned." Large and ineffective states of the ISI period were scaled back and weakened in the neoliberal era. As usual, regional differences apply. Jennifer Holmes and Sheila Gutiérrez de Piñeres conclude in this volume that greater state presence in Colombian frontier areas has reduced the violence undertaken by guerrillas and paramilitary groups struggling for control over oil and other assets. In contrast, William Barndt argues in this volume that the more active role of the state in Bolivian regions has exacerbated violence, as the government forcefully intervened to disrupt coca-growing in the central valleys in 2001–2002; and the Morales government's efforts to recentralize governance, undertake land reform, and enact other populist reforms in the eastern lowlands in 2007–2008 resulted in a huge spike in violence. This is consistent with the generally acknowledged phenomenon that weakly institutionalized democracies (especially those who have factional political competition) are particularly prone to social violence.

Long-Term Consequences of Liberalization

Liberalization has changed the nature of confrontations between governments and citizens. While police incursions into neighborhoods dominated by gangs have occasionally been met with violence, violent confrontations between governments and citizens over price hikes have been declining because of the reduced incidence of flashpoints triggered by increases in consumer prices. Insofar as liberalization eliminates or at least greatly reduces the incidence of high consumer subsidies, there are fewer occasions when budgetary pressures require the drastic reduction of the subsidies and the possibility of price riots. However, reactions to the global crises to which liberalized economies are exposed have culminated in riots. Peter Kingstone in this volume cites the urban riots in Argentina stemming from unemployment. Liberalization (or marketization) has also been associated with violence in instances where the state has privatized important services such as water.

Political Mobilization

The spread of communications and literacy has contributed to the political mobilization of previously excluded populations. Except for the remnant populations living isolated in the deep forest, low-income populations have more resources to devote to organizing. With this greater capacity, after decades of bitter struggle, lower-income groups have gained the rights to participate politically. Most countries in Latin America democratized in the 1980s. Nongovernmental organizations have proliferated, providing another form of mediation between the aggrieved and their governments. However, this process has been far from straightforward. Some scholars point out that under neoliberalism, democratic consolidation faces a largely distinct set of challenges: the under articulation of societal interests, pervasive social atomization, and socially uneven political quiescence undermined the efficacy of democratic representation and, consequently, regime legitimacy (Kurtz 2004). In the aftermath of neoliberal restructuring, labor movements are less organized than those in Europe 50 years ago. In most Latin American countries, labor is organizationally fragmented and detached from its allies (Levitsky and Roberts 2011, 415).

Eclipse of Overt Military Governance

In part because of economic failures, the assumption, once widely held within military circles, that the armed forces could impose societal discipline in order to foster rapid economic development, whether through rightist or leftist strategies, has largely disappeared. The Peruvian military government of 1968–1975 attempted a leftist economic strategy of nationalization, land reform, and the creation of cooperatives in both industry and agriculture—all steps that resulted in economic failure (Ascher 1984; Hudson 1992). As Kingstone (in this volume) notes, the Argentine military government of 1976–1983, in a heavy-handed liberalization effort, decimated the domestic industrialists, the middle class, and the organized working class, without producing new growth or eliminating inflation. The Brazilian military administrations fared very poorly in the 1980s in the face of high energy prices, high debt service, and rampant inflation; yielding government back to civilians in 1990 reflected the reversal of early economic success. Only the Chilean military yielded control (also in 1990) with the economy in good shape and sound policies that the civilian regime could continue to embrace.[25]

The consequences of this evolution on the viability of armed antigovernment leftist movements have been striking. The eclipse of outright coercive right-wing authoritarian governments, whether military or civilian, along with the demise of the Soviet Union and the end of Cuba's international adventurism, has greatly reduced the rationale and support for radical armed leftist movements.

The "New Left" and Reemergence of Populism

Yet rather than resulting in the conventional democratic interest-group politics of the developed nations—which had been the hope of the "modernization theory" underlying the US "Alliance for Progress" in the 1960s—in some countries a state-led radical economic populism has emerged. Although all "New Left" governments, once in power, have indeed expanded their developmental, redistributive, and social welfare roles, in practice they have been pursuing rather diverse agendas. Some have been more willing than others to use state power to regulate markets, alter property relations, and redistribute income (Levitsky and Roberts 2011, 3). The Chávez government exemplifies statist policies of systematic expansion of state regulation and control of the economy (see Norden, this volume). On the other side, leftist governments in Brazil, Chile, and Uruguay chose to maintain the relatively orthodox macroeconomic policies and liberal democratic constitutions they inherited from their predecessors: they generally maintain strict fiscal and monetary discipline, as well as uphold (or expand) private ownership of productive sectors and let markets determine wages, prices, and labor relations. Left governments in Argentina, Bolivia, Ecuador, and Nicaragua fell between these two poles, using a variety of economic strategies that involve a mix of orthodox and statist policies: using selective forms of state intervention without fully abandoning the market-led model or making the state the primary engine of development (notwithstanding rhetoric of socialism and "endogenous development").

In the absence of military governments, candidates for government office cannot ignore lower-income populations. In combination with the "lost decade" of the 1980s and structural adjustment in the 1990s, this has given rise to two forms of leftist political-economic orientations. The full-blown populism of Hugo Chávez in Venezuela, Juan Evo Morales Ayma in Bolivia, and possibly newly elected Ollanta Humala of Peru have featured denunciations of the neoliberal "Washington Consensus" with greater state intervention, price controls, more confrontations with foreign companies, and more direct redistributive efforts. One political result is that these governments have co-opted the radical impulses of the low-income groups most likely to be resentful of what the leaders characterize as the unequal income distribution within the country and the unfair global system.

While the strongly populist approaches of Bolivia and Venezuela have largely preempted antigovernment confrontations, the possible implosion of the economies, and the polarization stirred by confrontational discourse (particularly the ethnically oriented discourse of Chávez[26] and Morales), impart considerable fragility to the political futures of these countries. If elections lead to conservative or centrist administrations, or if the military intervenes in situations that they see as threatening public order, the violence of ideological confrontation may reemerge.

There is also a much more moderate leftist strain that has grown out of more populist roots and maintains populist rhetoric: the administrations of Lula da Silva and Dilma Rousseff in Brazil, Nestor and Cristina Kirchner in Argentina, Michelle Bachelet in Chile, Mauricio Funes in El Salvador, and Tabaré Vázquez in Uruguay. These leaders emerged from formerly radical movements, and have retained much of the symbolism of their movements but with far more centrist economic policies, pursuing redistribution through higher budget allocations for education, health, and income support for the poor rather than through more directly confrontational means. They have also been able to co-opt most of the leftist sentiment, while maintaining higher economic growth rates through the combination of market-oriented policies and fortuitously high prices for their major exports.

Persistence of Poverty and the Rise of Street Violence

Most Latin American nations, as "middle income" countries, have been able to finance social safety-net programs. As Judith Teichman notes in this volume, Mexico pioneered the significant conditional cash transfers for low-income families, beginning in rural areas but later extended into urban areas as well. Kingstone notes the largely successful parallel program in Brazil, and Argentina's emergency cash-transfer program. However, these programs generally have been too little and too late to prevent the rise of street violence, although Kingstone argues that Argentina's Plan de Jefes y Jefas probably had a significant deterrent effect on crime even if its long-term impact on job creation is arguable. The limitations of the social safety-net programs begin with the fact that the financing of social-protection programs does not guarantee that the poorest segments of the population will be the beneficiaries. Contributory pension plans, for which the poorest families are ineligible, are subsidized significantly more than the transfers for social assistance targeting the poor. Thus Lindert, Skoufias, and Shapiro (2006, 68) report the greater net budget transfers to the upper-income quintiles than the poorer quintiles in five of the seven Latin American countries they assess (Argentina, Brazil, Chile, Peru, and Mexico); and negligible transfers for any income group in Colombia and Guatemala.[27] Second, low investments in education, though they have improved overall literacy and skill levels, have left many children of low-income families without the skills to enter the formal-sector workforce.

Persistent poverty, bleak employment prospects for the poor, and the lack of alternative avenues for upward social mobility certainly provide an important source of the criminal violence that has risen so sharply in many Latin American countries. It is important to note that the individuals involved in the criminal violence that has largely replaced ideologically driven violence are not a "counter-elite" contesting for governmental control. Earlier violent confrontations frequently entailed guerrilla groups trying to topple governments—the Montoneros in Argentina, the VAR Palmares in Brazil, Colombia's M-19 and FARC, Peru's Shining Path, et cetera. The leaders of these movements aspired to become the government elite. In contrast, today's criminal gangs aspire to wealth and respectability, and typically are content to coexist with the government, military, and police; they battle with the state only out of defensiveness. As Judith Teichman's chapter in this volume notes, the Mexican drug traffickers coexisted (and colluded) in relative peace with the dominant Institutional Revolutionary Party (PRI) before it lost its monopoly over the national government; the violence began to escalate under the efforts of President Vicente Fox (the full-scale confrontation between Mexican drug cartels and the Mexican state erupted after Mexican president Calderón launched the offensive against the cartels). However, in one respect the largely nonideological gangs have indeed become counterelite, albeit reluctantly. In urban neighborhoods where government services are low, gang leaders provide some of these services, extract resources from residents, and mete out "rough justice"; in short, it is the classic "mafia" outcome of the vacuum of official governance.

Perceptions of Economic Justice

From the perspective of the poor, both the resentment against wealthier groups and the rationalizations for criminal behavior are shaped in part by perceptions of economic justice. From the perspective of the non-poor, the legitimacy of government transfers to the poor depends on explanations for poverty: if the poor are viewed as lazy or wasteful, they are owed nothing; if the income distribution is viewed as unfair, the obligation to redistribute is more compelling. It would seem obvious that the perception of economic unfairness would closely correspond to the degree of inequality. Yet this is not correct: there is very little correlation between inequality and perceptions of economic unfairness. Figure 1.1 displays the percentage of people in the 18 largest Latin American countries (excluding Cuba) who deem the income distribution as "fair" or "very fair" according to the latest Latinobarometro survey, and the most recent estimates of the Gini index of inequality.[28] The obvious outlier is Venezuela, and although some skepticism has been expressed about the reliability of official figures, it is generally acknowledged that the overall income distribution has become more equitable (Gasparini, Cruces, and Tornarolli 2009).[29] According to the Latinobarometro surveys, a higher percentage of Venezuelan respondents judged the income distribution as fair or very fair than in other Latin American countries in 2010. Yet the percentage of respondents judging the Venezuelan income distribution as fair or very fair declined 7 percentage points from 2010 to 2011, without a change in the regime. In contrast, Ecuador, with a relatively unequal distribution of income, experienced an increase of 10 percentage points in the same measure over the one-year period, giving it the highest score of all. This

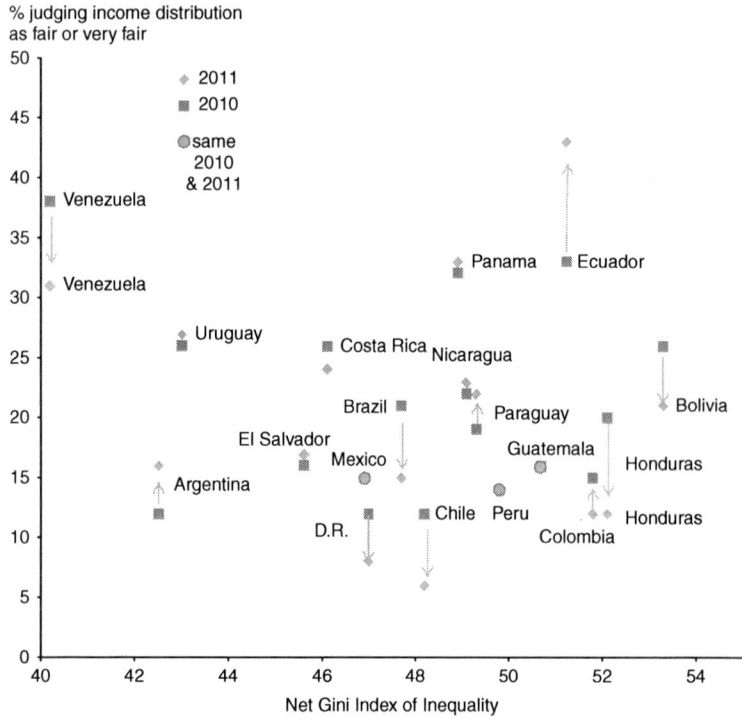

Figure 1.1 Income distribution and perceptions of income fairness, major Latin American countries.

Source: Corporación Latinobarometro 2011.

coincides with the Ecuadorean government's high-profile announcement of its intentions to create a price-control superintendency, to rein in alleged monopolistic behavior by large-scale businesses, and to gain greater control of the banking system (Dabes 2011; Gill 2011). The perceptions of the fairness also shifted substantially for Honduras, Bolivia, Chile, Brazil, and the Dominican Republic. Any real changes in the distribution of income from 2010 to 2011 could only be minimal, and certainly cannot account for the changes in perceptions.

The Venezuelan case helps to understand the lack of straightforward correspondence between actual levels of equality and perceptions of fairness. The most reliable time series of the Venezuelan Gini index, as displayed in Table 1.2, demonstrates a narrow range over nearly three decades, compared to the range for other countries,[30] and little change over the Chávez years up to the latest year covered by the estimates. One interpretation is that the

Table 1.2 Gini index of inequality, Venezuela, 1985–2007

	Solt 2010	Huber et al. 2006
1980	42.4	47.5
1985	42.0	44.9
1990	40.6	44.0
1995	43.5	46.6
1996	45.1	49.7
1997	44.8	49.4
1998	43.7	47.2
1999	43.2	47.0
2000	42.1	44.1
2001	42.7	46.4
2002	42.5	47.5
2003	43.3	46.4
2004	42.7	45.4
2005	42.1	47.6
2006	41.2	
2007	40.2	

Sources: Solt 2010; Huber et al. 2006.

heavily publicized efforts to redistribute income have had impacts on perceptions beyond what the actual trends would warrant. However, the problem with assessing income distribution in Venezuela is that efforts to diminish poverty and alleviate inequality have mostly come from direct social spending through the so-called Bolivarian Missions (largely volunteer-staffed programs providing social services, subsidized food, and other poverty-targeted assistance), mainly out of hidden budgets.

In contrast, the Argentine case demonstrates that the magnitude of strife over income distribution—any observer of Argentina would acknowledge that this strife has been very high for many decades—strongly promotes perceptions that the distribution of income is unfair. The irony is that this contention has impelled periodic movements to greater equality, but we may speculate that contention has heightened the sensitivity to existing inequalities.

Economic Policy Discourse and the Formation of Identifications

In addition to the impacts of economic outcomes, the discourse employed in deliberating over and announcing economic strategies and policies contributes to the shaping of politically relevant identifications. Race and ethnicity have always been relevant in Latin America, since darker skin is correlated with poverty and a lack of political power. However, historic policies of assimilation, along with sustained myths of "racial democracy," have kept them hidden. For various reasons, these have recently become more salient in several countries. The rhetoric of the populists in Venezuela and Bolivia, though basically focusing on class differences, has strong ethnic overtones. The Brazilian government's surprising adoption of affirmative action for Afro-Brazilians in 2000 has highlighted a racial distinction that had never been recognized formally in Brazil. It is striking, however, that affirmative-action programs in most of Latin America are understood to be programs to channel funds and special programs to relatively isolated, low-income rural areas, where indigenous groups reside, rather than to explicitly privilege indigenous or Afro-Latin-American individuals for jobs, government contracts, or reserved seats in institutions of higher education.[31]

The following chapters go into far more contextualized analysis of the experiences of nine Latin American nations. Judith Teichman's chapter on Mexico emphasizes the delayed consequences of the social exclusion caused by the series of economic policies, whether the earlier inward industrialization or the later economic liberalization. She argues that after the commitments to improve rural infrastructure and small-scale agricultural productivity of the 1930s gave way to sectoral policies favoring industry and large-scale, export-oriented agriculture, the rural areas experienced land consolidation and declining productivity of the communal lands *ejidos*,[32] which, because of the inalienability of their landholdings, could not secure capital from private sources to offset the decline of public expenditure. The long-term consequences have included periodic rural uprisings, in reaction to favoritism to large landholders and the threat of foreign competition; the migration of the rural poor to cities; and the susceptibility of low-income youth to the allures of drug trafficking and other violence-prone activities. She also links the rise in violence to the recently competitive nature of Mexican politics, which undermined the previous collusion between the former authoritarian government and the drug traffickers. Teichman also underscores the importance of the government's efforts to end the drug trade through increasing the activities of military and security forces.

Gustavo Arcia's chapter contrasts the extraordinarily violent patterns of El Salvador and Guatemala with distinctively peaceful Costa Rica, also arguing that economic policies in the two more violent countries stem from socioeconomic exclusion, traced back to raw-commodity promotion in the beginning of the twentieth century and the industrial protection policies from 1930 to 1980. Favored entrepreneurs allied with the political elite, excluding indigenous peoples and the rural poor. Governments neglected the public goods of education, fair legal institutions, or productivity-enhancing reforms. He argues that this socioeconomic exclusion provoked radical movements, countered by military governments or military-dominated governments, and the civil wars that wracked both El Salvador and Guatemala. The aftermath of the wars overwhelms the impacts of contemporary economic policies, as the die was cast once the brutality of wars infected the culture, Salvadoran and Guatemalan youth became involved in US-originated gangs, and the poverty remained entrenched. Arcia's chapter contributes to our appreciation of the sway of perceptions over realities, noting that Costa Rica's peace is reinforced by the false impression that the country is truly a land of small farmers. However, he points out that criminal violence is growing in Costa Rica as well, a disturbing reminder of the contagion of criminal violence.

Jennifer Holmes and Sheila Gutiérrez de Piñeres demonstrate how guerrilla activity in Colombia has tended to coincide with areas dominated by labor-intensive commodities, whereas paramilitary violence dominates in places driven by capital-intensive commodities. Contrasting the different regions producing oil, coca, and coffee, they isolate the impacts of specific economic policies from the trends and conditions affecting the country as a whole. Different patterns of land consolidation, drug eradication, and vulnerability to international market fluctuations help to account for different levels of violence across Colombia. Despite the multiple triggers of violence, they argue that established state institutions can dampen violence significantly during economic change. They argue that improving services and strengthening of rule of law and property rights may be a more viable strategy than attempting another round of land reform or rural development to address the violence. They are generally optimistic that across all regions, services have been improved and state presence is growing, which may eventually deter or at least effectively respond to violence. The nature of the economic resources may matter less than the way in which they are managed and reinforced by state institutions in preventing conflict and violence.

To account for the shift from relatively peaceful 1990s to the highly violent decade following, William Barndt's chapter on Bolivia also takes the approach of contrasting different regions within the country. He similarly employs the regional contrasts to clarify the impacts of economic policies in areas that have experienced violence at different times. Barndt acknowledges that the liberalization initiatives of the 1980s and the populist initiatives of the Morales government since 2006 have had widespread impacts all over Bolivia. Yet he argues that the violence of the 2000s must be understood in terms of more specific policies. In 2001–2002, efforts to eradicate Central Valley coca production unleashed conflict; in 2006–2008, it was not wholesale abandonment of the liberalization strategy, but rather the government's challenging the economic position of the established middle class, which triggered violence in eastern and western Bolivia; Western Highlands violence was a reaction to the Morales government's attempt to recentralize revenues. Barndt's analysis provides a cautionary lesson on the danger of overgeneralizing the impacts of broad development strategies. He also clarifies that although ethnic identity has been heightened over the past two decades, in part due to economic policies, it is not ethnicity per se that triggered violence, as demonstrated by the fact that the reversal of the policies reduced the violence.

Deborah Norden's chapter on Venezuela accounts for the origins and later shift from a relatively peaceful and democratic nation to a more polarized, conflict-ridden one. She argues that until the unraveling of the 1990s, Venezuela's leaders had carefully negotiated political and economic accords among most social sectors and political groups, based on high levels of spending financed through oil revenues. Yet the neglect of investment in alternatives to the oil industry, as well as in education and other aspects of human capital development, left the Venezuelan inefficient, heavily subsidized rentier state vulnerable to disillusionment, and populist mobilization of the groups left out of the distribution of oil-based benefits. She also notes that President Hugo Chávez has capitalized on the previously latent ethnic differences among Venezuelans to heighten the animosity among groups.

Emily Penner takes a different approach in comparing the consequences of policies in the crucial education sector. Latin America is particularly ripe for identifying examples of education strategies that have influenced conflict, both because of the evolving nature of its politics and education policies and because of its history of violent conflict. Considering how much of the conflict of Latin America has been rooted in the frustrations of undereducated, underemployed youth, her assessment of the policies dictating the breadth and quality of education is clearly relevant to all cases. Penner's analysis is focused on Chile and Venezuela; in both countries, education has been at the forefront of domestic policy, and their past political experiences, current policy agendas, and policy climates are impacted by education. While both are pursuing aggressive agendas of education expansion, comparing their respective education policies highlights important differences with regard to conflict. In Chile, education is currently a source of political unity and is being used to help to recover from past conflicts. In contrast, the Venezuelan government has used education policy in an effort to rectify past inequalities, in addition to attempting to marginalize the political opposition. Additionally, education has been politicized in terms of instructional content, with the aim of enhancing Chávez's Bolivarian ideals and increasing participants' willingness to resort to violence to defend the Bolivarian Revolution. Penner's examination of the remarkably variable patterns in both countries goes beyond the question of education as an input to productivity, by analyzing the ideological implications of the control over education, its pedagogical content, and the identifications that arise out of different educational practices. Her analysis highlights why, for education to contribute to peace rather than conflict, policymakers must be conscious of the policies they pursue (and those they neglect to pursue) as well as the contexts into which these policies are inserted.

Peter Kingstone's chapter compares the cases of Argentina and Brazil. Despite their violent and unstable pasts, both countries currently stand out for their apparent success in overcoming their respective struggles over economic development as well as relatively positive cases of democracy and political stability. Kingstone presents the contrasting patterns of political violence in these two countries first in the context of industrial development under ISI strategy and, subsequently, in the context of neoliberal reforms and democratization. Kingstone demonstrates that Brazil's political violence has been replaced with very high levels of violence among urban youths while Argentina's violence has declined, but continues to have political underpinnings. He shares with the other contributions the emphasis on the transformation of ideological-based violence to criminal violence and the diagnosis of socioeconomic exclusion: the shift to a more market-oriented economy has been accompanied by tremendous dislocation and weakening of state support for the poor and vulnerable, and criminality has risen in both countries in direct relation to the breakdown of economic opportunity and state-protection mechanisms. Yet Kingstone highlights the distinctive success of both countries' governments in moderating populist commitments. He also chronicles the recent social safety-net programs that have addressed severe inequality in Brazil and employment instability in Argentina. Finally, the author posits that the relative stability of the prevailing economic model—a "pragmatic neoliberalism" in Brazil and a somewhat more statist version of the same model in Argentina—conceals the enduring limits to development in both countries. Kingstone states that though the young and the poor have not been self-identified as a group in either country, the effects of "structural violence" are quite systematic in their effects. To address this phenomenon and to prevent further spread of criminality, the governments of Argentina and Brazil need to secure better economic opportunities for young people, address inadequacies in their educational institutions, and pursue well-designed police reforms.

Notes

1. Since the late 1970s, very few redemocratized countries have collapsed and returned to more authoritarian regimes.
2. These data, from various issues of the Pan American Health Organization's (PAHO) quadrennial *Health Conditions in the Americas* and the renamed *Health in the Americas*, have been cross-checked with the UN Crime Trends Surveys, United Nations Drugs and Crime, and Interpol data. Police forces often report different levels than the governments' reports to the Pan American Health Organization. The data for Bolivia and Peru are so contradictory that the statistics for these countries do not warrant inclusion.
3. In Caribbean countries, unemployment rates among young people (aged 15 to 24 years) are two to four times those of the adult population (ILO 2011); they account for between 40 and 60 percent of the unemployed in the subregion.
4. Chávez's ascendance to power was quickly followed by Socialist candidate Ricardo Lagos in Chile (2000), Workers' Party (PT) leader Luiz Inácio Lula da Silva in Brazil (2002), Peronist Nestor Kirchner in Argentina (2003), Tabaré Vázquez of the leftist Broad Front (FA) in Uruguay (2005), and Evo Morales of the Movement toward Socialism in Bolivia (2005). By the end of the decade, leftist candidates won presidencies in Nicaragua, Ecuador, Paraguay, and El Salvador. Mexico's radically populist PRD candidate, Andrés Manuel López Obrador, came close to winning the 2010 presidential election.
5. Levitsky and Roberts (2011, 6) define populism as the top-down mobilization of constituencies by personalistic leaders who challenge established elites on behalf of the "people." They stress ontological and historic distinctions between this phenomenon and "leftism" in Latin America. The programmatic content of populist appeals has varied across countries and over time; in the 1990s, it actually took right-wing and even neoliberal form, as political outsiders organized the poor against a political and economic elite associated with the ISI state (ibid.).
6. This issue has been addressed by Yashar 2011.
7. The UN Economic Commission for Latin America and the Caribbean (2010, 11) has calculated that the proportion of people in 18 Latin American countries living in extreme poverty fell to 13 percent in 2009 from 22 percent in 1990; the proportion in poverty (including those in extreme poverty) fell to 33 percent from 48 percent. While any poverty statistics are shaped by the somewhat arbitrary cutoff points defining the poor and the extremely poor, these trends are quite striking.
8. OECD (The Organisation for Economic Co-operation and Development) data shows that the contribution of social programs to inequality reduction in the region is far less than for European countries. Most scholars agree that the nature of employment generation is probably the key factor in addressing high and pervasive inequality in the region.
9. While conditional cash-transfer programs had a positive effect on income and consumption in the least favored sector of society, which led to a decrease in

poverty level, their effect on intergenerational mobility seems to be insignificant. Moreover, they do not usually cover households that are in transitory situation of poverty (due to acute economic crisis or extreme weather-related phenomena) (UN Development Program 2010, ch. 5). Argentina in the early 2000s may be an exception.
10. Even so, Chile, Argentina, and Uruguay also depended on primary products for their export earnings.
11. In this process, much of the indigenous peasantry was displaced to marginal regions and lands. In some countries of the region, the expansion of the estates at the expense of community lands continued well into the middle of the twentieth century (Kay 2000, 7).
12. As promotion of agricultural exports usually meant support for big commercial agriculturalists using capital-intensive methods, small landowners, tenants, and rural workers again found themselves at disadvantage.
13. While some scholars present these reforms as successful (Sparovek and Maule 2009; Deininger 2003), others assess their results as limited, if not disappointing (Borras 2003).
14. This dynamic is most prominently presented by Hirschman (1963) with respect to Chile.
15. The interest rates on existing private international loans vary daily according to the current rate.
16. Another explanation of course is not the reformers' political prudence but the fact that Latin America does not rank high in indices of policy quality: noncooperative political coordination among different governmental agencies, subnational authorities, and other actors involved in the policymaking processes hamper policy implementation.
17. Of the countries with more modest scope of reforms, Uruguay had thorough financial-market reform and significant trade reform; Costa Rica significant fiscal and trade reform; El Salvador thorough financial-market reform; Nicaragua significant financial-market reform and privatization. Argentina had significant financial-market reform; Guatemala significant trade reform; Paraguay significant financial-market reform. Brazil, Ecuador, Honduras, Peru, and Venezuela had no significant liberalizations in any of the areas.
18. The regional average of the overall "structural reforms index" began at 0.341 in 1985, was at 0.384 in 1989, and was 0.583 by 1999. Of course, the changes in the indices for specific countries varied considerably, yet every country showed an increase from 1990 to 1999 (except Nicaragua, for which data were not available for 1990) (Lora 2001, 30).
19. For example, Lastarria-Cornhiel (2006, 17) asserts that "[t]he adoption of neo-liberal economic policies and economic re-structuring became widespread in Latin America beginning in the early 1980s."
20. Several other scholars have commented on this phenomenon (see, e.g., Lucero 2008; Van Cott 2007).
21. The "Beijing Consensus" has emerged as an alternative approach to economic development aimed to use "economic and governance to improve society." The

term was introduced into the mainstream political lexicon by J. C. Ramo, a former senior editor of *Times Magazine* (Ramo 2004).
22. In Argentina, the largest nationalization project was the reversal of the privatization of two airlines.
23. These are budget allocations instituted in Peru in the mid-1970s but with increasing shares of oil and mining revenues going to the extractive areas. See Arellano-Yanguas 2011.
24. World Bank: World Development Indicators, various years.
25. One can argue though that economic upturn in Chile from 1987 was largely the result of increase in copper prices. Also, the increase in nontraditional agricultural exports that led growth was started under Frei before the military took over. On the other side, Judith Teichman (2001, ch. 4) posits that in their pursuit of capital liberalization policies the military in Chile made mistakes that were economically and socially costly, for instance, the Chilean taxpayers are still paying down the "subordinated" debt accrued when the military government bailed out the banks.
26. See Deborah Norden's chapter in this volume for an analysis of the implications of Chávez's discourse.
27. For Argentina, the equivalent of US$60 per capita for the top quintile compared to US$10 for the bottom quintile; Brazil and Chile, US$50 for the top quintile and US$10 for the bottom quintile; Peru, nearly US$30 for the top quintile and nearly zero for the lowest quintile; Mexico, US$15 for the top quintile and nearly zero for the lowest quintile. In Colombia and Guatemala, the transfers were less than US$10 across all quintiles.
28. The Latinobarometro figures can be found in Corporación Latinobarómetro 2011, 34.The Solt estimates of Gini indices correlate at 0.90 with the estimates of the UN Development Programme for the "income Gini coefficient." The UN Development Program estimates are from the World Development Indicators Database (World Bank 2011); the Solt estimates can be found at http://dvn.iq.harvard.edu/dvn/dv/fsolt/faces/study/StudyPage.xhtml?studyId=36908&tab=files. The Solt estimates have the advantage of being more up-to-date, and having smoothed the apparent anomalies found in other Gini index time series. Also it is not clear to what year each UNDP estimate pertains.
29. For further cross-checking on the Venezuelan inequality trends, two different measures are reported in Table 1.2: the net Gini index from Solt 2010 and the estimates generated by Huber et al. 2008, which represent the gross Gini index. See also Huber et al. 2006. The reassuring point is that the changes from the average 1995–1999 Gini indices to the average 2000–2005 indices are quite similar: a reduction of inequality to 42.6 from 44.1 for the Solt measures; to 46.2 from 48.0 for the Huber et al. 2008 measures.
30. Brazil, 55.8 in 1980 and 47.7 in 2008; Argentina, 39.6 in 1982 and 47.5 in 2002; Mexico, 44.9 in 1985 and 49.1 in 2000; and Colombia, 55.8 in 1980 and 47.7 in 1990. From Solt 2010.

31. Besides Brazil, Chile, with a relatively small indigenous population, has a modest indigenous scholarship program. For inventories of programs targeting the low-income rural areas, see Gajardo 2004; Grosh et al. 2008.
32. *Ejidos* are village lands held in the traditional Indian system of land tenure in Mexico and assigned in small parcels to the villagers to be farmed.

References

Arellano-Yanguas, Javier. 2011. Aggravating the resource curse: Decentralisation, mining and conflict in Peru. *Journal of Development Studies* 47(4): 617–638.

Ascher, William. 1984. *Scheming for the poor: The politics of income redistribution in Latin America*. Cambridge, MA: Harvard University Press.

Bautista, Romeo, and Alberto Valdés, eds. 1993. *The bias against agriculture: Trade and macroeconomic policies in developing countries*. San Francisco: ICS Press.

Beall, Jo. 2006. Cities, terrorism and development. *Journal of International Development* 18(1): 105–120.

Binswanger-Mkhize, Hans, Camille Bourguignon, and Rogier van den Brink, eds. 2009. *Agricultural land redistribution: Toward greater consensus*. Washington, DC: World Bank.

Borras, Saturnino. 2003. Questioning market-led agrarian reform: Experiences from Brazil, Colombia and South Africa. *Journal of Agrarian Change* 3: 367–394.

Centeno, Miguel Angel. 2002. *Blood and debt: War and the nation state in Latin America*. University Park: Pennsylvania State University Press.

Corporación Latinobarómetro. 2011. *Informe 2011*. October. http://www.latinobarometro.org/latino/latinobarometro.jsp. Accessed November 12, 2011.

Crisp, Brian, and Michael Kelly. 1999. The socioeconomic impacts of structural adjustment. *International Studies Quarterly* 43(3): 533–552.

Cruz, José Miguel. 2008. *Violence and insecurity as challenges for democratic political culture in Latin America*. Latin American Public Opinion Project, Nashville, Vanderbilt University

Dabes, Cintia. 2011. Ecuador: Anti-monopoly bill passes. *The Argentina Independent*, September 30. http://www.argentinaindependent.com/currentaffairs/newsfromlatinamerica/ecuador-anti-monopoly-bill-passes-/ Accessed November 13, 2011.

Davis, Diane. 2006. The age of insecurity: Violence and social disorder in the new Latin America. *Latin American Research Review* 41 (1): 178–197.

DeFerranti, David, Guillermo Perry, Francisco Ferreira, and Michael Walton. 2004. *Inequality in Latin America. breaking with history?* Washington, DC: World Bank.

Deininger, Klaus. 2003. *Land policies for growth and poverty reduction*. Washington, DC: World Bank.

De Janvry, Alain, Elisabeth Sadoulet, and Wendy Wolford. 2001. The changing role of the state in Latin American land reform. In *Access to land, rural poverty, and public action*, edited by Alain de Janvry, Gustavo Gordillo, Jean-Philippe Platteau, and Elisabeth Sadoulet, 279–303. Oxford: Oxford University Press.

Edwards, Sebastian. 1995. *Crisis and reform in Latin America: From despair to hope.* New York: Oxford University Press.

———. 2010. *Left behind: Latin America and the false promise of populism.* Chicago: University of Chicago Press.

Gajardo, Marcela. 2004. América Latina: políticas educativas de acción afirmativa: Situación, tendencias, perspectivas. In *Políticas educativas y equidad: Reflexiones del seminario internacional*, edited by Juan Eduardo García Huidobro, 101–118. Santiago, Chile. http://wwwfs.mineduc.cl/Archivos/ConvivenciaEscolar/doc/archivo_372.pdf#page=103. Accessed November 10, 2011.

Gasparini, Leonardo, Guillermo Cruces, and LeopoldoTornarolli. 2009. Recent trends in income inequality in Latin America. La Plata, Argentina: CEDLAS, Universidad Nacional de La Plata, August.

Gill, Nathan. 2011. Ecuador economic policy minister king announces resignation, *Bloomberg News*, October 26. http://mobile.bloomberg.com/news/2011-10-26/ecuador-s-economic-policy-minister-king-announces-resignation. Accessed November 13, 2011.

Graham, Carol. 2002a. Crafting sustainable social contracts in Latin America: Political economy, public attitudes, and social policy. Washington, DC: The Brookings Institution Center on Social and Economic Dynamics Working Paper Series No. 29, July.

———. 2002b. Public attitudes matter: A conceptual frame for accounting for political economy in safety nets and social assistance policies, Social Protection Discussion Paper Series. Washington, DC: World Bank Social Protection Unit, December.

Graham, Carol, and Eduardo Lora, eds. 2009. *Paradox and perception: Measuring quality of life in Latin America.* Washington, DC: The Brookings Institution.

Grosh, Margaret, Carlo del Ninno, Emil Tesliuc, and Azedine Ouerghi. 2008. *For protection and promotion: The design and implementation of effective safety nets.* Washington, DC: World Bank.

Hammond, J. L. 1999. Law and disorder: The Brazilian Landless Farmworkers' Movement. *Bulletin of Latin American Research*, 18: 469–489.

Hirschman, Albert O. 1963. *Journeys toward progress: Studies of economic policy-making in Latin America.* New York: Twentieth Century Fund.

Huber, Evelyne, François Nielsen, Jenny Pribble, and John D. Stephens. 2006. Politics and inequality in Latin America and the Caribbean. *American Sociological Review* 71(6): 943–963.

Huber, Evelyne, John D. Stephens, Thomas Mustillo, and Jennifer Pribble. 2008. Social policy in Latin America and the Caribbean dataset, 1960–2006, University of North Carolina. http://www.unc.edu/~jdsteph/common/data-common.html

Hudson, Rex, ed. 1992. *Peru: A country study.* Washington: GPO for the Library of Congress.

Imbusch, Peter, Michel Misse, and Fernando Carnon. 2011. Violence research in Latin America and the Caribbean: A literature review. *International Journal of Conflict and Violence*, 5(1): 87–154.

International Labor Organization. 2011. *Global employment trends for youth: 2011 update*. ILO: Geneva.
Kaufman, Robert. 2011. The political left, the export boom, and the populist temptation. In *The resurgence of the Latin American left*, edited by Steven Levitsky and Kenneth Roberts, 93–116. Baltimore, MD: John Hopkins University Press.
Kay, Cristobal. 2000. *Conflict and violence in rural Latin America*. ISS Working Paper No.312. The Hague: Institute of Social Studies.
———. 2006. East Asia's success and Latin America's failure: Agrarian reform, industrial policy and state capacity. In *Political conflict and development in East Asia and Latin America*, edited by Richard Boyd, Benno Franciscus Galjart, and Tak-Wing Ngo, 21–52. London: Routledge.
Kirby, Peadar. 2009. Neo-structuralism and reforming the Latin American state: Lessons from the Irish case. *Economy and Society* 38(1): 132–153.
Kurtz, Marcus. 2004. The dilemmas of democracy in the open economy: Lessons from Latin America. *World Politics* 56(2): 262–302.
Lanzaro, Jorge. 2011. Uruguay: A social-democratic government in Latin America. In *The resurgence of the Latin American left*, edited by Steven Levitsky and Kenneth Roberts, 348–374. Baltimore, MD: Johns Hopkins University Press
Lastarria-Cornhiel, Susana. 2006. Feminization of agriculture: Trends and driving forces. Rimisp-Latin American Center for Rural Development, November. Background paper for the World Bank World Development Report 2008. http://siteresources.worldbank.org/INTWDR2008/Resources/2795087-1191427986785/LastarriaCornhiel_FeminizationOfAgri.pdf. Accessed September 27, 2011.
Levitsky, Stephen, and Kenneth Roberts, eds. 2011. *The resurgence of the Latin American left*. Baltimore, MD: John Hopkins University Press.
Lindert, Kathy, Emmanuel Skoufias, and Joseph Shapiro. 2006. *Redistributing income to the poor and the rich: Public transfers in Latin America and the Caribbean*. Washington, DC: World Bank.
López-Calva, Luís Felipe, and Nora Lustig, eds. 2010. *Declining inequality in Latin America: A decade of progress?* Washington, DC: Brookings Institution Press and United Nations Development Programme.
Lora, Eduardo. 2001. *Structural reforms in Latin America: What has been reformed and how to measure it*. Washington, DC: Inter-American Development Bank, December.
———. 2007. *The state of state reform in Latin America*. Washington, DC: Inter-American Development Bank..
Lucero, José Antonio. 2008. *Struggles of voice: The politics of indigenous representation in the Andes*. Pittsburgh: University of Pittsburgh Press.
Madrid, Raul. 2011. Origins and policies of the Movimiento al Socialismo. In *The resurgence of the Latin American left*, edited by Stephen Levitsky and Kenneth Roberts, 239–259. Baltimore, MD: John Hopkins University Press.
Mahon, James. 2009. Tax reforms and income distribution in Latin America. Williamstown, MA: Williams College. Prepared for delivery at the XXVIII

Congress of the Latin American Studies Association, Rio de Janeiro, June 11–14.

Moser, Caroline, and Cathy McIlwaine. 2006. Latin American urban violence as a development concern: Towards a framework for violence reduction. *World Development* 34(1): 89–112.

Navarro, Zander. 2009. Expropriating land in Brazil. In *Agricultural land redistribution: Toward greater consensus*, edited by Hans Binswanger-Mkhize, Camille Bourguignon, and Rogier van den Brink, 267–290. Washington, DC: World Bank.

Pan American Health Organization. Various years. *Health conditions in the Americas*. Washington, DC: Pan American Health Organization.

———. Various years. *Health in the Americas*. Washington, DC: Pan American Health Organization.

———. 2011. Statistics on homicides, suicides, accidents, injuries, and attitudes towards violence. http://www.paho.org/english/hcp/hcn/vio/violence-graphs.htm #homicides-n-sa. Accessed October 25, 2011.

Pinstrup-Andersen, Per, ed. 1988. *Food subsidies in developing countries: Costs, benefits, and policy options*. Baltimore: The Johns Hopkins University Press.

Ramo, J. C. 2004. *The Beijing consensus*. London: The Foreign Policy Center.

Rodgers, Dennis. 2009. Slum wars of the 21st century: Gangs, *mano dura* and the new urban geography of conflict in Central America. *Development and Change* 40: 949–976.

Rodgers, Dennis. 2006. The state as a gang. Conceptualizing the governmentality of violence in contemporary Nicaragua. *Critique of Anthropology*, 26 (3), 315–330.

SEHLAC Group. 2010. Instruments for measuring armed violence in Latin America and the Caribbean. Seguridad Humana en Latinoamérica y el Caribe. Discussion Document, Santiago, Chile, June.

Sloan, John. 1984. *Public policy in Latin America: A comparative survey*. Pittsburg: University of Pittsburg Press.

Solt, Frederick. 2009. Standardizing the World Income Inequality Database. *Social Science Quarterly* 90(2): 231–242. SWIID Version 3.0, July 2010.

Solt, Frederick. 2009. Standardizing the World Income Inequality Database. *Social Science Quarterly* 90(2): 231–242. SWIID Version 3.1, December 2011.

———. 2010. Standardized World Income Inequality Database, Version 3.0 Southern Illinois University. http://dvn.iq.harvard.edu/dvn/dv/fsolt/faces/study /StudyPage.xhtml?studyId=36908&tab=files. Accessed October 22, 2011.

Sparovek, Gerd, and Rodrigo Fernando Maule. 2009. Negotiated agrarian reform in Brazil. In *Agricultural land redistribution: Toward greater consensus*, edited by Hans Binswanger-Mkhize, Camille Bourguignon, and Rogier van den Brink, 291–309. Washington, DC: World Bank.

Stallings, Barbara, and Wilson Peres. 2011. Is economic reform dead in Latin America? Rhetoric and reality since 2000. *Journal of Latin American Studies* 43: 755–786.

Teichman, Judith. 2001. *The politics of freeing markets in Latin America: Chile, Argentina, and Mexico.* Chapel Hill: University of North Carolina Press.
Themnér, Lotta, and Peter Wallensteen. 2011. Armed conflict 1989–2010. *Journal of Peace Research* 48: 525–536.
Timmer, C. Peter, ed. 1991. *Agriculture and the state: Growth, employment, and poverty in developing countries.* Ithaca, NY: Cornell University Press.
UN Development Programme. 2010. *Regional human development report for Latin America and the Caribbean.* New York: United Nations.
UN Development Programme. 2011. *Human development report 2011. Sustainability and equity: A better future for all.* New York: United Nations
UN Economic Commission for Latin America and the Caribbean. 2010. *Social panorama of Latin America.* Santiago, Chile.
———. 2011. *Social panorama of Latin America.* Santiago, Chile.
United Nations Office on Drugs and Crime. 2011. Global study on homicide 2011. Vienna, Austria: UNODC. http://www.wider.unu.edu/research/Database/en _GB/wiid/_files/79789834673192984/default/WIID2C.xls. Accessed September 27, 2011.
UNU-WIDER. 2008. World Income Inequality Database, Version 2.0c, May 2008. http://www.wider.unu.edu/research/Database/en GB/database/.
Van Cott, Donna Lee. 2007. *From movements to parties in Latin America: The evolution of ethnic politics.* New York: Cambridge University Press.
Wolf, Eric. 1999 [1969]. *Peasant wars of the twentieth century.* Norman: University of Oklahoma Press.
World Bank. 2011. World Development Database. Washington, DC: World Bank. http://data.worldbank.org/data-catalog/world-development-indicators
Yashar, Deborah. 2011. The left and citizenship rights. In *The resurgence of the Latin American left*, edited by Stephen Levitsky and Kenneth Roberts, 184–211. Baltimore, MD: John Hopkins University Press.

CHAPTER 2

Violent Conflict and Unequal Development: The Case of Mexico

Judith Teichman

In the last 15 years, Mexico has experienced high levels of both political and criminal violence. While the Zapatistas are the most well-known insurgent group in southern Mexico, by the twenty-first century various sources were reporting guerrilla activities in the majority of states and in the Federal District.[1] In addition, drug trafficking and drug violence have expanded throughout the country. These problems have long historical roots and spring from a variety of interrelated social, political, and economic factors. This chapter will focus on the country's development trajectory from the mid-nineteenth century to the early twenty-first century and will make the case that even when the Mexican economy was growing and social peace appeared to prevail, inequality and exclusion persisted. I will further argue that the failure to mitigate these negative aspects of the country's development trajectory has contributed to the current high levels of criminal and political violence. However, poverty and inequality, by themselves, did not produce political violence in Mexico; a key ingredient was a particular kind of state response to societal grievances: one that combined encouraging promises with minimal real concessions, supplemented by brutal repression of those reaping the least from economic policies. Politicizing agents, who contributed to the collective awareness of grievances, also played a crucial role.

This analysis adapts Johan Galtung's concept of "structural violence" (1969). Structural violence, the essence of which is inequality in political power, is distinguishable from other forms of violence in that it is not carried out by a specific actor or actors who intend physical harm (Galtung 1969, 169). It arises from the confluence of state economic and social-policy actions and inactions that, even if unintended, cause physical and psychological harm.[2] Galtung acknowledges that deprivation in basic material needs can cause psychological harm because material deprivation diminishes dignity. This observation is particularly salient in the Mexican case where over history public policies have contributed to the social and political marginalization of culturally distinct (indigenous) peoples whose material deprivation became integral to issues of collective identity and survival. While structural violence under certain conditions may engender violent collective political action, it can also produce high rates of crime due to the social discord it creates. Inequality has been strongly associated with criminal violence (Wade 2004, 582; Fajnzylber, Lederman, and Loayza 2002, 1328), particularly in Latin America. At the same time, regimes engaging in structural violence may also employ direct physical violence (repression) to maintain the level of material deprivation of the oppressed. Both structural violence and direct state repression are integrally intertwined in the Mexican case.

Whether or not collective political violence occurs is heavily contingent on group members' perceptions of deprivation; that is, a group must *recognize* its deprivation. Ted Gurr's notion of "relative deprivation" is helpful in understanding the emergence of collective violence in southern Mexico. Gurr defines relative deprivation as "an actors' perception of the discrepancy between their value expectations and their capabilities" (1970, 24)—put more simply, the gap between what people view as rightfully theirs and what they believe they are able to actually obtain and keep. Hence, expectation and hope for both the present and the future are key ingredients of feelings of relative deprivation, an emotional state that must be felt both broadly and intensively if it is to produce violent collective action (Gurr 1970, 27, 29). This concept is particularly useful in the Mexican case because the rise of opposition in southern Mexico was closely related to the gap between the social justice expectations raised by the Mexican Revolution and its aftermath and the decreasing commitment and ability of the postrevolutionary leadership to deliver on those promises, particularly after the mid-1980s.[3] The relative deprivation gap provided an essential context for activities of a variety of politicizing agents and circumstances. In Mexico, collective feelings of relative deprivation were forged politically over a period of 50 years because of historical events, the construction of historical memories, and the activities of politicizing agents.[4] All of this would not have been possible without structural violence. Hence, the role of the Mexican state in contributing to the circumstances that gave rise to political and criminal violence is central to this analysis. While Mexican insurgent groups have certainly seen their difficulties as stemming from the power of ranchers, big landowners, industrialists, and politicians, their political struggles and insurgencies have, as we shall see, generally been directed against the Mexican state, perceived as not living up to its obligations.

The Historical Origins of Violence in Mexico

Collective political violence in Mexico has long historical roots, stemming from a persistent history of structural violence. Conquest, colonial rule, and the establishment of a primary export economy dependent on cheap Indian labor shaped the emergence of a hierarchical social and political order with marked racial and cultural features. By mid-twentieth century, the indigenous population, the poorest of the country's citizens, were concentrated in south central Mexico, constituting between 28 percent to 37 percent of the total population (Lambert 1967, 42). In time, a majority mixed-blood *mestizo* population came to constitute the middle levels of a social hierarchy that placed a small white minority (around 10 percent) at the pinnacle of economic and political power.

Incessant civil conflict during the first part of the nineteenth century involved fierce struggles that stymied the establishment of national power for many years. When centralized authority finally emerged, it was with the dictatorship of Porfirio Díaz (1876–1911), a regime whose activities marked the epitome of structural violence. Its leadership believed strongly that economic modernization required the application of modern science by a white *criollo* class of industrialists and bankers. It vigorously and successfully pursued measures to increase foreign capital investment in mining and commercial export agricultural production. As a consequence, silver production quadrupled, Mexico became the world's second-largest copper producer (Miller 1985, 275), and a dynamic manufacturing sector arose in the city of Monterrey in northern Mexico. The public treasury, empty when Porfirio Díaz took power, was in surplus and the country acquired a solid international credit rating (Cumberland 1968, 231).

Yet the economic model was a socially exclusionary one, involving a high concentration in ownership of both industry and land and a marked decline in living standards of the mass of the population. The facts that there were high levels of protection and government-granted monopoly concessions in industry (Haber 1989, 44), that industrialists preferred capital-intensive methods, and that entrepreneurs were uninterested in obtaining export markets, all resulted in inadequate employment expansion in industry. The most devastating social consequences occurred in the rural sector, however, where the presence of *ejidos* (communal landholdings) were regarded by the Porfiriato as impediments to economic modernization. The confiscation of Indian lands and land grants to foreign land developers, railway survey companies, and regional political leaders produced an enormous concentration in land ownership (Hart 1997, 129; Haber 1989, 29; King 1970, 5; Cumberland 1968, 198). By 1910, less than 3 percent of the population-owned land and the real wage of the agricultural laborer had dropped to one-quarter of what it had been in 1800 (Tannenbaum 1968, 140; Parkes 1960, 262). Famine stalked dispossessed peasants and the working class. Life expectancy and infant mortality rates deteriorated in the last decades of the Porfiriato (Hart 1997, 158; Cumberland 1968, 192). In addition, the regime was brutally repressive, making social and political change through peaceful means impossible.

The dispossessed popular classes—Indian peasants, small landowners, and workers—fought in the Mexican Revolution (1910–1920), many mobilized by strong and charismatic leaders drawn from their own ranks, such as Emiliano Zapata and Pancho Villa. However, middle-class schoolteachers, shopkeepers, small and medium farm owners (*rancheros*), and some wealthy landowners also supported the revolution. With the political defeat of Zapata and Villa, the rising middle class took control of the revolutionary leadership, and its emerging vision of modernization took hold in the decades to come (Bennett and Sharpe 1982, 175; Smith 1979, 76). However, as we will see, the middle-class revolutionary elite could not dismiss the social justice aspirations of workers and peasants either quickly or easily.[5] In particular, Zapata's revolutionary aspirations for a return of *ejidal* (communal) land became stamped in the historical memory of the Indian peasantry and would be invoked in future struggles.

The immediate postrevolutionary period of ongoing uprisings and repression was only resolved when President Plutarco Elías Calles created a new political party that incorporated state political machines and used patronage to keep violent conflict in check. This party would eventually become the Institutional Revolutionary Party (PRI), a crucial component of the "perfect dictatorship," and instrumental in ensuring decades of political stability and relative social peace after 1940.[6] When the onset of the Great Depression meant that the postrevolutionary leaders could no longer ignore the clamor for redistributive measures, the administration of Lázaro Cárdenas (1934–1940) improved wages, expanded social security protection, and between 1935 and 1940 distributed a total of 45 million acres of land, more than two times what had been distributed by all of the previous governments combined (Parkes 1960, 343). Landless workers declined from 68 percent to 36 percent of the rural workforce between 1920 and 1940

(Hewitt de Alcántara 1976, 4). By the early 1940s, more than one-half of the rural population belonged to *ejidos*, which accounted for more than one-half of total cropland (Parkes 1960, 351). In this way, poor Indians became the co-owners of new large farms. The creation of *ejidos* was accompanied by significant public investment in roads, irrigation works, schools and medical services, and access to credit. The result was an increase in both *ejido* holdings and productivity.

The Cardenista reform experience, in benefiting workers and peasants in ways that no previous regime had, established the PRI as the party of the Mexican Revolution, thereby setting the stage for the years of political stability that would follow. Peasants who did get land became strong regime supporters because the agrarian reform program gave hope to others that someday they too would be beneficiaries, just as urban dwellers who had not yet benefited from improved wages and social improvements believed that they would (Hansen 1980, 173). The failure to live up to these expectations in the decades to come and, later, the PRI's perceived abandonment of this *agrarista* vision would fuel rural mobilization and recourse to political violence.

The antagonism of the increasingly powerful business sector (Saragoza 1988, 192) concerned about the high level of worker and peasant political mobilization and the growing public deficit ushered in the "counterreform"— the post-1940 period. Now the political leadership moved toward a more authoritarian and exclusionary economic model.[7] The emergence of a new wealthy northern commercial agricultural group, with its origins in the postrevolutionary middle class, was the driving force behind these developments. The post-1940 period witnessed the decline of worker and peasant power through the institution of authoritarian corporatist mechanisms of political containment and control. The political leadership (the president, and those closest to him) handpicked the official peasant and worker leaders and party candidates, replacing radical workers and peasant leaders with more acquiescent ones. The 1931 labor code, a law requiring labor organizations to obtain legal recognition from the state, reinforced this control of peasant and worker leaders. From the late 1960s, marketing boards and state farm banks, especially the National Bank of Rural Credit (BANRURAL), which provided support for *ejidos*, became the most important institutions for political control in rural areas. One of the most important factors in the containment of popular unrest was the opportunity for personal enrichment-afforded labor and peasant leaders, who, in return, ensured that their rank and file voted for the PRI at election time.[8]

Insofar as these political arrangements operated to mitigate dissent, they also contributed to what was becoming an evermore exclusionary economic model. Agrarian policy moved away from support for small and ejidal agriculture to an explicit slant toward big commercial export agriculture. Powerful northern agriculturalists close to the presidency and hostile to the collective ejidal received generous support from the state in the form of loans and irrigation works (Hewitt de Alcántara 1976, 177).[9] Meanwhile poor peasant producers in south and central Mexico, dependent upon rain-fed lands and facing a variety of other challenges,[10] saw a steep decline in land redistribution and in the quality of lands received when redistribution did occur (Esteva 1983, 39). Loans available to small and ejidal farmers also fell off while the terms of repayment tightened and the state fertilizer company favored big farmers and made it difficult for small and ejidal farmers to obtain fertilizers (Hewitt de Alcántara 1976, 63, 66). The Green Revolution further deepened the impact of the skewed support for big commercial farmers, since it privileged the new technological packages that small and ejidal farmers could neither afford nor manage successfully. The large commercial farms successfully adopted the new methods and increased their output while small farmer and ejidal yields fell by the 1960s.[11] Increasingly indebted and then bankrupt, small farmers sold their land and *ejiditarios* (members of *ejidos*) rented theirs. Both sought wage labor. As big farms mechanized, however, there was less and less need for paid labor, a reality that contributed to a growing problem of rural unemployment and increased rural-urban migration. However, for reasons explained below, most of these migrants did not find employment in the urban sector either.

From the mid-1950s on, public policy became even more supportive of industrial development, providing a panoply of industrial promotion measures such as high-tariff protection and tax advantages to encourage industry. Manufacturing grew at an average annual rate of 8.7 percent between 1953 and 1970, while agricultural growth slowed to 3.8 percent (Solís 1981, 198). As import substitution in light consumer goods diminished, intermediate, capital, and durable consumer goods production began to take the lead in industrial growth (Aspra 1977, 114; Solís 1981, 171). Importantly, however, these newer dynamic industries were capital intensive (and therefore not important in employment generation) and were dependent upon the importation of inputs and machinery—a feature of Mexican industry with roots in the Porfiriato. The capital-intensive (nonlabor-absorbing) nature of industry, a attribute encouraged by a variety of public-policy measures,[12] meant that industry in urban areas did not provide expanded employment opportunities for rural-urban migrants, and hence the urban informal sector (disguised unemployment) increased. One of the major features of Mexican manufacturing industry continued to be excess capacity attributable to its lack of competitiveness and inability to acquire foreign markets (King 1970,

113). Introduced in 1965, the Border Industrialization Program, involving the establishment of export processing zones that allowed the protection-free importation of industrial inputs for products to be exported, was an attempt to confront the lack of sufficient employment generation. However, a high level of underemployment remained. The high level of rural-urban migration combined with the weak employment-generating capacity of industry resulted in the existence of a very large informal sector, estimated at between 40 and 60 percent of the economically active population by the late 1960s.

While the Mexican middle class grew rapidly during the period (Gilbert 2007, 29), the benefits of prosperity left out a significant proportion of the population. During the 1940 to 1950 period, the bottom 20 percent of the population experienced a worsening of income while the top two quintiles—the beneficiaries of the country's economic growth—saw a substantial improvement in their relative and absolute position (de Navarrete 1967, 154). Between 1963 and 1968, the Gini coefficient remained high at between 0.55 and 0.57, and either continued to increase thereafter or stagnated (Olson 1985, 19; Felix 1982; Glade 1986).[13] Asset inequality was rife in the rural sector where, by the mid-1950s, landownership was once again heavily concentrated (Cockcroft 1983, 178; Aguilar and Carmona 1972, 53).

The social impact of Mexican development was particularly detrimental for rural dwellers. As agricultural salaries declined from 26.7 percent to 21 percent of agro livestock GDP between 1950 and 1967, by 1960, the majority of Mexican cultivators and landless dwellers could not meet basic needs (Hewitt de Alcántara 1976, 129, 133). By 1970, rural poverty stood at 49 percent of the households (with overall poverty at 34 percent), more than 3 million rural workers were without any land at all, and half the rural labor force was working as day laborers (Aguilar and Carmona 1972, 208). There was a sharp inequality between northern and central regions, where industrialization produced greater prosperity and less poverty, and the south, where the largest concentration of indigenous population lived and engaged in traditional agriculture.

Resistance to the "Perfect Dictatorship," Development Failures, and the Rise of Violence

From the mid-1940s, regionally based independent peasant movements emerged as peasant disillusionment with the reversal of the Cardenista reform agenda gathered momentum. In the state of Morelos, where Zapata's spirit flourished, between 1942 and 1962, peasants led by Rubén Jaramillo took up arms on three occasions in their struggle for better crop prices, credit, and land reform.[14] On these occasions, the recourse to arms followed on the heels of broken government promises and brutal state repression (Padilla 2007). Sporadic resistance, including violent resistance, to the decline of government support for the peasantry continued through the 1950s and into the 1960s drawing on the historical legacy of Zapata, as later guerrilla movements would. For the most part, however, rural leaders pursued legal and electoral means, resorting to violence when the state responded with repression to their demands.

In the 1960s and the early 1970s, two small but significant armed movements operated in the state of Guerrero, one of the poorest states in Mexico: the National Revolutionary Civic Association (ACNR), led by Genaro Vásquez, and the Party of the Poor, led by Lucio Cabañas. Both leaders were rural schoolteachers. A bastion of Zapata support during the Mexican Revolution, Guerrero politics and economy continued to be dominated by a handful of powerful families. Cabañas took up arms in 1967 following government repression of an opposition rally in which eight people were killed. Although the guerrilla band itself was small, it took seven years, 24,000 army troops, and the initiation of a "dirty war" to defeat the guerrilla threat in Guerrero. This difficulty no doubt stemmed from what the CIA, in its analysis of the movement, refers to as Cabañas's "widespread support and sympathy among peasants" (Doyle 2003, 1). Other organizations, such as the General Union of Mexican Workers and Peasants (UGOCM), and the Independent Peasant Confederation (CCI), demanded land redistribution through the 1950s and the 1960s and met with state repression (Harvey 1998, 123).

By the early 1970s, rural unrest and a marked rise in independent unionism were further stimulated by the influx of students, radicalized by the 1968 student massacre in Mexico City, into rural areas for the purpose of organizing (Hansen 1980, 229). Faced with rising popular pressure, President Luís Echeverría (1970–1976) began to make concessions to rural dwellers: His government expanded credit, guaranteed agricultural prices, restored ejidal lands to original owners, and purchased land to create additional *ejidos*. These concessions, however, stimulated further rural unrest, as peasants recognized that the regime could be compelled to make concessions. When a rash of land invasions occurred in the state of Sonora in 1975, the government expropriated 4,387 hectares of irrigated land and distributed it among 433 peasants (Sanderson 1981, 40). This act was followed by more land invasions in the states of Durango and Sinaloa and the granting of additional lands to *ejidos*.

These developments caused increasing alarm among the country's powerful private sector, concerned both with the threat to property rights and with the rapid rise in public spending (Ayala Espino 1988, 295, 60). By

1976, capital flight had assumed disastrous proportions (Fitzgerald 1979, 49) and, as the current account shot up, the government signed a politically unpopular agreement with the International Monetary Fund in 1976. The following administration of José López Portillo (1977–1982), in seeking to jump-start economic growth through developing the country's vast petroleum reserves, reinforced the predisposition to capital-intensive economic growth. His plan called for the doubling of crude production and refining capacity in six years and for the tripling of the country's production of basic petrochemicals (Teichman 1988, 60). While state-led petroleum-based expansion saw growth rates averaging 8.5 percent per year between 1978 and 1981, in the long term, the strategy worsened the situation of the urban and rural poor and set the stage for rising political unrest for the reasons explained below.

The new strategy changed the structure of the Mexican economy: Whereas in 1976 petroleum and its derivatives accounted for 16.8 percent of the value of exports, by 1981, this figure reached 74.4 percent. The rapid growth and its capital-intensive nature based on petroleum extraction and petrochemicals increased the country's appetite for imports and allowed the country to borrow heavily on the international market. It did so at floating interest rates, an imprudent strategy that would have devastating economic and social consequences. With petroleum export-led growth, Mexico began to suffer from the "Dutch disease" in which the inflationary pressures caused by the inflow of capital produced an overvalued currency that made nonpetroleum exports uncompetitive. The share of manufacturing of exports began to decline (Teichman 1988, 75) and agriculture fell into crisis (Esteva 1983, 9). By 1980, food exports dropped and one-quarter of all foodstuffs had to be imported.

Given its capital-intensive nature, the petroleum-export strategy was not an effective job producer—so it did not address the plight of the country's large informal sector workers (Székley 1983, 109). As the inflow of capital stimulated inflation, the purchasing power of the population declined. Real minimum salaries fell by an accumulated index of 12 percent between 1977 and 1980 (134). After 1980, the programs for the poorest that had been initiated by Echeverría were dropped and land reform was declared to be no longer the objective of rural policy (Sanderson 1981, 1). Finally, there were no fiscal redistributive arrangements in place to ensure that the wealth generated from this capital-intensive model would be allocated to the social classes and regions that needed support. Prior to the 1991 fiscal reform, federal revenue sharing was distributed to states based on their individual collection efforts, which meant that the poorer states received about one-third of the amount per capita received by richer states (Rodríguez 1997, 91).

While urban areas were calm, the petroleum-export strategy galvanized opposition from peasants in petroleum-producing regions. As Ascher observes, resource development inevitably entails the enrichment of particular groups and the relative deprivation of others (Ascher 1999, 182). Although, as he points out, this does not necessarily result in political opposition, it did in the case of Mexico. A variety of state actions, in violating expectations instilled by the Mexican Revolution and its attendant promises, propelled rural dwellers into protest. A law passed in 1977 stipulated that all lands were to be subject to immediate expropriation if oil and gas deposits were discovered, thereby giving the state petroleum company, Petróleos Mexicanos (PEMEX), control over all surface and subsoil rights, including those of ejidal and communal lands—an action specifically violating the assumption of the state as the protector of ejidal lands. Although the law provided for compensation, it was slow in coming and generally inadequate. The consequence was growing unrest in the petroleum-producing states of Tabasco, Chiapas, and Veracruz. In 1977 and 1978 alone, there were 42 blockades of PEMEX installations (Prevot-Schapira 1982, 166). Such incidents escalated after 1978.

However, while the petroleum boom was an important contextual contributor to unrest, the growing strife in Chiapas also built upon long-standing grievances of earlier years. The Mexican Revolution, the land redistribution during the Cárdenas years, and President Echeverría's brief foray into land reform, all contributed to the expectation that peasants without land would eventually be able to obtain it. However, in Chiapas, petitions for land had been largely ignored in the face of a particularly intransigent landowning class, and so peasants began to invade the lands for which they had been unsuccessfully petitioning and were met with state repression (Harvey 1998, 92).

Meanwhile, the socioeconomic changes wrought by resource development had a profound impact on rural welfare. Beginning with President Echeverría and accelerating during the López Portillo years, the federal government invested heavily in infrastructure and oil production in the Chiapas. Although rich in natural resources (oil, natural gas, coffee, and hydroelectric power), Chiapas remains one of the poorest states in Mexico. As traditional farming declined and state investment in oil production increased, employment generation was inadequate, and the rural population became increasingly differentiated between those (relatively few) able to take advantage of the new opportunities and the majority who could not (Collier 1994, 97).[15] Those able to accumulate extra cash were able to improve their farm production acquiring the land of poorer peasants without financial resources, who became landless wage laborers.[16]

While competition for resources was intense and economic hardship widespread in Chiapas, conflicts among the poor along ethnic and religious lines were not the main source of violent conflict. Rather, conflict occurred largely between poor indigenous groups, on the one hand, and powerful groups such as ranchers,[17] logging companies, and the state, on the other. The general absence of violent ethnic and religious conflict among peasant groups was likely related to a number of factors that dulled potential sources of hostility. Indigenous people saw themselves as sharing a common condition of deprivation; land colonization did not cause peasants to lose land to other peasants, since the programs involved the occupation of vacant land or land claimed by logging companies and significant out-migration from the state may have alleviated pressures that could have contributed to conflicts (Villafuerte Solís 2005, 477).

The economic changes that had occurred in Chiapas—changes that involved increasing socioeconomic polarization followed by a clear message that state support would no longer be forthcoming—set the stage for an intensification of feelings of relative deprivation. By the mid-1970s, new actors galvanized these feelings of popular discontent. In 1974, the Indigenous Congress, organized by Bishop Samuel Ruiz, was instrumental in the subsequent rise of the radical peasant movement in Chiapas. The Congress, which involved Indian communities in ongoing discussions, focused on pressing social issues, later taken up by the Zapatistas: land, health care, sufficient food, and education. In bringing together indigenous people from throughout the state, the Congress helped develop an awareness of shared problems and inspired the emergence of a number of independent peasant organizations (Collier 1994, 65–76). At this time, however, the leaders who emerged from the Congress and their organizations did not advocate armed struggle but insisted on a strategy of gradually building up independent organizations.

Marches and demonstrations accelerated through 1981 and 1982. These activities were met with repression and the arrests of leaders (Harvey 1998, 110). Under the weight of the sharp economic downturn linked with the debt crisis, its attendant economic restructuring, and growing political repression, popular support for peasant organizations would soon shift to the Zapatistas and armed struggle.

From the Debt Crisis to Market Reform:
The Expansion of Guerrilla and Drug Violence

The debt crisis triggered profound economic policy changes. Faced with a decline in petroleum prices, increased interest rates, and capital flight,

Mexico experienced its worst recession since the Great Depression. Two administrations, those of Miguel de la Madrid Hurtado (1983–1988) and Carlos Salinas de Gotari (1989–1994) oversaw the rise and implementation of market liberalizing reforms. Ultimately, these reforms contributed to greater poverty, particularly in southern Mexico.[18] Indeed, as the 1982, economic crisis was followed by another economic downturn in 1985 and the peso crisis of 1995, both widespread poverty and inequality remained intractable problems everywhere in Mexico. These economic events contributed both to the rise of guerrilla activity and criminal violence related to the drug trade. Their contribution, however, was integrally intertwined with politics and the political response of the state.

In 1985, trade liberalization went forward rapidly; from 1989, the government initiated the most important privatizations; and in 1994, Mexico signed the North American Free Trade Agreement (NAFTA) with the United States and Canada. One of the most controversial market reforms involved the reform of Article 27 of the constitution in 1992. This reform declared the end of land redistribution and effectively put an end to the *ejido*, the collective landholdings of much of the country's poorest peasantry. With the aim of stimulating investment and export competitiveness in the agricultural sector, the reform gave communal farmers the legal right to hold title to land and therefore the right to sell or rent the land and to form joint ventures with private agribusinesses.[19] In addition, the new law deleted the section of the constitution that had allowed peasants to petition for land redistribution. The new law, in combination with the increasing hardship faced by farmers (explained below), was instrumental in convincing the mass of poor indigenous peasantry, long hopeful that the state would fulfill the peasant aspirations of the Mexican Revolution, that the state had abandoned them. While big ranchers applauded the reform, it fuelled peasant fears that land would become increasingly concentrated.[20] The impact in Chiapas was particularly acute because there was an unusually high number of unresolved land petitions in that state, and peasants now feared that all of the unresolved petitions would be rejected (Harvey 1998, 188). Hence, many peasants now lost all hope of ever obtaining a piece of land. In the words of Neil Harvey, the privatization of the *ejido* "constituted a symbolic break with the past" while offering no guarantees of improvement in the future (188).[21] In addition, the lack of access to land on the part of many young indigenous men fuelled disputes over land, increasing desperation particularly in Lacandon region, the very region that would provide the strongest base of Zapatista support (191).

As the country's political leaders dismantled the state, small and ejidal farmers, who had gained the least from the economic growth of the last

40 years, now lost the minimal state support of earlier years. Marketing boards, such as the Mexican Coffee Institute (Instituto Mexicano del Café, INMECAFE) and the coffee marketing board, were abolished. Credit from the bank providing funds to the ejidal sector was first reduced and then the bank itself was eliminated. Guaranteed farm prices were removed from all products except corn and beans, and import licenses were abolished for all agricultural products except corns, beans, wheat, and powdered milk (Martínez and Fárber 1994). Lustig concludes that the dismantling of state support during the early 1990s likely left many indigenous communities worse off than before (Lustig 1998, 209).

NAFTA, combined with the skewed nature of the new agricultural support system put in place to help farmers face changes in protection, had a devastating impact on the country's small and ejidal farmers. While the NAFTA agreement provided for a 15-year phase-in period for the removal of tariffs and import quotas for maize and beans (produced by indigenous peasants in south central Mexico), the Mexican government accelerated the liberalization process arguing the need to avoid national shortages (Acuña Rodarte 2003, 135).[22] The consequence was a rapid rise in the exportation of much cheaper maize and bean imports.[23]

The impact was dramatic. Farm employment dropped dramatically from 23 percent of total employment in 1990 to 12 percent by 2008 (Fox and Haight 2010, 29). A Carnegie report, documenting the effects of NAFTA, estimates that 1.3 million rural jobs were lost by 2002 (Polaski 2003, 17, 29) while another study puts the figure at 2 million (Fox and Haight 2010, 29). Rural day laborers faced deterioration in pay and worsening working conditions (López Gámez and Ovallo Vaguera 2001, 90). However, while there is no doubt that US imports drove the price of Mexican corn down and contributed to rural unemployment, corn production did increase within Mexico. There were two reasons for this. Large commercial producers, including multinational ones, increased production because of their access to various generous government support programs established specifically for them; indeed, many commercial farmers received government support from several such programs (Fox and Haight 2010, 134). Even the Farmer's Direct Support Program (PROCAMPO, Programa de Apoyos Directos al Campo), instituted to compensate farmers faced with competition from imports, has mainly benefited larger farmers having more than 5 hectares of land, while subsistence farmers with fewer than 5 hectares received only 8 percent of PROCAMPO payments (Corbacho and Schwartz 2002, 8). It is important to underline that this program provided no benefits to the landless. At the same time, farmers on small plots have also continued to grow corn in the absence of resources that would have allowed them to switch to alternative crops or due to their inability to find alternative employment (Henriques and Patel 2004, 4). One study suggests that while older small corn farmers continued to produce corn, their unpaid family labor (sons and daughters) were forced to leave the farm and migrate. Family members leaving farming probably form the bulk of the rural unemployed (Fox and Haight 2010, 33).

While southern rural farmers have been particularly disadvantaged, Mexico's social situation in general has been poor. Sharp upswings in poverty followed each economic downturn with persisting high levels of inequality. The decline in wages that had begun in the aftermath of the debt crisis continued to be a feature through the 1990s (Dussell Peters 2000, 157). When salaries fell, incomes of those in the informal sector also faired badly as they depended upon purchasers in the formal sector. Poverty, at 32 percent of the population in 1977, had increased to 39 percent by 1984, and, following the 1995 peso crisis, reached a high of 46.9 percent before declining to 41.1 percent by the year 2000 (Wilkie 1999, 428; ECLAC 2007, 299–300).[24] Faced with the financial crisis in 1995, the government removed subsidies on corn and tortillas, causing increased hardship among the urban poor. The marked regional dimension to poverty in Mexico, not illustrated by aggregate national figures, is important. Much higher levels of poverty existed in rural areas where poverty stood at 56 percent in 2000 (ECLAC 2007, 299–300). However, even higher levels were present in the southern states of Chiapas, Guerrero, and Oaxaca—areas of high concentration of the indigenous population (Lustig 1998, 205). Finally, income distribution remained unchanged or worsened during the 1990s with an increasing concentration of income in the top 10 percent of the population (Dussell Peters 2000, 156).

The deteriorating social situation had spurred the establishment of a new type of social program by 1989: The National Solidarity Program or PRONASOL provided federal matching funding for local improvement projects. Widely accused of being used for political purposes, it provided more support to Chiapas than to any other state. However, the program failed to shore up political support for the PRI in that state. Indeed, the administration of the program further angered peasants because municipal mayors loyal to the PRI denied the funds to independent peasant organizations. The accumulated grievances of recent years would eventually be channeled by the Zapatistas.

Beginning in the early 1980s, there is a notable decline in electoral support for the PRI and a rise in electoral absenteeism in rural Mexico (López Gámez and Ovallo Vaguera 2001, 109). The continuation of violent government repression of independent peasant organizations after 1990 and divisions within these organizations, rendering them increasingly incapable of defending peasant interests, were probably the most important proximate factors producing growing support for the Zapatistas—support that would be sufficient to launch an armed uprising (Harvey 1998, 197). When the Zapatista rebellion burst forth in January 1994, its declaration demanded "jobs, land, housing, food, heath, education, independence, liberty, democracy, justice and peace" (Russell 1995, 38). Later, the Zapatistas demanded a "radical transformation of the national pact" that would include regional/local political autonomy for indigenous communities (EZLN 1995). They also declared resistance to all aspects of the country's neoliberal development model (EZLN 2005). By 1999, at least 14 additional rebel groups had been identified in the region, a number that increased thereafter. Mexico's southern states remain highly militarized.

By the mid-1990s, guerrilla activity in Guerrero, which continued to be inspired by the legendary guerrilla leaders, Zapata and Cabañas, was once again on the rise with various actions carried out by two organizations, the EPR (the Popular Revolutionary Army) and a splinter group, the Insurgent People's Revolutionary Army. The 1980s had also witnessed the growth of autonomous peasant organizations in that state and a number of them had joined together to support Cuauhtémoc Cárdenas's 1988 bid for the presidency. At the same time, the large-scale electoral fraud that blocked Cárdenas's victory in 1988, massive electoral fraud at the state and local levels, the slashing of farm subsidies, and the drop in corn and coffee prices, all fuelled growing farmer unrest in Guerrero. In 1994, peasants established a new organization, the Campesino Organization of the South Sierra (OCSS), to represent their interests. This organization was met with brutal state repression, stimulating support for the guerrilla organizations (Paulson 2000, 28). Members of Guerrero's persecuted peasant organizations welcomed the emergence of the EPR (Velasco 2005, 39).

The economic changes instituted since the debt crisis have also contributed to the expansion of the drug trade and its attendant criminal violence. But the new economic conditions have operated in concert with historical contextual factors, with the process of transition to electoral democracy, and alongside the campaign against the Colombian drug cartels—a development that forced a shift of trafficking from Colombia to Mexico. In addition, the social and political realities of much of rural Mexico, characterized by widespread poverty, inequality, political repression, violent feuds between communities, and banditry, have provided fertile ground for the rapid expansion of organized criminal activity.

Although Mexico had been involved in the drug trade for several decades, the Mexican drug cartels have become more powerful since the demise of the Colombian Cali and Medellín cartels in the 1990s. There are currently seven cartels operating in Mexico, and their influence extends into most states of the republic (Cook 2007, 5). Violence occasioned by the drug trade is of several types. The drug cartels themselves carry out extensive violence against police, the military, and public officials, virtually taking control of entire towns that are then left without formal law enforcement. There is also violence between cartels over turf. Finally, the Mexican state itself has became a source of growing violence as various agencies of the state (the military, the federal police) have carried out ongoing campaigns against drug traffickers. Unlawful killings by state security forces, arbitrary arrests, and the use of torture by police are among the long list of transgressions identified by the US Department of State's Bureau of Democracy, Human Rights and Labor (2008).

Features of Mexico's authoritarian legacy, as described earlier, have facilitated the expansion of the drug trade. Not all political regimes give the drug trade the same opportunity to develop. Strong regimes with relatively little preexisting corruption, with well-paid police and government officials, and with strong civil societies, are far better equipped to confront and mitigate the expansion of the drug trade and its attendant violence. Mexico's preexisting levels of political corruption, stemming from the years of PRI rule and its political control mechanisms that promoted the exchange of material rewards for political support, made police and government officials open to the further corrupting tactics of drug traffickers.

At the same time, the neoliberal economic model also made an important contribution to the rise of the drug trade and violence. NAFTA fostered the growth of the drug trade because its trade routes could now be used to smuggle narcotics across the border with more ease. The value of drugs crossing the Mexican border into the United States is estimated at US$20 billion (Miller 2008; Dermota 2007; Weinberg 2002, 18). The combination of the withdrawal of state support for agriculture, the biased nature of the new agricultural supports, which disadvantaged small farmers, and the influx of traditional agricultural products against which domestic farmers could not compete are among the factors pushing poor farmers toward drug production (Weinberg 2002, 23; MacDonald 2005, 115; Malkin 2001, 121). Individualized responses to feelings of relative deprivation are evident among poor single men who leave their local communities to participate in drug trafficking in order to make their fortunes. Many of these returning "narco migrants," having succeeded in amassing some wealth, have used it to buy land and become farmers (MacDonald 2005, 121). It is estimated that the number of people making a living from marijuana and opium cultivation may be as high as 300,000 (Velasco

2005, 94), a figure that does not include the other direct and indirect jobs created by the industry in packaging, transportation, security, and money laundering.

Moreover, lack of opportunity has also encouraged the urban poor to turn to the drug trade. Indeed, the expanding informal economy—an economy that has its origins deep in the country's economic history—is characterized by precarious and poorly paid employment and has provided a reservoir of labor for illegal drug activities (Serrano 2008). The informally employed are easily recruited as mules for the drug traffickers and into the drug cartels' armies. The vast majority of those arrested on drug charges are those of scarce economic means who have been drawn into these lower-level drug activities (Velasco 2005, 108). In the general climate of unemployment and poverty, the young are particularly vulnerable to involvement in illegal activities, including the drug trade (Geffray, Fabre, and Schiray 2002, 11), as they experience social exclusion and may feel a sense of injustice (Moser and Van Bronkhorst 1999). Indeed, one recent study shows that even a small increase in employment opportunities can reduce drug crimes among young males (Ihlanfeldt 2007). The Zetas, an organization of former police officers involved in fighting the drug trade, became the enforcement arm of the powerful Gulf Drug Cartel; its camps recruit and train 15–18 year olds (Grayson 2008). Finally, low public salaries, another symptom of the country's failed development, facilitate drug traffickers' corruption of police and government officials and make recruitment into the cartels relatively easy (Eskridge 2001). Police receiving low pay are particularly vulnerable when given the choice between accepting a bribe and providing protection to drug traffickers versus rejecting the bribe and endangering not only their own lives but also that of their families.

In southern Mexico, an additional ingredient exacerbating the level of violence has been the emergence of paramilitary groups since 1995. It is not entirely clear who directs these violent groups and what exactly their interests are. Nevertheless, they are most assuredly a legacy of the country's authoritarian rule and its attendant social and economic exclusion. In Chiapas, paramilitaries appear to have been linked to the PRI and to have been involved in violent action against political opponents. They also seem to be heavily involved in drug production and trafficking. In Guerrero, the paramilitaries appear to be armed bands controlled at the state level. Velasco characterizes the conflict between the paramilitaries and the guerrillas in the poor southern states of Mexico as involving competition for scarce resources between impoverished groups, some of whom are sympathetic to the government and others who are opposed (Velasco 2005, 55).

Violence and Development in the Twenty-First Century

The election of President Vicente Fox of the right-of-center PAN (Popular Action Party) in the year 2000 marked an important milestone in the Mexican political transition, as the election brought a non-PRI candidate to the presidency for the first time. In the 2006 national election, the PAN presidential candidate, Felipe Calderón, won by such a narrow margin that his victory was contested by the opposition left Party of the Democratic Revolution (PRD). Calderón declared his support for the market economy, for privatization, and for a campaign against the drug trade. The post-2000 period has witnessed both a continuation of rural guerrilla and state violence and a marked upsurge in drug-related violence.

One of the most important factors in the rising drug violence is, paradoxically, the very efforts of recent governments to curb it. Drug production and trafficking has a long history in Mexico going back to the 1930s facilitated by the corruption permeating the state apparatus right down to the federal police who were supposed to be fighting it. However, it is only very recently, since the achievement of electoral democracy, that the trade has engendered such high levels of violence. Indeed, as long as the PRI was in power, the most reprehensible consequences of the drug trade were contained because high-level control of the drug trade was part of an array of hierarchical control mechanisms. Power concentrated in the hands of the president made possible government protection of the trade in exchange for a piece of the action. Hence, the biggest drug traffickers invariably had close ties to high-ranking PRI politicians who, if they were not directly involved in the drug trade, operated to protect it and benefited from it financially. Mexican president Carlos Salinas's brother Raúl, for example, was linked to top drug traffickers through his involvement in money laundering.

Hence, the transition to electoral democracy has contributed to a marked rise in the level of violence. It has unraveled the past-centralized control that kept drug violence in check. Furthermore, as Presidents Fox and Calderón have sought to reduce drug trafficking and its attendant corruption through increasing the numbers of soldiers and police involved in the antidrug trade activities, violence and corruption have increased. Because drug profits are so high (due to the illegality of drugs), drug cartels can afford to meet government-sponsored police and military action against their operations with even higher levels of violence (private armies) and bigger payments to police and government officials. Battles in northern Mexico between drug traffickers and police are becoming the norm. Journalists who write about the drug trade are now at serious risk. According to the Inter-American Commission on Human Rights, in 2006, Mexico outranked Colombia in the number of assassinated journalists (Inter-American Commission on Human Rights 2007, 16–17). In addition to the execution of police and state prosecutors, judges have become targets (Schwartz 2008). At the same time, the government's increased zeal in pursing drug traffickers has continued to result in human rights violations against citizens.

The failure of the neoliberal economic model remains an important factor in the escalation of drug violence. Mexico's continuing poverty and lack of economic opportunity means the cartels will continue to find people to join their ranks. The predisposition of the centre-right Fox and Calderón governments to rely largely on the market as the main instrument for economic growth and employment generation has contributed to this difficulty. Fox's main poverty program, Oportunidades, was a continuation and expansion of the targeted conditional cash-transfer program (Progresa) introduced by his PRI predecessor.[25] While the program no doubt improves the lives of the extremely poor, critics have pointed to deficiencies such as neglect of the moderately poor and the need for complementary programs such as income-generating activities (Teichman 2008; Rawlings 2005).

Neither Fox nor Calderón have addressed the pressing rural grievances adequately, so guerrilla insurgency has continued. Following President Zedillo's rejection of the agreement negotiated with the Zapatistas, another proposal, drawn up under President Fox, became law in 2001. This law fell far short of meeting indigenous aspirations, however. It did not allow local indigenous communities much autonomy and failed to give them control over natural resources, one of their key demands. The likelihood of a PAN government achieving an agreement with the Zapatistas is probably remote, since the most vociferous opposition to the originally negotiated agreement came from the private sector and from the PAN (Hernández Navarro and Carlsen 2004, 453).

An addition to the NAFTA agreement, the regional defense-based initiative called the Security Prosperity and Partnership Agreement (SPP) is yet another factor likely to contribute to the ratcheting up of the level of violence. Although justified by the need to fight drug trafficking and terrorism, the agreement has drawn considerable criticism because it can be used to criminalize social protest (Sciacchitano 2008; Pickard 2007).[26] The lines between the War on Drugs and Terrorism and the war against the popular opposition may be blurred. Market liberalization and NAFTA have meant a continuation, if not deepening, of structural violence, now supplemented by state repression justified on the grounds of terrorist threats and drug trafficking. This structural violence is integrally linked to rising political and criminal violence and to direct violence carried out by the state.

Conclusions

Despite the fact that, in many respects, Mexico's economic strategies have changed substantially over time, I argue that structural violence is an apt characterization of the consequence of economic policies from the late nineteenth century onwards. All of the country's various economic programs have involved the use of capital-intensive methods with scant regard for the implications for employment, small and communal agricultural production, and human welfare in general. The initial drive for modernization carried out at the end of the nineteenth century involved a heavy focus on infrastructural development, capital-intensive industrialization, and free rein for foreign investment, particularly in resource development. The Mexican Revolution gave rise to a much more nationalistic economic model that entailed public ownership and development of natural resources, heavy protection for a growing industrial sector, and restrictions on foreign capital investment. As the postrevolutionary model ran out of steam, the political leadership turned to petroleum as the new basis for export-led growth and the country witnessed a brief period of petroleum-led growth. When this strategy imploded with the drop of petroleum prices and the debt crisis, policymakers initiated the dismantling of many of the interventionist instruments of the past: They dramatically reduced protection on imported products, privatized public companies, and signed NAFTA. None of these economic strategies provided the necessary conditions for sustained improvements in social wellbeing.

While there were periods during which land redistribution and support for small and *ejido* agriculture occurred in the postrevolutionary years (most notably under Presidents Cárdenas and Echeverría), governments mostly supported big commercial export agriculture, a feature that contributed to landlessness and rural-urban migration. The country's industrialization and petroleum-export strategy were also anti poor in their use of capital-intensive methods and neglect of employment generation. In addition, there was an important regional bias in Mexican development from the onset. Economic growth has been especially favorable to northern Mexico—where industrialization and commercial export agriculture has benefited from its proximity to the US market. The more inward industrial-development strategy that got under way after 1940 gave attention to industrial development in and around Mexico City. In southern Mexico, the country's rulers have been primarily preoccupied with resource extraction, showing relatively little concern for the plight of small and communal farmers. Following the debt crisis, economic policy, in the form of structural adjustment, continued to contribute to inequality and poverty: Urban wage laborers lost their jobs while cheap imported agricultural products and a biased agricultural support system contributed to rural unemployment.

Engagement in the drug trade with its high level of violence was an integral offshoot of an economic model that failed to provide economic opportunities. The rapid increase in criminal violence has been encouraged by the lack of economic opportunity and the presence of a high degree of socioeconomic inequality. Government policies, combined with NAFTA, have had a devastating impact on rural employment, encouraging some to turn to drug production. Because aspirations for land and improved living standards could no longer be met by legal means, there is a strong incentive to turn to illegal ones—particularly the drug trade.

While Mexico's exclusionary development has provided one set of underlying conditions contributing to political and criminal violence, the country's authoritarian political arrangements and their fallout gave rise to the awareness of social injustice and precipitated the eventual recourse to violent political resistance. The mechanisms of the "perfect dictatorship," involving as they did the hegemony of a political party claiming to be heir to the Mexican Revolution, held out the promise of land and a better life for the poor masses who supported the PRI. The party's leaders even partially delivered on some of these promises, while at the same time periodically exercising brutal repression against groups seeking to hold it to its presumed revolutionary credentials. The consequence of exclusionary economic policies, combined with this political strategy of containment, was that the government delivered less and less of what it promised, and, in fact, after the mid-1980s, the state began to be perceived as presiding over increased deprivation as it dismantled a variety of support mechanisms and ended the promise for land redistribution. The consequence was the emergence of ever-stronger sentiments of collective relative deprivation and, for some, a recourse to arms in the face of repression. Importantly, the country's guerrilla organizations tie their claims to the demands for social justice made by the peasant hero of the Mexican Revolution, Emiliano Zapata.

Mexican history is characterized by structural violence. The state has consistently pursued economic policies that have not only failed to reduce poverty and inequality sufficiently but have also likely contributed to both. Furthermore, the Mexican state has often exercised direct repression against those seeking to hold it to its revolutionary promises of social justice, thereby setting the stage for collective political violence. The country's political and economic conditions have also provided fertile ground for rising criminal activity, particularly the drug trade. Hence, providing economic opportunities through the pursuit of an economic model that generates higher levels of employment is essential to mitigate the social conditions underlying political and criminal violence.

Notes

1. Velasco (2005, 32) claims that guerrilla groups have been reported in 31 states. More conservative estimates claim that there are guerrilla activities in 19 states, including a number of northern ones. Most observers place the number of guerrilla organizations operating in the country at somewhere between 26 and 30 but acknowledge that it is difficult to know their size and presence (Delmonte 2008, 6; Castro Soto 2000; Turbiville Jr. 1997).
2. State violence includes any form of abuse that causes harm to body or soul. Not only can states create physical and psychological harm through their actions and policies but also those actions and policies can instigate violent behavior on the part of individuals and groups in society.
3. Lupsha (1971) claims that the concept of "indignation" is more useful than that of "relative deprivation." In conflating such a large variety of theories, however, his critique does not do justice to Gurr's concept, which is not simply a psychological theory and which does not preclude an actor's belief that an injustice has been committed. I have chosen to focus on the notion of "relative deprivation" because the key factor creating the basis for unrest in southern Mexico has been the *gap* between the expectations/hopes raised by revolutionary promises and the upsurge in state actions and inactions (especially from the mid-1980s) that convinced rural dwellers that those promises would never be fulfilled. Moral indignation no doubt occurred but it occurred because of this gap.
4. Although the concept of "relative deprivation" helps explain the Mexican case, I do not assume that an expect/get gap will *always* produce recourse to political violence; nor do I assume that *all* political violence involves such a gap. As this chapter will demonstrate, oppositional peasant groups were reluctant to resort to political violence, usually doing so only in the face of violent government repression.
5. The fact that the new revolutionary ruling class would eventually address many of the social justice aspirations of peasants and workers (particularly during the Cárdenas years) is a crucial ingredient contributing to the political stability that Mexico enjoyed for many years. However, the failure to continue to meet the expectations raised by this early foray into social reform after 1940 (and the consequent creation of feelings of relative deprivation) eventually contributed to unrest and political violence.
6. In 1990, during a debate with Mexican writer Octavio Paz, the Peruvian writer Mario Vargas Llosa described Mexico's political system as a "perfect dictatorship."
7. The extent of political exclusion varied. Highly organized strategic groups, such as workers in the mineral and petroleum sectors and state employees, had more access to the state and achieved greater economic benefits than did peasants,

unskilled workers, and workers in the informal sector who had little or no access to the state and, as we shall see, benefited far less from economic growth.
8. Although these arrangements contained unrest, they did not eliminate it. Independent union movements in the railway, petroleum, and miners' unions, for example, emerged in the late 1940s and the early 1950s. The persistence of rural unrest, including violent insurgency, is discussed later in the chapter.
9. President Miguel Alemán (1946–1952) had close friends and allies among the landowners of northern Mexico (Cockcroft 1983, 294). Illegal large holdings in the north were often held by members of the Agricultural Department.
10. The total available cropland is slightly over 10 percent of the country. However, there is also a lack of adequate rainfall in many areas with potentially tillable land. Severe droughts have been an ongoing problem (Butler, Pick, and Hettrick 2001, 230).
11. In contrast, between 1941 and 1945, production in the *ejido* sector was the same or slightly better than that of large commercial producers (Hewitt de Alcántara 1976, 210).
12. Such policies include tariff reductions on capital goods and the rebates and tax holidays on imported capital goods.
13. The Kuznetian prediction that while inequality would rise during the early phase of modernization, it would subsequently decline as the labor force in the industrial sector expanded and as industry absorbed labor, has been questioned by an increasing number of studies, particularly with regard to Latin America (Deininger and Squire 1996; Bruno, Ravallion, and Squire 2000). Many economists now recognize that an improvement in equality is important in achieving economic growth (Birdsall, Pickney, and Sabot 1996; Cornia, Addison, and Kiiski 2004).
14. Jaramillo and many of his followers had fought in the Zapatista army. His peasant supporters saw him as Zapata's heir (Padilla 2007, 261).
15. In addition, resource development meant loss of cropland and relocation for peasant communities (Harvey 1998, 97; Benjamin 1996, 230).
16. Another factor contributing to Zapatista support in eastern Chiapas was the prevalence of conversion to Protestantism, which rendered the population more open to opposition to the status quo (Collier 1994, 95–99, 45).
17. Insofar as ranchers and government officials were *mestizo* and the owners of logging companies white, there is also, of course, a racial identity aspect to the conflict.
18. Market liberalization was not the only factor in the rise of poverty in southern Mexico. The decline in coffee prices in the late 1980s played an important role. However, as we shall see later in this discussion, the combination of the dismantling of state support along with the influx of agricultural products against which small farmers could not compete would have a devastating impact. Poverty statistics are given later in the chapter.
19. It therefore became possible for owners to use their land as collateral in order to borrow from private banks. With the dismantling of the state bank responsible for lending to ejiditarios, borrowing from private banks now became essential.

20. Here it is important to distinguish between the expectations of peasants, which fuelled unrest, and actual consequences. In fact, relatively few ejiditarios sought to privately title lands.
21. López Monjardin (1996, 444) also notes the deep symbolic and psychological impact of the reform.
22. Between 1996 and 1999, the Mexican trade minister authorized a total of 8.3 million tons of corn imports above the tariff-free quota established by NAFTA (Appendini 2003, 266).
23. With much higher levels of productivity and subsidies amounting to almost US$13 billion (MacDonald 2005, 210), corn is produced in the United States at roughly 40 percent of the cost of corn produced in Mexico (Acuña Rodarte 2003, 135).
24. By 2005, poverty had declined to 35.5 percent, slightly above its 34 percent level in 1970 (ECLAC 2007, 299–399).
25. Progresa, initiated in 1997, provided small amounts of money to the female heads of households in poor rural communities in exchange for commitments to keep children in school and to take them to health clinics regularly. Under President Fox, the program was expanded to a wider range of beneficiaries and to urban areas.
26. There is some anecdotal evidence that this is occurring. Observers claim that the SPP was behind attacks on autonomous Zapatista communities (on the grounds of involvement with illegal drugs), the murder and arrest of rural leaders in Chihuahua, who were demanding the renegotiation of NAFTA's agricultural terms, and the police repression and arrest of protesting flower growers in the state of Mexico in 2006 (Carlsen 2008, 3; Sciacchuitano 2008).

References

Acuña Rodarte, Olivia. 2003. Toward an equitable, inclusive and sustainable agriculture: Basic grains producers unite. In *Confronting globalization: Economic integration and popular resistance in Mexico*, edited by Timothy A. Wise, Hilda Salazar, and Laura Carlsen, 129–148. Bloomfield: Kumarian Press.

Aguilar, Alonso, and Fernando Carmona. 1972. *México: Riqueza y miseria*. Mexico City: Editorial Nuestro Tiempo S.A.

Appendini, Kirsten. 2003. The challenges to rural Mexico in an open economy. In *Mexico's politics and society in transition*, edited by Joseph S. Tulchin and Andrew D. Selee, 255–276. Boulder, CO: Lynne Rienner.

Ascher, William. 1999. *Why governments waste natural resources: Policy failures in developing countries*. Baltimore: Johns Hopkins University Press.

Aspra, Antonio L. 1977. Import substitution in Mexico: Past and present. *World Development* 5(1–2): 111–123.

Ayala Espino, José. 1988. *Estado y desarrollo: La formación de la economía mixta mexicana (1920–1982)*. Mexico City: Fondo de Cultura Económica.

Benjamin, Thomas. 1996. *a rich land a poor people, politics and society in modern Chiapas*. Albuquerque: University of New Mexico Press.

Bennett, Douglas, and Kenneth Sharpe. 1982. The state as banker and entrepreneur: The last resort nature of the Mexican state's intervention, 1917–1970. In *Brazil and Mexico: Patterns in late development*, edited by Sylvia Ann Hewlett and Richard S. Weinert, 168–205. Philadelphia: Institute for the Study of Human Issues.

Birdsall, Nancy, Thomas C. Pickney, and Richard H. Sabot. 1996. Why low inequality spurs growth: Savings and investment by the poor. Washington: Inter-American Development Bank. Office of the Chief Economist. http://idb docs.iadb.org/wsdocs/getdocument.aspx?docnum=788146. Accessed August 15, 2009.

Bruno, Michael, Martin Ravallion, and Lyn Squire. 2000. Equity and growth in developing countries: Old and new perspectives on the policy issues. In *Distributive justice and economic development: The case of Chile and developing countries*, edited by Andrés Solimano, Eduardo Aninat, and Nancy Birdsall, 37–52. Ann Arbor: The University of Michigan Press.

Bureau of Democracy, Human Rights and Labor, U.S. Department of State. 2008. *Mexico: Country reports on human rights practices, 2007*. http://www.state.gov/g/drl/rls/hrrpt/2007/100646.htm. Accessed July 7, 2008.

Butler, Edgar W., James B. Pick, and W. James Hettrick. 2001. *Mexico and Mexico City in the world economy*. Boulder: Westview Press.

Carlsen, Laura. 2008. Armoring NAFTA: The battleground for Mexico's future. America's Policy Program Special Report. http://www.americaspolicy.org. Accessed September 15, 2009.

Castro Soto, Gustavo. 2000. Los grupos guerrillero y las elecciones. *Boletines de CIEPAC*. 200. http://www.ciepac.org/boletines/chiapasaldia.php?id=200. Accessed March 13, 2012.

Cockcroft, James D. 1983. *Mexico: Class formation, capital accumulation and the state*. New York: Monthly Review.

Collier, George. A. 1994. *Basta! Land and the Zapatista Rebellion in Chiapas*. Oakland, CA: The Institute for Food and Development Policy.

Cook, Colleen W. 2007. *Mexico's drug cartels*. Washington DC: CRS Report for Congress, Congressional Research Service.

Corbacho, Ana, and Gerd Schwartz. 2002. Mexico: Experiences with pro-poor expenditure policies. IMF Working Paper. Washington: IMF, Fiscal Affairs Department.

Cornia, Giovanni Andrea, Tony Addison, and Sampson Kiiski. 2004. Income distribution changes and their impact in the post Second World War period. In *Inequality, growth and poverty in an era of liberalization and globalization*, edited by Giovanni Andrea Cornia, 26–52. Oxford: Oxford University Press.

Cumberland, Charles C. 1968. *Mexico: The struggle for modernity*. New York: Oxford University Press.

De Navarrete, Ifigenia M. 1967. Income distribution in Mexico. In *Mexico's recent economic growth*, edited by Tom E. Davis, 133–199. Austin: University of Texas Press.

Deininger, K., and L. Squire. 1996. New ways of looking at inequality and growth. DEC Notes Research Findings. Washington: World Bank. http://go.worldbank.org/S9IS2SLEE0. Accessed October 26, 2008.

Delmonte, Luís Mesa. 2008. Violence and terrorism: a response from Mexico. *Defense against Terrorism Review* 1(2): 47–66.
Dermota, Ken. 2007. Snow fall. *The Atlantic*. http://www.theatlantic.com/doc/200707/cocaine#. Accessed October 22, 2009.
Doyle, Kate. 2003. The dawn of Mexico's dirty war: Lucio Cabañas and the party of the poor. The National Security Archive. http://www.gwu.edu/~nsarchiv/NSAEBB/NSAEBB105/index.htm#usdocs. Accessed October 3, 2009.
Dussell Peters, Enrique. 2000. *Polarizing Mexico: The impact of liberalization strategy*. Boulder, CO: Lynne Rienner.
ECLAC (Economic Commission for Latin America and the Caribbean). 2007. *Social panorama of Latin America*. Santiago: United Nations, Economic Commission for Latin America.
Eskridge, Chris. 2001. Mexican cartels and their integration into Mexican socio-political culture. http://www.customscorruption.com/mexican_cartels_integr.htm. Accessed June 12, 2009.
Esteva, Gustavo. 1983. *The struggle for rural Mexico*. South Hadley, MA: Bergin and Garvey Publishers Inc.
EZLN. 1995. The third declaration of the Lacandon jungle: EZLN communique. http://flag.blackened.net/revolt/mexico/ezlnco.html. Accessed October 20, 2009.
———. 2005. The 6th declaration of the Selva Lacandon. EZLN Communiqué. http://www.anarkismo.net/newswire.php?story_id=805. Accessed October 20, 2009.
Fajnzylber, Pablo, Daniel Lederman, and Norman Loayza. 2002. What causes violent crime? *European Economic Review* 46: 1323–1357.
Felix, David. 1982. Income distribution curves in Mexico and the Kuznets curve. In *Brazil and Mexico: Patterns in late development,* edited by Sylvia Ann Hewlett and Richard S. Weinert, 265–297. Philadelphia: Institute for the Study of Human Issues.
Fitzgerald, E. V. K. 1979. Stabilization policy in Mexico: The fiscal deficit and macroeconomic equilibrium, 1960–1977. In *Inflation and stabilization in Latin America*, edited by Rosemary Thorp and Laurence Whitehead, 23–64. New York: Homes and Meier.
Fox, Jonathan, and Libby Haight. 2010. Mexican agricultural policy: Multiple goals and conflicting interests. In *Subsidizing inequality: Mexican corn policy since NAFTA,* edited by Jonathan Fox and Libby Haight. Santa Cruz, CA: Woodrow Wilson Centre for Scholars and University of California.
Galtung, Johan. 1969. Violence, peace and peace research. *Journal of Peace Research* 6(l): 167–191.
Geffray, Christian, Guihern Fabre, and Michel Schiray. 2002. Main findings. In *Globalization, drugs and criminalization*, coordinated by Christian Geffray, Guihern Fabre, and Michel Schiray. http://www.unesco.org/most/globalization/drugs_1.htm. Accessed November 13, 2009.
Gilbert, Dennis. 2007. *Mexico's middle class in the neoliberal era*. Tuscon: The University of Arizona Press.

Glade, William. 1986. Distribution and sectoral problems in the new economic policy. In *Mexico's political stability: The next five years*, edited by Roderic A. Camp, 73–94. Boulder, CO: Westview Press.

Grayson, George. 2008. Los Zetas: The ruthless army spawned by a Mexican drug cartel. E-Notes. http://www.fpri.org/enotes.grayson.loszetas.html. Accessed June 2, 2008.

Gurr, Ted. 1970. *Why men rebel*. Princeton, NJ: Princeton University Press.

Haber, Stephen H. 1989. *Industry and underdevelopment: The industrialization of Mexico, 1890–1940*. Stanford: Stanford University Press.

Hansen, Roger D. 1980. *The politics of Mexican development*. Baltimore, MD: The Johns Hopkins University Press.

Hart, John Mason. 1997. *Revolutionary Mexico: The coming and process of the Mexican revolution*, tenth anniversary edition. Los Angeles: University of California Press.

Harvey, Neil. 1998. *The Chiapas rebellion: The struggle for land and democracy*. Durham, NC: Duke University Press.

Henriques, Gisele, and Raj Patel. 2004. NAFTA, Corn and Mexico's trade liberalization. America's Program. Interhemispheric Resource Center. www.americaspolicy.org. Accessed March 10, 2012.

Hernández Navarro, Luís, and Laura Carlsen. 2004. Indigenous rights: The battle for constitutional reform in Mexico. In *Dilemmas of political change in Mexico*, edited by Kevin J. Middlebrook, 440–465. London: Institute for Latin American Studies.

Hewitt de Alcántara, Cynthia. 1976. *Modernizing Mexican agriculture: Socio-economic implications of technological change, 1940–1976*. Geneva: U.N. Institute for Social Development.

Ihlanfeldt, K. 2007. Neighborhoods drug crime and young males' job accessibility. *The Review of Economics and Statistics* 89(1): 151–164.

Inter-American Commission on Human Rights. 2007. *Annual report of the inter-American commission on human rights, 2006*, Vol. II. Washington DC: General Secretariat, Organization of American States.

King, Timothy. 1970. *Mexico: Industrialization and trade policies since 1940*. London: Oxford University Press.

Lambert, Jacques. 1967. *Latin America: Social structures and political institutions*. Berkeley: University of California Press.

López Gámez, Emilio, and Fredrico Ovallo Vaguera. 2001. *Poscampo*. Chapingo: Departamento de Sociedad Rural, Universidad Autónoma Chapingo.

López Monjardin, Adriana. 1996. A contracorriente: Expresiones de la resistencia a las reformas de la legislación agraria. In *Neoliberalismo y organización social en el campo*, edited by Hubert Carton Grammont. México City: UNAM, Institución de Investigaciones Sociales.

Lupsha, Peter A. 1971. Explanations of political violence: Some psychological themes versus indignation. *Politics and Society* 2(89): 90–104.

Lustig, Nora. 1998. *Mexico: The remaking of an economy*, second edition. Washington, DC: The Brookings Institute.

MacDonald, James H. 2005. The Narco economy and small town rural Mexico. *Human Organization* 64(2): 115–125.
Malkin, Victoria. 2001. Narco-trafficking, migration and modernity in rural Mexico. *Latin American Perspectives* 28(4): 101–128.
Martínez, Gabriel y Guillermo Fárber. 1994. *Desregulación económica (1989–1993)*. Mexico City: Fundo de Cultura Económica.
Miller, Michael. 2008. The age of innocents. *Newsweek*, November 3. http://www.newsweek.com/id/165678. Accessed August 5, 2009.
Miller, Robert Ryal. 1985. *Mexico: A history*. Norman: University of Oklahoma Press.
Moser, Caroline, and Bernice van Bronkhorst. 1999. Youth violence in Latin America and the Caribbean: Costs, causes and interventions. LCR Sustainable Development Working Paper No. 3. Washington DC: The World Bank.
Olson, Wayne. 1985. Crisis and social change in Mexico's political economy. *Latin American Perspectives* 23(3): 7–25.
Padilla, Tanalís. 2007. From agrarista to guerrilleros: The Jaramillista Movement in Morelos. *Hispanic American Historical Review* 87(2): 255–292.
Parkes, Henry Bamford. 1960. *A history of Mexico*. London: Eyre and Spotiswoode.
Paulson, Joshua. 2000. Rural rebellion in southern Mexico: The guerrillas of Guerrero. *NACLA report on the Americas* 23(5): 26–48.
Polaski, Sandra. 2003. Jobs, wages and household income. In *NAFTA: Promise and reality: Lessons for the hemisphere*, edited by John Audley, Sandra Polaski, Demetrios G. Papademetriou, and Scott Vaughan, 11–37. Washington DC: Carnegie Endowment for International Peace.
Prevot-Schapira, Marie France. 1982. Trabajadores del Petróleo y poder syndical en México. In *Energía en México: Ensayos sobre el pasado y presente*, coordinated by Miguel S. Wionczek, 143–169. Mexico City: El Colegio de México.
Pickard, Miguel. 2007. Ten easy questions and ten tougher ones regarding SPPNA (Security and Prosperity Partnerships of North America). *Boletines de CIEPAC*. 541. http://www.commonfrontirs.ca/Documents/SPP_docs/20questionsSPP_hi-res.pdf. Accessed March 8, 2012.
Rawlings, Laura B. 2005. a new approach to social assistance: Latin America's experience with conditional cash transfer programs. *International Social Security Review* 58(2–3): 133–161.
Rodríguez, Victoria E. 1997. *Decentralization in Mexico: From Reforma Municipal to Solidaridad to the Nuevo Federalismo*. Boulder, CO: Westview Press.
Russell, Philip L. 1995. *The Chiapas rebellion*. Austin Texas: Mexico Resource Center.
Sanderson, Steven E. 1981. *Agrarian populism and the Mexican state: The struggle for land in Sonora*. Berkeley: University of California Press.
Saragoza, Alex M. 1988. *The Monterrey elite and the Mexican state*. Austin: University of Texas Press.
Schwartz, Jeremy. 2008. Judges latest targets in Mexico drug war. Cox Newspapers Washington Bureau, February 2. http://www.coxwashington.com/reporters

/content/reporters/stories/2008/02/02/MEXICO_JUDGES02_COX.html. Accessed July 7, 2008.
Sciacchitano, Katherine. 2008. Here come the security and prosperity partnerships but—what security? whose prosperity? *Dollars and sense: Real world economics.* http://www.dollarsandsense.org/archives/2008/0108sciacchitano.html. Accessed March 8, 2012.
Serrano, Monica. 2008. The parallel economy. BBC Radio World Service. http://www.bbc.co.uk/worldservice/news/2008/11/081029_narcoeconomy.shtml. Accessed August 13, 2009.
Smith, Peter H. 1979. *Labyrinths of power.* Princeton: Princeton University Press.
Solís, Leopoldo. 1981. *La realidad económica Mexicana: Retrovisión y perspectivas.* Revised. Mexico City: Siglo XXI.
Székley, Gabriel. 1983. *La economía política del petróleo en México, 1976–1982.* Mexico City: El Colegio de México.
Tannenbaum, Frank. 1968. *Mexico: The struggle for peace and bread.* New York: Alfred A. Knopf.
Teichman, Judith. 1988. *Policymaking in Mexico: From boom to crisis.* Boston: Allen and Unwin.
———. 2008. Redistributive conflict and social policy in Latin America. *World Development* 36(3): 446–460.
Turbiville Jr., Dr. Graham H. 1997. Mexico's other insurgents. *Military Review* 77. http://struggle.ws/mexico/usa/army_on_epr.html. Accessed March 12, 2012.
Velasco, José Luís. 2005. *Insurgency, authoritarianism and drug trafficking in Mexico's democratization.* London and New York: Routledge.
Villafuerte Solís, Daniel. 2005. Rural Chiapas ten years after the armed uprising of 1994: An economic overview. *The Journal of Peasant Studies* 32(3–4): 461–483.
Wade, Robert Hunter. 2004. Is globalization reducing poverty and inequality? *World Development* 32(4): 567–589.
Weinberg, Bill. 2002. Drugs, guerrillas and politics in Mexico. *NACLA report on the Americas* 24(2): 18–26.
Wilkie, James W. ed. 1999. *Statistical abstract of Latin America*, Vol. 3. Los Angeles: UCLA Latin American Centre Publications, University of California.

CHAPTER 3

The Evolution of Violence: Economic Development and Intergroup Conflict in Guatemala, El Salvador, and Costa Rica

Gustavo Arcia

This chapter reviews the incidence of violence and intergroup conflict in three countries in Central America: Guatemala, El Salvador, and Costa Rica, to develop a typology of violence and its links with social and economic policies. The root causes of violence in Central America have always been traced to poverty and inequality, which in turn are perceived to be the root cause of the political violence experienced by the region during the 1980s. Between 1975 and 2008, Guatemala underwent a low-intensity conflict in which as much as 200,000 people died. El Salvador suffered the loss of 75,000 people during a decade of armed conflict that ended in 1992. Costa Rica, one of the most peaceful countries in the world, is now concerned about drug trafficking and street crime, both of which are main topics of public opinion and political discourse (Arroyo and Espinoza 2001).

Guatemala, with a large proportion of indigenous population for whom Spanish is a second language, was run by a small but powerful nonindigenous group that controlled the large indigenous labor force and most of the land. This conflict between the landed elite and indigenous people has been a recurrent theme in Guatemala's modern history. Now that the political conflict has reached a peaceful transition, Guatemala is being affected by violence associated with drug trafficking and gang warfare (UNDP 2007).

El Salvador, very small in area and with a larger proportion of people of mixed blood—*mestizos*—underwent a violent decade of conflict and civil war in the 1980s. After working out an admirable peace agreement that evolved into a working democracy, gang warfare and violent crime are a big concern of the citizenry, many of whom claim that the widespread possession of small arms and the mistrust of the justice system lead people to take personal action instead of relying on the rule of law. For El Salvador, violent crime is an economic phenomenon explained by the lack of employment opportunities for the young and the presence of gangs as an alternative social structure for youth (FUSADES 2005).

Costa Rica has been different from the beginning, since it was populated by colonizers from Spain who could not rely on the small indigenous population to work the land. As a result, Costa Rica became a country of small landholders with a democratic sociopolitical structure that reflected its social origins. Although Costa Rica has slowly evolved into a country with problems of inequality in land distribution and ethnic disharmony, the country's self-image is still rooted in the democratic principles of its past (Seligson 1975; Huhn 2008; Vargas, Rosero, and Seligson 2006; Chomsky 1996).

Crime, especially violent crime associated with drug trafficking and gang warfare, now is high on the list of problems cited by citizens in Central America (Boraz and Bruneau 2006; World Bank 2011). However, the crime prevention and crime reduction policies being implemented by Central American governments are not yet in full effect, and their impact remains to be determined. Are current policies and programs going in the right direction? Are the roots and proximate causes of violence and crime being addressed by such policies? These are the main questions underlying this chapter.

Violence Is a Regional Problem

Central American countries are among the most violent in Latin America (Figure 3.1). In Honduras, there are 86 homicides for every 100,000 people; in El Salvador, there are 71; in Belize, 42; and in Guatemala, 39. Venezuela, a middle-income country, has 67 homicides per 100,000 people. What the statistics suggest, however, is that poverty alone does not explain violent crime—Haiti has only 6.9 homicides per 100,000 people and Nicaragua 13—which also suggest that reducing violence and intergroup conflict requires a careful analysis of its root causes.

Violence in Latin America is costly (Table 3.1). The human capital losses due to violence can be equal to almost 2 percent of GDP—as in the case

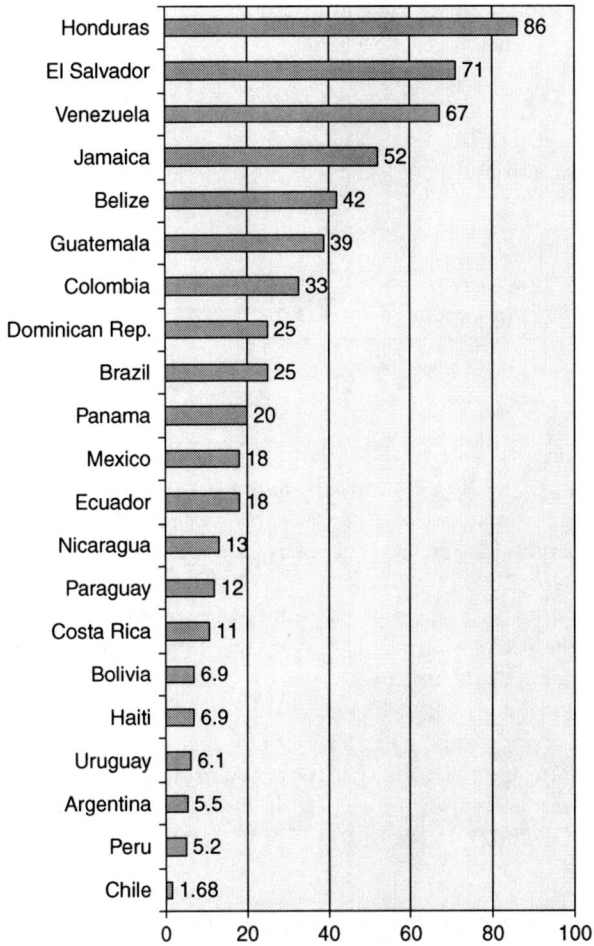

Figure 3.1 Homicide rates per 100,000 people, 2011.
Source: Prepared by the author with data from UNODOC 2011.

of El Salvador—and can cost upward of US$2.5 billion per year for Latin America (World Bank 2010). The loss due to violence in Central America equals what the region spends in primary education. Its effects on investment losses can be staggering: the equivalent of 4.8% of GDP (Londoño and Guerrero 1999), about one-half of private investment.

There have been many studies and fora about violence in the region, and most have concluded that curbing small arms and clamping down on gangs

Table 3.1 Economic value of violence and crime in Central America per year*

	% of GDP	Millions USD
Costa Rica	0.58	96
El Salvador	1.99	271
Guatemala	1.43	289
Honduras	1.31	61
Nicaragua	0.96	38
Panama	0.63	76
Latin America	1.2	2,500

Note: *Economic value of disability-adjusted life years.
Source: Adapted from World Bank 2010, 27.

will go a long way to reestablish the rule of law and peaceful coexistence (Fundación Arias 2001). This may be only a partial solution, since they do not address the root causes of violence: the victimization of some groups within society and the exclusion of others from social and economic progress (Carrillo Flórez 2009).

Among most policymakers in Central America, it is a foregone conclusion that the use of violence to resolve civil disputes makes difficult the implementation of the rule of law and the implantation of a participatory democracy (Salomón 2001; Castellanos 2001). However, others point out that a lack of understanding of the root causes of crime, the lack of investment in youth, and the inability of the region to recognize and deal with its post-traumatic collective disorder is at the heart of the problem (FUSADES 2005; UNDP 2007).

Exploring the Links between Development Strategies and Intergroup Conflict

Are the patterns of economic development implemented by the Central American countries unrelated to social conflict? A quick review of the histories of conflict and violence in Guatemala, El Salvador, and Costa Rica yield patterns of violence that can be traced back to economic and social policies that—to put it mildly—had unintended consequences. Table 3.2 presents a conceptual framework with which one could analyze intergroup conflict in Central America and help define better policies by anticipating their unintended consequences on intergroup violence. This framework assumes that economic-development policies have spillover effects and potential negative impacts on some sectors of the population. In countries where economic

Table 3.2 A conceptual framework for analyzing the links between the risk factors and economic variables affecting social welfare

Risk factors	Links to economic and social variables
Income inequality • Low availability of public goods • Weak legal institutions • Undeveloped opportunities for economic mobility • Gross market imperfections • Income growth accrued to unequal resource ownership	• Exports concentrated on commodities with low product transformation • Investment in technology not transferable to wider internal markets • Low tax base and low investment in public infrastructure • Unequal enforcement of property rights • Little attention to increasing productivity: poor and expensive
Political corruption • Political power linked to economic power • Rent seeking by political party leaders • Use of violence as a tool for keeping political power • Influence trafficking • Uneven application of the rule of law • Low or no accountability	• Economic opportunity linked to party affiliation • Use of insider information for economic gain • Tax avoidance and lower government revenues • Low private investment by those not affiliated to the party in power
Social exclusion • Discrimination or exclusion of native populations • Discrimination or exclusion of Afro-descendants	• Unequal public investment patterns • Regional autonomy as a euphemism for benign neglect • Tolerance for economic abuse of discriminated populations
Low human capital formation • Low education among the poor • Low human capital investment overall	• Low investment in education • Low quality of education • Low returns to education • The cost of crime is included in the variable cost of production, reducing private investment • Capital flight • Brain drain

Source: Prepared by the author.

inequality is high and where powerful elites have a large degree of influence over policies and laws, there is a high probability that rent-seeking behavior by powerful economic actors could produce large welfare losses among less-powerful groups.

Some of the negative consequences of economic and social policies implemented with the intention of generating benefits to specific groups may take a long time to develop. The assumption that powerful economic groups are also rational may suggest that such rationality in the pursuit of increased economic gain may not take into account two issues: the unintended consequences of such policies on other groups in society and the negative long-term consequences of the policies themselves. Under this framework, intergroup conflict becomes a manifestation of the accumulation of negative consequences of policies that benefit only the richer group within society, generating a deterioration of social welfare among the poor and disadvantaged groups.

The first category of risk factors in Table 3.2 addresses income inequality, which evolves from several factors, including the underinvestment in public goods (education, health, and public infrastructure); the inattention to legal institutions, which result in ineffective or corrupt judicial systems; the inattention to the development of economic mobility and the resulting lack of a middle class that could be the engine of more opportunities for employment; and the inattention to gross inequalities in resource ownership. Exclusion of the majority of the population from capturing the benefits of income growth goes a long way to explain why some societies grow peacefully and reach a high standard of living (Acemoglu and Robinson 2012). The links between inequality and economic variables are many, including the lack of product transformation in the country, which could be crucial for increasing the productivity and incomes of the poor; the lack of investment in technology, which can also increase labor productivity; the avoidance of taxes; and the lack of enforcement of property rights, which can reduce private investment. The net result of income inequality and its associated economic policies is a poor labor force with low opportunity for increasing its income and welfare.

The second risk factor—and its links with bad economic behavior—is political corruption, which can be summarized as the use of public institutions and of economic policies for the benefit of powerful elites. Even in weak-functioning democracies, the use of economic policies (e.g., tariffs, export taxes, exchange rates, and promotional export programs) to benefit those in power can produce indirect damages to the rest of society by increasing income inequality, reducing public investment, and creating an unfavorable legal climate. The effect of corruption on violence is direct:

those excluded by the selective application of the law are bound to take violent action as a group (Carrillo Flórez 2009). The net result of corruption is a lower rate of growth due to a reduction in private investment and no opportunities for improving the income of those who suffer net economic losses as a result of corruption.

The third risk factor is social exclusion of native populations and of populations of African descent. This risk factor is now being recognized as a key element in the formulation of social sector policies, even though it has been long known that indigenous groups and Afro-descendants have less access to economic opportunity, lower levels of public investment, and lower levels of social inclusion. Moreover, these populations have been the victims, instead of the aggressors, in the history of intergroup conflict in the region (Dulitzky 2005; Hall and Patrinos 2006).

The fourth risk factor is the low level of human capital formation—characterized by the low levels of public investment in education and health for minorities and by the low quality of services in basic education, basic health, and economic infrastructure (Hall and Patrinos 2006). The net impact of this underinvestment is chronic poverty, low income mobility, and little economic opportunity. What is even worse for society is that among those with little or no access to education and higher labor productivity, crime—as a means of producing income or as response to social neglect—can easily become an economic activity.

This conceptual framework fleshes out in greater detail what other analysts have concluded about the role of crime in reducing labor productivity. A recent survey of entrepreneurs in Costa Rica, El Salvador, and Guatemala indicated that reducing crime would have the most effect in improving labor productivity, followed by compliance with tax laws and corporate governance rules (Alaimo et al. 2009). Crime—defined as losses from theft, the cost of security, and the payment of bribes—seems to have the biggest impact on investment decisions in these three countries. Hence, the framework can be used to determine policy priorities that can structurally reduce crime and violence.

Historical Foundations of Inequality and Conflict in Central America

From 1524 to 1821, colonial institutions fostered the exploitation of indigenous groups and people of African descent in those countries with sizable indigenous populations or population of African descent. Only when there was little or no population to exploit was there an opportunity for the development of a more egalitarian society. Between independence and the Cuban

Revolution, Central America was a net exporter of agricultural commodities—coffee, sugar, bananas—and beef produced by landed elites and large foreign companies, such as United Fruit. Central American economic and social policies were designed to complement the interests of both groups, leaving the poor behind (Torres Rivas 1993). The gross inequalities in initial land tenure and patterns of agricultural development lead to completely different rates of distribution of the benefits of agricultural and economic growth for the past two-hundred years (Deininger 2004).

The Cuban Revolution in 1959 brought about a coalition of intellectuals and the poor—which included the indigenous populations—that tried to bring political change, resulting in armed conflict in Guatemala, El Salvador, and Nicaragua. The success of the insurgency movements in Nicaragua and El Salvador brought about some significant structural changes in politics and policies, generating more public investment in education and poverty alleviation. Political upheaval in Central American stopped at the beginning of the 1990s, and the incidence of poverty—particularly extreme poverty—has declined in both countries, but not enough to generate enough income growth among the poor to forestall crime.

In Costa Rica, where there have been only a few episodes of intergroup violence in the life of the republic, the foundations of inequality and conflict have been minimized, even though it is widely recognized that discrimination against its Afro-Caribbean population is still a significant social issue (Bourgois 1989; Immigration and Refugee Board of Canada 2002). Costa Rica was just a passageway from South to North America, with little potential for intergroup conflict because there was little competition for land resources. Intergroup conflict arose after the arrival of workers of African descent in the 1800s, who were brought in to work in the banana plantations in the Atlantic coast, and who were not formally recognized as Costa Ricans until they were granted the rights to citizenship in 1949. Still, the integration of Afro-Costa Ricans has been difficult and full integration into Costa Rican society is still a work in progress (Purcell 1993; Chomsky 1996; Harpelle 2001; Senior Angulo 2007).

This brief historical summary provides a context to the groups in conflict in the three countries, where four basic groups have been in conflict at one time or another:

- *The nonpoor, with caveats*: The rich in Guatemala has been in conflict with the poor, with indigenous groups, and with any other group that have tried to reduce their economic and political power (Hernández Pico 2012).

- *The poor*: In all the countries in Central America, including Costa Rica, the poor as a group is a difficult constituency. The low indicators of education and health among the poor are just symptoms of past neglect. Although there is no reported causal relationship between poverty and violence in Central America, there is correlation between deprivation and high rates of homicide (World Bank 2011).
- *Indigenous populations*: As a group, indigenous populations in Guatemala have been the subject of direct violence and institutional neglect. During the 30 years of low-intensity civil war, the indigenous populations were mistreated and attacked by the military (Hernández Pico 2012.
- *People of African descent*: People of African descent have been the victims of past violence and now are the victims of economic and social discrimination and neglect, resulting in a slow rate of inclusion in society (Harpelle 2001; Hall and Patrinos 2006).

Is the Proof in the Pudding?

Comparing the three countries, one finds a common pattern: Costa Rica, a small country initially populated by white small farmers, consistently shows better social and economic indicators than El Salvador and Guatemala (Table 3.3). Is equality a precondition for better socioeconomic performance? Probably yes, but it cannot be proved with just a table. However, it is certain that Costa Rica has consistently invested its peace dividend in education and in the development of its institutions. The results in Table 3.3 are probably the net result of this investment.

If Costa Rica is used as an example for equality and democracy, the empirical evidence shows that such an approach to development did work. However, it is difficult to prove that if Guatemala had taken the same approach as Costa Rica, the large proportion of indigenous population would have produced the same results. The empirical evidence of export agriculture in the Guatemalan altiplano, where indigenous groups now produce high-priced vegetables for exports in tiny plots of land, suggests that it can be done at the economic level. However, the original conflict between indigenous groups and the Spaniards was based on ethnic and cultural differences that became determining factors in the country's development because of the large number of indigenous people. In Costa Rica, where only 2 percent of the population is black, and 1 percent is indigenous, it may have been easier to develop economically without

Table 3.3 Comparison of selected social and economic indicators in the three Central American countries, 2009.

Indicator	Guatemala	El Salvador	Costa Rica
Infant mortality rate (per 1,000 live births)	29	21	10
Life expectancy at birth, total (years)	70	71	79
Total adult literacy rate (% of people ages 15 and above)	73	82	96
Exports of goods and services (% of GDP)	20	28	46
GDP growth (average of the last five years, %)	4	3.2	6.6
GDP per capita, PPP (constant 2000 international $)	4,400	6,280	10,390
Population, total (in millions)	13.6	6.1	4.5
Poverty headcount ratio at national poverty line (% of population)	56.2	48.3	22
Poverty headcount ratio at rural poverty line (% of rural population)	74.5	55.7	25.5
Poverty headcount ratio at urban poverty line (% of urban population)	27.1	43.1	19.2

Source: Prepared by the author with data from the DATAGOB database available at http://www.iadb.org/datagob/

generating a level of intergroup conflict that could have had a negative national impact.

The differences between Costa Rica, and Guatemala and El Salvador apply also to the rule of law, whose fairness and application is considered by local analysts as a key component of social and economic development (Table 3.4). Confidence in the judiciary, the respect for civil liberties, press freedom, and trust in the police are a few of the indicators that clearly show a difference between an egalitarian democratic system, such as the one in Costa Rica, and the systems in Guatemala and, to a lesser extent, in El Salvador. Evidently, disrespect for the rule of law is a consequence—not a cause—of intergroup discrimination that has prevailed since colonial times.

As in the case of socioeconomic indicators, the indicators of the rule of law are manifestations of past and existing inequities, which have been amply documented to work against the welfare of indigenous groups in Guatemala, and against the poor in El Salvador.

Table 3.4 Indicators of the rule of law in the three countries in Central America, 2010 and 2011.

Indicators	Guatemala	El Salvador	Costa Rica
Confidence in judiciary: Percentage of those who have a lot or some confidence in the judiciary.	19.5	23.1	45.9
Corruption Perceptions Index: Scale ranges from 10 (highly transparent) to 0 (highly corrupt).	3.1	3.9	5.1
Percentage of those surveyed who believe that crime has increased a lot or some in the last year.	87.8	75.7	93.4
Civil liberties: 1 (highest) to 7 (lowest). Scores based on evaluations by a team of regional experts and scholars in relation to freedom of expression, freedom of organization, freedom of assembly, property rights protection, equality under the law, etc.	4	3	1
Confidence in the police: Percentage of those surveyed who responded that they have a lot or some confidence in the police.	15.7	36.8	42.1
Freedom of the press: A score of 0 to 30 is considered "Free"; 31 to 60, "Partly Free"; and 61 to 100, "Not Free."	58	42	19
Percentage of those surveyed who responded that to a great extent or a fair amount the justice system punishes the guilty.	29.6	25.9	46
Political rights: People participate freely in the political process (1=highest degree of freedom, 7=lowest).	3	2	1
Time (days) for dispute resolution	1,459	1,010	550

Source: Prepared by the author with data from the DATAGOB database available at http://www.iadb.org/datagob/

Three Decades of Social Conflict

At first, it was political violence, armed conflict of low and high intensity, that lasted about 20 years. Then peace was followed by nonpolitical violence that has lasted 10 years. Intergroup inequity was the root cause of the problem, and the resulting armed conflict was just its principal symptom. This section describes the social inequities among different groups and its violent consequences.

Guatemala

Guatemala is a clear case where all the risk factors alluded to in the conceptual framework—income inequality based on rent seeking, the use of political patronage to favor a business elite, ethnic discrimination, and unequal access to education and health created the ideal conditions for intergroup conflict.

Intergroup conflict in Guatemala has been of two basic kinds: A long-standing oppression and neglect of indigenous groups by other members of society, particularly the rich, and political persecution and the perpetration of violence to indigenous groups opposed to the military governments. From these two types of conflict, a sequel has emerged: the high level of gang violence prevailing today.

Between 1901 and 1944, banana cultivation dominated the economy, and the United Fruit Company became very influential and politically powerful, controlling about 40 percent of the arable land. By 1945, 2 percent of the population controlled 70 percent of the land, but only 12 percent of the total land was in cultivation. To address this imbalance, the government initiated a process of agrarian reform in 1945, but in 1954, a military coup (rumored to have been sponsored by the CIA) toppled the government of Jacob Arbenz, who was considered sympathetic to leftist ideas. A military junta was installed in its place, initiating a period of persecution of anyone suspected of having leftist ideas (PNUD 2007).

In 1960, the success of the Cuban Revolution served as motive for persecuting leftist leaders in Guatemala, resulting in a systematic and brutal repression of people of indigenous origin in the altiplano region of the country. Between 1982 and 1986, the military government of General Rios Montt implemented a violent antiguerrilla campaign that resulted in the death of thousands of people, mostly of Indian extraction. In entire communities, all the males were killed by the army, claiming that they were Communist guerrillas.

Beginning in 1986, the level of repression scaled down; Guatemalan society was exhausted and everyone wanted peace. This exhaustion led to the signing of the peace accords of 1996, in which indigenous populations were taken into account as recipient of social and economic benefits previously denied to them. Since then Guatemala has lived in relative political peace, but civil violence has escalated with the emergence of youth gangs, drug trafficking, and street crime. In 1999, for example, there were 2,650 homicides in a country of 12 million. By the year 1995, there were 19.7 homicides per 100,000 people; by 2011, this rate had increased to 39. The consensus is that the country's high incidence of homicides is due to the existence of violent youth who are still suffering the alienation and trauma of the civil war.

The Guatemalan Peace Accords

The peace accords between the government of Guatemala and the Guatemalan National Revolutionary Unity (URNG) in 1996 show the areas where the group conflict originates and, as a result, where development policy needs to be redefined.

The talks between the government and the insurgency covered themes that had been restricted before, such as human rights, the role of the army, and the rights of indigenous people. To give the dialogue broad-based legitimacy, Guatemala created the Assembly of Civil Society (ASC), an umbrella organization that included all sectors of society, except big businesses, whose representatives preferred to participate as a separate entity. Given the broad base of the ASC, the discussions had to lead to a broad consensus on every point. The net result was a document with genuine agreements and serious limitations, but a document that made the signing of a peace accord possible.[1]

The accords were preceded in 1994 by a Human Rights Accord, in which the government and URNG agreed to allow a United Nations Verification Mission (MINUGUA) to monitor compliance with human rights by both sides of the conflict, creating a space for discussions where a third party could help keep both sides from stretching the truth. By 1995, the talks had evolved enough to reach an accord on the identity and rights of indigenous people, who accounted for 56 percent of the total population. As such, the accord defines Guatemala as multiethnic, multicultural, and multilingual, with direct consequences for the operation of all areas of government.

As talks progressed, both parties signed a demilitarization accord in 1996, in which the role of the army was well defined. This was a key consensus that helped seal peace, since it signified passing constitutional reforms that restricted the functions of the army to defense of the borders and the maintenance of Guatemala's territorial integrity. The accord also eliminated paramilitary groups, reduced the size of the military, and created a new civilian police force for ordinary security. The accord also addressed judicial reform to eliminate impunity for those committing violent political crimes.

The accords have held, and Guatemala continues to be peaceful. The conflicts associated with the diversity of its population are being addressed.

For example, the Ministry of Education now publishes primary-school textbooks in 12 indigenous languages, and political activity by indigenous candidates for local government is now a normal event.

El Salvador

From 1931 to 1979, El Salvador had a succession of authoritarian governments controlled by the military, or by civilians who were aligned with the military. Between 1931 and 1944, a series of internal conflicts occurred, in which interparty struggles were combined with popular insurrections by small farmers and the poor. The military government reacted with violence, killing more than 10,000 people.[2]

Between 1944 and 1960, the military governments repressed anyone suspected of leftist or Communist tendencies. In the midst of this low-intensity conflict between the Right and the Left, El Salvador experienced a period of high export growth. Coffee prices were high, but an increasing population and public investments in infrastructure near large cities generated a high rate of urbanization. El Salvador became heavily urbanized, and the urban poor began to demand more education and employment.

The Cuban Revolution became a model for local insurgencies. By 1970, the first armed guerrilla groups began to appear in the rural areas of Chalatenango, and by 1980, a full civil war was in effect.[3] Paramilitary groups began to execute anyone suspected of being a guerrilla or a sympathizer, and thousands of people disappeared to be found dead later in the outskirts of San Salvador. The war lasted from 1980 to 1992 and left about 75,000 people dead. The peace agreements signed in 1992 continue to hold and El Salvador began a process of democracy that has proven to be very effective in restoring economic growth and political tolerance. Currently, violence is still a problem, but it is perpetrated by youth gangs who grew up in exile, and who were deeply affected by the war.

The Salvadoran Peace Process

On January of 1992, the government of El Salvador and the Frente Farabundo Martí para la Liberación Nacional (FMLN) signed a peace agreement that took seven years to come to fruition. In the mid-1980s, the first dialogue efforts took place, but it was not until 1989, during the Cristiani government, that peace negotiations took shape, ending in the peace agreement reached in Mexico City three years later.

Dialogue between the government and the FMLN revolved around the observance of human rights, the passing of some key reforms related to the role, restructuring, and reduction of the army, and constitutional changes related to election laws and the judicial system. In addition, the business sector wanted to maintain a market economy, while accepting more attention to poverty alleviation. Compliance would be verified by the United Nations and several countries forming the Group of Friends.[4] Four years later, this same approach would also succeed in Guatemala.

One key element of the agreement was the reincorporation of army soldiers and guerrilla fighters into civilian life. By the time the peace agreement was signed, the reincorporation programs were ready for implementation. This approach defused any source of dissatisfaction by soldiers and guerrilla combatants and helped consolidate the peace process. Finally, the peace accords were accompanied by a five-year Economic and Social Development Plan, aimed at employment creation and poverty reduction.

The peace accords were very successful in establishing a democratic process. El Salvador had several presidential elections since the signing of the accords, and the transfer of power from one government to another has been completely normal. In fact, the new government installed in June 2009 is led by President Mauricio Funes, a member of the FMLN.

Costa Rica

Intergroup conflict in Costa Rica has been relatively small but well defined: The clear resistance to integrate its Afro-Caribbean population.[5] Afro-Caribbean immigration to Costa Rica began in the middle of the nineteenth century, coming mostly from Jamaica, Panama, and San Andrés (Colombia). In 1834, Great Britain freed the slaves in Jamaica, and the economic crisis of 1850 set up massive emigration of workers of African descent to Central America. In Costa Rica, there was a need for manual labor to build the railroad from the Central Valley to the Atlantic to ship the coffee out of the country. To that end, the town of Limón was created with this immigrant labor, of which two-third was black and one-third was Chinese.

Government leaders excluded nonwhites from residency and citizenship, arguing that the imported labor was not on par with the cultural and sanitary norms of the white population. Immigrant labor was accepted under the condition that they leave at the end of the construction period. By 1906, the United Fruit Company had hired 4,000 Jamaican workers for its banana plantations around Limón, which became the main Afro-Caribbean city in Costa Rica. Because of the temporary nature of these workers, the central government invested little in schools and other government services and the region lagged behind the rest of the country in quality and coverage of government services.

It was until 1948, under the administration of President José Figueres, that Afro-Caribbeans born in Costa Rica were given full rights to citizenship. By 1963, the vast majority of dwellers in Limón were Costa Rican citizens. Discrimination does exist against blacks and people of indigenous origins, but it is reported to be subtle and nonviolent.[6] Today, Limón Province houses most of the Afro-Caribbean population, and their social and economic indicators lag well behind the rest of the nation. They now represent 3 percent of the total population. Even though efforts have been made in the last decade to increase access to health and education, past discrimination has led to call for self-determination and complete regional autonomy (Stewart 2004).

President Figueres abolished the army in 1949, leaving only a small police force in its place. Since then, Costa Rica's political parties reached political accords that allowed the functioning of democratic elections that allowed it to invest in the technical and civic education of its citizens, becoming a small economy with a high standard of living. Ecotourism, electronics, and software now generate more income than agriculture. However, during the export-boom years between 1955 and 1970, the benefits of agricultural prices were distributed widely among the population because the Costa Rican economy was based on small coffee farms. Where plantation agriculture was the dominant source of income, the winners were corporate institutions, as in the case of the United Fruit holdings in the Atlantic coast, which used disenfranchised labor as its main factor of production. One can argue that because of their small numbers and because of efforts by the government to redress past discrimination, ethnic violence has not been necessary. Instead, street violence, especially street crime and drug running, has become the main problem since 2000 (Huhn 2009a). What is striking to find is that many analysts are discovering that Costa Ricans themselves are now beginning to cope with the image of civil violence in a country whose cultural self-image was always associated with *political* nonviolence (Huhn 2009b).

Explaining Present Violence in the Region

About ten years after the signature of the peace accords in El Salvador, the country began to suffer the effects of gang violence and the use of gang members for drug trafficking on a large scale. Initial assessments indicated that many of the children of Guatemalan and Salvadoran émigrés working in the United States had become gang members in Los Angeles. Soon this pattern of gang growth began to spread to Honduras (Bruneau 2005; Boraz and Bruneau 2006).

Known as the *maras*, the gangs were divided into groups with their own codes of allegiance and a pattern of extremely violent behavior.[7] Although the gangs began as an association of youth in search of identity and self-protection, they quickly became a vehicle for crime. The US Immigration Service began to deport large numbers of gang members to their countries of origin, mainly El Salvador, Guatemala, and Honduras, and their violent behavior moved in with them. Although the region had achieved political peace, it is now in a war with crime, in which there seem to be different interpretations of the roots of crime and different policies to deal with it (Demoscopía 2007).

The number of gang members is difficult to determine, and this lack of precision can be seen from the homicide figures by the country and the corresponding estimate of gang numbers, as shown in Table 3.5. The correlation is certainly weak. Very poor countries like Haiti and Nicaragua show relatively small gang activity. Moreover, there is no linear pattern that can be established in the relationship between gang numbers and crime numbers. El Salvador has 80 percent more crime than Guatemala but 20 percent fewer gang members. Honduras has only 20 percent more crime than El Salvador but 300 percent more gang members.

Even peaceful Costa Rica is not exempt from the current wave of violence. Between 1997 and 2008, the percentages of households reporting that a household member had been the victim of street robbery more than tripled: from 3.3 percent to 11.1 percent. Robbery attempts increased more than two times, and assaults increased almost threefold, as shown in Table 3.6. According to Arroyo and Espinoza (2001), the economic recession of the early 1980s reduced safety-net coverage, with corresponding increase in crime that caught the Costa Rican state by surprise. Violent crime, low by Central American standards, is now acknowledged to be a big problem for all citizens.

Table 3.5 Rate of homicides per 100,000 people and estimated number of gang members by country

Country	Rate 2011	Number of gang members
Guatemala	39	14,000
El Salvador	71	11,000
Honduras	86	36,000
Nicaragua	13	4,500
Costa Rica	11	2,700

Sources: Prepared by the author with data from UNODOC 2011 and World Bank 2010, vii.

Table 3.6 Percent of Costa Rican households reporting a crime committed against a household member

	1997	2008
Burglary	7.9	7.2
Street robbery	3.3	11.1
Attempt of robbery	2.4	6
Assault	0.8	2.2

Source: Adapted from World Bank 2010, 13, using data from 1997 and 2008 household surveys.

Most explanations of the gangs' growth revolve around two root causes: the trauma of the wars and the arrival of emigrant youth who became gang members in the United States. According to Cruz (2005), these theories fail to explain why Honduras, which did not have a civil war, has a serious gang problem. Nicaragua and Mexico, both of which had many youth sent back by the US Immigration Service, do not have a similar gang problem. Cruz's theory is that gangs evolve out of dysfunctional families deeply affected by the war, the systematic neglect of the poor by their own societies, and a culture of violence; gangs are the product of weak institutions that fail to guarantee and respect the rights of children and the young. The results of a large study by Demoscopía (2007) seem to confirm this analysis.

In a forum about violence in Central America, the main diagnosis revolved around two themes and a context: a weak justice system and the abundance of firearms within a context of high tolerance for violence in society—consequences of the wars (Fundación Arias 2001). The main manifestations of the problem are street crime, large-scale drug trafficking, organized crime, and intrafamily violence. At a more fundamental level, others conclude that the current wave of violence reflects the legacy of an authoritarian political culture combined with the intrusion of party politics on the judiciary, resulting in a dysfunctional justice system. Under this assumption, people feel helpless before the state, inducing the use of private violence as a tool for accountability (Salomón 2001).

Current Approaches for Reducing Violence

El Salvador has made the most concerted effort to address gang violence. Aside from creating an Observatory of Violence (OCAVI), to record and disseminate information about violent crime in the Central American region, El Salvador has invested human and monetary resources in studying the root causes of violent crime and ways to stop it (FUSADES 2005). So far, there is a broad consensus in El Salvador about the causes of violent crime in the country:

a. *Violent crime is a side effect of the civil war.* After the cease-fire, the programs designed to incorporate soldiers and combatants to civilian life were incomplete or inadequate.
b. *Weakness in the judicial system.* The level of impunity is high, leading to a mistrust of the justice system by the population. As a result, crimes are not reported, and victims are afraid of retaliation by their victimizers.
c. *The erosion of values*, where violent force is considered a legitimate avenue for redress, especially among those affected by forced migration, the disintegration of their families, and the lack of opportunities for work among the youth.
d. *The expansion of organized crime*, drug traffic, and other activities that use gang members as day laborers.
e. The *easy availability of firearms*, which promotes the private settling of scores outside of the law.

Each country in Central America has tried to develop its own strategy (Peetz 2008). In El Salvador, the *maras* are considered as a threat to security, and the government has implemented a mix of activities around law and order and repressive policies aimed at protecting citizens against violence. In Costa Rica, the approach has been slower and less coherent, relying more on rehabilitation, but still tentative about direct courses of action.

- In Guatemala, police repression and activities by paramilitary groups have been more common. The current approach is for citizens to defend themselves and for the government to rely on police action to combat crime. There is little effort to address any of the root causes of youth alienation that leads them into gang membership.
- According to FUSADES (2005), a respected think tank in San Salvador, the repressive measures being implemented—and which have been implemented in the past—are ineffective. The country needs to implement preventive measures and generators of social capital in order to deal with the root causes of violence.
- In Costa Rica, a consensus has been built around prevention, with the government implementing a multifaceted plan in which several line ministries and other institutions work jointly to prevent drug abuse, sexual violence, street crime, and reinforce mental health.[8]

From the Outside Looking in

The first step taken by Central American countries has been to raise awareness about the roots of violence and the need to start keeping accurate records in centralized databases. While the OCAVI is a first step in this direction, similar efforts are in progress at the United Nations Development Program (UNDP), and through bilateral programs with some countries in North America and Europe. In the meantime, the UNDP has focused its efforts at creating working groups on violence and conflict, especially in relation to disarmament and policies related to small firearms and their links to street crime and family violence.

A thorough analysis of violence and conflict in Latin America from the perspective of social exclusion has been published by the Inter-American Development Bank (IDB) (Carrillo Flórez 2009). It argues that the export of raw commodities until the 1920s, and the policy of industrial protection from 1930 until 1980, actually contributed to the disempowerment of large segments of the population in Latin America. Such policies favored the creation of a small group of rich entrepreneurs and politicians and created favorable conditions for the exclusion of indigenous groups, the rural poor, and other segments of the population, including the political opposition. Social exclusion is now more visible in urban areas and among young adults, producing fertile grounds for radical extremism and political populism. The eventual imbalance of power created by ruling elites has resulted in the steady erosion of political parties, the weakening of public institutions, and the inability of the state to deliver public services—including justice—to the excluded segments of the population. In this regard, the IDB study concludes that the reform of the justice system is of high priority to address violence and conflict.

The World Bank Group has built a program on Urban Crime and Violence Prevention for the Latin American and Caribbean regions. Its objective is to reinforce community and government capacity for addressing public insecurity through municipal/urban renewal and preventive strategies. Its goal is to implement comprehensive interventions at the neighborhood level in coordination with other relevant municipal, government, and nongovernment programs addressing crime and violence and their causes. This program published two comprehensive reports on violence and crime in Central America, which suggest that the Central American countries will begin to pay close attention to the root causes of violence in the near future (World Bank 2010; World Bank 2011).

What is needed now is for the countries to look into themselves and implement long-term coherent policies. That will require a review of the issues like those listed on the conceptual framework and a realization that inclusive growth is the only way to reach a state of nonviolence in their societies

Notes

1. An extended version of this discussion can be found in North American Congress on Latin America (NACLA 1997).
2. This section is based on the chapter on El Salvador in Torres Rivas (1993).
3. At the time, the guerrilla movements in Guatemala, El Salvador, and Nicaragua followed the Cuban model, with a rural-based insurgency generating the momentum to spillover into urban areas. Cuban support was evident inasmuch most guerrilla leaders had spent time training in Cuba and time developing their internal organization before becoming a strike force.
4. The leaders of Colombia, Mexico, Panama, and Venezuela formed a *Grupo de Paises Amigos* and took an active role in promoting dialogue and reaching a consensus between the FMLN and the Salvadoran government.
5. This section summarizes the works of Purcell 1993, Chomsky 1996, Harpelle 2001, and Senior Angulo 2007.
6. There are about 90,000 Costa Ricans of African descent, and about 40,000 of indigenous origin. The total population is 4.5 million. Rebeca Grynspan, former vice president of Costa Rica and now under-secretary-general and associate administrator of the UNDP, has referred to these two groups as the "invisible population" in her efforts to bring attention to their problems.
7. The name *mara* is a short derivative of *marabunta*, a word describing a large concentration of legionnaire ants eating everything in their path.
8. This plan coordinates the individual plans of different line ministries: National Mental Health Plan (Ministry of Health), National Plan against Drugs (coordinated by the Costa Rican Institute against Drugs), National System for the prevention and treatment of intrahousehold violence (National Institute for Women), Strategic Plan for Road Safety (Ministry of Transportation), National Plan for the Prevention of Violence (Ministry of Education), and the National Plan for the Eradication of the Sexual Exploitation of Children and Youth (National Children Council [Patronato Nacional de la Infancia]).

References

Acemoglu, Daron, and James Robinson. 2012. *Why nations fail: The origins of power, prosperity and poverty*. New York: Random House.

Alaimo, Verónica, Pablo Fajnzylber, J. Luís Guasch, J. Humberto López, and Ana María Oviedo. 2009. The investment climate in Latin America. In *Does the investment climate matter? Microeconomic foundations of growth in Latin America*, edited by Pablo Fajnzylber, José Luís Guasch, and J. Humberto López, 49–112. Washington DC: World Bank.

Arroyo, Viviana, and Ana Nancy Espinoza. 2001. Análisis comparativo: Armas y violencia social en Centroamérica. In *El arsenal invisible: Armas livianas y seguridad ciudadana en la postguerra centroamericana*, 357–398. San José, Costa Rica: Fundación Arias para la Paz y el Progreso Humano.

Boraz, Steven, and Thomas Bruneau. 2006. Are the Maras overwhelming governments in Central America? *Military Review* November–December: 36–40.

Bourgois, Philippe. 1989. Blacks in Costa Rica: Upward mobility and ethnic discrimination. In *Costa Rica*, edited by Marc Edelman and Joanne Kennan, 161–169. New York: Grove Press.

Brunneau, Thomas C. 2005. The Maras and national security in Central America. *Strategic Insights* 4(5): 1–12.

Carrillo Flórez, Fernando. 2009. La lucha contra la exclusión social en América Latina—Una mirada desde Europa. Washington DC: Banco Interamericano de Desarrollo.

Castellanos, J. M. (2001). *El Salvador 1930–1970. Antecedentes históricos de la guerra civil.* San Salvador: Dirección de Publicaciones e Impresos.

Chomsky, Aviva. 1996. *West Indian workers and the United Fruit Company in Costa Rica, 1870–1940*. Baton Rouge: Louisiana State University Press.

Cruz, José Miguel. 2005. The gangs of Central America. Project Syndicate. http://www.project-syndicate.org/contributor/777. Accessed March 18, 2012.

Deininger, Klaus. 2004. Land policies and land reform. Technical Note. Land Policy and Administration Thematic Group. Washington DC: World Bank.

Demoscopía S.A. 2007. *Maras y pandillas, comunidad y policía en Centroamérica*. San José,, Costa Rica

Dulitzky, Ariel. 2005. A region in denial: Racial discrimination and racism in Latin America. In *Neither enemies nor friends: Latinos, Blacks, Afro-Latinos*, edited by Anani Dzidzienyo and Suzanne Oboler, 39–62. New York: Palgrave Macmillan.

Fundación Arias para la Paz y el Progreso Humano. 2001. El arsenal invisible: Armas livianas y seguridad ciudadana en la postguerra centroamericana. San José, Costa Rica.

Fundación Salvadoreña de Desarrollo. 2005. Consideraciones sobre la criminalidad en El Salvador. Primera Parte. Boletín No. 55, Departamento de Estudios Legales, San Salvador.

Hall, Gillette, and Harry Patrinos, eds. 2006. *Indigenous peoples, poverty and human development in Latin America*. London: Palgrave Macmillan.

Harpelle, Ronald H. 2001. *The West Indians of Costa Rica: Race, class, and the integration of an ethnic minority*. McGill-Queen's Studies in Ethnic History. Montreal and Kingston: McGill-Queen's University Press.

Hernández Pico, Juan. 2012. Guatemala. The impenetrable wall built by the rich. *Envío Digital*, No. 299. http://www.envio.org.ni/articulo/3313. Accessed March 18, 2012.

Huhn, Sebastian. 2008. A History of Nonviolence: Insecurity and the Normative Power of the Imagined in Costa Rica. Working Paper No. 84. German Institute of Global Area Studies. Hamburg.

———. 2009a. The culture of fear and control in Costa Rica (I): Crime statistics and law enforcement. Working Paper No. 104. German Institute of Global Area Studies. Hamburg.

———. 2009b. The culture of fear and control in Costa Rica (I): The talk of crime and social changes. Working Paper No. 108. German Institute of Global Area Studies. Hamburg.

Immigration and Refugee Board of Canada. 2002. *Costa Rica: Reports of severe discriminatory practices against black or Afro-Costa Rican citizens, particularly refusal to assist if these citizens are targeted by criminal gangs, and possibility of redress through the Office of the Ombudsman or other legal process*, CRI37851. http://www.unhcr.org/refworld/docid/3df4be2614.html. Accessed March 18, 2012.

Peetz, Peter. 2008. Discourses on violence in Costa Rica, El Salvador, and Nicaragua: Youth, crime, and the responses of the state. German Institute of Global and Area Studies No. 80, Hamburg.

Purcell, Trevor W. 1993. *Class, color, and culture among West Indians in Costa Rica*. Los Angeles: UCLA Center for Afro-American Studies.

Programa de Seguridad Ciudadana y Prevención de la Violencia, Programa de las Naciones Unidas para el Desarrollo (PNUD)Guatemala. 2007. *Informe estadístico de la violencia en Guatemala*. Guatemala: PNUD.

Salomón, Leticia. 2001. Las armas y la cultura de violencia. In *El arsenal invisible: Armas livianas y seguridad ciudadana en la postguerra centroamericana*. San José, Costa Rica: Fundación Arias para la Paz y el Progreso Humano.

Seligson, Mitchell. 1975. Agrarian capitalism and the transformation of peasant society: Coffee in Costa Rica. Special Studies Series, Council on International Studies, State University of New York at Buffalo.

Senior Angulo, Diana. 2007. La incorporación social en Costa Rica de la población afrocostarricense durante el siglo XX, 1927–1963. MSc Thesis, Universidad de Costa Rica, San José.

Stewart, Rigoberto. 2004. *The Limón REAL Project. Creating a free and autonomous region in Costa Rica*. Raleigh, NC: Free Nation Foundation.

Torres Rivas, Edelberto. 1993. *Historia general de Centroamérica*. Madrid: FLACSO.

United Nations Development Program. 2007. *Informe estadístico de la violencia en Guatemala*. Guatemala: Magna Terra Editores.

United Nations Office of Drug and Crime. 2011. *Global study on homicide*. New York.

Vargas, Jorge, Luís Rosero, and Mitchell Seligson. 2006. The political culture of democracy in Costa Rica: 2006. Washington DC: Democracy and Governance Program, United States Agency for International Development.

World Bank. 2010. *Crime and violence in Central America, Vol. II*. Sustainable Development Department and Poverty Reduction and Economic Management Unit, Latin America and the Caribbean Region. Washington DC.

———. 2011. *Crime and violence in Central America: A development challenge*. Sustainable Development Department and Poverty Reduction and Economic Management Unit, Latin America and the Caribbean Region. Washington DC.

CHAPTER 4

Violence and Sectoral Development in Colombia

*Jennifer S. Holmes and
Sheila Amin Gutiérrez de Piñeres*

Colombia is often portrayed as a country plagued by interminable internal conflict. However, behind this pessimistic generalization is a variegated reality of peaceful areas and bloody fighting. In this chapter, we examine specific sectors in Colombia to ask the question: when does sectoral development increase versus decrease conflict? This chapter has a targeted focus on economic sectors typically associated with higher conflict: coffee, oil, plantation agriculture (ranching and African palm), and coca. Our analysis extends to examining the following intervening factors: government policy, commodity prices, the provision of basic services, and overall state presence. We examine in depth case studies to identify the contextual factors that influence the relationship between development of distinct commodities and violence. Finally, what are the lessons learned about how to pursue development opportunities without increasing conflict?

In Colombia, there are two main types of nonstate political violence. First, leftist guerrilla groups, such as the Revolutionary Armed Forces of Colombia (FARC) and the National Liberation Army (*Ejército Liberación Nacional*, ELN), emerged in the 1960s, although they have earlier precursor groups.[1] These groups mobilized partially in response to the National Front period when the traditionally dominant Liberal and Conservative parties had a power-sharing agreement but excluded other parties and movements.

Second, Decree 3398 of 1965 and Law 48 of 1968 legalized the formation of rightist paramilitary groups with the hopes of fighting leftist guerrillas. By 1989, paramilitary groups were declared illegal because of their increasing violence. We will examine both types of violence in this chapter.

Scholars studying Colombia have identified possible linkages of violence and development including price shocks, legal versus illegal crops, differential impact of agricultural policies on landowners versus rural populations, capital- versus labor-intensive products, and average landholding size. Some have focused on specific commodities. Holmes, Piñeres, and Curtin (2008) found the coffee sector to be a significant predictor of guerrilla violence and the ranching sector and coca to be associated with paramilitary violence in Colombia. Rettberg (2010) and Dube and Vargas (2009) also found the contextual changes in the coffee sector to be a significant predictor of guerrilla violence. Dube and Vargas (2009) focus primarily on oil and coffee to examine the impact of price shocks, as mediated by the resource intensity of the product (labor versus capital). They conclude that "the prices of agricultural commodities (which are labor-intensive) are negatively related to conflict: when the price rises, conflict falls differentially in the municipalities that produce more of these agricultural goods. In contrast, the prices of natural resources (which are capital intensive) are positively related to conflict: when the price rises, conflict rises differentially in municipalities that produce more of these natural resources" (Dube and Vargas 2009, 2). Scholars such as Arbeláez, Echavarria, and Gaviria (2002, 42–43) have found onset of violence in areas "related to the sudden development of primary products (gold, emeralds, oil, bananas, cocaine)" especially in the context of low state presence. Similarly, in the Pacific, new palm-oil farms also create displacement or an intensification of conflict (Elhawary 2008) as land is seized for commercial use (Escobar 2003; Goebertus 2008) The varied results of past research motivate the need to study a subset of sectors across departments and time to determine if in fact a differential impact exists.

Land in Colombia

It is important to recognize that Colombia has suffered from numerous waves of internal conflict, much of it over land.[2] Richani (1997, 38) states: "If there is an epicenter, or flashpoint, that could have set the process leading to the war system... it would be the conflicts that have surrounded the distribution of land in Colombia ever since it became independent." Guerrero Baron and Mond (2001, 13) argue that "there is consensus that great social inequality and instability give rise to a dynamic that confers legitimacy on revolutionary projects and violent alternatives." Rural areas are neglected, receive little investment, have few poverty-reduction programs, low government services (Khan 2001), high poverty, and low productivity (Heshusius Rodríguez 2005). Long-standing issues of land inequality have led to "underutilization of cropland and overuse of pasture areas," low investment by local government, and high levels of violence (World Bank 2004, 2–3). In general, agricultural exports tend to be associated with exclusionary patterns of growth (increasing concentration of land and unstable employment (Carter and Mesbah 1993). In particular, there are additional aspects of land use that may affect conflict in Colombia. These include drug-related money laundering, both conflict- and development-induced internal displacement, and Colombian policies that favor large farms (World Bank 2004; see also Jaramillo 2001). These tensions have worsened as commercial agricultural activity increased (McLean 2002, 125) or as new areas were colonized and brought into cultivation. Damiani (2003, 84–88) argues that scholars who focus on the negative effects of agricultural exports typically associate the sector with low wages, seasonal or low need for labor, policies that discourage unions and lower the influence of labor in general, but that other effects are possible if factors include a shortage of skilled labor, year-round demand for labor that facilitates unionization, and links between local unions and the International Labor Organization (ILO). Unfortunately, in rural Colombia, these favorable conditions did not exist. Union members are often repressed or killed by right-wing paramilitary groups, and the average unemployment from 1990 to 2006 was 13.5 percent (Economic Commission for Latin America and the Caribbean). In many years during this time period, more trade unionists were killed in Colombia than in the rest of the world combined, according to the International Trade Union Confederation. The transformation of land from subsistence to commercial agriculture must be accompanied by increased demand for labor; otherwise, standards of living fall and poverty increases. Finally, the increase in cultivation of illegal drugs has created an environment where peasants have been forced out of traditional agricultural commodities. The substitution of employment in the legal for the illegal sector, referred to as the criminalization of the peasant, could have magnified preexisting violence (González 2002) in the context of the transition from a traditional agricultural economy to one dominated by more specialized, and often export driven, agricultural commodities.

Government and Land Policies

Instead of mediating the conflict over land, Colombian government policies toward land and rural development intensify it. Many early programs to rectify land issues have failed. Instead, resources were captured by the existing dominant large landowners and rural elites (Galli 1978). Deininger (1999, 655–656) argues that before 1994, Colombian policies exacerbated the extreme maldistribution of the land that dated back to the Spanish conquest. Specifically, lucrative tax incentives encouraged wealthy individuals to invest in land. Land was repurposed to crops needing little labor, due to sector-specific credit subsidies and protectionism. Additionally, in the 1980s, many *narcos* bought land to launder drug assets. Moreover, sharecropping was either illegal or discouraged, which further reduced opportunities for the small landowner or peasant. The 1993 Agrarian Law not only provided credit subsidies to small farmers but also created the Incentive to Rural Capitalization (ICR) that provided as much as 40 percent of the cost of investments that could be taken advantage of by larger farmers who were ineligible for the other programs (Guterman 2007, 21). In general, the commercial agricultural economy benefited from these policies (Jaramillo 2001, 822–824). After 1994, attempts were made to improve the implementation of the Colombian Land Reform Law. Despite intent to redistribute a million hectares, grants were used only to purchase land, and subsidies were captured by the well connected as opposed to the original targets of the program (Deininger 1999). Guterman (2007, 25) concludes by stating that "within the agricultural sector, the development and growth of the rural sector has favored large farmers, and land ownership continues to be highly concentrated. Very few of the benefits of agricultural reform have reached small farmers." Attempts at integrated rural-development programs, such as Colombia's Fondo de Desarrollo Rural, (Integrated Rural Development Program) have not benefited the small farmer either. Instead, "those best able to exploit market opportunities" have gained the most. Moreover, these policies tend to be developed with an aim of gaining rural political support instead of necessarily helping small farmers who do not have great influence (Redcliff 1989, 374).

Time Frame and Data Sources

This study begins after the most recent liberalization of the Colombian economy in the early 1990s. This opening also coincided with an initial drop in global commodity values. However, the impact of commodity prices was not consistent, and Colombia fared well compared to the rest of Latin America. This time period also coincided with a period of decentralization, which not only shifted the responsibility for the provision of basic services to the local governments and municipalities, but also provided significant transfers to the regional governments, due to mandates from the 1991 Constitution (Faguet and Sánchez 2008, 1298). This is a significant change for a country that in the past had invested only about half of the already-low Latin American average of public investment in education and health (López 2003, 272).

This increase in resources to the newly empowered local officials has been accompanied by more comprehensive efforts to improve security in addition to expanding and strengthening the capacity of the state. After his election in 2002, President Álvaro Uribe announced his Democratic Security Policy, which explicitly stated the importance of following up security gains with other aspects of state capacity. The plan recognized the historical lack of state control and capacity throughout much of the country and called for a permanent presence in all the municipal capitals, improvement in the judicial system, and increased coordination of efforts. This general strategy was continued after his reelection in 2006 with the Strategy of Strengthening Democracy and Social Development (2007–2013) and the National Development Plan of 2006–2010. As a result, Colombia has made significant improvement in security and the provision of services.

Departments were chosen based on percentage of departmental GDP dedicated to a certain commodity or relative dependence on a sector to isolate the effect of that sector on paramilitary and guerrilla-violence trends. Antioquia, because of its overall violence and complex-diverse economy, was not included, since it would be impossible to isolate the impact of any given commodity. Production and violence levels change year by year, so we analyze violence and trends by actor.

The figures in this chapter are based on the following data sources. Production and GDP data are in millions of 1994 pesos from Departamento Administrativo Nacional de Estadística/ National Administrative Department of Statistics (DANE). Poverty estimates are from the 1993 and 2005 censuses. The Gini estimates have been provided to from the authors by Sánchez 2003. GDP per capita estimates (in constant 1994 pesos) come from DANE's *Cuentas Nacionales Departamentales* (1991–2007). Estimates of levels of basic services and justice spending are from the Departamento Nacional de Planeación. The human rights violations data are from Centro de Investigación y Educación Popular (CINEP). These estimates are the annual number of politically motivated human rights violations from CINEP's Base de Datos, vintage 2007. Murder rates from *Instituto Medicina Legal*. Coca-cultivation numbers are from the United Nations Office on Drugs and Crime. General commodity prices come from the World Bank Commodity Price Data and are reported in constant US$2,000.

Oil

Scholars have advocated treating oil separately from agricultural products and other primary exports. Fearon and Laitin (2003) find oil to be associated with higher levels of insurgency and civil war, but believe that this may be due to the tendency for oil-producing countries to be weak states. We include oil because it is traded on the world market in international currency. In Colombia, oil is a capital intensive, parastate product that provides resources to local governments. In general, oil prices were stable or slightly decreasing from $23.8 in 1990 until $14 in 1998. Afterwards, oil prices began to increase, reaching $59 in 2006 (World Bank Commodity Prices). Increasing prices fueled the oil-related revenue of the municipal governments. Municipalities receive royalties redistributed from the national government via royalties proportionate to local production. Additionally, municipalities receive a transport tax proportionate to the length of local oil pipelines in their jurisdiction. Dube and Vargas (2009, 19) believe that this "raises the incentive to predate on these resources." Since it is a capital-intensive industry, as opposed to a labor-intensive industry, the effect of increasing oil prices on wages was minimal. Therefore, guerrillas and paramilitaries can also benefit from oil-related wealth, in terms of predation, in these areas (Elhaway 2008, 94).

We focus the examination of the two largest oil-producing departments: Casanare, which experienced rapid growth in oil production in our time frame, and Arauca, which had historically been a major oil-producing region. Both departments have varying levels of violence. There are no oil-producing departments without violence. Given this, we examine how violence evolves, in response to increasing oil production and state response.

Both Arauca and Casanare (see Table 4.1) are frontier, historically isolated departments and were chosen by Pearce (2007) for an in-depth historical analysis of oil production (see Figure 4.1) and conflict. Both departments had preexisting conflict and a weak state presence that predate our time period.

Arauca as a department has a history of strong peasant resistance. Specifically, the leftist guerrilla group, the ELN, historically recruited here among dissatisfied oil workers (Pearce 2007, 226). Despite its historical frontier status, Arauca was prioritized for security spending due to the presence of oil. For example, from 1993 to 2003, the combined per capita justice and security spending was higher than average for the country (900,000 pesos per capita).[3] Arauca experienced significant changes during this time period. The influx of oil resources assisted in the reduction of poverty, but an increase in inequality. Population almost doubled in this time period,

Violence and Sectoral Development in Colombia • 101

Table 4.1 Select indicators for Arauca and Casanare

Department	Arauca	Casanare
Average years of schooling (1993 to 2005)	5.9 to 7.0	5.5 to 6.7
Percent homes with water and sewage (2005)	78 (water) 70 (sewer)	65 (water) 58 (sewer)
Population enrolled in *Seguridad Social* (%) (1996 to 2005)	10 to 70	33.7 to 95.6
Poverty (%) (1993 to 2005)	53.7 to 35.5	52.1 to 35.5
Gini (1992 to 2002)	0.63 to 0.69	0.77 to 0.76
GDP per capita (1990 to 2002) (constant pesos)	4,685,435 to 1,849,519	2,794,981 to 5,132,517
Per capita justice and security spending	1,700,000	1,600,000

Source: Departamento Nacional de Planeación, Sánchez 2003, DANE; Departamento Nacional de Planeación 1999, SISD Boletín 20: Indicadores de política social; Departamento Nacional de Planeación, 2008. SISD Boletín 37: Indicadores Sociales Departamentales; Departamento Nacional de Planeación, 2002, Indicadores de coyuntura y económicos, DANE. 1993; Censo Nacional DANE. 2005; Censo Nacional Sánchez, Fabio. 2003.

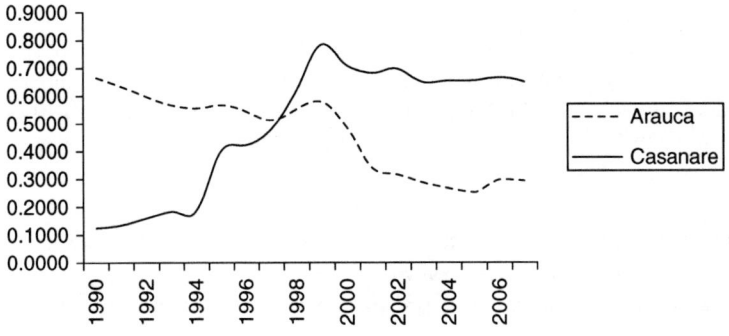

Figure 4.1 Oil as a proportion of departmental GDP, 1990–2007.

outpacing departmental GDP growth, resulting in a decline in GDP per capita.

In the 1980s, and especially after the activation of the Caño Limón oil field in 1986, local and regional governments benefited greatly from the oil-related resources, but corruption limited its effectiveness. "A large amount of resources became available to a territory where politics was still a struggle for personal accumulation of wealth and power based on relationships with vote-delivering clients. The weakness and venality of local institutions and the growing power of armed groups, in particular the ELN guerrillas, meant that oil revenues failed to bring serious benefits or sustainable development to the people of Arauca" (Pearce 2007, 227). Pearce does not isolate oil as the source of conflict, but instead highlights contextual factors that allowed oil resources to fund armed groups. In her view, the government did not provide professional and accountable security or promote the rule of law. The lack of professional protection of the pipeline resulted in human rights violations. State presence was sparse and institutions that were in place performed poorly, were unresponsive to broader demands, were clientelistic, and failed to provide public policies to resolve issues related to demographic change and land use. In general, the local governments were responsive to interests of private interest as opposed to the "common good." According to Pearce (2007, 225–228), these shortcomings of the Colombian governments, at all levels, created a context of increasing conflict, despite the attempt of dominant oil-producer BP-Amoco to change its policies in response to well-publicized charges of collusion with armed groups, who were able to predate upon the pipeline and other oil-related infrastructure.

Figure 4.2 presents human rights violations on noncombatants by actor in Arauca. The successful recruitment of oil workers by the ELN is reflected in the constant level of leftist guerrilla violations through the mid-1990s, followed by a period of fluctuation. After 2002, there is a significant spike in human rights violations by paramilitary groups. Despite the apparent increasing conflict in this period, the murder rate actually declined from 95 per 100,000 in 1998 to 78 per 100,000 in 2005. Pearce (2007) expresses concern that high levels of conflict may be difficult to reverse, once established. Our analysis supports this, since Arauca's human rights violations spiked despite increased government resources and a decline in the relative importance of oil on the economy.

Like Arauca, Casanare is also a frontier department that historically had a very weak state presence (see Figure 4.1). In fact in 1993, there was no justice spending. Afterward, more resources were invested in justice and security spending, giving the department a higher level of per capita spending than the average. It was a department with an economy initially dominated by the ranching sector, with almost 62 percent of the departmental GDP attributed to animal-related products in 1990. However, during this time period, oil production began, rapidly changing the character of the economy. By 2006, just fewer than 8 percent of the departmental income came from the ranching sector. Despite an increase in the population by

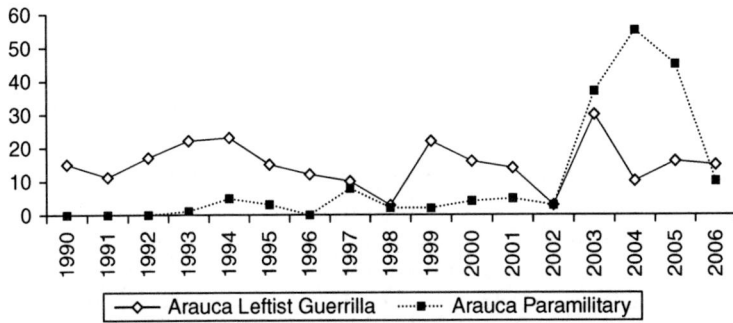

Figure 4.2 Human rights violations with attributions of responsibility in Arauca.

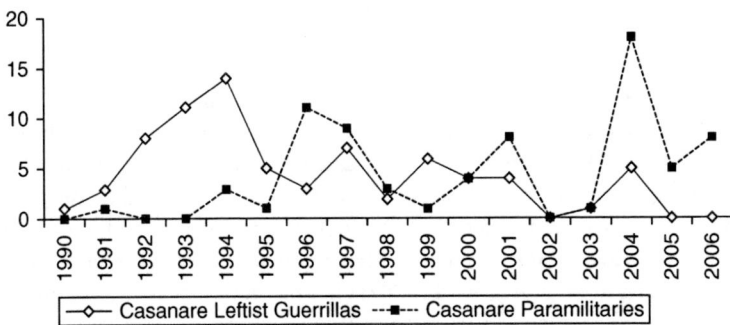

Figure 4.3 Human rights violations with attributions of responsibility in Casanare.

about a third, income per capita increased and poverty declined. Inequality has remained relatively high.

Casanare had prominent and powerful cattle families, who were easily able to form paramilitaries to counter any emergent guerrilla threat. Additionally, as oil revenues increased starting the mid-1990s, cycles of paramilitary violence reached new levels, while leftist guerrilla violence generally decreased. In Casanare, the overall murder rate declined from 109 per 100,000 in 1998 to only 53 per 100,000 in 2005.

The different patterns of these two departments reflect the intensification of preexisting, underlying conflict in a context of a weak and clientelistic state presence that allowed rent-seeking behavior of nonstate violent groups. Arauca was a department with dominant guerrilla activity and influence, whereas Casanare was dominant in ranching, with eventual higher paramilitary activity when challenged by guerrilla actions. However, both departments have also experienced increased state capacity in terms of higher than average justice and security spending. Improvement is evident in the statistics of the provision of basic services in both Casanare and Arauca. This strengthening of state presence may improve the chances of these departments to develop without creating negative cycles of rent seeking and predation of oil resources by nonstate violent groups, especially in the cases of areas like Casanare, where efforts to strengthen state capacity were contemporary to the resource booms, and not after them, as in Arauca. Therefore, a policy of linking increased state presence, and development/expansion of oil production has the potential to dampen violence and prevent the onset of violence despite the strategy of oil promotion.

Coffee

Historically, coffee has been an anchor of prosperity to the Colombian economy. However, when the international coffee market collapsed, what had been a source of stability became an economic drag in coffee-producing areas. The coffee economy has changed dramatically in recent years, as prices fell and government support to smaller producers disappeared through the end of the time period studied here (prices have since rebounded). Moreover, crop-substitution plans to replace coffee production have not been successful, resulting in deterioration of rural economic conditions. Guerrilla groups have taken advantage of this crisis in traditional coffee regions to recruit (Richani 1997; Trujillo and Badel 1997, 273–275; Holmes, Gutiérrez de Piñeres, and Curtin 2008).

Two studies have focused primarily on the coffee-conflict nexus. Rettberg (2010) is clear that coffee as a commodity is not a cause of conflict. The context of the production and the sale of this commodity determine the relationship. In fact, she clearly demonstrates that in the past, Colombia's coffee regions were "considered a safe haven from armed conflict and poverty" (Rettberg 2010, 112). What has changed is the following: the dissolution of the International Coffee Agreement in 1989, the collapse of coffee prices, the penetration of coca cultivation into coffee-growing regions, processing and drug trafficking in these regions, the weakening of the National Coffee Federation and its support to small cultivators and its general promotion of political stability, and the transition from many small landholders to a concentration of landholding. In addition to these changes, the Colombian coffee industry suffered from disease and currency revaluation during the 1990s. Dube and Vargas (2009) focus on the impact of price shocks and wages in the case of a labor-intensive commodity such as coffee. They do not find a major impact on local government revenue. "Our interpretation of this evidence is that when agricultural laborers in the coffee region face lower wages, this raises their incentive to join armed groups. The availability of cheaper recruits also leads armed groups to scale up recruitment activities in these areas" (Dube and Vargas 2009, 21).

This study begins years after the peak of coffee prices. The 1990 price, in constant US cents per kilogram, was a mere 191 compared to the 1977 peak of 908, which was followed by a general decline. The market bottomed out at 129 in 1992. The years of 2001–2003 also came close to that historic low. During 2000–2005, producers received a direct price support, instead of being taxed as during previous years (Guterman 2007, 14). However, during most of this period, coffee as a crop had a negative rate of assistance, according to Guterman (2007, 30): -6.1 percent from 1990 to 1994, -21.4 percent from 1995 to 1999, but mildly positive (6.2 percent) from 2000 to 2005. Unlike many export commodities that received subsidies, coffee was instead taxed to generate revenue for government expenditures. During this same time, Colombia also began to face competition from Vietnamese and Brazilian coffee.

The three traditional coffee-producing departments are Caldas, Tolima, and Quindio. Of these three departments, Tolima has the most violence and Quindio the least. Figure 4.4 demonstrates the generally declining importance of coffee in these traditional coffee-producing departments. The economy of Caldas, despite the relative decline of coffee, was still heavily dependent on coffee during this time period. Ranching and other agriculture each

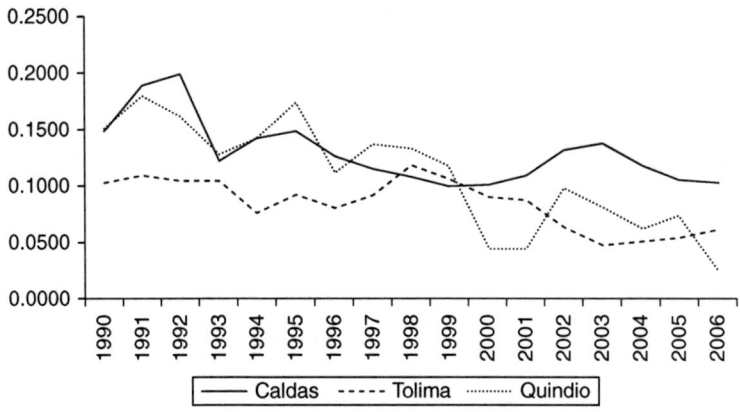

Figure 4.4 Coffee, as a proportion of departmental GDP.

contributed generally less than 5 percent of departmental GDP during this time period. Tolima had generally minimal production of ranching-related animals and stable production of other agricultural products during this time period. The coffee sector in Quindio dropped in importance. Ranching and other agriculture remained stable at about 15 percent of GDP.

Tolima and Caldas have similar patterns of violence but different patterns of coffee production. Rettberg (2010, 126) notes that the guerrillas made a strategic plan to move into coffee-producing areas in response to the crisis in this region in the early 1990s. The paramilitaries entered around 1996, as landownership patterns changed and concentrated. These decisions made by warring armed groups are reflected in Figures 4.5–4.7. In all departments, levels of human rights violations by all groups are low through the mid-1990s. In Caldas, there is a slight but steady increase in leftist guerrilla violations from 1993 to 1996, but that activity spikes in 1999. Soon after, the new presence of paramilitaries is seen, with increases in the early 2000s. Added together, conflict in Caldas was highest around these later low-coffee-price years. In Tolima, there is similar calm until the spike of guerrilla violations in 1996, which was followed by rapidly increasing violence by both guerrillas and paramilitaries. Notably, both departments experienced rapid declines in all types of violence in 2006. Interestingly, Quindio did not suffer from much if any political violence until a spike in paramilitary violence in 2006.

The statistics in Table 4.2 demonstrate that both Caldas and Tolima had generally high levels of development prior to the period of this study. Nonetheless, there is still improvement during this time period. Caldas

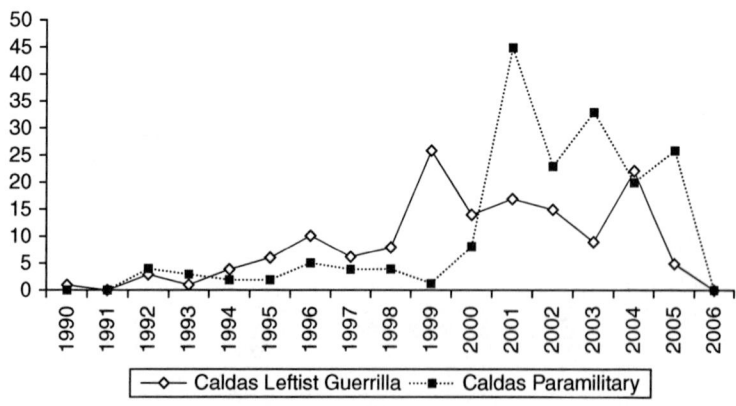

Figure 4.5 Human rights violations with attributions of responsibility in Caldas.

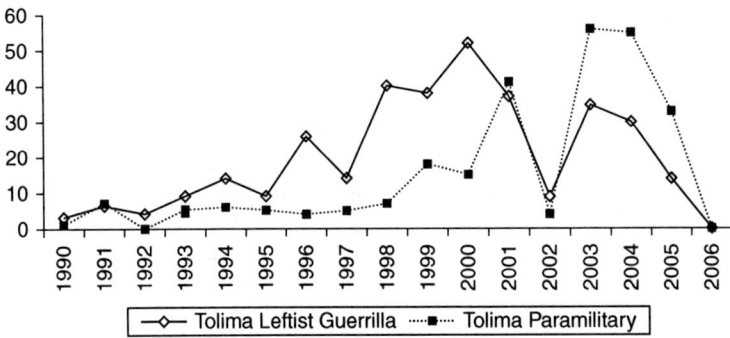

Figure 4.6 Human rights violations with attributions of responsibility in Tolima.

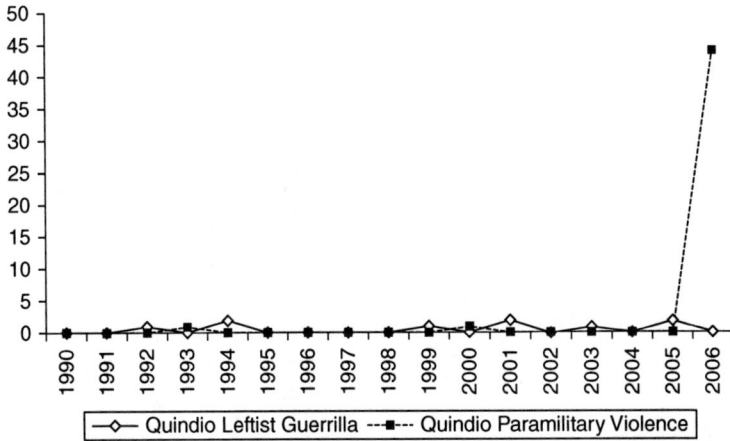

Figure 4.7 Human rights violations with attributions of responsibility in Quindio.

improved the average years of schooling. The percentage of homes with access to water and sewer was already high in 1993 and remained constant through 2005. The population enrolled in *Seguridad Social* increased. These statistics reinforce Rettberg's conclusion that before the change in the coffee economy, these departments were better off than the average Colombian rural areas due to the previously strong employment opportunities for rural workers. From 1993 to 2005, poverty declined; even though, inequality (Gini) increased. GDP per capita increased modestly despite 15 percent

Table 4.2 Select indicators for Caldas, Tolima, and Quindio

Department	Caldas	Tolima	Quindio
Average years of schooling (1993 to 2005)	5.9 to 7.0	5.5 to 6.7	6.4 to 7.8
Percent homes with water and sewage (1993 to 2005)	77 (water) 85 (sewer)	60 (water) 63.5 (sewer)	91 (water) 87 (sewer)
Population enrolled in *Seguridad Social* (%) (1996 to 2005)	36.7 to 58.8		36 to 70
Poverty (%) (1993 to 2005)	28.9 to 17.7	39.2 to 29.8	24 to 16
Gini (1992 to 2002)	0.69 to 0.72	0.73 to 0.68	0.71 to 0.68
GDP per capita (1990 to 2002) (constant pesos)	1,307,083 to 1,544,289	1,234,517 to 1,565,789	1,235,385 to 1,295,551
Per capita justice and security spending	1,400,000	560,000	

Source: Departamento Nacional de Planeación, Sánchez 2003, DANE; Departamento Nacional de Planeación 1999, SISD Boletín 20: Indicadores de política social; Departamento Nacional de Planeación, 2008. SISD Boletín 37: Indicadores Sociales Departamentales; Departamento Nacional de Planeación, 2002. Indicadores de coyuntura y económicos, DANE. 1993; Censo Nacional DANE. 2005; Censo Nacional Sánchez, Fabio. 2003.

population growth. Caldas's per capita justice and security spending was also higher than the department average of 900,000 pesos. Tolima's poverty declined. Per capita justice and security spending was lower than the department average. Inequality fell slightly. GDP per capita increased while the population did not increase during this time period. In terms of social services, the average years of schooling increased as did the percent of homes with access to sewer. Quindio was even better off than the other two with its average years of schooling, and homes with access to water and sewer being higher. The percent of the population in *Seguridad Social* increased and poverty declined steeply, although per capita income was stagnant. Its homicide rate fell from 58 in 1998 to 26 in 2005. Inequality remained high.

Despite the conflict in these departments, violence trends do decrease in this time period, as efforts to increase the depth and breadth of state capacity continued after 2002. These public policies may have been successful because of the stronger government presence prior to the collapse of the coffee market and supporting state institutions, matched by the eventual improvement in tax policies toward the sector.

Plantation-Based Agriculture and the Ranching Sector

Some of the more commercially based, export-oriented agricultural products, such as palm, bananas, and other plantation-based crops, share similar characteristics with the ranching sector. Moreover, many of the departments that have dominant sectors of plantation agriculture also have strong ranching sectors, making it difficult to differentiate the impact of one from the other. Historically, products for export such as meat products and coffee, and other agricultural products with industrial uses, were favored by government policies. These sectors, unlike coffee, tend be more capital intensive. The ranching sector benefited greatly from government economic policies. For example, Guterman (2007, 30) calculates the nominal rate of assistance to beef and milk as the following: 8.9 percent and 18.4 percent from 1990 to 1994, 6.4 percent and 44.4 percent from 1995 to 1999, and -9.5 percent and 94.5 percent from 2000 to 2005 respectively. We report both beef and milk subsidies, even though beef subsidies are small, since both are products of large ranches.

We focus on these agricultural products because they tend to be dominated by large landowners. Plantation-based export crops have been associated with development-induced displacement in Colombia (Palacios 2010; Escobar 2003; Calado and Medrano 2006). "The rural areas from which poor peasant and indigenous populations were expelled by force include territorial zones traditionally used by small peasants and settlement areas;... territories required for large agro-industrial plantations, such as African palm; cocaine plantations; indigenous people's traditional preserved territories, or *resguardos*; and strategic corridors for arms and drug trafficking" (Calado and Medrano 2006, 236). Subsequently, it may be useful to examine this sector along with the effects of the ranching sector, which is strongly associated with paramilitary violence in Colombia (Holmes, Gutiérrez de Piñeres, and Curtin 2008). This sector has been associated with conflict in other countries as well. Williams (1986), in a study of cattle ranching in Central America, documented displacement of peasants, increased protests, and early rebellion in these areas where ranching expanded. The theorized causal linkages between these sectors of development and violence are very similar: large landowners either fund or affiliate with paramilitary groups to displace individuals or to discourage protest. It must also be noted that although indigenous groups or small landowners may have land rights that would be recognized, the historical weakness of the state and the rule of law diminish the effectiveness of potential legal claims in light of overwhelming private force and the lack of a mediating government presence. The ranching sector has historically been associated with paramilitary violence, since these traditional large landowners were some of the first to create their own self-defense forces, paramilitaries, to fight leftist guerrillas. As patterns of landownership changed, new large landowners, including those who were investing drug money, also funded paramilitary groups.

Many, such as the *Oficina del Alto Comisionado de las Naciones Unidas para los Refugiados* ACNUR (2005), Elhawary (2008), and Mingorance (2006), have linked African oil palm plantations in Colombia to conflict-induced displacement and violence. Palacios (2010) makes the claim that palm plantations have caused more forced displacement than even coca. The Pacific province of Chocó, historically one of the poorest departments in Colombia, experienced the new development in the 1980s, including the rapid expansion of African palm plantations. The small and communal landowners were displaced by the large-plantation owners. These plantations have been linked to development-induced displacement by the paramilitaries. "The paramilitaries forged alliances with private investors to invest in the crops for which they received subsidies and incentives from the state as part of its rural development agenda" (Elhawary 2008). In fact, the palm industry has received subsidies since the 1950s and recently was favored by the ICR program that encouraged the formation of new farms. Palm oil also received price-stabilization funds (Guterman 2007, 10, 24). Guterman's calculation of the rate of assistance to palm oil is 33.3 percent from 1990 to 1994, 13.7 percent from 1995 to 1999, and 44.9 percent from 2000 to 2005, making it one of the most favored products.[4] According to the *Federación Nacional de Cultivadores de Palma de Aceite* (FEDEPALMA),[5] Meta is the department with the most palm production, followed by Cesar, Santander, Magdalena, Nariño, and Casanare.

The trend for plantation agriculture is mixed, with declines in Cesar, Caquetá, and Chocó, but stability in Meta throughout this period with the exception of Caquetá, which has a spike in 1998 (see Figure 4.8). Ranching has greater fluctuations. Here Caquetá has more than a quarter of its GDP in ranching until a decline that starts in 1996, bottoming out in 1998 with 16 percent, but it builds back up to 27 percent in 2003. Meta has stable proportions of GDP in ranching, around 12–16 percent. There is a slight downward trend in Cesar (from around 20 percent in 1990 down to 13 percent in 2006). Chocó's peak of ranching is 1991 with 19 percent of department GDP, but then declined to just below 8 percent in 2006. Meat prices were relatively stable during this time period. In 1990, the value was 250 cents per kilogram. Prices slowly declined to 155 cents in 1996, but slowly recovered to a peak of 237 cents in 2005. Palm oil prices increased from 290 cents in 1990 to 691 cents in 1998. Then prices fell to 285 cents in 2001 before stabilizing around 450 cents in the end of the period.

Caquetá's economy is the most heavily dominated by these two sectors. Caquetá was relatively peaceful until the late 1990s, when increases in guerrilla violence were matched with increases in paramilitary violence (Figure 4.9).

Reflecting the gradual decline in the two main drivers of its economy, GDP per capita measured in constant pesos fell. It peaked at 1,662,409 in 1998 but dropped back in 2002. The provision of services increased such as the average years of schooling, access to water and sewer. The percentage of workers enrolled in *Seguridad Social* also increased. Although these numbers indicate improvement, the provision of services is still lower than the average.[6] The homicide rate fell from 109 in 1998 to 58 in 2006. Poverty fell

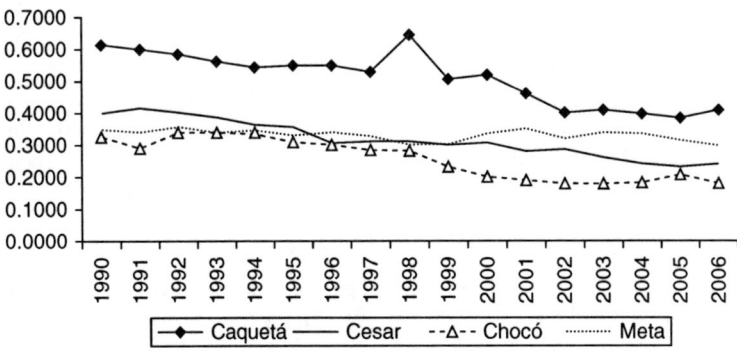

Figure 4.8 Proportion of departmental GDP that is ranching and plantation agriculture.

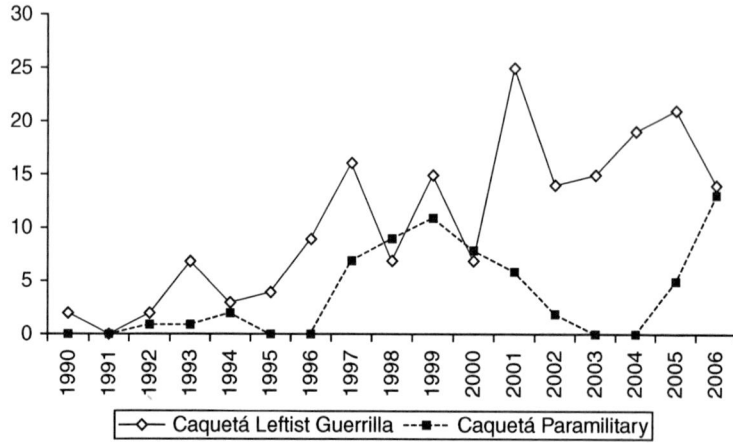

Figure 4.9 Human rights violations with attributions of responsibility in Caquetá.

while inequality remained fairly constant. Caquetá's per capita justice and security spending was much lower than average (see Table 4.3).

Chocó is not a major palm producer, but is an example of recent production that has resulted in development-induced displacement, despite a 1993 law that tithed almost half of the department's land to the Afro-Colombian communities in the area. The year of the handover of land, 1996, marked the beginning of a paramilitary offensive and the establishment of new palm plantations (Oslender 2008, 87–92).

The spikes in paramilitary violence from the CINEP data reflect the use of paramilitaries to displace the small landowners to pave the way for large plantations (Figure 4.10). Hernandez (2010) reports on an instance of displacement in which two Afro-Colombian communities were forced off their traditional lands in the late 1990s by paramilitaries. In 2010, 24 representatives of the palm companies were arrested and charged with the displacement of these indigenous communities. As mentioned earlier, Chocó is one of the poorest departments in Colombia and also has high inequality. Its GDP per capita is the lowest in Colombia. Provision of services is also particularly low. The average years of schooling and access to services remained low. The percentage of the population enrolled in *Seguridad Social* increased. Chocó's per capita justice and security spending during this time was about average (see Table 4.3).

The legal drivers of Meta's economy were stable during this time period. Although there is a small increase in paramilitary violence in 1992, the

Table 4.3 Select indicators for Caquetá, Chocó, Meta, and Cesar

Department	Caquetá	Chocó	Meta	Cesar
Average years of schooling (1993 to 2005)	4.5 to 6.1	4.6 to 5.6	5.6 to 7.4	5.2 to 6.6
Percent of homes with water and sewage	47.1 to 62.7 (water) 36.9 to 54.7 (sewer)	<20 (water) 14 (sewer) remains unchanged	66 to 75 (water) 60.7 to 75 (sewer)	73 to 76 (water) 38.5 to 61 (sewer)
Population enrolled in *Seguridad Social* (%) (1996 to 2005)	17.9 to 54.7	22.9 to 65.6		
Poverty (%) (1993 to 2005)	58.2 to 41.5	80.4 to 79.2	41.3 to 25	56.1 to 44.7
Gini (1992 to 2002)	0.53 to 0.56	0.67 to 0.67	0.69 to 0.59	0.64 remains constant
GDP per capita (1990 to 2002) (constant pesos)	1,114,538 to 1,034,640	686,148 to 697,707	1,680,277 to 2,016,192	1,099,646 to 1,394,793
Per capita justice and security spending	380,000	970,000	790,000	310,000

Source: Departamento Nacional de Planeación, Sánchez 2003, DANE; Departamento Nacional de Planeación 1999, SISD Boletín 20: Indicadores de política social; Departamento Nacional de Planeación, 2008. SISD Boletín 37: Indicadores Sociales Departamentales; Departamento Nacional de Planeación, 2002, Indicadores de coyuntura y económicos, DANE. 1993; Censo Nacional DANE. 2005; Censo Nacional Sánchez, Fabio. 2003.

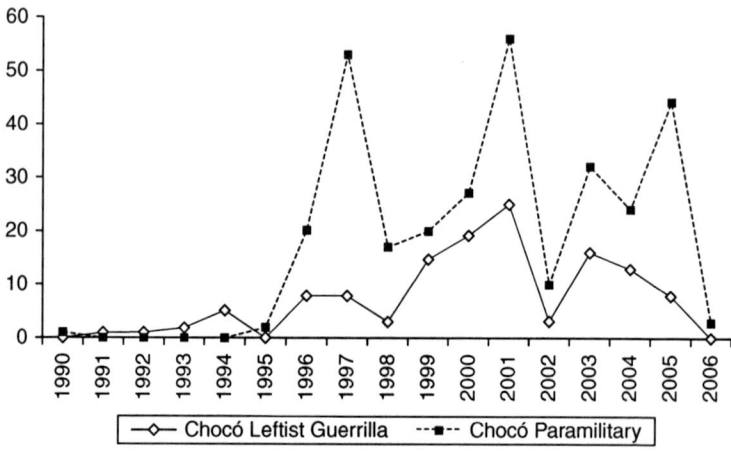

Figure 4.10 Human rights violations with attributions of responsibility in Chocó.

violence trends are relatively low until the significant increases in paramilitary violence in 2003 (Figure 4.11). Meta also experienced new coca cultivation in 1999 with over 11,000 hectares cultivated, which remained constant until a peak of almost 19,000 hectares in 2004. New coca production may be driving the spike in paramilitary violence more than production of agricultural goods or the ranching sector.

Poverty decreased and GDP per capita increased. Inequality also decreased. Per capita justice spending was less than average. The provision of services, initially relatively high, further increased during this time (see Table 4.3). Despite this general improvement, guerrilla violations remain constant, although paramilitary violence has declined. Homicide rates increased from 47 in 1998 to 105 in 2006, reflecting a continued context of conflict.

Cesar experienced a steady decline in the importance of ranching and plantation agriculture, from 40 percent of departmental GDP to 24 percent in this period. The violence in Cesar slowly winds down, after the peak of guerrilla violence in 1994 and paramilitary violence in 1997 (Figure 4.12). The homicide rate also declined from 47 in 1998 to 29 in 2006. Per capita justice and security spending was low—just slightly greater than one-third of the department average. Inequality remained constant while poverty fell and GDP per capita increased. Provision of services also increased. The average years of schooling and provision of services increased (see Table 4.3).

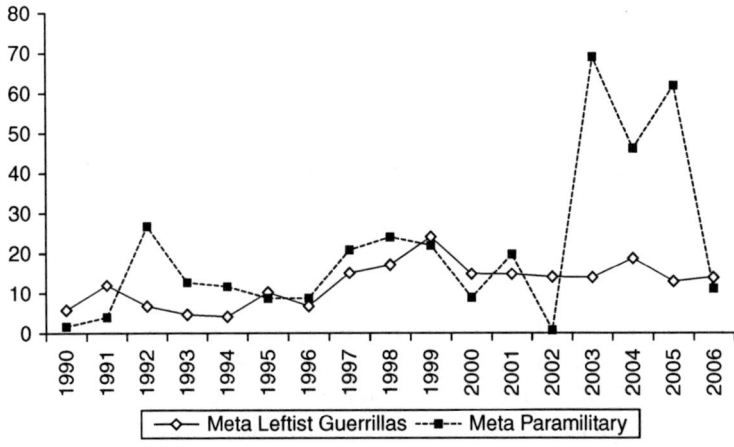

Figure 4.11 Human rights violations with attributions of responsibility in Meta.

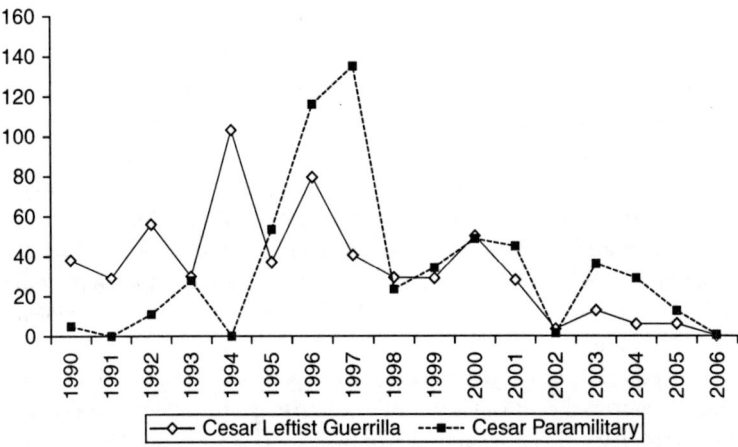

Figure 4.12 Human rights violations with attributions of responsibility in Cesar.

There is an improvement in standards of living and declines in violence but the question remains as to whether this is due to a more fortified position by the paramilitary or more state presence. Additionally, in general, these departments are starting from an overall lower level of services than average. Meta's conflict levels fell in terms of overall homicide and have a continued relatively constant-level activity of guerrillas while experiencing a spike in paramilitary violence. However, this may reflect the dynamics of new cultivations of coca in a context of preexisting conflict, more than any simplistic relationship between the economy and violence. The case of other agricultural commodities is much more difficult to isolate and may require even more disaggregated case studies given the conflicting results found in Chocó and Meta.

Coca

Coca is a crop that, because of its illegality, does not involve agreement with the state, should be treated differently than other primary exports. Specifically in Colombia, the destruction of the main cartels in the 1980s and the 1990s allowed the FARC, and other nonstate violent groups, to be more directly involved and benefit directly from the drug trade. Numerous scholars and policy experts cite the importance of coca production in fueling conflict and terrorism (Rochlin 2003; Byman et al. 2001; Le Billon 2001). Peceny and Durnan (2006) examine the effects of US drug policy in Colombia and the status of coca as an illegal product (which prevents state participation in the extraction of the coca) following the argument of Snyder (2006). Holmes, Gutiérrez de Piñeres, and Curtin (2008) find a connection between leftist violence and coca cultivation from 1993 to 1998, but not from 1999 to 2002. However, in both time periods, they find a positive relationship between coca cultivation and paramilitary violence.

Here, we examine three coca-producing departments: Putumayo, Guaviare, and Nariño. Putumayo has the greatest coca production in 2000, while Guaviare has the most consistent level of production. Nariño had none until 1999, after which production increased until stabilizing around 15,000 hectares a year (Figure 4.13). On average, Nariño has more violence relative to Putumayo and Guaviare.

The spikes in Putumayo's violence seem unrelated to the coca-cultivation trends. Toward the end of this period, leftist guerrilla violence declines, but paramilitary violence continues to increase (Figure 4.14). Despite these increases, the homicide rate greatly decreased from 108 per 100,000 in 1998 to only 30 in 2006. Putumayo, in addition to having significant coca cultivation, also has a major component from other agriculture (from 20 to 65 percent of GDP). It also has livestock and oil, which can vary from approximately 5 to 10 percent of GDP. During this time period, inequality and poverty decreased. GDP per capita increased despite a population growth of one-third. Putumayo historically has had very low access to services and per capita justice and security spending was much lower than average (see Table 4.4). Even with improvements, Putumayo remains near the bottom of services and economic development.

Violence and Sectoral Development in Colombia • 117

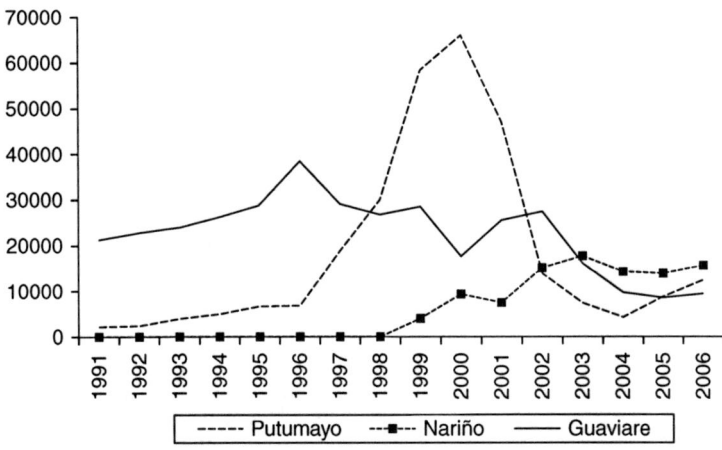

Figure 4.13 Coca cultivation in hectares.

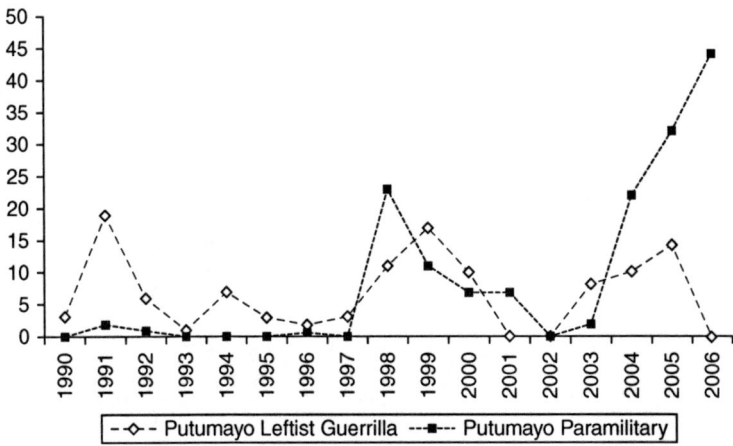

Figure 4.14 Human rights violations with attributions of responsibility in Putumayo.

Nariño lacked coca cultivation until 1999 and then rapidly increased through 2006.

The department also became home to new cultivation of African palm, with the associated development-induced displacement (Escobar 2003, 158). In Nariño, the spike in both guerrilla and paramilitary violence

Table 4.4 Select indicators for Putumayo, Nariño, and Guaviare

Department	Putumayo	Nariño	Guaviare
Average years of schooling (1993–2005)		4.8–6.4	Not available
Percent homes with water and sewage	33.1–39 (water)	59–65 (water)	22.7–32.4 (water)
		34.6–43.4 (sewer)	7.9–33.4 (sewer)
Population enrolled in *Seguridad Social* (%) (1996–2005)	2.7–65	27.8–61.7	6.8–58.2
Poverty (%) (1993–2005)	78.8–34.5	56.3–43.6	Not available
Gini (1992–2002)	0.72–0.69	0.67 remained constant	Not available
GDP per capita (1990–2002)	662,508–812,446	687,454–856,772	2,724,613–1,668,396
Per capita justice and security spending	255,000	276,000	54,000

Source: Departamento Nacional de Planeación, Sánchez 2003, DANE; Departamento Nacional de Planeación 1999, SISD Boletín 20: Indicadores de política social; Departamento Nacional de Planeación, 2008. SISD Boletín 37: Indicadores Sociales Departamentales; Departamento Nacional de Planeación, 2002, Indicadores de coyuntura y económicos, DANE. 1993; Censo Nacional DANE. 2005; Censo Nacional Sánchez, Fabio. 2003.

seems to be associated with new coca cultivation (Figure 4.15). Its homicide rate was 23 in 1998 and increased slightly to 26 in 2006. Nariño was slightly more developed than Putumayo with more access to water and sewer and people were enrolled in *Seguridad Social*. Average years of schooling and GDP per capita increased. Per capita justice and security spending was very low. Poverty decreased slightly while inequality was stable (see Table 4.4).

Interestingly, Guaviare's spikes in violence correspond to the height of coca cultivation in 1996, and the subsequent decline, which began in 2004 (Figure 4.16).

During this time period, the homicide rate was 122 per 100,000 in 1998 and actually increased to 138 in 2006. Guaviare is also a department with historically extremely low rates of service provision and state presence such as access to water and sewer. The percentage of the population enrolled in *Seguridad Social* increased from one of the lowest rates in the country. GDP per capita dropped. During this time, population increased by approximately half. Justice spending was practically nonexistent in Guaviare during this time (see Table 4.4). The overall per capita justice and security spending was the lowest in Colombia. Typical of historically isolated departments, neither poverty nor Gini coefficients are reported for this time period. Guaviare's legal economy was dominated by plantation agricultural products in 1990, composing approximately 80 percent of department GDP. This fell below

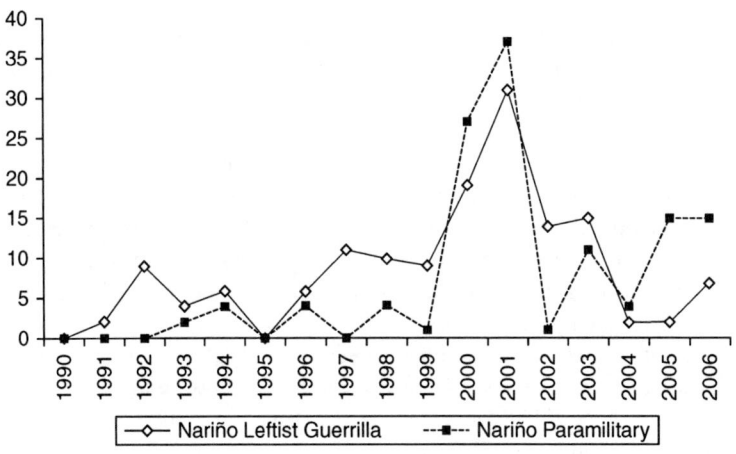

Figure 4.15 Human rights violations with attributions of responsibility in Nariño.

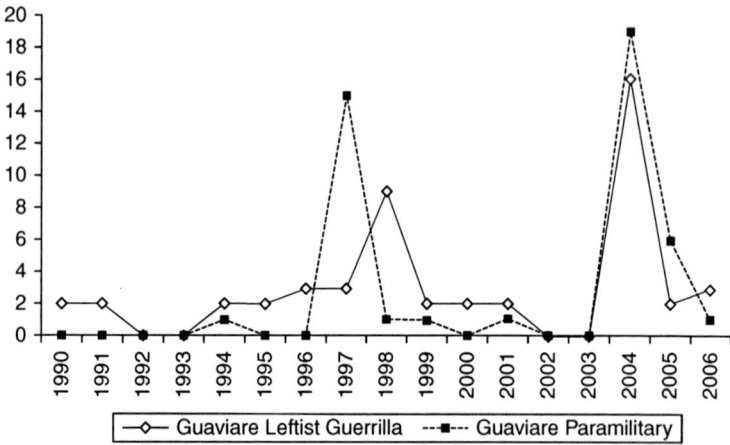

Figure 4.16 Human rights violations with attributions of responsibility in Guaviare.

50 percent in 2004. It appears that the state presence in Guaviare and Putumayo is still insufficient to be able to moderate or discourage conflicts. The experience of Nariño reinforces the danger of new production of illegal crops such as coca, without a strong government presence.

Conclusions

Examining violence, development, and commodity production at the department levels demystifies any simplistic association among them. The analysis does reveal that guerrilla activity dominates in labor-intensive commodities and paramilitary in capital-intensive commodities. In departments where there is a change in production from capital-intensive to labor-intensive or labor-intensive to capital-intensive, we see entry of other violent actors matched by increases in violence. However, the presence of the state can prevent increases in violence during economic change. In Colombia, spikes in violence are associated with new cultivation or production, especially in the context of weak state presence and contested land rights. Government policy favored commercial agriculture over the interests of small farmers, but this has not uniformly resulted in higher levels of violence. There are many factors that impact the nexus between development and violence. State presence, rule of law, and the protection of property rights (not just of large landowners) mitigate inflammatory effects of development and reduce violence. Improvement in the provision of services may be a more viable option than attempting another round of land reform or rural development plans. While we recognize that land reform is the first-best policy solution, it is also the least viable. In light of this, a second-best solution of investment in human and social capital is recommended. Investment in human and social capital allows the citizenry to capture benefits and improve standards of living and does not trigger another round of land-related conflict.

In the Colombian case, the main intervening factor is state presence. In the case of coca, violence coincides with increased or new cultivation and a lack of effective government interventions. However, Colombia has started to make progress with this historical challenge. Across all departments, there is a general improvement in services and state presence that may eventually deter and effectively respond to violence. Additionally, it is also likely that if a nonstate actor provides stable order, an influx of resources may not result in higher violence. To conclude that development or increased production of a specific commodity leads to violence is much too simplistic a statement. This supports the works of others, like Snyder (2006), who look at the influence of the state, its institutions, and arrangements with private actors for extraction or production. Snyder and Bhavnani (2005) find that it is not just the resources that affect conflict, but the interaction with patterns of state spending, the overall resource profile of the country, and the mode of extraction. Policy implications include improving "management of the extraction process and better usage of resource revenues that are controlled by states" (Humphreys 2005, 534). Even within a single country like Colombia, there is sufficient variation of initial and current conditions to reveal a differing impact of development, partially driven by distinct state presence and rule of law. Lessons learned from the Colombia case are that types of violence associated with particular commodities may vary by the characteristics of the commodity. For example, development of a labor-intensive commodity in an area heavily dominated by a capital-intensive commodity is likely to be followed by violence as new actors enter the area. Structural changes in the economy must be predated with government presence and infrastructure to aid those affected by the changes. The impact of the development of specific sectors is influenced by the political environment and initial conditions in which the development occurs.

Notes

1. See Pécaut (1997), Sánchez, Díaz, and Formisano (2003), and Holmes, Gutiérrez de Piñeres, and Curtin (2008) for additional discussions of violence in this period.

2. See Miguel Ortiz Sarmiento (1991). See also Medina Gallego (1990).
3. Only Santa Fé de Bogotá, Antioquia, and Valle de Cauca had higher per capita spending totals. This estimate was generated by combining the total justice and security spending from 1993 to 2002 and using the 2002 population estimates.
4. Only sugar, rice, and milk have higher rates of assistance.
5. http://www.fedepalma.org/oil_palm.htm. Accessed December 15, 2011.
6. According to the Departamento Nacional de Planeación, nationwide 78 percent of homes had access to water and 68.5 percent had access to sewer in 2005. The national average for the years of schooling was 7.8 in 2005 and 74 percent of people were enrolled in *seguridad social*.

References

Arbeláez, Maria Angelica, Juan José Echavarria, and Alejandro Gaviria. 2002. Colombian long run growth and the crisis of the 1990s. Report submitted to Global Development Network/Interamerican Development Bank Project on "Economic Growth in Latin America and the Caribbean."

Byman, Daniel, Peter Chalk, Bruce Hoffman, William Rosenau, and David Brannan. 2001. *Trends in outside support for insurgent movements*. Santa Monica, CA: Rand Corporation.

Calado, Fernando, and Diana Medrano. 2006. Prolonged internal displacement: Durable solutions amidst violence in Colombia. In *Intra-caribbean migration and the conflict nexus*, edited by Taryn Lesser, Berta Fernández-Alfaro, Lancelot Cowie, and Nina Bruni. Human Rights Internet, Ottawa, Canada.

Carter, Michael R., and Dina Mesbah. 1993. Can land market reform mitigate the exclusionary aspects of rapid agro-export growth? *World Development* 21(7): 1085–1100.

Damiani, Octavio. 2003. Effects on employment, wages, and labor standards of non-traditional export crops in northeast Brazil. *Latin American Research Review* 38(1): 83–112.

DANE Departamento Administrativo Nacional de Estadística, 1991–2007. *Cuentas Nacionales Departamentales. Base 1994*. Santafé de Bogotá.

Deininger, Klaus. 1999. Making negotiated land reform work: Initial experience from Colombia, Brazil, and South Africa. *World Development* 27(4): 651–672.

ECLAC (Economic Commission for Latin America and the Caribbean): Cepalstat Database. Available online: http://www.eclac.org/estadisticas/. Accessed December 15, 2011.

Elhawary, Samir. 2008. Violent paths to peace?: Rethinking the conflict-development nexus in Colombia. *Colombia International* 67: 84–100.

Escobar, Arturo. 2003. Displacement, development, and modernity in the Colombian Pacific. *International Social Science Journal* 175(55):157–167.

Faguet, Jean-Paul, and Fabio Sánchez. 2008. Decentralization's effects on educational outcomes in Bolivia and Colombia. *World Development* 36(7): 1294–1316.

Fearon, James D., and David Laitin. 2003. Ethnicity, insurgency, and civil war. *American Political Science Review* 97(1): 75–90.

Galli, Rosemary. 1978. Rural development and social control in Colombia. *Latin American Perspectives* 5(4): 71–89.

Goebertus, J. 2008. Palma de aceite y desplazamiento forzado en zona bananera. *Colombia Internacional* 67: 152–175.

González, Fernán. 2002. "Colombia entre la Guerra y la paz. Aproximación a una lectura geopolítica de la violencia colombiana," Revista Venezolana de Economía y Ciencias Sociales 8/2: 13–49.

Guerrero Baron, J., and D. Mond. 2001. Is the war ending? Premises and hypotheses with which to view the conflict in Colombia. *Latin American Perspectives* 28(1): 12–30.

Guterman, Lisa. 2007. Distortions to agricultural incentives in Colombia. Agricultural Distortions Working Paper 14. Washington, DC: World Bank.

Hernandez, Sandra. 2010. Palm oil businessmen arrested over forced displacement in Choco. *Colombia Reports*, May 20.

Heshusius Rodríguez, K. 2005. Medición del impacto de un programa de reforma agaria en Colombia. *CEDE Documento 2005–28*.

Holmes, Jennifer S., Sheila Amin Gutíerrez de Piñeres, and Kevin Curtin. 2008. *Guns, drugs and development in Colombia*. Austin: University of Texas Press.

Humphreys, M. 2005. Natural resources, conflict, and conflict resolution. *Journal of Conflict Resolution* 49(4): 508–537.

Jaramillo, Carlos Felipe. 2001. Liberalization, crisis, and change: Colombian agriculture in the 1990s. *Economic Development and Cultural Change* 49(4): 821–846.

Khan, Mahmood Hasan. 2001. Rural poverty in developing countries implications for public policy. Economic Issues No. 26. International Monetary Fund.

Le Billon, Philippe. 2001. The political ecology of war: Natural resources and armed conflicts. *Political Geography* 20(5): 561–584.

López, Ramón. 2003. The policy roots of socioeconomic stagnation and environmental implosion: Latin America 1950–2000. *World Development* 31(2): 259–280.

McLean, P. 2002. Colombia: Failed, failing or just weak? *The Washington Quarterly* 25(3): 123–134.

Medina Gallego, C. 1990. Autodefensas, paramilitares y narcotráfico en Colombia: Origen, desarrollo y consolidación. El caso de Puerto Boyacá. Bogotá: Editorial Documentos Periodísticos.

Oslender, Ulrich. 2008. Another history of violence: The production of "geographies of terror" in Colombia's Pacific coast region. *Latin American Perspectives* 35(5): 77–102.

Palacios, Paola. 2010. Forced displacement: Legal versus illegal crops. Working Paper. Bogotá: Universidad de los Andes.

Pearce, Jenny. 2007. Oil and armed conflict in Casanare, Colombia: Complex contexts and contingent moments. In *Oil Wars*, edited by Mary Kaldor, Terry Lynn Karl, and Yahia Said, 225–273. London: Pluto Press.

Pécaut, Daniel. 1997. Presente, pasado y futuro de la violencia en Colombia. *Desarrollo Económico* 36(144): 891–930.
Peceny, Mark, and Michael Durnan. 2006. The FARC's best friend: U.S. antidrug policies and the deepening of Colombia's civil war in the 1990s *Latin American Politics & Society* 48(2): 95–116.
Redcliff, Michael. 1989. The environmental consequences of Latin America's agricultural development: Some thoughts on the Brundtland Commission report. *World Development* 17(3): 365–377.
Rettberg, Angelika. 2010. Global markets, local conflict violence in the Colombian coffee region after the breakdown of the International Coffee Agreement. *Latin American Perspectives* 37(2):111–132.
Richani, N. 1997. The political economy of violence: The war system in Colombia. *Journal of Interamerican Studies and World Affairs* 39(2): 37–81.
Rochlin, James. 2003. Vanguard revolutionaries in Latin America: Peru, Colombia, Mexico. Boulder, CO: Lynne Rienner Publishers.
Sánchez, Fabio, Ana Maria Díaz, and Michel Formisano. 2003. Conflicto, violencia y actividad criminal en Colombia: Un Análisis Espacial. Documento CEDE, March 2003–2005.
Sarmiento, Carlos Miguel Ortiz 1991. Violencia política de los ochenta: Elementos para una reflexión historica. *Anuario Colombiano de Historia Social y de la Cultura* 18: 245–280.
Snyder, Richard. 2006. Does lootable wealth breed disorder? a political economy of extraction framework. *Comparative Political Studies* 39(8): 943–968.
Snyder, Richard, and Ravi Bhavnani. 2005. Diamonds, blood, and taxes: A revenue-centered framework for explaining political order. *Journal of Conflict Resolution* 49(4): 563–597.
Trujillo, E., and M. E. Badel. 1997. Los costos económicos de la criminalidad y la violencia en Colombia: 1991–1996. *Planeación y Desarrollo* 28(4): 266–308.
United Nations Office on Drugs and Crime. Various years. *Colombia: Monitoreo de cultivos de coca.*
Williams, Robert G. 1986. *Export agriculture and the crisis in Central America.* Chapel Hill: University of North Carolina Press.
World Bank. 2004. *Colombia land policy in transition.* Report No. 27942-CO.

CHAPTER 5

On the Brink of Violence: Work, Fear, and the State in the Bolivian Regions

William T. Barndt

During the past decade, Bolivia twice experienced intense and prolonged political violence. In neither of those two periods, however, was the violence equally distributed across the country. In 2001–2002, violence was concentrated in the central valleys. Between 2006 and 2008, violence sprung up in both the eastern lowlands and western highlands. Why was this decade so violent for Bolivia? And why was that violence concentrated in particular regions, rather than spread uniformly across the country?

This chapter argues that the roots of Bolivia's recent violence can be found in a series of choices that recent governments made about economic development. The shift to a liberal development strategy in the 1980s generated a fragile, but relatively peaceful, equilibrium during the 1990s. The shattering of this equilibrium during the 2000s resulted directly from attempts by the state to disrupt the economic livelihood of significant economic sectors in particular regions of Bolivia: coca-growers (*cocaleros*) in the central valleys in 2001–2002 and the urban middle class in the eastern lowlands and western highlands in 2006–2008. In response to these disruptions, leaders of the threatened economic sector(s) mobilized their followers into protest. And in both instances this led to regionally concentrated intergroup violence.

The chapter begins by describing trends in Bolivian political violence between 1985 and 2008, identifying 2001–2002 and 2006–2008 as anomalously violent periods. The second part shows how particular policies associated with Bolivia's liberal development strategy contributed to the chain of events that led to the violence of the 2000s. The chapter then explains the origins of violence in the central valleys during 2001–2002. The next part takes up the more complex increase in eastern and western political violence between 2006 and 2008. The final part concludes by drawing lessons from Bolivia about the relationship between economic development strategies and intergroup violence.

Political Violence in Bolivia (1985–2008)

To identify patterns in Bolivian political violence, this chapter relies on a new-count dataset of "incidents of political violence" in the country since 1985.[1] After a minor uptick in 1986, the country experienced little violence from 1989 through 2000. This changed in the 2000s. In 2001, Bolivia experienced a startling 29 incidents of political violence—more than it had experienced in the previous seven years combined. Wide-scale violence then declined (though brief notable explosions occurred in 2003) before beginning to rise sharply in 2006 and again reaching significantly high levels in 2008. Compared to the late 1980s and 1990s, that is, the 2000s were a remarkably violent decade in Bolivia (see Figure 5.1).

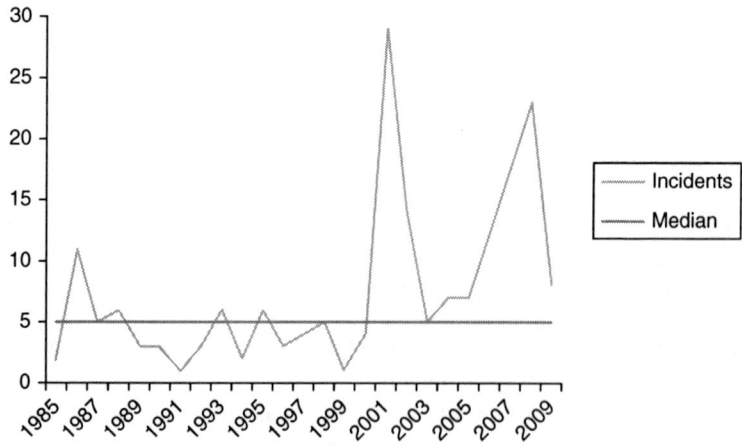

Figure 5.1 Political violence in Bolivia, 1985–2008.

Yet this national-level analysis disguises important regional-level trends. Bolivia is broadly divided into three separate regions: the western highlands, the central valleys, and the eastern lowlands. Each of these regions has a distinct geography, economy, and (arguably) culture. Moreover, each corresponds roughly to different sets of "departments," the largest subnational unit of government in Bolivia. And as it turns out, each region has experienced a distinct pattern of political violence since 1985.

The Central Valleys

The central valleys of Bolivia, located primarily in Cochabamba department, have served as the country's breadbasket since colonial times. They host an important indigenous presence, consisting of both highland migrants and permanent residents (the two groups blur significantly). Over the past four decades, the Cochabamban economy came to rely increasingly on coca, the shrub whose leaves provide the main derivative for cocaine. The 1980s in particular saw a shift of production into Cochabamba, as rising international demand for cocaine and a devastating economic crisis led more highlanders to migrate into the region. Many of these individuals settled in the Chapare region of Cochabamba,[2] which became a center of illegal coca-growing (Sanabria 1993; Painter 1994; Leons and Sanabria 1997).

Political violence in the central valleys remained virtually absent until the mid-1990s, when the central government sporadically and ineffectively increased its efforts to reduce illegal coca-growing (Kurtz-Phelan 2005). Still, violence in the central valleys remained relatively low until 2001–2002, when the region exploded following the first committed attempt by the central government to eradicate illegal coca-growing in the Chapare (see Figure 5.2 below). In fact, the spike in political violence at the national level during 2001–2002 was constituted almost entirely by violence in the central valleys, particularly in the Chapare. This explosion of violence, however, diminished as quickly as it had appeared: after 2002, levels of political violence rapidly returned to 1990s levels.

The Eastern Lowlands

The eastern lowlands of Bolivia—which include the departments of Santa Cruz, Pando, Beni, and (arguably) Tarija and Chuquisaca—compose some of the most sparsely populated regions of the country. Culturally, the lowlands are rather divided. The region's major urban centers are dominated by nonindigenous settlers, many of whom closely identify with their European roots. But the lowlands also represent the center of Amazonian and Guarani

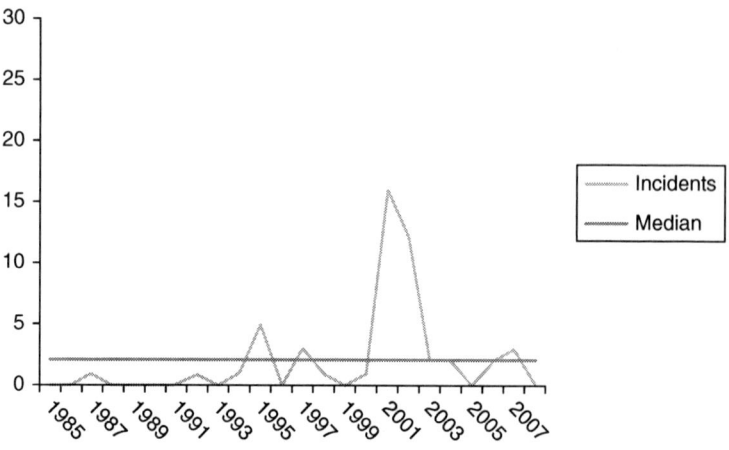

Figure 5.2 Political violence in the central valleys, 1985–2008.

indigenous populations, who organized the strongest indigenous association in the 1990s. Traditionally dominated by large-scale agriculture and forestry (including ranching and timber), the regional economy has shifted in recent years to include competitive agro-industries (most importantly soybeans) and hydrocarbons (most importantly natural gas).[3] In addition, the region contains two major cities, Santa Cruz and Sucre, both of which are centers of middle-class employment.

Until recently, the eastern lowlands were the least violent region of Bolivia. Then, in 2007 and 2008, incidents of political violence became nearly *15 times* as frequent as they had been during the previous two decades (see Figure 5.3 below). During those two years, a significant eastern opposition movement grew up in response to the government of President Evo Morales and his *Movimiento al Socialismo* (MAS) Party. This opposition engaged in deadly clashes with supporters of the Morales government, culminating in a September 2008 lethal assault on the Morales supporters in Pando.

The Western Highlands

The Bolivian western highlands—including most of the departments of La Paz, Oruro, and Potosi—consist largely of a high plateau sandwiched between two Andean ranges. As the historic home of the Aymara, highland Bolivia is often described as the most indigenous region of the country. The highland economy has long been driven by the mining industries in Potosi

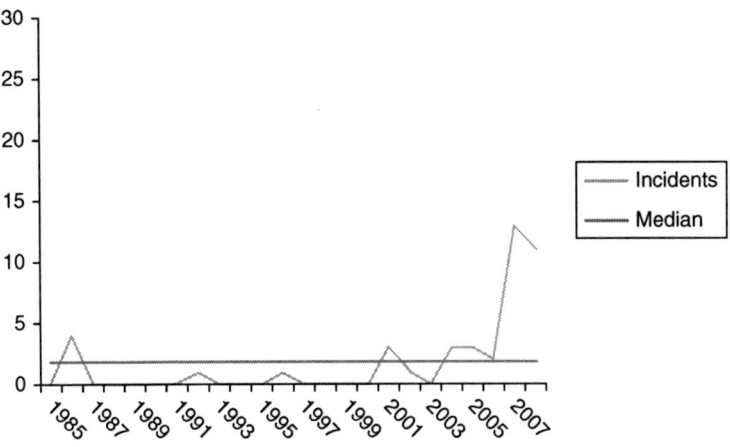

Figure 5.3 Political violence in the eastern lowlands, 1985–2008.

and Oruro, though significant portions of the population also remain tied to subsistence agriculture. Government employment has provided another important component of the economy, particularly for the urban middle class, as the city of La Paz is the seat of the executive and legislative branches.

During the economic restructuring of the 1980s, the central government used violent states-of-siege to break up protests and exile opposition leaders to remote outposts. Throughout the subsequent decade, however, the Bolivian highlands remained remarkably free of violence: only seven incidents were reported during all of the 1990s (see Figure 5.4 below). Violence began to leach back into the region during the early 2000s. As peasants and the urban lower class organized protests against the state's attempts to deepen economic liberalization, the government responded with violence similar to that which it had employed during the earlier restructuring. Highland violence then rose to significantly high levels in 2006,[4] after Bolivia inaugurated President Morales. This violence then diminished rapidly in 2007, before again rising to record levels in 2008.

Summarizing the Puzzle

The record levels of political violence that Bolivia experienced during the 2000s actually reflected much more *regionally contained* outbreaks in violence. In 2001–2002, Bolivia experienced an explosion of violence concentrated in

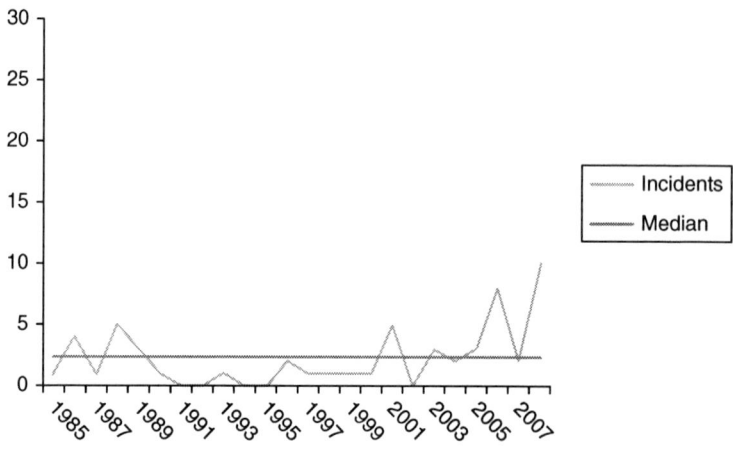

Figure 5.4 Political violence in the western highlands, 1985–2008.

the central valleys. Between 2006 and 2008, violence shifted back and forth between the eastern and western highlands. Understanding why the 2000s have been so violent for Bolivia thus requires careful examination of the causes of these spikes of violence in the regions.

Setting the Stage for Violence: Liberal Development Strategy in Bolivia (1985–2000)

Any account of the violent 2000s must begin with the major shift in development strategy that occurred in Bolivia during the mid-1980s: this shift in strategy set the stage for both the relatively peaceful 1990s and the much more violent 2000s. The shift began in 1986, when newly elected President Victor Paz Estenssoro, an architect of the state-capitalist strategy that had anchored development since the 1950s, adopted a liberal development strategy (Gamarra 1994; Conaghan and Malloy 1994; Brysk and Wise 1997). The new strategy involved a variety of policies, including the removal of price controls, exchange-rate devaluation, wage freezes, the opening of debt negotiations with international creditors (Conaghan and Malloy 1994, 140), increasing foreign investment, and the liberalization of land and labor markets. Together, the set of reforms that constituted this new strategy radically reshaped state-society relations in Bolivia (Yashar 2005). Yet, it was two particular policies that set the stage for the violent 2000s: (1) a shift toward promoting new capital-intensive sectors and (2) a selective reduction of public employment.

The State as Midwife to Capital-Intensive Sectors

A critical component of this liberal development strategy was the emergence of competitive export sectors capable of driving economic growth in Bolivia. To this end, the state actively encouraged private investment in promising export industries. Two capital-intensive industries—hydrocarbons and soybeans, both in eastern Bolivia—became prime foci of this new policy.

The Bolivian hydrocarbons industry remained under the control of a state company, Yacimientos Petrolíferos Fiscales Bolivianos (YPFB) from the 1930s through the early 1990s. Upon the election of President Gonzalo Sánchez de Lozada in 1993, however, the Bolivian government relaxed its grip on the industry. The Sánchez de Lozada administration initiated a "capitalization" program that sought to attract foreign investment for natural-gas exploration and extraction.[5] In effect, this program allowed the state to bring in private-sector companies as 50-percent investment partners and full-time managers of hydrocarbons projects (Valdez 1998). As a result, foreign investment poured into the natural-gas sector during the 1990s: British Petroleum, Petrobras, Repsol YPF, and Total, all became involved in developing the Bolivian reserves. By the late 1990s, Bolivian state finances began to benefit from increased revenues associated with the growing sector.

In addition to hydrocarbons, the government sought to aid the emergence of competitive export-oriented agro-industry in eastern Bolivia. As Eaton (2007) rightly observes, this was not an entirely new policy: the government had been "funneling" economic assistance to this region for decades (see also Conaghan and Malloy 1994, 57–58). During the 1990s, however, the state took up the project with renewed vigor, directing "over half... of the agricultural credits and international development grants" to eastern Bolivia in 1997 and "targeting" more than 80 percent of "all public-sector investment" between 1997 and 2002 for modern agriculture (Economist Intelligence Unit [EIU] 2002). This new phase of assistance privileged capital-intensive agro-industries, most prominently soybeans, that promised to generate significant export earnings.[6] Indeed, these policies helped soybeans become a major agricultural export during the late 1990s and the 2000s.

Change and Continuity in Public Employment

With its shift toward a liberal development strategy, the Bolivian state also sought to reduce public employment across the board. This plan became a reality for state-dependent working-class Bolivians in 1985 and 1986, when the state severely reduced its subsidization of labor associations (such as the Central Obrera Boliviana [COB]) and labor-intensive industries. These cuts were most pronounced in the western highlands, where the mining industry had produced strong unions over the course of the twentieth century. Indeed, the state-mining company Corporación Minera de Bolivia (COMIBOL) saw its workforce cut by more than 20,000 during this period (Gamarra 1994; Conaghan and Malloy 1994).

Faced with unemployment, many of these working class, largely highland Bolivians, were displaced. They not only poured into the urban informal sector in highland cities (generating staggering population growth around La Paz), but also moved eastward into the central valleys and (to a lesser extent) eastern lowlands. Most importantly for this argument, many unemployed and underemployed Bolivians settled into illegal coca-growing in the Chapare. In effect, the end to working-class subsidies induced significant internal migration in Bolivia (Lucero 2008, 89). Reducing state-sponsored working-class employment thus became a de facto policy of promoting working-class migration.

The liberal development strategy came with a promise to reduce all public-sector employment. Yet in practice, the Bolivian government reduced only working-class employment: the state remained a major employer of middle-class Bolivians throughout the 1990s: "Following the initial cutbacks between 1986 and 1988, public employment... increased dramatically. According to one estimate, in [1989–1990] as many as twenty thousand new employees [were] hired" (Gamarra 1994, 115). Indeed, Malloy (1991, 45) argues that the lion's share of growth in state employment since 1952 had been devoted to the middle class: "Given the fact that Bolivia's... export-oriented economy has provided a very limited set of opportunities for the urban middle class, the state has become the main source of financial support for them." For example, the possibility of migration to the United States or Europe has been constrained by stringent visa requirements. And new businesses have often fared best when they have gained the support of political patrons; that is, the possibility of successful entrepreneurship on the part of middle-class individuals is endogenous to their access to state resources. In an economic environment where few other opportunities existed to attain and preserve middle-class status, the Bolivian urban middle class became dependent on urban public-sector jobs, provided (as discussed below) through party-based patronage (Malloy 1970; Gamarra 1994). As such, the decision by the state to leave middle-class patronage intact during the 1980s and the1990s in effect saved the Bolivian urban middle class.

The Liberal Peace of the 1990s

This situation became a relatively stable equilibrium in Bolivia during the 1990s. As the state promoted capital-intensive industries in eastern Bolivia, urban middle-class Bolivians remained ensconced in cocoons of state patronage. At the same time, the state-dependent working class was cut off from subsidies and forced to migrate to the outskirts of major cities, the Chapare region of Cochabamba, and further eastward. The protest that might have been generated by these displaced and unemployed workers was defused, at least in part, by the fact that some could sustain themselves by growing coca illegally. Recognizing this stabilizing effect of the illegal coca economy, successive governments in the 1980s and the 1990s undertook no serious attempt to eradicate it. Yet this equilibrium—the liberal peace that held throughout all three Bolivian regions during the 1990s—would prove remarkably brittle.

From Coca to Violence and Back Again: The Central Valleys (2001–2002)

Beginning in the mid-1990s, the central valleys experienced a handful of violent incidents a year. As the United States ratcheted up its opposition to the coca trade and its funding for alternative development, the Bolivian government sought to diminish coca production in the region (Sanabria 1997, 174; Painter 1994; Sanabria 1993). Yet throughout most of the 1990s, the Bolivian government's commitment to these efforts was uneven, in large part because it recognized coca's importance to the informal economy (Gamarra 2002; Kurtz-Phelan 2005). In 1990, for example, the Bolivian government estimated that there were 300,000 workers in the illegal coca-cocaine industry, which may have generated more than 200 million dollars that remained in-country and represented more than a sixth of export revenues (Painter 1994, 50–51). Thus, while eradication forces[7] came into regular conflict with coca-growers, no full-scale attempt to eradicate illegal coca was undertaken. And though significant lip service was paid to the promise of internationally sponsored crop-substitution programs (primarily tropical fruits and spices), these efforts were widely recognized as unlikely to succeed (EIU 2001; EIU 2002). In short, the Bolivian state followed a de facto coca-tolerance policy throughout most of the 1990s.

This changed sharply with the inauguration of President Hugo Banzer in 1998. Unlike its predecessors, the Banzer government mounted a serious campaign to eradicate illegal coca production (Gamarra 2002). While the motivations behind this shift were complex, it seems clear that international pressure was not sufficient to provoke it. This effort—dubbed *Plan Dignidad*—"targeted precursor chemicals, suspended compensated eradication, and militarized the Chapare." According to Gamarra, the effort was initially quite successful: "In three years, one less than the Plan anticipated, Bolivia eradicated over 30,000 hectares of coca and all but eliminated the

Chapare's role in the drug industry. In June 2001 the Bolivian government claimed it had achieved the elusive goal of 'coca cero' by 2002" (Gamarra 2002, 1–2).[8]

Because of *Plan Dignidad*, large numbers of *cocaleros* and their families were forced to abandon production. Many moved to towns and cities. Some began to organize landless movements, largely in the eastern lowlands. Yet employment opportunities were severely limited in all these regions. Further eastward migration was made difficult by the shift to large-scale capital-intensive agro-industry over the course of the 1990s, which diminished the need for additional labor. Moreover, the informal sector in urban areas was already saturated, a result of the absence of growth in labor-intensive sectors. In short, *Plan Dignidad* disrupted the fragile equilibrium of liberal Bolivia: by eradicating coca-growing in the Chapare, the Bolivian state left *cocaleros* without viable options for employment.

Lacking economic alternatives, the *cocaleros* responded to *Plan Dignidad* with protest and violence. Bolivia was thus rocked in 2001 by a pronounced spike in political violence. This violence was unsurprisingly concentrated in the Chapare region of Cochabamba, where much illegal coca production occurred—and where *Plan Dignidad* was focused. The *cocaleros'* violence took two forms. First—in keeping with past practice—*cocaleros* and their supporters began prolonged blockades of the major highways through the central valleys, leading to sporadic violence between the *cocaleros* and the police, and military troops ordered to dislodge them. Yet the scale of these clashes was much greater than in the past: "Facing an inevitable mobilization of the coca growers federations in the Chapare, Quiroga secretly ordered the entry of 4,000 military and police troops into the Chapare" (Gamarra 2002, 7) Second, coca-growers began engaging in more regular offensive maneuvers against the coca-eradication forces. In 2001, for example, *cocaleros* began attempting to invade and occupy military installations in the Chapare. The same year, booby traps began to cause casualties among eradication troops; though it remains unclear who set the traps, it likely was dispossessed *cocaleros*.

This violence was facilitated by the fact that, far from being a disorganized set of independent farmers, the *cocaleros* had been building organizational capacity for a decade. During the 1990s, Morales "[became] the undisputed leader of the emerging *cocalero* movement. The movement affiliated with the [peasant federation] CSTUCB...[and] gained prominence within the CSTUCB in the 1990s, as illustrated by the election of [Morales ally] Roman Loayza as the Secretary General at the 1996 conference of the peasant federation" (Yashar 2005, 186–187).[9] Ironically, this increased organizational capacity in part sprouted from *cocaleros'* attempts to respond to previous, less serious eradication campaigns (Spedding 1997, 135). As Lucero (2008, 141) puts it: "The *cocalero* movement was quite literally made possible (and necessary) by Washington Consensus economic policies that relocated workers from the highlands of Bolivia and a Washington-led war on drugs that kept coca prices high but made coca production dangerous."

Then, in 2003, violence in the central valleys declined as sharply as it had begun. Although incidents continued through 2006, the sharp spike in violence that had led some Bolivians to speculate about civil war dissipated. This abrupt end coincided precisely with the decision of a new Bolivian government to enter into negotiations with the *cocaleros* over the eradication program in late September 2002. Although those talks broke down—leading to a brief period of renewed violence between the state and *cocaleros* in January 2003—the new government would last only another nine months (Ledebur 2004, 163). And the government that succeeded it, that of Carlos Mesa, quickly negotiated a deal with *cocalero* leader Morales that allowed for the renewed cultivation of coca in the Chapare (Kurtz-Phelan 2005, 107). Between 2003 and 2007, the number of hectares eradicated by the government fell by 50 percent. As the eradication campaign faltered, coca production again began to rise. Although illicit coca production has not regained its previous scale, the most recent figures show that it nearly doubled between 2000 and 2008 (UNDOC 2008a; 2008b).

In short, the violence of 2001–2002 did not simply occur because organized *cocaleros* in the central valleys had lost their livelihoods. Instead, it was that the coca-eradication program launched in 1998 disrupted the coca economy *without providing any plausible economic alternatives for coca growers*. If coca had been the alternative to state-subsidized employment in the late 1980s, no similar alternative to coca now existed for working-class Bolivians. By eradicating coca, the Bolivian government effectively created a new, large, dispossessed, organized, angry population with plenty of time on its hands—and it was this population that struck back against the state in 2001–2002. The violence only declined when subsequent governments began to back away from the "zero coca" policy in late 2002, allowing some *cocaleros* to return to work. Had the state not relented, it is likely that the violence would have continued to escalate, perhaps even under increasingly radical peasant leaders.

Though fleeting, the violence in the central valleys of 2001–2002 had profound effects on Bolivia's political trajectory. Perhaps most importantly, it propelled the leader of the *cocalero* movement, Morales, to a position of national prominence—at the expense of more strident indigenous leaders. As Lucero notes, it was neither the strong Confederación de Indígenas del Oriente, Chaco, y Amazonia de Bolivia (CIDOB)[10] nor the radical indigenous nationalist Felipe Quispe, but rather Morales with his "more inclusive popular-indigenous discourse and party" who came to lead the opposition movement in the 2000s (Lucero 2008, 139–141). This is important because Morales was first and foremost a *cocalero* who sought to include diverse social movements in his new political party, rather than pursue the types of ethnically exclusive organization being advocated by other leaders (Van Cott 2007).[11] As a result, his leadership diluted the extent to which the new opposition was defined by a clearly ethnic component. In this way, the rise of the *cocalero* movement may have precluded the possibility of a potentially more divisive ethnic identity emerging as a pillar of popular-sector opposition in Bolivia—a fact which would arguably become critical during the next bout of violence in 2006–2008.[12]

The Rise and Fall of Middle-Class Violence

The Western Highlands and Eastern Lowlands (2006–2008)

Following 2003, violence declined sharply in Bolivia.[13] Yet this trend changed after the inauguration of President Morales. In 2006, the Morales government's initial pursuit of land reform brought a significant uptick of violence against opposition-affiliated media by government partisans in the western highlands. But it was the following year, 2007, that political violence really exploded in the eastern lowlands. By 2008, violence wracked both the eastern lowlands and western highlands. These spikes in highland and lowland violence were primarily driven by the Morales government's attempt to "recentralize"[14] departmental revenues. Faced with the threat of recentralization, a de facto alliance emerged in eastern Bolivia between large landowners and an urban middle class that depended for their status on decentralized revenues, distributed through departmental representatives of the old parties. This alliance mobilized significant violence against the government and its supporters in eastern Bolivia, violence that was perpetrated largely by the old eastern middle class. When this fight over the distribution of state revenues was (at least temporarily) resolved in late 2008, the eastern middle class became much less willing to engage in antigovernment violence. As a result, eastern landowners were left without allies who could organize mass protest and violence against the government—and eastern violence diminished accordingly.

Yet the events of 2007–2008 had stoked worries among *newly ascendant middle-class clients of the Morales government in the western highlands.* Just like the old middle class that had preceded it, this new highland middle class depended on the central government's access to revenues that could be used for patronage; the stalling of fiscal recentralization thus threatened this new middle class. As such, during 2008, this group turned to violence against politicians who sought to derail the government's attempt to recentralize state revenues. In short, the violence of 2007–2008 was perpetrated largely by the Bolivian urban middle class. Different middle-class factions turned to violence because the government threatened to disrupt the flow of state revenues to their patrons, thus removing the only plausible livelihood that allowed them to maintain their status.

Eastern Impotence and Emergent Highland Violence (2006)

The nationally significant spike in violence of 2007–2008 was preceded in 2006 by a regionally significant uptick in violence in the western highlands. Though not a cause of the violence that would wrack Bolivia during the following two years, the highland violence of 2006 sheds light on the coalition that supported it; as such, this period merits discussion.

Throughout the 2005 campaign, Morales had declared his support for the redistribution of large tracts of "unproductive" land. When he took office in January 2006, threatened eastern agro-industrialists and ranchers employed "friendly" media to incite fear about the new administration. Consider, for example, the coverage offered by Unitel, a television station owned by the Monasterios, a major ranching family and chief shareholders of the Bolivian Cattleman's Bank (*Banco Ganadero*) in Santa Cruz. From inauguration day forward, Unitel provided biased, borderline racist, coverage of the Morales government. Such partisanship within the eastern media transformed opposition-affiliated journalists into ready targets for radical government supporters during 2006, primarily (though not exclusively) in the MAS-dominated western highlands.

This antimedia violence by government supporters took off in June 2006, following Morales's announcement that the government would begin redistributing 12 million acres of land (Reel 2006). Though this land was public, the Morales administration received a critical media response. In response, the administration assaulted the media more directly. In May, Morales declared Monasterio "an enemy of the government," and less than four weeks later "asked Unitel journalists to identify themselves before a large audience of MAS party members before he verbally attacked Unitel." Four days later, "presidential security guards assaulted nearly a dozen journalists during a ceremony in Caracallo, Oruro." (US Department of State 2006). From June through early October, attacks by government partisans on opposition-affiliated media became common. That is, the brief 2006 spike in violence in the western highlands occurred when the government turned its supporters against representatives of the media whose owners opposed the initiation of land reform.

Somewhat surprisingly, eastern agriculturalists did not respond with organized violence of their own. The reasons behind this tactical choice are difficult to untangle, but three factors seem important, given subsequent events. First, the threat of land reform had not yet become acute. Moves toward land reform in mid-2006 focused on the redistribution of unproductive *public* land, rather than *private* lands (though this would change by the end of the year). Second, any violent tactics adopted by eastern landowners would necessarily have been capital intensive: eastern landowners had no natural mass-based constituency of their own to mobilize. But hiring mercenaries may have seemed a rather drastic step in mid-2006. Third, and probably most importantly, eastern agriculture could, during most of 2006, still depend on significant aid and comfort from *subnational governments*, even as the national government became more threatening. To understand why this was the case, I now turn to the Morales government's attempt to recentralize subnational revenues, which catalyzed the violence that began in late 2006 and escalated until late 2008.

The Suddenly Violent Urban Middle Class (2006–2008)

In late 2006, a new Constituent Assembly, dominated by representatives from Morales's MAS party, began to debate questions of natural-resource ownership and the autonomy of departments to raise their own resources (EIU 2003; 2007).[15] This debate raised the possibility that the national government would recapture the rapidly growing[16] fiscal resources that currently accrued to departmental governments. (These fiscal resources had become available as a result of the capitalization policy pursued as part of the liberal development strategy of the 1990s.) While the pursuit of land reform had threatened only large agriculturalists, this new debate over the redistribution of state revenues threatened *agriculturalists, departmental prefects (governors), and much of the urban middle class*. This was because revenue redistribution threatened to restrict the state patronage and credit on which those sectors had depended.

Between 1985 and 2005, this patronage had been distributed by the major political parties that dominated the electoral arena since the return to civilian rule: the Movimiento Nacionalista Revolucionario (MNR) and Acción Democrática Nacionalista (ADN)—and to a lesser extent the Movimiento Izquierda Revolucionaria (MIR), Unidad Cívica Solidaridad (UCS), and Conciencia de Patria (CONDEPA). This distribution of patronage among the urban middle-class clients of these parties was facilitated by the electoral system, which mandated that Congress choose the president if no candidate won a majority of votes in the election. As no party ever won a majority of votes, presidential elections were invariably followed by monumental "horse-trading" between the parties. In order to gain a majority of congressional votes—and thus be elected president—a candidate needed to distribute patronage-rich positions widely across the different parties represented in Congress. This often resulted in expansive multiparty government coalitions (Gamarra 1994). In 1998, for example, Banzer was elected by what came to be known as the "mega-coalition," which included every major party except the MNR. As discussed above, the Bolivian urban middle class has always been dependent on state patronage. As a result, any attempt to strip the urban middle class of state patronage is, in effect, an attempt to strip it of its middle-class status.

Eastern agriculturalists had for decades also relied on these same parties for assistance (Eaton 2007; Gil 1987; Torrico 1978). As discussed above, the first Sánchez de Lozada and Banzer-Quiroga administrations (1993–2002) had actively supported the rapid development of the soya industry in Santa Cruz. This was facilitated, as Eaton (2007) notes, by the close ties that eastern agriculturalists maintained with the national-level politicians who came from their regions. Just as the urban middle class depended on the patronage of the major parties in power, so also large-scale agriculturalists relied on these parties to funnel state credit and aid to the eastern lowlands.

As such, the election of Morales and his MAS party in 2005 should have threatened both the urban middle class and eastern agriculturalists in two specific ways. First, Morales had developed his own party organization—the MAS—separate from all existing parties. The victory of Morales thus threatened to disrupt long-standing patronage networks. Second—and even more concretely—Morales won *a majority of the vote* in the 2005 presidential election. As such, no "horse-trading" among parties in the Congress was necessary. Consequently, the election of Morales threatened to cut this old middle class off from the revenues that had sustained its livelihood for 20 years. At the same time, eastern agriculturalists were threatened by the displacement of eastern-friendly parties from the executive (and much of the legislative) branch. Faced with drastic threats to their livelihoods, both groups might have been expected to turn to antigovernment violence.

Yet neither did. Most surprisingly, the middle-class clients of the old parties did not initially react violently to Morales taking office—not even as the newly inaugurated administration replaced public officials with its own allies. This is particularly shocking given the subsequent willingness of these middle-class individuals to turn to violence in 2007 and 2008. Why did the change in government not produce a more serious outbreak of violence, given that it effectively ended the ability of the old parties to channel support from the national government to their middle-class dependents?

The explanation seems to be in another change heralded by the 2005 elections. In 2005, Bolivians also directly elected—for the first time—departmental governors or "prefects." Prior to 2005, prefects had been appointed by the president (as part of the patronage-based "horse-trading") and served at his discretion. This change from appointment to direct election effectively released prefects from executive control, allowing them to act as more independent agents. Beginning in January 2006, the new prefects also had more autonomous—though still contested—control over departmental finances, including a plurality of the growing revenues generated from the export of natural gas and other hydrocarbons.

This first crop of directly elected prefects included supporters of Morales: Alberto Luís Aguilar in Oruro, Mario Virreira in Potosi, and David Sánchez in Chuquisaca. Yet opposition candidates won in five other departments[17]: all five of these opposition prefects were deeply tied to the parties that Morales had displaced from control of the central government.[18] These newly elected prefects thus provided a clear way both to maintain pre-Morales patronage networks for the old middle class in 2006 and to continue to support large-scale eastern agriculture. Instead of providing jobs and aid out of central government revenue, these representatives of the old parties could provide them out of *departmental revenue*. Coincidentally, the prefects' ability to do just this was enhanced by the ongoing boom in hydrocarbon revenues in 2005 and 2006, a plurality of which were then transferred to departmental control (Weisbrot and Sandoval 2009).

Because opposition prefects could continue to support both the urban middle class and large-scale eastern agriculture, neither the election nor the inauguration of Morales provoked violence—even after the Morales government began installing its own allies in public positions. As long as the newly elected opposition prefects could dole out jobs and agricultural assistance, there was no economic imperative to turn to violence against the government.

The peace was not to last, however. Fall 2006 brought debates in the Constituent Assembly over revenue redistribution. These debates came to a head in late 2006, when the Morales government began to push for plenipotentiary powers for the Constituent Assembly. This was a procedural issue with serious substantive consequences: if the assembly had plenipotentiary powers, it could pass reforms with a simple majority of delegates, while under existing constitutional rules it needed the support of two-thirds of delegates. Given that the opposition controlled over a third of the seats in the assembly, maintaining the existing rules allowed the opposition to veto any controversial motion proposed by the MAS delegates (Lehoucq 2008). Were the government to receive plenipotentiary powers, that veto power would be lost—and with it the opposition's capacity to protect the livelihoods of landowners and the prefect-dependent old middle class.

Indeed it was in response to the government push to grant the assembly plenipotentiary powers that opposition began to crystallize at the departmental level. This opposition was led by the newly elected prefects and departmental "civic committees," which had been established years earlier to help articulate departmental goals and demands (EIU 2008a; 2008b; Eaton 2007). Across the eastern departments, these civic committees tended to be dominated by the local professional class and businessmen, including large-scale agro-interests.[19] In other words, the threat of revenue redistribution effectively forged alliances between prefects (and their middle-class clients) and local businessmen (including agriculturalists) throughout the opposition-controlled departments of the eastern lowlands.

It was at this moment that the organized violence on the part of the opposition began to appear in Bolivia, primarily in the eastern lowlands. Unsurprisingly, it was the eastern middle class that led the violence. Like the *cocaleros*, this old middle class became violent when the central government threatened to undercut its livelihood. Faced with the loss of prefectural patronage, groups from this old middle class began in 2007 to strike at pro-government targets. In December 2006, the Unión Juvenil Cruceñista (UJC) attacked the leader of a local human rights group in Santa Cruz. The UJC, dominated by middle- and upper-class residents of Santa Cruz, was an affiliate of the Santa Cruz civic committee that Ruben Costas had led prior to becoming prefect. The following month, young middle-class supporters of Cochabamba's prefect, Manfred Reyes Villa, fought against supporters of MAS in a battle that led to a handful of deaths and scores of injuries. Three months later, violence between state and the opposition broke out in Tarija and Beni. In August 2007, residents of Sucre began harassing MAS delegates to the Constituent Assembly in Chuquisaca over their attempts to bypass the question of whether that city should become the capital of Bolivia (with all the opportunities that would imply, including patronage). In September 2007, supporters of the Santa Cruz prefect attacked the government-affiliated television station in Santa Cruz. And in November, urban residents of Chuquisaca and Pando attacked MAS partisans. Throughout the year, state security forces and government partisans responded in turn. While the scale of these incidents varied, they clearly demonstrated escalating broad-based violence.

Eastern agriculturalists supported this escalation, especially as the government implemented additional new policies that threatened their interests.

In response to inflationary pressures, the government opened Bolivia to duty-free agro-imports, undermining the boom-time profits of eastern farmers (EIU 2008d). Then, in late 2007, the Bolivia government prohibited the export of rice, corn, wheat, beef, tomatoes, potatoes, sugar, and oil—and set price ceilings for beef (*Los Tiempos* 2007). This ratcheted up the pressure on eastern agriculture, further inflaming the tension between government and landowners and almost certainly increasing the sector's willingness to stoke middle-class violence.

The situation did not descend into chaos, though, until the very end of 2007—when a series of moves by the Morales administration further crystallized the threats to the urban middle class (and large agriculturalists). In October 2007, Morales made three announcements regarding the redistribution of hydrocarbons revenues that at that time were being transferred to subnational governments. First, he announced that a portion of these revenues would be used to fund a pension for senior citizens, reducing the revenues available to distribute at the subnational level. Second, he promulgated Executive Decree 29322, which shifted the bulk of hydrocarbons revenue transfers from departmental prefects to municipalities. The percentage of these revenues that went to prefects dropped from 57 percent to 24 percent, while the percentage distributed to municipalities increased from 34 percent to 67 percent (*La Prensa* 2008b).[20] Third, Morales took fiscal oversight of municipalities away from the prefects and gave it to the central government.[21] At the same time, the government began pushing even harder to grant the Constituent Assembly plenipotentiary powers, now via "unconventional" means. Convening only the government-supportive assembly delegates, the Morales administration declared a quorum and manufactured a two-thirds majority that approved a draft of the new constitution. The draft was then sent to Congress for its approval on December 14 and approved in February 2008 by a session of Congress that opposition deputies were prohibited from attending. In two months, that is, the Morales government ratcheted up the threat to the prefects and their local allies. A corresponding escalation of open dissent among opposition prefects and (at least initially) local governments alike followed.

As the battle over control of state revenues heated up,[22] the middle-class allies of the prefects mobilized more violence against the government. Between May and September, organized supporters of the prefects attacked government partisans, installations, and the state security forces in Chuquisaca (May), Santa Cruz (July and August), Tarija (September), and Pando (September).[23] These largely middle-class individuals were often affiliated with departmental civic committees (e.g., through the UJC in Santa Cruz)—and sometimes even employees of the prefect itself (as in Pando).

Perpetrators of opposition violence, in other words, did not represent wide swaths of the Bolivian population. Rather, they were members of the group most directly affected by the government's attempts to undermine the fiscal position of the prefects: those factions of the old middle class who had transferred their loyalties from the national to the departmental level.

The violence came to a head in September 2008, when supporters of the prefect of Pando attacked rural supporters of the central government, causing nearly 30 deaths, and leading Morales to declare martial law. Following this melee, however, lowland violence declined sharply in late 2008: the urban middle class seemed to withdraw from violent activity throughout the eastern lowlands, ignoring impassioned appeals by the prefects and landowners for action after opposition congressmen negotiated compromises with the central government over gas revenues and land reform in November (EIU 2008c; 2009a).

This failure to mobilize additional antigovernment violence in late 2008 can be traced directly to the effects of two new government policies on the old middle class. First, following the September violence, the prefects (represented by Tarija's prefect, Mario Cossio) and municipalities (represented by the national organization of municipalities, FAM) both entered into negotiations with the Morales government (*La Prensa* 2008b). While negotiations with the prefects fell apart, negotiations with the municipalities moved steadily forward. This was possible in part because Morales's decision to transfer the bulk of subnational revenues from the prefects to the municipalities in late 2007 led to a boom in municipal revenue. As the municipal revenue began to flow into the *local level,* opportunities undoubtedly began presenting themselves for the old middle class to (once again) transfer their loyalties downward, this time from prefects to mayors. Second, Morales himself began to court the old middle class in opposition departments (EIU 2009b). Once the national government reopened the possibility of providing patronage to the eastern middle class, significant parts of that class were apparently willing to realign themselves away from their old patrons. This shift, it should be noted, was facilitated by the fact that the Morales government had not defined itself as an exclusively indigenous movement. By defining itself in looser "popular" terms, the administration effectively created a political tent broad enough to encompass middle-class defectors from the old order. This served it quite well for defusing the violence of 2007–2008.

By providing new patronage opportunities at the local and departmental levels, Morales succeeded in fracturing urban middle-class support for violence in the eastern lowlands. In Beni, local shopkeepers threatened to go on strike against the civic committee (*La Prensa* 2008a). In Tarija, members of the civic committee apparently went into revolt against their (detained) leadership, calling for less violence and more mediation (García Pérez 2009). And, perhaps most surprisingly, the UJC in Santa Cruz split when a significant faction of it decided to support a MAS candidate (*Latin American Newsletters* 2009). That some of the armed middle-class youth who had led the Santa Cruz violence were willing to support a government-backed candidate spoke volumes to the splintering of the old middle-class opposition—not to mention the fickleness of its political alliances. As the dependence on the old middle class in opposition prefects thus declined, so too did the ability of those prefects to mobilize violence against the government.

Yet the national spike in Bolivian violence in 2008 was driven not only by events in the eastern lowlands. During 2008, frustrated highland supporters of the Morales government also began to turn to violence. This bout of highland violence was more clearly directed at politicians than that of 2006–2008 witnessed five separate incidents of attacks (two of which led to fatalities) on highland dissidents (including within the MAS), while opposition lawmakers were harassed and blocked from entering government buildings on two important occasions.[24] Arguably, this targeting of highland politicians can also be attributed to emergent fights within a newly assertive MAS-affiliated middle class. During 2007, the Morales administration had greatly expanded central government patronage among its partisans, leading to "[frequent] fights for jobs in the central government between the different factions of organized labor and social movements that compose the MAS" (EIU 2007). As the departmental autonomy movement asserted itself in 2007–2008—potentially derailing the further expansion of central government patronage—upwardly mobile highland supporters of the government turned to violence against those politicians who obstructed the administration's agenda. In doing so, they provided more evidence that violence may be the most plausible option available to the Bolivian middle class when it finds its access to state patronage threatened.

New Choices for Eastern Agriculture?

Following the pacification of the old middle class, eastern agro-industrialists appeared to return to their situation of mid-2006: angry but without mass-based allies. In fact, their situation had deteriorated. Not only did they now lack well-funded prefectural allies, but also the national government now seemed intent on redistributing *private* land. Given this situation, some eastern interests may have turned briefly to a form of political violence that they had previously eschewed: in 2009, the Bolivian government arrested a small group of reputed international terrorists, reportedly funded by agriculturalists in Santa Cruz. Yet such activities have not become widespread. This may be because most eastern agriculturalists have more palatable economic alternatives to violence than either the *cocaleros* of 2001–2002 or the middle class of 2006–2008. Faced with increasing pressure from the central government, large eastern agro-industrialists may well shift out of agriculture, perhaps into financial services for the hydrocarbons industry, perhaps into cocaine manufacturing, or perhaps into commercial trading (this last seems especially plausible should Bolivia's exchange rate become increasingly overvalued due to the onset of Dutch disease associated with the hydrocarbons industry). If their assets are liquid, these agriculturalists may respond to government pressure not with violence, but rather by moving their investments elsewhere.[25] In fact, declining investment in eastern agro-industry was reported as early as February 2008 (EIU 2008d).

In short, the violence that consumed Bolivia during 2006–2008 resulted from Morales's upsetting of long-standing patterns of public employment among the urban middle class. Like the *cocaleros* of the central valleys during 2001–2002, these factions of the Bolivian middle class only turned to violence during 2006–2008 when the government threatened to remove the only plausible livelihood for maintaining their middle-class status. Faced with the loss of patronage, different middle-class factions mobilized against their opponents in both the eastern lowlands and, arguably, the western highlands. Perhaps this dynamic should not be surprising. Fifteen years ago, Eduardo Gamarra (1994, 117) warned: "Unless Bolivian rulers can address the issue of patronage rotation among all sectors of the dependent middle class, democratic stability will be in question." This difficult balancing act continues today.

Conclusions

The escalation of violence in Bolivia during 2001–2002 and 2006–2008 resulted from government policies that undermined the livelihood of important regional economic sectors without providing those sectors with plausible alternatives that would allow them to maintain their income or status. Such attempts led those threatened sectors that had the capacity to mobilize popular support into violent clashes with the government. Whether they were *cocaleros* or the urban middle class, Bolivians turned to violence only when the government threatened to leave them with no clear alternative. Conversely, the diminution of violence in Bolivia in the central valleys after 2002 and the eastern lowlands in late 2008 resulted from the government's ability to shift course and provide the threatened sectors with clearer alternatives. As soon as the government removed the immediate threat to their livelihood, the *cocaleros* and urban middle class alike withdrew from antigovernment violence. Given the paucity of alternative employment opportunities—as discussed above—neither working- nor middle-class Bolivians can afford to sit by while the government seeks to undermine the bases of the local economy in which they are embedded. What has motivated working- and middle-class Bolivians to rebel against the state over the past decade has been, in short, the possibility that they may lose the only job that enables them to maintain their current status.

This chapter also suggests that three pieces of conventional wisdom about the recent violence in Bolivia might merit further discussion. First, it was not the attempt by the Morales government to shift away from a liberal development strategy that caused the violence. Although Morales has done so, the violence that followed was not a direct response to that shift but rather to eventually unnecessary attempts to undercut the livelihood of the old eastern middle class. Second, the *presence* of gas revenues alone certainly did not cause the violence in Bolivia. For much of 2006, in fact, natural-gas revenues may have *mediated* the violence by allowing opposition prefects to provide employment to displaced old middle class.

Third, some argue that the recent conflict in Bolivia has been driven by a heightened sense of ethnicity. Over the course of the 1990s, the Bolivian liberal development strategy helped forge well-organized indigenous movements (Yashar 2005; Brysk and Wise 1997) that were shut out of the commanding heights of the Bolivian state. As a result, ethnicity became a highly salient political cleavage in Bolivia over the course of the 1990s. This has led to claims that the violent 2000s in Bolivia were the *result* of increasing indigenous mobilization; that the conflicts of the 2000s were first and foremost *ethnic* conflicts. Yet it was neither the existence—nor even the demands—of these movements that led to violence. It was instead the attempt by the Bolivian government to recentralize revenues.

Now there is no doubt more open discussion (and fear) of indigenous identity among many nonindigenous Bolivians today then there was in, say, the early 1990s. Yet I would argue that these fears have actually shrunk (even as racist rhetoric has increased) since 2001–2002 when,

> As one Bolivian politician described it, the country was on the brink of a racially based civil war between those who believed that the country was the shining example of democracy and economic reform and the vast majority who felt excluded completely from the benefits (Gamarra 2002).

This is arguably due to the fact the Morales government, while clearly identifying with Bolivia's indigenous majority, has not relied on the more divisive discourses associated with other indigenous leaders (notably Felipe Quispe). This weaker ethnic identification enabled the government to defuse conflict in the eastern lowlands by courting the nonindigenous urban middle class in cities like Santa Cruz (as discussed above). Such rapprochement would have been much more difficult had the Morales government defined itself in more exclusive ethnic terms.

It would be ideal if some broader policy lesson could be drawn from this facet of the Bolivian case. Unfortunately, the rise of a less exclusive "indigenous" political leadership in Bolivia seems more the result of stochastic elements of the country's trajectory than the result of conscious political strategizing. It was *Plan Dignidad* that helped bring Morales and the *cocaleros* to prominence in an environment where other, more radical movements remained real possibilities. Nonetheless, this is a historical accident worth noting. Where the possibility of "racially based civil war" is openly discussed, it may be those political movements that both incorporate and dilute ethnic-based claims that most effectively undercut the possibility of sustained and broad-based ethnic violence.

Notes

I would like to thank the Pacific Basin Research Center for their generous support of this project and William Ascher, Natalia Mirovitskaya, and other participants at the workshops for their helpful comments.

1. The data were compiled from Annual Human Rights Reports on Bolivia issued by the US Department of State, which track many things, including political violence. An incident was identified whenever the report mentioned any of these events: an arbitrary or unlawful deprivation of life; a disappearance; an attack constituting cruel, inhuman, or degrading punishment; an arbitrary arrest or detention; a violent violation of civil liberties; or another similar act of political violence. The reports usually included sufficient information to code where the incident occurred, which allowed for the regional analysis below. Additional information available from author.The scale of incidents could not be consistently scored given available data. That said, the recent spikes in violence all included incidents of intergroup violence that resulted in multiple deaths and hundreds of injuries. Intergroup violence of this scale was absent in Bolivia from 1985 through the 1990s. As such, I am confident that the spikes in violence during the 2000s represent real increases in both the frequency and the severity of intergroup violence. Details about particularly egregious incidents are included in the text.
2. The possibility of intergroup violence accompanying this migration was low for two reasons. First, short-term labor flows between the highlands and valleys had a long history (Painter 1994, 5): the migration did not consist of "outsiders"

unknown to permanent residents. Second, the Chapare, at least that time, was sparsely populated.
3. During the 1980s, Pando, Santa Cruz, and Beni were also centers of cocaine manufacturing (Leóns and Sanabria 1997).
4. The 2003 incidents were a harbinger of the violence to come.
5. Capitalization strategies were pursued in other sectors, but were most lucrative in hydrocarbons.
6. Moreover, the land reform adopted by President Sánchez de Lozada in 1996 redefined productive land in terms of taxpaying rather than idleness (Lucero 2008; Yashar 2005). Because only unproductive land could be redistributed, this policy secured the rights of commercial agriculturalists.
7. Both the Unidad Móvil Policial para Áreas Rurales (UMOPAR) (*Mobile Police Unit for Rural Areas*), the state coca-eradication force, and the state coca-eradication unit, Dirección de la Reconversión de la Coca (DIRECO) (Coca Eradication Directorate
8. These figures were subsequently contested.
9. Morales and Roman Loayza were elected to the legislature between 1997 and 2002 (Yashar 2005; Van Cott 2007).
10. CIDOB, which represented the indigenous peoples of eastern Bolivia, was the strongest indigenous organization in Bolivia. Yet it remained regionally fragmented from other indigenous organizations (Yashar 2005).
11. A split opened up between Quispe and Morales in the early 2000s.
12. That possibility was greatly feared by some eastern Bolivians. As one civic leader in Tarija put it to me in 2001: "There could be war" (Author interview, Tarija, August 2001). Gamarra (2002) reports similar findings.
13. Between 2000 and 2005, Bolivia experienced significant popular protest against the privatization of public services, the liberalization of the natural-gas industry, and coca eradication. Yet the majority of the *violence* that occurred was related to coca eradication, concentrated in the central valleys during 2001 and 2002. The year 2003 saw significant violence surrounding a police strike and the deposal of President Sánchez de Lozada, but overall brought fewer violent incidents than 2006–2008.
14. On recentralization, see Eaton and Dickovick (2004).
15. The Constituent Assembly also considered aggressive land reform.
16. Under the 2005 Hydrocarbons Law, a plurality of the revenues from the increasingly lucrative natural-gas industry was transferred directly to the departments (Weisbrot and Sandoval 2009).
17. In La Paz, José Luís Paredes was elected for the opposition, realigned with the government, then again distanced himself from Morales.
18. To be specific, four of the five newly elected opposition prefects had served as key nodes in the pre-Morales government-based patronage network—and the fifth represented the prime beneficiaries of pre-Morales agricultural credit.
19. In both Santa Cruz and Beni, there were preexisting links between the prefects, on whom the urban middle class depended, and agro-interests.

20. The remaining percentage is distributed within the national government and among other state agencies, including universities.
21. It also allowed for pro-government municipalities to organize without worrying about fiscal harassment from prefects.
22. In response to the administration's policies, eastern opposition prefects independently declared "departmental autonomy." The first eight months of 2008 were thus dominated by a series of elections, in which the government and opposition struggled over their relative powers. On these events, see Lehoucq (2008).
23. At the same time, landowners pressured the central government via other means. For example, in August 2008, ranchers in Beni and Santa Cruz announced they would stop sending beef to the highlands in order to force up prices and undermine the Morales government (Chávez 2008).
24. Though four separate incidents of attacks on journalists did occur, similar to those of 2006.
25. But those with illiquid assets (e.g., ranchers) may still be disposed to violence.

References

Brysk, Alison, and Carol Wise. 1997. Liberalization and ethnic conflict in Latin America. *Studies in Comparative International Development* 32(2)(Fall): 76–104.
Conaghan, Elizabeth, and James Malloy. 1994. *Unsettling statecraft: Democracy and neoliberalism in the Central Andes*. Pittsburgh PA: University of Pittsburgh Press.
Chávez, Frank. 2008. Beef producers' boycott—Latest opposition strategy. *Inter Press Service*, August 22. http://ipsnews.net.news.asp?idnews=43640. Accessed June 9, 2010.
Eaton, Kent. 2007. Backlash in Bolivia: Regional autonomy as a reaction against indigenous mobilization. *Politics & Society* 35(1): 71–102.
Eaton, Kent, and Tyler J. Dickovick. 2004. The politics of recentralization in Argentina and Brazil. *Latin American Research Review* 39(1): 90–122.
Economist Intelligence Unit. 2001. *Country Profile: Bolivia*.
———. 2002. *Country Profile: Bolivia*.
———. 2003. *Country Profile: Bolivia*.
———. 2007. *Country Report: Bolivia* (February).
———. 2008a. *Country Report: Bolivia* (January).
———. 2008b. *Country Report: Bolivia* (March).
———. 2008c. *Country Report: Bolivia* (December).
———. 2008d. *Country Report: Bolivia* (April).
———. 2009a. *Country Report: Bolivia* (January).
———. 2009b. *Country Report: Bolivia* (October).
Gamarra, Eduardo A. 1994. Crafting political support for stabilization: Political pacts and the new economic policy in Bolivia. In *Democracy, markets, and structural reform in Latin America*, edited by William C. Smith, Carlos H. Acuña, and Eduardo A. Gamarra, 105–128. New Brunswick, NJ: Transaction Publishers.

Gamarra, Eduardo A. 2002. Has Bolivia won the war? Lessons from Plan Dignidad. April 2002 draft of paper originally prepared for delivery at the Conference on the Political Economy of the Drug Industry, Utrecht University, June 14, 2001.

García Pérez, Leticia. 2009. Tarija: El Comité Cívico ha perdido el rumbo. *La Epoca* (La Paz), February 3.

Gil, Lesley. 1987. *Peasants, entrepreneurs, and social change: Frontier development in lowland Bolivia.* Boulder, CO: Westview Press.

Kurtz-Phelan, Daniel. 2005. Coca is everything here: Hard truths about Bolivia's drug war. *World Policy Journal* (Fall): 103–112.

La Prensa. 2008a. La media luna afronta fractura tras movilizaciones por el IDH (La Paz). September 18.

———. 2008b. Tres discrepancias frenan un acuerdo final sobre el IDH. *La Prensa* (La Paz). September 26.

Latin American Newsletters. 2009. Bolivia: Morales seeks out middle class support. *Latin American Regional Report: Andean Group* (November).

Ledebur, Kathryn. 2004. Bolivia: Clear consequences. In *Drugs and democracy in Latin America: The impact of U.S. Policy*, edited by Coletta Youngers and Eileen Rosin, 143–185. Boulder, CO: Lynne Rienner Publishers.

Lehoucq, Fabrice. 2008. Bolivia's constitutional breakdown. *Journal of Democracy* 19(4) : 110–124.

Léons, Madeline Barbara, and Harry Sanabria, eds. 1997. *Coca, cocaine, and the Bolivian reality.* Albany: State University of New York Press.

Los Tiempos. 2007. Inflación: El Gobierno aprueba decretos y la compra de carne, (Cochabamba). November 15.

Lucero, José Antonio. 2008. *Struggles of voice: The politics of indigenous representation in the Andes.* Pittsburgh: University of Pittsburgh Press.

Malloy, James M. 1970. *Bolivia: The unfinished revolution.* Pittsburgh: The University of Pittsburgh Press.

———. 1991. Democracy, economic crisis, and the problem of governance: The case of Bolivia. *Studies in Comparative International Development* 26(2) (June): 37–57.

Painter, James. 1994. *Bolivia and coca: A study in dependency.* Boulder CO: Lynne Rienner Publishers.

Reel, Monte. 2006. Bolivia plans to redistribute idle farmland. *Washington Post*, May 18.

Reporters without Borders. 2006. Media become leading targets in tit-for-tat violence between government and opposition. December 14. http://www.rsf.org/Media-become-leading-targets-in.html. Accessed June 9, 2010.

Sanabria, Harry. 1993. *The coca boom and rural social change in Bolivia.* Ann Arbor: The University of Michigan Press.

———. 1997. The discourse and practice of repression and resistance in the Chapare. In *Coca, cocaine, and the Bolivian reality*, edited by Madeline Barbara Léons and Harry Sanabria, 169–194. Albany: State University of New York Press.

Spedding, Alison L. 1997. Cocataki, Taki-Coca: Trade, traffic, and organized peasant resistance in the Yungas of La Paz. In *Coca, cocaine, and the Bolivian reality*, edited by Madeline Barbara Léons and Harry Sanabria, 117–138. Albany: State University of New York Press.

Torrico, José Isaac. 1978. The public sector in Bolivian agricultural development. In *Modern-day Bolivia: Legacy of the revolution and prospects for the future*, edited by Jerry R. Ladman, 233–254. Tempe: Center for Latin American Studies, Arizona State University.

United Nations Office on Drugs and Crime. 2008a. *World drug report*. Vienna, Austria: UNODC.

——— . 2008b. *Global illicit drug trends*. Vienna, Austria: UNODC.

US Department of State. 1986–2009, annual editions. *Annual report on human rights: Bolivia*. Washington, DC.

Valdez, José A. 1998. Capitalization: Privatizing Bolivian style. *Economic Reform Today* (1): 20–24.

Van Cott, Donna Lee. 2007. *From movements to parties in Latin America: The evolution of ethnic politics*. New York: Cambridge University Press.

Weisbrot, Mark, and Luís Sandoval. 2009. The distribution of Bolivia's most important natural resources and the autonomy conflicts. Issue Brief, Center for Economic and Policy Research (January). http://www.cepr.net/documents/publications/Bolivia-hydrocarb-update-2009-01.pdf. Accessed June 9, 2010.

Yashar, Deborah J. 2005. *Contesting citizenship in Latin America: The rise of indigenous movements and the postliberal challenge*. New York: Cambridge University Press.

CHAPTER 6

Sowing Conflict in Venezuela: Political Violence and Economic Policy

Deborah L. Norden

Venezuela's Shifting Exceptionalism

From the 1960s through the 1980s, Venezuela was lauded as the paragon of democracy and stability in South America. While throughout the region, military regimes reigned with a previously unknown ferocity, Venezuelan democracy appeared to flourish. Yet by the end of the 1980s, Venezuela was becoming one of South America's more conflict-ridden countries. This chapter seeks to explain the shift in Venezuela's level of conflict and internal violence relative to others in the region, with particular attention to the effects of economic conditions and policies on shifting levels of social conflict.

First, it is important to note that lower political violence *relative to others* in the region at any point of time does not mean low political violence per se, or even lower than at other times within that particular country. Venezuela did, in fact, experience political violence during the 1960s, including military insurrection, guerrilla warfare, and state repression. During the turbulent 1960s and 1970s, however, the "norm" for political violence within the region was extremely high, with both guerrilla movements and virulent state responses to popular insurrection. Venezuelan exceptionalism during this period stemmed from the fact that, unlike most South American countries, it did not experience military rule during the 1960s to the 1980s. The severity and duration of Venezuela's guerrilla challenge also paled in contrast to later movements in neighboring Andean countries, especially Colombia and Peru. Yet by the early 2000s, the level of social conflict in Venezuela surpassed that of other Latin American countries.

What then explains Venezuela's differing experiences with conflict during these periods? The potential for social conflict emanates from a range of factors, including political exclusion (especially either increasing exclusion or increasing *awareness* of exclusion as a consequence of social modernization); policies that emphasize divisions within society (economic, ethnic, or other); mounting intensity and/or salience of social cleavages; and deteriorating economic conditions, either generally or for a particular subgroup. Social tensions may be expressed either through violence or nonviolent contentious action. However, the combination of deteriorating conditions, salient social cleavages, and perceived or increasing political exclusion enhance the likelihood of overt conflict. Consequently, I suggest that the economic policies that are most likely to lead to violence are those that exacerbate divisions within society, especially those distancing the government from significant social sectors; those that rapidly increase transfers from one sector to another; and—often more difficult to identify—those that may lead to overall economic decline. Such policies highlight each group's relative loss compared to more privileged sectors. The counterpart to this is that those economic policies that simultaneously minimize costs to most sectors of society and alleviate differences would help support a peaceful society. The problem is that the state spending required for this approach may eventually become unsustainable, forcing painful policy reforms. This is especially the case if, as was the case in Venezuela, spending is based on volatile energy exports rather than more consistent productivity.

Peace and Conflict in Venezuela

In Venezuela, the relatively peaceful "Punto Fijo" period (a democratic period initiated in 1958 through elite-negotiated pacts) was characterized by difference-alleviating policies such as those mentioned above, while the Chávez period is characterized both by policies that intensified latent cleavages within the society, overtly identifying winners and losers, and consequently by more conflict. To clarify these patterns and illuminate which conditions and policies may have contributed to relative peace or violence, this chapter thus looks at three major periods: the Punto Fijo period of relative democratic stability; the decline of democratic stability, from about 1989 to 1998; and Hugo Chávez's "Bolivarian Revolution," from 1999.

In comparison to conditions elsewhere in the region, the Punto Fijo period in Venezuela was relatively peaceful and stable. To be sure, during the early 1960s, not long after the 1958 transition from military rule to democracy, the country experienced military insurrection, guerrilla warfare, and state repression as government troops sought to counter the guerrilla threat. Yet, the Venezuelan government succeeded in containing threats from both military rebels and guerrillas within the framework of democracy. The preservation of democracy prevented both the expansion of guerrilla warfare—since authoritarianism provides justification for revolutionary movements—and the scale of state repression. In Venezuela, government forces are estimated to have killed hundreds of people, in comparison to thousands or tens of thousands in other South American countries (Wickham-Crowley 1990, 204). During the 1970s, when violence peaked in countries like Argentina and Chile, Venezuela experienced very little political conflict; the battles of the transition period appeared to be resolved. The Punto Fijo two-party democracy began its struggle to maintain legitimacy and control once the economy began to slide, starting noticeably in the early 1980s. This period concluded with a confusing episode in 1988, when the military killed 14 Venezuelan fishermen in the border town of Amparo, whom they accused, apparently falsely, of being Colombian guerrillas. This presumably unprovoked violence, subsequently explained as the government's misplaced attempt at building legitimacy, suddenly made Venezuela's democratic regime look frighteningly similar to the rapidly vanishing military regimes to the South.

For most observers, however, Venezuela's transformation from the democratic stability to conflict-ridden decline began in 1989. In the 1989 *Caracazo*, Venezuela experienced an explosion of riots in response to President Carlos Andrés Pérez's package of neoliberal economic reforms (López Maya, 2003). The ensuing repression left hundreds dead and helped provoke disgruntled military officers to launch the first of two coup attempts in February 1992 (Norden 1998a). The coup failed, but brought coup-leader Lt. Col. Hugo Chávez to the public's attention, eventually enabling him to win the 1998 presidential election.

Chávez assumed the presidency in 1999, with a clearly transformational and increasingly socialist political agenda, unavoidably resulting in further social tensions. While most of Latin America enjoyed relative peace and stability, Venezuela has endured considerable political conflict, ranging from protest to military coups. Venezuela's levels of political conflict, violence, and instability again made the country an exceptional case within the region, now at the other end of the spectrum.

Economic Policies, Economic Outcomes, and Conflict

Given their importance in determining the relative wellbeing of different groups within societies, economic policies play an important role in fomenting or deterring conflict. Economic *policies* only partially shape economic *outcomes*, however, and the latter may be at least as important as policies in determining relative peace or conflict within a society. This assertion has at least two components. First, economic outcomes result from the combination of policies with circumstances often beyond the control of national policymakers. Despite the country's substantial resources, Venezuelan policymakers cannot control the price of oil, but they do need to deal with the consequences. Second, economic *outcomes* generally trail economic policies, sometimes by quite a few years. Carlos Andrés Pérez's neoliberal economic policies clearly triggered the riots of 1989, yet what motivated those difficult reforms? The decision to implement the reforms was shaped by the government's considerable economic constraints at the time, which in turn were a product of both prior economic policies and the global environment.

Significant economic outcomes include changes in wealth, both relative to past conditions and to other groups within society. Overall wealth over time can be measured by factors such as per capita GDP and real wages. In an oil-producing country like Venezuela, oil revenues are particularly important in generating wealth, and have a strong influence on consumption. However, as will be discussed, oil revenues can vary dramatically over time, reverberating throughout the domestic economy. Complicating this further is the fact that oil prices are notoriously difficult to control by any single producer country (even a leading Organization of the Petroleum Exporting Countries [OPEC] member), soaring or plummeting as a consequence of such factors as faraway wars or international recessions. Since few oil-producers manage to avoid having this resource dominate their economies, these swings can have devastating effects on both the economy and political stability; "outcomes" not easily managed by "policies." Regardless of the causes, deteriorating economic conditions such as high inflation, declining productivity and its corollary, and rising unemployment contribute to "relative deprivation" among a large proportion of the population, greatly increasing the likelihood of conflict (Gurr 1970).

Wealth and the distribution of wealth may generate significant rifts within the population, but can be difficult to assess. Actual "wealth" includes income, as well as earnings from investments and government-provided benefits, but standard measures of income distribution like the Gini coefficient generally only look at wages and salaries. Even more difficult to measure is "quality of life." Beyond wages and other earnings, state-provided benefits such as public schools, public health benefits, or free or subsidized food distributions—critical elements of Chávez's development strategies—can substantially mitigate poverty. Public goods, such as access to clean water and sanitation, also contribute to people's standard of living and overall wellbeing, despite having no direct impact on income distribution or measurable "wealth." It is in part for this reason that the UN Development Programme's "Human Development Index" includes not only per capita gross domestic product (GDP/PC), but also measures of education and life expectancy (UNDP 2009).

Government policies may influence wellbeing and the distribution of wealth more rapidly than they can shift income distribution. For example, public spending in such areas as education and health may diminish dissatisfaction from income inequality, since investments in these areas both improve quality of life and can reasonably raise expectations for future earnings. Short-term poverty relief can also appease the poor. Notably, both forms of distribution may antagonize wealthier sectors of the society if they feel that they are unjustifiably footing the bill for these expenses.[1] Thus, economic policies both contribute to the overall wellbeing of the population and help determine society's relative winners and losers, potentially stimulating "losers" to intensify their claims against "winners," or impacting the likelihood of conflict between different nonprivileged groups over the distribution of resources.

Policies and Politics during the Punto Fijo Period (1958–1988)

The Punto Fijo period, from 1958 until around 1988, avoided many of these divisions through two-party dominance and a spirit of political compromise. The "Punto Fijo" pact committed the two parties that would dominate the next four decades, *Acción Democrática* (AD) and *Comité de Organización Política Electoral Independiente* (COPEI), as well as the short-lived *Unión Republicana Democrática* (URD), to respect electoral outcomes, consult about policy, and refrain from personal attacks during campaigns (Karl 1987, 83). A second document, the "Minimum Program of Government," directly addressed the policy concerns of the relatively smaller and pro-business COPEI, by promising to respect private property, "subsidize the private sector through the Corporación Venezolana de Fomento [Venezuelan Development Corporation]," and avoid uncompensated land expropriations (Karl 1987, 84). The document thus ensured that economic elites would not be threatened, and that COPEI and their allies would not again revert to advocating military intervention.

The Punto Fijo period was not without conflict, however. The major incidents of political violence were at the beginning and end of the period. Early violence took the form of military insurrection and guerrilla warfare. Repeated military coup attempts failed largely because in an atmosphere of political compromise and hope, would-be coup leaders encountered insurmountable opposition both from civilians and from other groups in the military (Trinkunas 2005, 118–120). A 1960 assassination attempt against President Rómulo Betancourt also failed, although seriously injuring the president (Trinkunas 2005, 119). The greatest threat to political stability emanated from guerrilla warfare, however, especially given the widespread wave of revolutionary idealism that followed the 1959 Cuban Revolution.

Domestically, political exclusion likely motivated Venezuela's guerrilla movement at least as much as economic causes. The Venezuelan Communist Party (PCV) was the one important Venezuelan party excluded from the Punto Fijo pact of 1958, despite their prior involvement in the opposition movement against Pérez Jiménez. Although the older generation in the party still leaned toward democracy, the younger generation embraced more revolutionary aspirations. On the other hand, the Movement of the Revolutionary Left (MIR) was a new party, formed by leftist youth from Betancourt's *Acción Democrática* in response to the party's determination to remain firmly in the center (Ellner 1986, 83). As the government clamped down on the young leftists' protests, the two groups became increasingly radicalized, eventually joining forces in 1963.

The guerrillas' base remained mostly confined to the universities, however, with little support from the rural poor they sought to recruit (Levine 1973, 53). This was partly because oil had already transformed Venezuela's economy and society well before 1958, significantly reducing the proportion of the population employed in agriculture (Karl 1987, 69). The government also carried out a major land reform program, redistributing "land to 150,000 families during the early 1960's" (Wilpert 2003). Since many agrarian elites had also moved into oil-related endeavors, the land program caused less opposition from elites than might have been expected.

In essence, prior transformations to Venezuelan society, along with deliberate policies, limited both the potential salience of an urban-rural cleavage, as well as the likelihood of tension between capital and workers. The wealth from the oil economy, including the highly paid oil workers, "meant that a largely nonproductive urban middle class actually preceded and outnumbered the slowly growing working class" (Karl 1987, 71). The government also spent generously on social programs. As Wilpert writes, "[D]uring the boom years, anti-poverty policies meant providing free universal education, free health care, a decent minimum wage, and massive public works projects" (Wilpert 2003). The 1976 nationalization of oil also led to expanded public-sector employment (Mahler 2009, 13), substantially easing unemployment and increasing the size of the middle class. Like the agrarian reform, these programs could be provided at little cost to economic elites, funded instead by abundant oil revenues. Under these conditions, revolutionary ideologies enticed few recruits, and provoked only a limited backlash from the government.

Policies and Politics During the Decline of Punto Fijo (1989–1998)

According to many observers, Venezuela's economic decline began as early as the late 1970s, moving toward "crisis by the mid-1980s" (Coronil and Skurski 1991, 292). Popular responses to gradual economic decline tend to build up slowly, however, in part because the people may not immediately identify the incumbent government as responsible for the conditions—correctly so, given the multiple causes of economic conditions. Nevertheless, President Carlos Andrés Pérez's efforts to respond to the emerging crisis meant that he would ultimately shoulder the blame for Venezuela's economic woes.

Venezuela thus moved in the opposite direction from much of Latin America since the early 1980s. Indicators of the brewing problem included increasing protests and strikes in the mid-1980s and the 1988 Amparo incident. According to López Maya, Lander, and Ungar, "[T]he number of protests steadily grew since 1980, and many of them were confrontational and violent" (López Maya, Lander, and Ungar 2002, 201). Protests were particularly high in 1985, for example, with 262 protests registered by the El Bravo Pueblo Database, after which they declined to 70 and 83 protests per year in 1986 and 1987, respectively; protests rose again in 1989, with 213 protests (López Maya, Lander, and Ungar 2002, 202).[2] Within this context, the Amparo Incident appears to have been a misplaced effort to focus on an external threat. After a bloody military offensive left 14 dead, the government reported that the bodies belonged to Colombian guerrillas who had crossed into Venezuelan territory. Local residents, however, countered that the dead were innocent Venezuelans, victims of a government-concocted show to regain legitimacy (Coronil and Skurski 1991, 301, 306). The 1995 judgment of the Inter-American Court on Human Rights backed the latter interpretation, subsequently awarding reparations to two survivors and the families of the assassinated victims (IACHR 1995; 1996).

It was the 1989 *Caracazo*, however, that marked the demise of the AD-COPEI dominated party system. On February 27, Venezuela's poor took to the streets en masse, in an explosion of riots following the sudden implementation of neoliberal economic reforms. Frustrated from years of burgeoning poverty and unemployment, and infuriated by the government's imposition of still more sacrifices, angry citizens looted the markets, venting their rage and stocking their empty pantries. As the chaos built, looters turned to more expensive items, taking clothes, furniture, and equipment, and vandalizing businesses and automobiles. After days of chaos, the president finally called in the military. Prepared more for warfare than policing, the armed forces now trained their weapons on their own people. The anarchy was eventually controlled, but with a heavy toll; ultimately, an estimated 396 people died in the conflict (López Maya, Lander, and Ungar 2002, 198).

Two coup attempts, in February and November of 1992, further shook a country long unaccustomed to military insurrection. Despite limited casualties in the first attempt, any coup attempt is intrinsically violent, given the implicit *threat* of force. Furthermore, the February coup attempt, led by a group of army lieutenant colonels, inspired more congratulations than condemnation on the part of the people, indicating the government's profound loss of legitimacy. The second coup attempt, largely carried out by the air force, caused relatively more significant destruction and casualties, provoking much stronger public disapprobation. Both the coup attempts and the ultimate election of Lt. Col. Hugo Chávez to the presidency can be seen as a further response to the conditions and policies triggering the *Caracazo*, and ultimately, ending the Punto Fijo era.

Politically, the death of Punto Fijo can be traced to a collusive two-party system that lost its ability to respond to a changing society (Norden 1998b). The principles of collaboration and consultation, initially forged in the 1950s to protect democracy from interparty hostility, created multiclass parties poorly adapted to channel the new class cleavages that developed in the 1980s (Roberts 2003). Thus, Morgan describes a situation in which the dominant parties' relatively stable support began to decline by the late 1980s, with "AD support [falling] precipitously after the reelection of AD's Carlos Andrés Pérez in 1988" (Morgan 2007, 82). These new divisions emanated from deteriorating economic conditions, caused by earlier Venezuelan policies, as well as shifting international oil prices, and an International Monetary Fund (IMF)-dominated international environment, along with more immediate policy decisions by national leaders. As Kenneth Roberts writes, "Starting in the late 1980s,... recurrent political and economic crises gradually polarized the political arena around an elite-mass cleavage for the first time in a generation" (Roberts 2003, 56). This cleavage then reverberated into the political sphere, placing new stress on the Punto Fijo system and ultimately creating the political opportunity for Chávez's "Bolivarian Revolution."

Venezuela's economic decline can be traced to the early 1980s. Shortly after Mexico's 1982 debt crisis, Venezuela's leaders sought to address their country's own building debt, stagnating productivity and increasing capital flight. Thus, on February 18, 1983, the government announced the first devaluation of the national currency in 20 years (López Maya, Lander, and Ungar 2002, 186). A year later, President Jaime Lusinchi initiated a broader economic plan that included further devaluing the currency and concomitantly establishing exchange rate controls, moderately increasing prices for gasoline, and committing to lower state spending (López Maya, Lander, and Ungar 2002, 187). The plan was not only ineffective, but according to Briceño-León, detrimental as well: "[It] encouraged corruption, monopolization and caused a remarkable shortage of products as basic as milk, sugar or feminine sanitary towels" (Briceño-León 2006, 319–320). In December 1988, about a month before leaving office, Lusinchi ceased payments on the national debt (López Maya, Lander, and Ungar 2002, 187).

By the time Carlos Andrés Pérez took office in early 1989, conditions had only gotten worse. By the end of 1988, oil prices had declined to a level not seen since for more than 15 years, while both inflation and poverty soared (see Figure 6.1). After negotiating with the IMF, Pérez introduced neoliberal economic reforms that included eliminating price controls and subsidies for basic goods; increasing prices for state-provided services; establishing a floating interest rate; and lowering tariffs (Coronil and Skurski 1991, 295; López Maya, Lander, and Ungar 2002, 187). By the 1990s, the Pérez government had privatized Compañía Anónima Nacional Teléfonos de Venezuela (CANTV, the telephone company) and Venezolana Internacional de Aviación S.A. (VIASA), the state-owned airline; Siderúrgica del Orinoco (SIDOR), the state steel industry, followed a few years later, under Caldera (Ellner 2008, 90; McCoy 1998, 10). The government proposed various social policies to soften the blow, especially the Plan to Confront Poverty (PEP), "designed to supply the basic necessities to vulnerable groups" (Lacruz 2006, 148; translation mine). Programs involved nutritional support, including food subsidies and a maternal-infant program, as well as provision of school uniforms and some fees, and an expansion of preschools. Nevertheless, overall social spending dropped precipitously in 1989, including substantial declines in both health care and education spending (López Maya, Lander, and Ungar 2002, 192; García and Salvato 2006 253). Thus, overall, the costs of the reforms were much more widely distributed than the

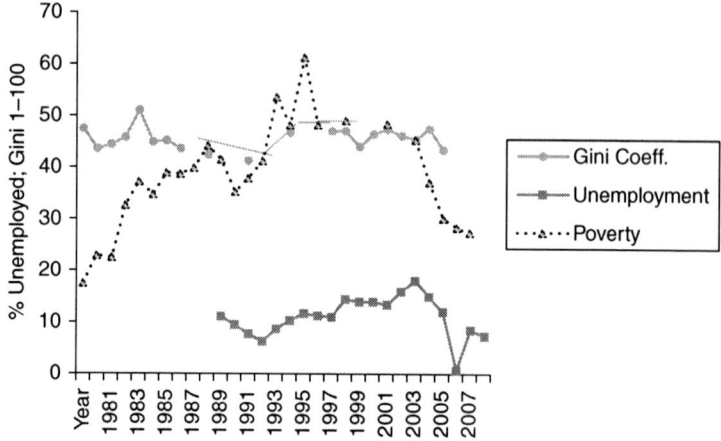

Figure 6.1 Inequality and poverty in Venezuela.

Sources: Gini coefficient: 1989–2006, from SEDLAC; 1980–1987, from UNU-WIDER; Unemployment, 1990–2008: IADB, Latin American and Caribbean Macro Watch; Poverty:1980–1997, López Maya, Lander, and Ungar 2002, 193; 1999–2008, CEPAL.

benefits, creating a much larger pool of relative "losers" in this new economy with respect to "winners."

The element in Pérez's reform policies most immediately felt by the Venezuelan people involved gasoline prices. The government doubled the price of gasoline almost instantly. It sought to convince the National Transport Federation to cap bus and taxi fares increases at 30 percent in order to limit the popular impact; however, the privately owned transportation companies rebelled and more than doubled their fares, setting the scene for the February *Caracazo* riots.

According to Coronil and Skurski, raising gasoline prices violated "imagined shared ownership of the nation's petroleum resources based on its founding legal code. The state's legitimacy was intimately tied to its ability to control the nation's formerly foreign-owned oil industry in the name of the entire pueblo" (Coronil and Skurski 1991, 314). Thus beyond its pocketbook impact, the increase was perceived as a betrayal, a source of "moral indignation." The people revolted against the policies, the leaders, the parties, and the entire political system created by the pact of Punto Fijo. Venezuela was now en route to becoming one of the most violent in the region.[3] In February 1992, a leader of a failed military coup became the new hero of the Venezuelan people; nine years later, he became their president.

Venezuela's Bolivarian Revolution: The First Decade

Hugo Chávez Frías took office in 1999, following an electoral campaign focused on ousting the purportedly corrupt and elitist AD- and COPEI-party rule and rewriting the Venezuelan Constitution. His "Bolivarian" movement and Movimiento Quinta República (MVR) political party (named for the MBR-200 military movement that launched the February 1992 coup attempt) constituted a major break from Venezuela's long-established two-party system. In contrast to the country's historically cooperative political leadership, Chávez emphasized conflict—allies and revolutionaries versus the enemies of his Bolivarian Revolution—rejecting neoliberalism, US international domination, and the entire old political elite. He sought to concentrate power in the presidency; to redistribute wealth and power within Venezuela; and to use the power of the bursting Venezuelan purse to buy international allies and challenge the United States. In the process, Chávez deepened social cleavages in Venezuela, excluded and discriminated against former political and economic elites, and made little effort to appease the affected groups. By increasing the salience of social differences like ethnicity and, in particular, socioeconomic class, Chávez's policies augmented social conflict. As Steve Ellner writes, "Venezuelan politics under Chávez has become a zero-sum game at the same time that discourse reflects a clear social bias. Never before in Venezuela has the head of state declared that assisting the poor is more important than serving other sectors of the population" (Ellner 2008, 133; also see Roberts 2003). Rather than purporting to be a government of and for all Venezuelans, the Chávez government consistently portrayed themselves as the voice of the downtrodden, economically deprived, and ethnically darker skinned.

Chávez's Economic Policies

The major thrust of Chávez's economic policies was thus to expand government control over the economy, in order to shift greater resources toward the poor. Given its overwhelming significance in the Venezuelan economy, the new government first focused on the oil industry. The government also sought to provide a range of social benefits to the poor, albeit mostly with short-term, populist distributive programs, while moving gradually toward more consequential and divisive policies, such as land reform and nationalization of enterprises.

Oil policy provoked a particularly intense backlash, including the April 2002 coup and the general strike of 2002–2003, during which time Petróleos de Venezuela (PDVSA) management led almost a total shutdown of the oil industry (Webber 2010, 26–27).[4] Chávez sought to reclaim control over the oil industry, redirecting oil proceeds toward his political project. The 2001 Hydrocarbons Law was an important step toward this control, establishing "majority government ownership of all mixed companies in charge of primary oil operations" to reverse economic liberalization (Ellner 2008, 113). The government also reined in PDVSA's famous autonomy, expanding oversight by the Ministry of Mines and ultimately firing several of PDVSA's top executives. Notably, the ensuing protests by PDVSA personnel generated little sympathy among the people, for whom the organization represented elite privilege more than modernization (Tinker-Salas 2009, 233). Under Chávez's authority, the company became directly involved in many of the government's social programs, a strong contrast to the previous, highly professional model.

Social Policies

Not surprisingly, social programs have been a centerpiece of the Chávez government, although their relative success in reducing poverty and inequality has remained highly debated (Corrales 2010; Wilpert 2003). Many of these programs were designed to have an immediate impact on the beneficiaries. For example, the Plan Bolivar 2000 engaged the armed forces in programs ranging from providing police services in remote regions, to fixing refrigerators, distributing food, or repairing schools and homes. Beginning in 2003, the government began a new approach, launching various social or Bolivarian "Missions," which sought to address specific issues in an intense and focused way, similar to Cuban campaigns during its revolutionary period. The majority of the Missions have dealt with health care and education issues, with the help of Cuban literacy workers and around one thousand Cuban doctors (Wilpert 2003). Other Missions were designed to provide subsidized food, help with job training, or facilitate land titles for indigenous people. As the Missions have been financed by surplus funds from PDVSA, directly under the control of the president and outside of the formal budgetary process, these expenditures—while significant—do not necessarily appear in standard accounts of social spending in Venezuela, making it difficult to track actual spending over time (Penfold-Becerra 2007, 64). All evidence, however, indicates that social spending has grown substantially under Chávez, and increasingly so with rising oil prices.

The government's social policies provoked various criticisms, particularly by those concerned with the strong Cuban role, whether due to a fear of communism or a fear of competition from the Cuban doctors. However, realistically, the Plan Bolivar 2000 and the Bolivarian Missions imposed few actual costs on major sectors of society, and did benefit the poor. In contrast, Agrarian Reform and nationalization policies did pose a meaningful threat to economic elites. The 2001 Land Reform Law sought to redistribute land to Venezuelan families both for equity purposes and to increase the country's self-sufficiency in food production, an area that had suffered a decline over the years. For the initial years of the land reform, the program mostly drew from the government's extensive properties, distributing land to approximately 130,000 families by 2003, while also attempting to provide the support necessary for the new farmers to succeed (Wilpert 2003). In 2005, however, the government shifted toward more radical land distribution, deliberately seeking to break up large-landed estates and permitting squatters to occupy land even before the transfer was legally authorized. According to Ellner, "These actions contrast with traditional agrarian reform in Venezuela, which concentrated on the distribution of public land that had always abounded in rural areas" (Ellner 2008, 125). Nationalizations and government expropriations also accelerated. For the most part, nationalization occurred with compensation, as the government purchased majority shares in a few large companies, mostly those that had been state owned until the 1990s. Various failing companies were also expropriated, however, legalizing the situation of workers who had taken control when owners had abandoned their enterprises; other businesses were given the option to accept government aid in exchange for allowing workers to share in the management if owners wished to avoid expropriation (Ellner 2008, 125, 127). While most of these policies were implemented after violence peaked in 2004, enough were initiated previously to consolidate a determined political opposition, desperate to prevent the loss of their property, and increasingly unable to effectively defend their interests through institutional channels.

Ethnic policies and, in particular, discourse helped to also highlight heretofore latent ethnic cleavages in Venezuela, as well as the parallels between ethnic and socioeconomic cleavages within Venezuelan society. The influence of race and ethnicity in Venezuela has been historically masked by the relatively early process of miscegenation, particularly between those of European and African origin, given Venezuela's relatively small indigenous population. According to Barry Cannon, "[B]y the end of the colonial era 60 percent of Venezuelans had African origins and of the 25 per cent classified as white probably some 90 per cent had some African ancestry" (Cannon 2008, 10). This intermixing has continued over the years; by the beginning of the twenty-first century, approximately 67 percent of the population was of mixed race, with only 21 percent classified as white, 10 percent as black, and 2 percent indigenous (Library of Congress 2005, 7). With such blurred lines between ethnicities, Venezuela easily embraced the myth of "racial democracy," with its presumption that ethnicity is irrelevant. In fact, however, Venezuelan society and politics have been dominated by lighter-skinned peoples.

According to some, the illusion of equality began to shatter with Carlos Andrés Pérez's neoliberal reforms, while others trace the resurgence of open racism to the economic crisis of 1983 (Herrera Salas 2005, 99; Roberts 2003, 55). Both events brought into sharp relief the actual inequalities within Venezuelan society. As Barry Cannon writes, it was during the economic decline of the 1980s and the 1990s that "[r]acist discourse began to re-emerge amongst the upper and middle classes. The link between class and race became more explicit as Afro-Venezuelan and indigenous people became the scapegoats for Venezuela's economic failure" (Cannon 2008, 12).

Hugo Chávez made race even more salient by explicitly aligning and identifying himself with the darker and poorer sectors of Venezuelan society. According to Cannon, "[T]he poor's support for Chávez is based on the fact that he is like them: from a poor background and *pardo* (of mixed Indigenous, African and European descent)." At the same time, "the rejection of Chávez by parts of the middle and most of the upper classes in Venezuela is precisely due to a rejection of these very qualities: being poor and darkskinned" (Cannon 2008, 7). Chávez has sought by various means—starting with the 1999 Constitution—to both give more recognition to the indigenous population and to directly incorporate indigenous groups into the political process (Herrera Salas 2005, 107). Yet it his discourse that seems to most inspire his darker-skinned allies and provoke his lighter-skinned opponents, helping to define not only their relationship to the president, but also to each other.

Conflict and Political Violence under Chávez

During the first decade of the Chávez administration, Venezuela thus suffered from considerable conflict and violence, ranging from protests and demonstrations, to coups and state repression. For example, protest data from Programa Venezolana de Educación-Acción en Derechos Humanos (PROVEA) indicates 855 protest actions in the 1998–1999 period, rising to 1,255 five years later and 2,893 by 2008–2009 (PROVEA 2009, 434). From 2002, following the November 2001 passage of 49 laws with a strongly nationalist and antiliberal thrust, until the failure of the August 2004 recall election, Chávez's opponents actively utilized multiple methods to try to remove the president from power. The government, however, was equally determined to remain in power, and also willing to use every resource to ensure that outcome.

The April 2002 military coups were a notable example of this. On April 11, 2002, "[s]everal general strikes called by the CTV [Venezuelan Workers' Confederation] and backed by the business organization FEDECAMARAS culminated in a violent confrontation in downtown Caracas... that resulted in nearly two dozen deaths and hours later gave way to a military coup" (Ellner 2008, 115). The military and civilian coup leaders promptly arrested Chávez and placed Federación de Cámaras y Asociaciones de Comercio y Producción de Venezuela (FEDECAMARAS) president Pedro Carmona at the head of the de facto government. Within two days, however, Chávez's allies—again, both military and civilian (particularly the poor)—had launched a countercoup and restored Chávez to power.

The opposition then took to the streets, launching a prolonged general strike in December 2002 that essentially shut down Venezuela's oil industry and devastated the economy. Protests during this period were especially violent; according to PROVEA reports, 19 percent of protests from October 2002 to September 2003 were violent, in contrast to only 7.6 percent of protests three years later, from October 2005 to September 2006, and 3.5 percent in the following year (PROVEA 2007, 390). The hotly contested 2004 recall vote seems to be at the center of the declining violence. Long avoided by the Chávez government, the recall vote marked the opposition's last serious effort to remove Chávez during this phase. Chávez's triumph at the polls both empowered him and deflated the opposition. Later protests focused less on ousting the government than questioning particular policies. Issues that provoked renewed street protests thus included growing restrictions on the media and a 2007 constitutional reform proposal that sought to establish a socialist state and end presidential term limits (the constitutional reform failed at this point, but Chávez subsequently managed to pass the term-limit abolition). Yet while the opposition moved toward moderation, the government began increasing its use of force. Thus, while state security forces blocked or repressed only around 3 percent of peaceful demonstrations from October 2002 to September 2003, by the 2006–2007 period, this had more than doubled (Provea 2007, 304).

Explaining Conflict under Chávez: Dividing Venezuelan Society

In some regards, increasing protest under Chávez can be seen as an indicator of more political freedom, at least initially. The Chávez administration reversed his predecessors' criminalization of protest, a legacy of the period of guerrilla conflicts in the 1960s. The 1999 Constitution thus prohibits state forces from using arms to repress protests. The protests also, however, reflect the broader social conflict spurred by the "Bolivarian Revolution," with its distinct winners and losers. During the earlier periods discussed, conflict tended to emerge either due to, first, the political exclusion of particular groups (the Venezuelan Left in the early 1960s, or remnants of the recently displaced military regime), and, second, the impact of declining oil revenues on social spending. Under Chávez, resources were somewhat limited for the first few years, but by 2003, oil wealth and renewed production once again meant prodigious revenues. However, the Chávez government actually intensified its polarizing policies during the period of abundance, imposing increasing burdens on the wealthy and middle class, while continuing to deliver the message that the Bolivarian Revolution would be the government of the poor—not a government of *all* the people.

What variables have helped define the lines of recent social conflict in Venezuela? While socioeconomic class has constituted by far the most significant cleavage under Chávez, other cleavages may be increasing in relevance. For example, regional divisions were historically important, as implied by the Andean domination of early Venezuelan politics; given the contrast between the relative wealth of the more industrialized Caracas region and the much poorer, more rural lowland, these regional divisions may be intensified as a parallel to the growing-class cleavage. Ethnicity also appears to be becoming more salient, as Chávez has sought to equate the darker skin with poverty and historical lack of political voice. While relatively subtle, the increasing salience of ethnicity, as well as possibly region, may be creating a problematic context of overlapping cleavages in Venezuela.

Explaining Peace, Political Violence, and Political Instability

Venezuela's shifting levels of conflict help to provide insight into some of the causes of relative social peace and its converse. Conflict, political violence, and instability and, by extension, their absence have been explained by various factors, including ongoing divisions within society, psychological reactions to changed conditions or aspirations, political exclusion, and declining legitimacy by political authorities. Rather than being mutually exclusive, these factors interact, potentially combining in ways that may exacerbate the likelihood of conflict.

First, what do we mean by conflict, political violence, and political instability? While these phenomena often coincide, they are nonetheless distinct. Conflict involves tension between or among different collective actors, whether defined by social characteristics (such as ethnicity, language, or religion), socioeconomic class, or political identity and role (i.e., government or opposition). "Conflict" implies expressing different interests, but not necessarily engaging in violence. Violence, on the other hand, involves the use or threat of force, whether mostly spontaneous, as with riots, or strategic, as in guerrilla warfare, terrorism, coups d'état, or state repression. The latter categories mentioned here are most obviously "political," as they either directly involve the government or seek to influence or replace it. However, since "politics" is essentially about power, other clashes between groups about relative power, whether regional or in relation to the government, would also be considered political violence. Relatively spontaneous events like riots (unless instigated by known agitators) may be more difficult to classify as political; however, these may still be an *effect* of government policies, as in the 1989 *Caracazo*. Finally, political instability involves conditions that threaten the continuity of the government or regime.

Among the conditions that may make political instability and political violence likely is the existence of substantial divisions between groups within the society.[5] Robert Dahl thus argues that democracy is "less likely in a country with sharply differentiated and conflicting subcultures," since "cultural conflicts can erupt into the political arena" (Dahl 1998, 150). Other authors, such as Seymour Martin Lipset (1960), have looked at social divisions in terms of "overlapping" and "crosscutting" cleavages, observing that differences are more likely to lead to conflict when sectors of the society are divided from each other along multiple lines. Cleavages may be ethnic, religious, linguistic, cultural, regional, or class based; they may also involve political ideology or preferences.

Differences, however, are not the same as cleavages, and may or may not have any political impact. In particular, concepts like ethnicity and socioeconomic class are *social constructs*, created by social recognition, rather than "true" characteristics of those involved. In that respect, they only exist to the extent that the people perceive them as distinguishing "us" from "them." Beyond this, recognized cleavages may or may not be *salient*. For example, indigenous identities have become much more salient in Latin America since the end of the twentieth century, in part because of international organizations and movements promoting indigenous rights, and in part because of policies that have heightened perceptions of group disadvantages (such as NAFTA in Mexico, or coca-eradication policies in Bolivia). In the Venezuelan case, as discussed, overlapping class and ethnic cleavages became increasingly salient immediately prior to and during the Chávez government, due both to economic conditions and government policies.

The increased salience of cleavages, in other words, and the likelihood that they may lead to political violence is often the consequence of changed conditions or expectations. As Ted Gurr explains, relative deprivation is "the tension that develops from a discrepancy between the 'ought' and the 'is' of collective value satisfaction, and that disposes men to violence" (Gurr

1970, 23). If changed policies or economic conditions align relative winners and losers along the lines of existing social cleavages, those cleavages then become both increasingly salient and potentially inflammatory. As William Ascher points out, this is particularly the case if the policies creating relative deprivation incur "moral indignation." Ascher argues that "the indignation that can arise when others are viewed as violating moral standards paradoxically can overcome the aversion to violence that we would otherwise associate with conscience" (Ascher 2009, 7–8). Expectations, then, are based not only on what groups have historically experienced, but also on cultural understandings of the rights of citizens or subgroups, and the respective obligations of the government. In Venezuela, cultural expectations of the state's obligation to utilize oil wealth to care for the people contributed to the political violence in 1989, when the state violated those expectations.

In a democratic context, the anger generated by shifting expectations may well be diffused if, first, the aggrieved are reasonably able to express their positions and hope for resolution *through* the democratic system; and second, if the government is generally recognized as legitimate. This leads to my third major point: political violence and instability are more likely when frustrated groups feel politically excluded, and/or when governments lose legitimacy. With respect to the first of these, in Albert Hirschman's terms (1970), opposition groups without a "voice" within the system may ultimately "exit." Exclusion or discrimination may be based on any of the characteristics described above as underlying social cleavages. Historically, we can identify many instances in which the ideological Left has recruited the politically excluded poor to engage in guerrilla warfare. Similarly, when governments have discriminated against the economically privileged to the extent that they felt unable to defend their core interests, the offended groups have often sought military allies to carry out a coup d'état. Venezuela's pacted Punto Fijo system faced its major challenge from the one important party it excluded, the PCV. Chávez, however, has opted to overtly favor the impoverished majority, excluding and antagonizing the wealthy (with the exception of the new "Boliburguesia," new economic elites who have positioned themselves in such a way as to profit from the Bolivarian regime).

In contrast, declining political legitimacy tends to result from more widespread government failures, particularly if a government seems unable to provide essential public goods such as security and economic stability. According to Juan Linz and Alfred Stepan, declining efficacy and effectiveness, and a corresponding loss of legitimacy, contributed significantly to the collapse of democratic regimes in the 1960s and the 1970s throughout Latin America (Linz and Stepan 1978,18–22). Governments may also initiate violence, however, either to maintain control or to help justify their position in light of waning legitimacy, as may have occurred with Venezuela's 1988 Amparo massacre (Coronil and Skurski 1991, 290–291).

Finally, how important are economic policies in explaining the presence or absence of social conflict and, in particular, political violence? I would suggest that economic policies may exacerbate or diminish the likelihood of either violent conflict but that this does not provide a sufficient explanation for whether peace or violence predominates in a society. Other factors are also critical, including not only those discussed above, but also people's ability to voice concerns and demands through institutionalized channels, the government's ability to respond to demands (Huntington 1965), and the extent to which government responses involve repression. Furthermore, while undeniably important, economic issues by no means constitute the sole concern of civilians. Environmental issues, education policies, infringements on media freedom, and demands for indigenous rights and autonomy have all triggered political contention within Latin America. That said, economic policies and conditions directly affect the wellbeing of the entire society and determine many of the relative losses and gains of different groups, thus making this a particularly critical issue.

Economic Policies, Economic Outcomes, and Conflict in Venezuela

In the Venezuelan case, shifting economic conditions interact with the government's choices about how it will utilize its alternately plentiful or meager resources. During the early years of Venezuela's democratic regime, abundant resources facilitated providing not only stability but also prosperity to citizens. Petroleum-led prosperity, substantial social spending, and economic protections for elites, combined with political inclusion successfully limited social conflict during the Punto Fijo period. Notably, during the Punto Fijo period, Venezuela enjoyed a comparatively more equitable income distribution than in most Latin American countries, as well as relatively high state spending on education and health (Di John 2009). Yet, policies during the 1960s and the 1970s also led to an insurmountable debt, while failing to develop adequate alternatives to oil dependency. The dramatic shifts in oil prices therefore hit Venezuela hard, especially the government, which has consistently relied on oil revenues. Successive governments delayed adjusting spending habits for some time, until Carlos Andrés Pérez enacted his incendiary reforms. During the Chávez period, social spending has again increased, but within the context of political exclusion and the economic elites' relative loss of privilege and protections, thereby leading to increased conflict as evidenced both by intensified protest and military insurrection.

Oil wealth has often anchored explanations of Venezuela's successful post-1958 political stability. According to Terry Karl, the oil industry drew many agrarian elites into trade and encouraged rapid urbanization, thereby diminishing the potential for urban-rural cleavages (Karl 1987). Oil wealth also meant that the government had sufficient resources to satisfy many different interests. The fact that Venezuela became less stable after oil prices declined in the early 1980s would appear to support the argument that oil income explains the shifts in political stability. Yet, increasing oil prices during the 1990s and early 2000s (with the exception of 2002–2003, during the PDVSA strike) did not suffice to prevent social conflict and political violence from plaguing the Chávez government. This indicates the importance of *policies*, versus mere resources. As various authors have observed, one reason for Venezuela's struggles has been its failure to maximize the benefits from petroleum. Venezuela's substantial oil reserves thus have not sufficed to ensure either economic prosperity or social stability.

Many of Venezuela's difficulties in fact may be endemic to oil-exporting states. As Karl explains, having a very valuable resource creates the temptation to spend heavily, using limited reserves to earn credit and using those funds to launch accelerated development (Karl 1997, 25). Oil revenues thus encourage the creation of a large state, accustomed to significant spending, which inevitably generates an unmanageable debt. At the same time, even with the best intentions of economic diversification, petroleum-rich states tend to continue relying on this single, exhaustible primary resource with considerable price volatility (Karl 1997, 47–48). As Figure 6.2 indicates, per capita GDP has increasingly followed oil prices, especially since the mid-1980s, demonstrating the strong and growing effect of oil prices on the Venezuelan economy.

However difficult managing oil may be, policymakers do have choices. In many respects, Venezuela's national oil company, PDVSA, appeared to offer a relatively successful model of oil management. Oil had begun feeding and transforming the Venezuelan economy as early as the 1920s, and helped fund the 1958 democratic transition and subsequent consolidation. Yet it was not until 1976 that Venezuela fully nationalized oil, just as oil prices were beginning to soar. This provided considerable income for the government. However, the PDVSA model also allowed considerable space for multinational companies to continue working in Venezuela, which many Venezuelans considered desirable, in part because foreign exports could contribute to the costly and complex process necessary to refine Venezuela's relatively poor quality crude oil. By the time Hugo Chávez came to power, PDVSA functioned much like a private oil company, with considerable autonomy for the management, and relatively little politically motivated

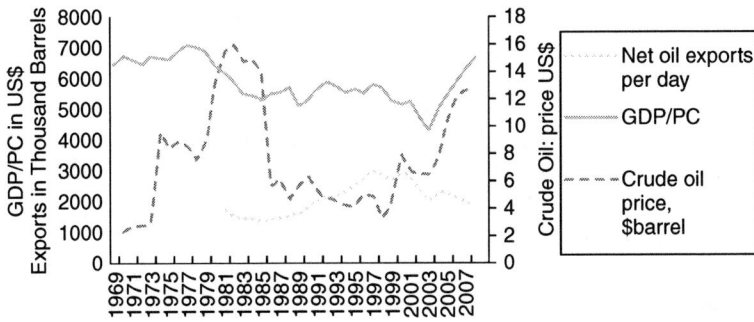

Figure 6.2 Oil and GDP/PC in Venezuela, 1969–2008.

Sources: Per capita GDP: World Bank World Development Indicators; Net oil exports per day and inflation-adjusted crude oil price:, Organization of Petroleum Exporting Countries, various years.

redirection of oil proceeds, beyond what might have been earned through taxes from a private company.

Nevertheless, Venezuela's pre-Chávez version of nationalized oil certainly was not flawless. Ascher points out various ways in which Venezuela failed to maximize its benefits from oil, including failing to "charge" the state oil company royalties for the crude oil itself (Ascher 1999, 16). Essentially, the oil company was permitted free access to the petroleum reserves, a strategy that not only risks depleting the resource, but also limited the government's ability to fully benefit from higher market prices. As Ascher notes, this also meant that PDVSA "retained revenues that depended much more on the world price of petroleum…than on the efficiency, true profitability or investment needs of PDVSA and its affiliates" (Ascher 1999, 213–214). This practice, however, coincided with the general belief that, as a shared patrimony, natural resources should be essentially free to all Venezuelans, a sentiment that also led to severely underpriced domestic gasoline. Although Chávez eventually did establish royalties for petroleum, the disastrous effects of price adjustments in 1989 discouraged touching the more politically sensitive issue of charging market rates for gasoline; as late as 2008, the price of gasoline at the pump thus remained around 12 cents a gallon (Wilson 2008).

Venezuela also failed to either adequately invest in oil, or to shift the economy beyond oil. According to Ascher, "PDVSA has had limited capitalization for oil exploration and production within Venezuela, thus limiting Venezuela's ability to sell oil when world oil prices are high" (Ascher 1999, 10). While an investment fund was set up to allow PDVSA to support its own needs, when times became tight, the Venezuelan government plundered that account to support other budgetary needs. Thus, instead of adequately funding exploration and development of new oil fields, which is essential even to maintain continued productivity, PDVSA sought to protect its closely guarded profits by transferring funds and investments outside the country (Ascher 1999, 217).

Other sectors of the economy were likewise neglected. As early as 1936, Venezuelan intellectual Arturo Uslar Pietri had posited "that oil profits could be reinvested and, like agricultural products, be harvested" (Tinker-Salas 2009, 189). Yet, the few seeds sown outside of the oil industry found little nourishment and failed to thrive. Often neglected, the non-oil economy began declining from the mid-1960s, and from 1980 to 2003, "output growth in the manufacturing sector...collapsed" (Di John 2009, vii). Jonathan Di John argues that Venezuela's difficulty in advancing industrialization and maintaining economic prosperity stemmed, in large part, from the difficulty of moving from the "easier" stage of import-substituting industrialization to a more difficult "big-push, natural-resource-based heavy industrialization strategy," without the concentration of political power that would permit the greater sacrifices of continued development (Di John 2009, 11–12).

In Venezuela, political institutions also seem to have had an impact on both economic consequences and relative political violence. Di John emphasizes problems stemming from clientelism, factionalism, and the eventual loss of the interparty collaboration that characterized the early Punto Fijo years. Others, however, blame the problem of corruption, itself the consequence of having too much wealth in the hands of government officials (Mahler 2009). According to López Maya, et al., the loss of political representation was even more central to the emerging crisis in the 1980s: "Even before the Lusinchi years [1984–1989], state and society relations, controlled by the parties, unions, and other associations based on the pacts of the 1958 transition to democracy, became less and less effective" (López Maya, Lander, and Ungar 2002, 201).

However, only since the late 1980s have observers seriously questioned what was *wrong* with Venezuela, or where Venezuelan policies failed. For the prior 30 years, Venezuela was seen as one of Latin America's few stable and peaceful democracies. Certainly, oil wealth was a boon, but Venezuela's political leaders had also carefully negotiated their new democracy, incorporating *most* major social sectors and political actors. They also put in place economic policies based on generous social spending, without needing to burden the economic elites with the costs. While it was a model that few countries could afford, and even Venezuela could not sustain, it is nonetheless a useful example for policymakers seeking to avoid political conflict.

Assessing Policies in Venezuela

This chapter has looked at a range of political, social, and economic factors, in order to determine which have supported peace and stability in Venezuela, and which have disrupted them. In brief, policies that *blur* differences between classes, ethnicities, and other social cleavages seem to have had more success in minimizing social conflict than those that emphasize those differences. This is the case even when this blurring masks actual inequalities and differences, as with the myth of racial democracy, which may have helped sustain racial inequality (as no one fights what they cannot see), but prevented overt conflict. This was the case during the Punto Fijo period, when discourse that described Venezuela as a racial democracy and development strategies designed to satisfy multiple, often competing, social sectors served to limit social conflict. In contrast, class-based politics, like those of Chávez, are intrinsically based on a conceptualization of a divided, as opposed to organic, society.

Likewise, economic policies that allow the illusion that all are potential "winners" provoke less conflict than those that highlight the unequal distribution of costs and benefits. Moderate policies that protect core elite interests, support middle-class concerns (e.g., education) enough to allow social mobility, and provide an ample cushion for the poor tend to bring relative stability, if the government has enough funds to pursue this path. In contrast, in Venezuela, conflict increased rapidly with either (a) government policies that had an immediate negative impact on working-class standards of living (for instance, the very sudden increase in public transportation rates in 1989); or (b) government policies that address poverty and inequality, but seriously threaten the core interests of elites, such as guarantees of private property or the use of state funds to support domestic enterprises.

To what extent do vagaries in oil wealth explain away the variations in social conflict? Prior to Chávez, this would seem to have been a reasonable explanation, since social conflict only began to emerge after the decline in oil revenues in the mid-1980s. However, during Chávez's government (1999 to the present), even very high oil revenues have not prevented increasing levels of social conflict. Higher oil revenues during Chávez's government suggest that policies—not just revenues—do matter. Policies that starkly divide losers from winners, enhancing subgroup identification and deepening cleavages between groups, or policies that threaten the present and future welfare of groups, who are simultaneously politically excluded, are most likely to provoke conflict.

Looking to Venezuela's Future

Hugo Chávez undeniably adopted many practices and policies that weakened Venezuela's democratic institutions, polarized the society, and consequently enhanced the possibility of further social conflict and political violence in Venezuela. Corruption and cronyism also increased at an astounding rate, with a loss of accountability and transparency that will inevitably prove detrimental to Venezuela's political and economic health for quite some time. In Transparency International's 2010 Corruption Perceptions Index, Venezuela was rated "highly corrupt," 164th out of the 178 countries surveyed, with the least corrupt countries placed at the top of the scale (Transparency International 2010, 79–80). This perceived corruption does little to create trust in the government and overcome social rifts.

At the same time, however, the Chávez government has taken some important measures toward diminishing the country's oil dependency, and conceivably protecting the resource itself. To begin with, the 2001 Hydrocarbons Law imposed royalties of 30 percent on all oil extracted from Venezuelan territory, thereby meeting one of Ascher's key recommendations for oil-producing states (República Bolivariana de Venezuela 2001; Ascher 1999). The Chávez government also consistently presented budgets based on extremely conservative estimates of likely oil prices (Corrales 2010, 38). The immediate result of this has been the creation of a substantial discretionary fund available to Chávez and his allies to spend as they see fit, often in ways that strengthen clientelistic networks and electoral possibilities more than economic development. However, limiting reliance on oil in the official budget helps provide at least *some* protection from the inevitable price swings. Finally, the government's National Service for Customs and Tax Administration (SENIAT) has sought to improve tax collection from businesses: "SENIAT, which hopes that tax collection will eventually ease the nation's dependence on oil income, has disproved the claim that in Latin America the income tax system can never be effectively implemented due to opposition from powerful business interests" (Ellner 2008, 126). The Chávez's governments social spending may also have long-range benefits for Venezuela's economic development, beyond the oil industry, by strengthening human capital through investments in health and education.

The Chávez administration, like its Punto Fijo predecessors, has relied on unsustainable oil revenues to fund its generous social spending. Yet other policies could help shield the government budget from some of the unpredictability of oil prices, while also building a stronger workforce. At the same time, punitive policies have pushed investment out of the country and created potentially enduring new lines of conflict. By deepening social cleavages, creating an atmosphere that excludes economic elites, allowing corruption to flourish, and distributing the costs of economic policies in a distinctly divisive manner, the government's policies have lent themselves more to political violence than to peace and stability, despite temporarily ample oil wealth.

Notes

1. This chapter does not explore the question of political culture. However, this is relevant. In longtime social democracies, paying relatively high taxes in order to support substantial social benefits is taken for granted, and is considered justified. Elsewhere, the political culture makes these distributional policies more difficult.
2. Note that the numbers of protests counted by El Bravo Pueblo Database (which uses *El Nacional* newspaper reports for its information) tend to differ significantly from those provided given by PROVEA, and should, therefore, only be used as an indicator of year-to-year violence. The BPD data is useful for this earlier period, however, since PROVEA data is not available prior to Hugo Chávez's government.
3. The UN Office on Drugs and Crime reports that in 2009, Venezuela had a homicide rate of 49 per 100,000 people. This was by far the highest rate in South America, with the next closest contender, Colombia, at 33.4 in 2010 (UNODC 2012).
4. The total cost of the oil strike to the Venezuelan economy was estimated to be around US$6 billion (Webber 2010, 26).
5. See Zuckerman's (1975) review of the many scholars contributing to the early conceptualization and analysis of "political cleavages." Seymour Martin Lipset's *Political Man* (1960) further explores the impact of overlapping and crosscutting cleavages on the likelihood of political conflict.

References

Anonymous. 2009. Cuestionan efectividad. *El Universal*, March 17, 2009.
Ascher, William. 1999. *Why governments waste natural resources: Policy failures in developing countries*. Baltimore: The Johns Hopkins University Press.
———. 2009. Psychological bases of resentment and perceptions of victimization arising from development strategies. Paper prepared for the annual research conference of the International Society for Political Psychology, Dublin.
Briceño-León, Roberto. 2006. Violence in Venezuela: Oil rent and political crisis. *Ciencia & Saude Colectiva* 11(2): 315–325.

Cannon, Barry. 2008. Class/race polarization in Venezuela and the electoral success of Hugo Chávez: A break with the past or the song remains the same? *Working Papers in International Studies* 9, Dublin: Centre for International Studies, Dublin City University.

Coronil, Fernando, and Julie Skurski. 1991. Dismembering and remembering the nation: The semantics of political violence in Venezuela. *Comparative Studies in Society and History* 33(2): 288–337.

Corrales, Javier. 2010. The repeating revolution: Chávez's new politics and old economics. In *Leftist governments in Latin America: Successes and shortcomings*, edited by Kurt Weyland, Raúl Madrid, and Wendy Hunter, 28–56. Cambridge: Cambridge University Press.

Dahl, Robert. 1998. *On democracy*. New Haven and London: Yale University Press.

Di John, Jonathan. 2009. *From windfall to curse? Oil and industrialization in Venezuela, 1920 to the present*. University Park: The Pennsylvania State University Press.

Ellner, Steve. 1986. The MAS Party in Venezuela. *Latin American Perspectives* 13(2): 81–107.

———. 2008. *Rethinking Venezuelan politics*. Boulder, CO: Lynn Rienner Publishers.

García, Haydée, and Silvia Salvato. 2006. Gasto social y equidad en Venezuela (1970–2004). In *Balance y perspectivas de la política social en Venezuela*, edited by Thais Maingon, 245–266. Caracas: Instituto Latinoamericano de Socio Investigaciones Sociales.

Gurr, Ted Robert. 1970. *Why men rebel*. Princeton: Princeton University Press.

Herrera Salas, Jesus María. 2005. Ethnicity and revolution: The political economy of racism in Venezuela. *Latin American Perspectives,* special issue on Venezuelan Exceptionalism revisited: The unraveling of Venezuela's model democracy, 32(2): 72–91.

Hirschman, Albert. 1970. *Exit, voice and loyalty*. Cambridge: Harvard University Press.

Huntington, Samuel. 1965. Political development and political decay. *World Politics* 17(3): 386–430.

Inter-American Court on Human Rights. 1995. El Amparo Case. Judgment of January 18, 1995. http://www1.umn.edu/humanrts/iachr/e!19elas.pdf. Accessed July 15, 2010.

———. 1996. El Amparo Case, Reparations (art. 63[1] American Convention on Human Rights). Judgment of September 14, 1996, Inter-Am. Ct. H.R. (Ser. C) No. 28 (1996). http://www1.umn.edu/humanrts/iachr/C/28-ing.html. Accessed December 28, 2009.

Inter-American Development Bank. Latin American andCaribbean macro watch. www.iadb.org/res/lmw.cfm. Accessed December 20, 2009.

Karl, Terry. 1987. Petroleum and political pacts: The transition to democracy in Venezuela. *Latin American Research Review* 22(1): 63–94.

———. 1997. *The paradox of plenty: Oil booms and petro states.* Berkeley: University of California Press.

Lacruz, Tito. 2006. Balance sociopolítico: Una ciudadanía social inacabada. In *Balance y perspectivas de la política social en Venezuela,* edited by Thais Maingon, 111–184. Caracas: Instituto Latinoamericano de Investigaciones Sociales.

Levine, Daniel. 1973. *Conflict and political change in Venezuela.* Princeton: Princeton University Press.

Library of Congress. 2005. Federal Research Division country profile: Venezuela (March). http://lcweb2.loc.gov/frd/cs/profiles/Venezuela.pdf.

Linz, Juan, and Alfred Stepan, eds. 1978. *Breakdown of democratic regimes.* Baltimore: Johns Hopkins University Press.

Lipset, Seymour M. 1960. *Political man: The social bases of politics.* Garden City, NY: Doubleday.

López Maya, Margarita. 2003. The Venezuelan *Caracazo* of 1989: Popular protest and institutional weakness. *Journal of Latin American Studies* 35: 117–137.

López Maya, Margarita, Luís Lander, and Mark Ungar. 2002. Economics, violence and protest in Venezuela: A preview of the future? In *Violence and politics: Globalization's paradox,* edited by Kenton Worcester, Sally Avery Bermanzhon, and Mark Ungar, 184–208. New York: Routledge Press.

Mahler, Annegret. 2009. Oil in Venezuela: Triggering violence or ensuring stability? A context-sensitive analysis of the ambivalent impact of resource abundance. *GIGA Working Papers (German Institute of Global Area Studies),* No. 112 (October).

McCoy, Jennifer, with Jeff Davis and Paul Foote. 1998. Reluctant reformers: Explaining privatization in Venezuela and Uruguay. Paper prepared for presentation at the Congress of the Latin American Studies Association, Chicago, September 24, 1998.

Morgan, Jana. 2007. Partisanship during the collapse of Venezuela's party system. *Latin American Research Review* 42(1): 78–98.

Norden, Deborah. 1998a. Democracy and military control in Venezuela: From subordination to insurrection. *Latin American Research Review* 33(2): 143–165.

———. 1998b. Party relations and democracy in Latin America. *Party Politics* 4(4): 423–443.

Organization of Petroleum Exporting Countries. Various years. *Annual statistical bulletin* Vienna.

Penfold-Becerra, Michael. 2007. Clientelism and social funds: Empirical evidence from Chávez's *"Misiones"* programs in Venezuela. *Latin American Politics and Society* 49(4): 63–84.

PROVEA. 2007. *Informe Anual 2006–2007.* www.derechos.org.ve. Accessed on June 8, 2008.

———. 2009. *Informe Anual 2009.* www.derechos.org.ve. Accessed on July 1, 2010.

República Bolivariana de Venezuela, Ministerio de Energía y Minas. 2001. Ley de Hidrocarburos Venezuela. Chapter VI, Royalties and Taxes, Section I, Royalties,

Article 40. http://www.leydehidrocarburos.gov.ve/ProyectdeLey.htm. Accessed on December 29, 2009.

Roberts, Kenneth. 2003. Social polarization and the populist resurgence in Venezuela. In *Venezuelan politics in the Chávez era: Class, polarization & conflict*, edited by Steve Ellner and Daniel Hellinger, 55–72. Boulder, CO: Lynne Rienner Publishers.

Tinker-Salas, Miguel. 2009. *The enduring legacy: Oil, culture and society in Venezuela*. Durham and London: Duke University Press.

Transparency International. 2008. 2008 Corruption Perceptions Index. www.transparency.ort/layout/set/print/news_room/in_focus/2008/cpi2008/cpi_2008/espanol. Accessed on July 25, 2010.

———. 2010. 2010 Corruption Perceptions Index. http://archive.transparency.org/policy_research/surveys_indices/cpi/2010/results.

Trinkunas, Harold. 2005. *Crafting civilian control of the military in Venezuela: A comparative perspective*. Chapel Hill: The University of North Carolina Press.

UN Development Programme. 2009. Human development report 2009. http://hdr.undp.org/en/statistics/indices/hdi/. Accessed December 23, 2009.

UN Office on Drugs and Crime. 2012. Homicide statistics. http://www.unodc.org/unodc/en/data-and-analysis/homicide.html. Accessed on March 29, 2012.

Webber, Jeffrey. 2010. Venezuela under Chávez: The prospects and limitations of twenty-first century socialism, 1999–2009. *Socialist Studies* 6(1): 11–44.

Wickham-Crowley, Timothy. 1990. Terror and guerrilla warfare in Latin America, 1956–1970. *Comparative Studies in Society and History* 32(2): 201–237.

Wilpert, Gregory. 2003. Venezuela's mission to fight poverty. *Venezuelanalysis*, November 11. www.venezuelanalysis.com/analysis/213. Accessed on December 25, 2009.

Wilson, Peter. 2008. Venezuela: Land of 12-cent gas. *Business Week*, May 23. www.businessweek.com/bwdaily/dnflash/content/may2008/db20080523_344156.htm. Accessed December 30, 2009.

World Institute for Development Economics Research, United Nations University. 2008. World income inequality database, V2.0c. www.wider.unu.edu. Accessed on December 24, 2009.

Zuckerman, Alan. 1975. Political cleavage: A conceptual and theoretical analysis. *British Journal of Political Science* 5(2): 231–248.

CHAPTER 7

Education Policy and Conflict in Latin America: Lessons from Chile and Venezuela

Emily K. Penner

Education policy can have a profound impact on political stability, revolution, and violent change, and thus plays an important role in creating or preventing conflict (Roberts-Schweitzer, Greaney, and Duer 2006, 2). Education can facilitate violent conflict by reinforcing confrontational political ideologies or training those who will become fighters (Leach and Dunne 2007, 23); likewise, the failure of an education system to provide a comprehensive education for students and support for educators can create fertile ground for protests and riots (Spencer and United States National Student Association 1965, 57). Alternatively, education can be used as a powerful tool for ameliorating hostility and restoring peace (Davies 2004, 8). The creation of new education policies can serve as a uniting force that works to heal tensions and rebuild nations after conflicts (Tawil and Harley 2004, 7). While instances of education instigating and curtailing conflict have been documented in numerous circumstances, the specific ways in which education policies create conflict or foster peace are not well understood. Research identifying education strategies that have ignited or extinguished political tensions and national conflicts is particularly limited. This chapter seeks to remedy this shortcoming by identifying specific education-policy strategies and policy contexts that either led to conflict or helped to prevent and end conflict.

The context of Latin America in the last century is particularly ripe for identifying examples of education strategies that have influenced conflict, both because of the evolving nature of its politics and education policies and because of its history of violent conflict. In the past century, various Latin American governments have transitioned from military dictatorships to socialist or communist states to puppet republics heavily influenced by the United States, and finally to emerging democracies. Throughout this process, countries once labeled as stable were later unsettled by civil war, while others, plagued with conflict earlier in the century, have more recently prospered peacefully. Here, as in previous research, inequality and development are at the core of conflict, but these cases reveal the particular importance of education policy in the midst of political struggles.

In two Latin American countries in particular, Chile and Venezuela, education has been at the center of political struggles over mobility and marginalization, attempts at reconciliation, and ongoing conflict. The cases of Chile and Venezuela implicate both education policy and the policy context in provoking or averting conflict. When comparing the historical experiences of these two cases, one finds examples of both constructive policies, which seek to lessen inequality, expand access, and improve quality, and obstructive policies, which create improvements for some groups while withholding opportunities from others, usually to shore up political support. One also finds examples of policy contexts that are collaborative, conciliatory, and provide fertile ground for helping education policies to flourish as well as other policy environments that are hostile, combative, repressive, and suspicious, which reject and corrupt even good policies. Thus, it is important to consider not only whether constructive policies are being pursued, but also if the policy environment is constructive or obstructive. It is important to examine the complementarities between the policy environment and the policy itself, or in other words the policy-environment fit. The seeds of conflict are sown when either the environment or the policy is obstructive, or there is a poor policy-context fit. It is not until policy decisions recognize and address the sources of conflict that conflict can be lessened and reconciliation can proceed. The cases and time periods that most aptly demonstrate the importance of the interaction of policy and policy context are presented in Table 7.1.

This table contrasts the constructive and obstructive education policies and policy environments used in both countries at different time points. The details of each of these examples will be discussed throughout the chapter.

At face value, Chile and Venezuela have many qualities in common, and thus serve as reasonable comparisons. Both have been internationally lauded as exemplars of a stable Latin American democracy at one point in their

Table 7.1 Historical comparison of constructive and obstructive education policies and policy environments in Chile and Venezuela

	Obstructive-policy climate	Constructive-policy climate
Obstructive education policies	Chile under Pinochet Venezuela under Carlos Andrés Pérez Venezuela under Chávez (recent)	Punto Fijo period in Venezuela
Constructive education policies	Chile under Allende Venezuela under Chávez (early)	*Concertación* period in Chile Chile under Frei Montalva

history, but struggled politically and economically at other times. They have also both enjoyed particular economic advantages because of their political organization and their natural resource wealth. Despite the potential for economic dominance, both also suffered through economic crises during the 1970s and the 1980s. Each country also experienced military dictatorships, several decades of relatively stable democracies, and democratically elected socialist leaders.

However, these commonalities belie dramatically different approaches to the use of education policy in attempting to address inequality and therefore also demonstrate dramatically different outcomes related to conflict. While both countries have historically struggled with the misalignment of education policy and policy environment, only one of these countries, Chile, has achieved a political situation in which education policies and the policy environment surrounding education have both been constructive.

The current state of politics in Chile and Venezuela provides a particularly informative comparison between constructive education policies and policy environment in Chile, and obstructive education policies and policy environment in Venezuela. The decades of the 1990s and the 2000s draw a sharp contrast in terms of how governments in the two countries used education policy to attempt to address mobility and inequality and how they used education more broadly to shape the larger political climate. In the *Concertación* period, Chile used education policy as an anchor of a larger policy agenda to involve opposing groups in planning the recovery from Pinochet's dictatorship. It pursued policies that targeted increased access and quality, attempting to address issues of inequality while also providing improvements to those already served by the system. In doing so, the country aligned constructive education policies with a constructive-policy environment, and enabled recovery from previous violence and conflict. In the later Chávez period, Venezuela also used education as an anchor of a larger policy agenda, attempting to gain political support from allies while marginalizing the opposition. Instead of structuring the education system to reconcile conflict, Chávez has used education policy to foment hostility. He has also pursued a policy of expansion, but did so by supplanting existing education structures while ignoring issues of quality and promoting ideology. In doing so, he aligned obstructive education policies with an obstructive-policy environment, and continues to escalate tensions. Although the environment in Chile has become more precarious with recent student protests and the environment in Venezuela may become less obstructive with upcoming presidential elections, the contrast of this recent period highlights starkly different approaches to education policy and different uses of education to shape political environments.

This chapter uses the historical and contemporary Chilean and Venezuelan cases to underscore the importance of the interaction of education policy and the policy environment by identifying specific examples of how and when education policy contributed to conflict and other instances when it contributed to peace. The contrasts between constructive and obstructive education policies highlight how education policy can contribute to preventing or fomenting conflict, depending on the context in which it is pursued. For both cases, the historical and current education policies and policy contexts are reviewed, highlighting how education contributed to conflict and cooperation. The effectiveness of current education policies is assessed, where research is available; and the manner in which current policies and policy environments in the two countries are working to move from or toward conflict is evaluated. Finally, a discussion of possible future outcomes is presented.

Chile—Education Policy at the Heart of Conflict, Reform, and Ongoing Challenges

Education policy has contributed to conflict in Chile for several decades, and was a prominent element of larger political discord at many key periods in Chilean history in the past century. At many moments, constructive policies aimed at lessening inequalities were met with resistance in the midst of contentious political climates, such as during the Allende period. In others, education was used as a tool for exclusion during an already-repressive political climate, such as under Pinochet. In both scenarios, conflict was the ultimate result. However, in contrast to historical disagreements about education policy, the post-Pinochet *Concertación* government expressly sought to avoid conflict over education policy, designating wide-reaching education reforms as a key pillar in the transition to democracy. This commitment to avoiding conflict helped to pacify the political climate surrounding education. In addition to reducing the conflict over education policy, the *Concertación* government developed several policies aimed directly at easing general political tensions and supporting conflict resolution. The combination of constructive policies and conciliatory political climate during this period demonstrates how education can be a powerful tool for overcoming a violent past.

Historical Education Policies and Policy Contexts

Early education policy change in Chile was characterized by repeated moves to expand access and a transition from private education (provided by the Catholic Church) to public education. While Catholic education has existed in Chile since its founding, Chile was the first country in Latin America to establish public education in 1842. Chile also became the first Latin American country to allow women into higher education in 1877. In 1920, education became free and compulsory for all students aged 7–13 years (Freeburger and Hauch 1964, 3).

President Arturo Allesandri promoted universal and compulsory primary education as a modernization tool for Chile in the 1930s (Farrell 1986, 20). In the ensuing three decades, the Ministry of Education remained committed to delivery of education by the government despite political transitions (Farrell 1986, 19). President Jorge Allesandri furthered his father's commitment to education by initiating a review of the Chilean education system from 1962 to 1964, identifying major inequalities inherent in the system (Schiefelbein and Davis 1974, 46). A proposal for the restructuring of basic education was pushed through by Eduardo Frei Montalva (Schiefelbein and Davis 1974, 46).

The education reforms of 1964 were some of the most significant in Chile's history and grew out of Frei Montalva's Christian Democratic Party's core belief that widespread education was essential to spurring economic growth because it improved opportunities for the middle and lower classes. The widely popular reforms focused both on improvements in education quality and access, and led to an attempt to more equitably distribute educational opportunities to lower- and middle-class children. The National Literacy Campaign was a keystone of Frei Montalva's presidency, and was met with public optimism (Austin 2003, 55, 65).[1] The reforms, which benefited from US financial support, were remarkably successful, especially among the urban poor who saw large increases in primary enrollment (Farrell 1986, 34). Funding was directed toward school construction and enrollment in primary and secondary school improved. Adult education was also of great political interest to Frei Montalva, and he announced reforms in this area soon after his inauguration (Austin 2003, 71). The education policies of funding school infrastructure in order to expand access, along with other wide-reaching education improvements, helped to support political cooperation during the 1960s and for much of Frei Montalva's tenure as president.

The election that followed Frei Montalva's presidency was very close. The Christian Democrats split between two candidates, and, thus, Salvador Allende of the Unidad Popular (a conglomeration of several socialist and other leftist parties) narrowly won. This left Allende with a limited popular mandate. Even within his party, Allende was not the most popular Figure (Farrell 1986, 50–53). The weak mandate from Allende's narrow election victory, coupled with rifts within the Popular Unity government and the Ministry of Education, eventually led to debate and disagreement throughout his later attempts to reform education policy and helped to chill the previously convivial political climate.

Although Allende adopted the policy prescriptions of the Frei Montalva reforms that called for the expansion of enrollment and school facilities and ending illiteracy (Vivallo Jara 1978, 135), some of his education policies were an ideological departure from Frei Montalva, calling for a reorientation of the education system and its foundations (Vivallo Jara 1978, 135). Allende's education strategy sought to strengthen the link between education and economic development by integrating work, study, socialist theory, and practice. To reinforce ideological changes, the plans aimed to devise an education system that would create the "New Man" to support socialist ideals, echoing the Cuban model. This ideological training would take place in the National Unified School (Escuela Nacional Unida or ENU) that would be constructed from a society reoriented by the socialist philosophy (Edholm 1982, 5; Farrell 1986, 49, 73).

Allende and the Ministry of Education attempted to work with other political parties while planning the ENU, but the political climate surrounding education policy was hostile. Many in both his political coalition and in the opposition were distrustful of Allende's proposals, fearing that they were an ideological indoctrination tool that would be used to make the nation's children more sympathetic to communism, would cut the education budget, and would eliminate funding for private schools (Vivallo Jara 1978, 300; Farrell 1986, 76). The opposition, influenced by the US Central Intelligence Agency, began to characterize all reforms of the Popular Unity government as "communist" attempts to impose a totalitarian ideology

(Farrell 1986, 54–56). Protests, mainly consisting of university students, became increasingly violent and regular, and newspapers openly called for military intervention (Farrell 1986, 202).

In early September of 1973, a successful compromise on education policy was reached with broad political, military, and religious support. This effort was seen as a final attempt to avoid a coup, but it was too late (Farrell 1986, 237). Military generals, led by Augusto Pinochet, seized control of the government and killed Allende on September 11, 1973 (Farrell 1986, 238). A Christian Democrat who worked on the education-policy compromise reached during Allende's final days concluded that "the ENU proposal was the single most important cause of the government's downfall" (Farrell 1986, 239). Allende's pursuit of education policies that heavily emphasized political ideology served to undermine political stability despite the positive elements of educational expansion and attempts to further combat illiteracy. The resistance from the Christian Democrats and others farther to the right, coupled with the Popular Unity's inner conflict and the intense media backlash, made education policy a political lightening rod for Allende and his government. Ultimately, the upper and middle classes as well as the military felt threatened by the moves of the Allende government and began to contemplate political intervention. As one scholar notes, the Frei Montalva reforms show that "Chileans were quite prepared to accept changes to [education]. But the hard-line socialist rhetoric in which the proposal was wrapped allowed it to be portrayed by the opposition as an attack on the *family* (socializing children into a value pattern which would alienate them from the beliefs of the parents) and their *religion* (particularly when the Church declared itself in opposition to the proposal)" (Farrell 1986, 244). With this perceived attack on the values of the opposition, discord over education policy opened the door for nearly two decades of violence and repression.

The coup led by Pinochet received support from the traditional right and the Christian Democrats who believed that it was necessary to prevent economic, political, and educational meltdown (Edholm 1982, 23). Within a few months, support for the regime had dwindled. The constitution was suspended, government industries were privatized, and activists from Popular Unity, as well as teachers, professors, and students suspected of leftist leanings, were tortured and killed (Oppenheim 1998, 120). The policy context surrounding education transitioned from hostile under Allende to combative and repressive under Pinochet.

Pinochet's early education agenda was simply to root out socialist influences, scale back the state social structure, and reinforce support for the dictatorship. He reversed Allende's reforms using violence, threats, and repression from 1973 to 1979 (Edholm 1982, 42). He worked to take power away from teachers' unions and universities in an effort to prevent any opposition groups from organizing. Pinochet cut education spending from 22 percent of the budget in 1970 to 12.5 percent in 1974 (Edholm 1982, 45). Those primarily impacted by the cuts were students from the lower class who had few opportunities to advance to secondary school. Pinochet also dramatically increased the role of private schools, placing higher expectations on what they taught, while requiring only the minimum from state-funded schools, which also exacerbated inequalities.

In 1979, Pinochet began to pursue education policy much more actively, launching his "Seven Modernizations" program in an attempt to change both the Chilean economy and society. This program aimed to strengthen the country by increasing privatization and competition. Pinochet's policies lauded nationalism and competitiveness and worked to institutionalize obedience (Austin 2003, 243). During the 1980s, education reform rose to the forefront of Pinochet's domestic agenda and was used as a tool to further implement his economic plans of liberalization and decentralization. A three-tiered university system that highly favored private institutions was developed. Market incentives were eventually used to stimulate demand for private schools even further (OECD and Centre for Co-operation with Non-members 2004, 107).

Education was also "municipalized" under Pinochet, beginning in 1980. The central-government appointed mayor of each town or city was in charge of appointing school administrators and teachers (Austin 2003, 238; Edholm 1982, 50, 53). The expectation was that having regionalized and private schools compete with public schools would improve quality in all schools. The result was that government spending on education decreased significantly and private spending on education became necessary. The universal access to education that had been developed under Frei Montalva and furthered under Allende was eroded by Pinochet's reforms, and the poor were largely excluded from education, particularly above the primary level (Oppenheim 1998, 152).

After a decade of a harsh political control and education policies that repeatedly eroded services for the poor and middle classes, underserved populations began to organize a resistance. During the 1980s, protests erupted over worsening social services, increased government oppression, and the disappearance of citizens of all social classes. Pinochet countered these protests with evermore violent repression. In turn, violent protests arose from the lower classes, particularly frustrated youths, who were being excluded from social services and education. Citizens of all ages became concerned with the rising level of violence. In 1986, several political parties, especially those of the center Left, organized the populace to vote against Pinochet in the upcoming plebiscite of 1988. The *Concertación para el No* movement unified the opposition and Pinochet was defeated. Competitive elections for the presidency and Congress were held in December of that year, and the *Concertación para el No* transformed into the *Concertación para la Democracia*.

The Current Education Policies and Policy Climate of Chile

The day after Pinochet's government ended, the democratic government that succeeded it began a series of major reforms aimed at reviving Chilean education and using it as a uniting force for a country emerging from 17 years of violence and oppression (OECD and Centre for Co-operation with Non-members 2004, 233). The *Concertación* government put special emphasis on educational reform as a way to combat the inequity and poverty that grew under Pinochet (Oppenheim 1998, 260). The cornerstone of the new strategy was a push to increase quality and equity throughout the educational system. The strategy focused significantly on increasing access to secondary schooling, especially in poor, rural areas. The Brunner Commission of 1994 worked to build political consensus for these reforms and to achieve continuous engagement from opposing parties throughout the process of reforms (OECD and Centre for Co-operation with Non-members 2004, 233). In 1996, President Eduardo Frei Ruiz-Tagle began a six-year education reform. Cox and Lemaitre (1999, 181) suggest that four conditions enabled the successful Chilean education reforms: (1) Political consensus about the need for changes; (2) political support at the highest level of the state; (3) sufficient financial resources to fund changes in the level of functioning systems; and, (4) a time horizon that was longer than the term of the government. The overlap of these conditions with mutual interest in building incrementally from the past led to an ongoing reform process. The political context of these reforms was an integral part of the reconciliation process, as the reforms themselves grew out of an enabling policy environment and led to several policies that help to mitigate conflict.

Several of Pinochet's education policies endured as part of the reforms of the 1990s, but they were modified significantly to expand education access and decrease systemic inequality. Policy reforms initiated by Pinochet—such as the decentralization of decisions regarding education funding, a mixed public and private financing system for primary and secondary schools, and a tiered public and private university system—continued under the *Concertación* government (Glenn and deGroof 2005, 124–126). These policies became successful at uniting the country, because they were modified creatively under democratic governments so that they generated wider-reaching benefits and did not just benefit the elite.

An important component of the reform process was increasing government spending on education. Public financing of education declined dramatically under Pinochet, and one commitment on the part of the *Concertación* government was to restore public funding and distribute it more equitably. Whereas under Pinochet, schools with the highest test scores got the most support (often leaving low-income schools with the least support), the new government sought to redistribute this money so that schools in poor and rural areas received the most support (Cox and Lemaitre 1999, 164).

The Ministry of Education also worked to change the culture of teaching (which had been traumatized by Pinochet) by developing a democratic atmosphere that would replace an environment of fear with a culture of professionalism and collegiality (OECD and Centre for Co-operation with Non-members 2004, 233). This new focus helped to revive the demoralized teaching force, improve a difficult political climate that surrounded schools, and gain their cooperation throughout the difficult reform process (Cox and Lemaitre 1999, 165). Several reforms were undertaken to improve pay and working conditions for teachers including changes to working conditions, salaries, and hours, as well as the development of teacher bonuses (Cox and Lemaitre 1999, 167).

In addition to improving the school experience for teachers, the Ministry of Education has emphasized improving the effectiveness and rigor as well as equity for students. The 1990 reforms focused on improving school quality (especially in low-performing schools), on extending the school day, and on improving teacher quality (OECD and Centre for Co-operation with Non-members 2004, 235). One particularly noteworthy program targeting school quality, the P-900 program, identified roughly 900 schools with the lowest national test scores each year and provided them with intervention, administrative support, and extra funding.

Education policies also targeted improvements in the areas of high school completion and early childhood education. In 2000, the High School for All (Liceos para Todos) program targeted schools with large concentrations of struggling (at-risk; poor?) students, predominantly in poor urban areas, and provided extra scholarship funding to students who were deemed at risk for dropping out. It also provided the schools with instructional support and help with designing programs to decrease dropouts (OECD and Centre for Co-operation with Non-members 2004, 104; Ruiz and Vergara 2005, 13–15). In 2001, the Junta Nacional de Jardines (JUNJI) helped expand early childhood education opportunities. The Chile Crece Contigo program was a hallmark initiative of the Bachelet presidency, creating an early child-care voucher for low-income mothers (Fort, et al. 2007, 3). The result of these and other initiatives is a growing public support system for education that regularly reevaluates existing requirements and coordinates public and private resources to target these needs.

Two aspects of this ongoing reform were specifically intended to address conflict. The first was directed at modern history instruction and curriculum. This component of the reform created a unit for tenth-year students to study and discuss recent historical events, including the coup that ended Allende's presidency, Pinochet's dictatorship, and the transition to democracy. When discussions over this course grew tense, the Ministry of Education again compromised between two opposing sides about how to present recent history and agreed to "present diverse historiographal positions to the students in order to prevent political conflict" (Magendzo and Toledo 2009, 452). The description and the content objectives for this unit of curriculum also extended the focus on avoidance of conflict. The purpose of this unit was to generate cohesion and national unity after a divisive political period (Magendzo and Toledo 2009, 448).

The second aspect of the reform was intended to address a larger dissatisfaction over the political marginalization of the indigenous population that was especially harsh during the Pinochet years (Austin 2003, 253). In 2008, President Bachelet made efforts to support indigenous education by establishing the National Academy for the Mapuche Language. In addition, the National Capacity-Building for Intercultural Conflict Prevention and Management Program was proposed between 2007 and 2009, in response to student protests. This program was recently funded by UNESCO, and has several key elements aimed at increasing the participation of indigenous students as well as providing them with more financial support for tertiary education. However, indigenous groups continue to press for more reforms to improve quality and services (Minority Rights Group International 2008, 1).

Evaluation of Recent Education Policies and Reforms

The prior and ongoing education reforms have been successful in uniting a previously divided political field on a contentious issue, and have also succeeded in creating widespread improvements to the education system at all levels. During this time, socioeconomic gaps in overall enrollments have shrunken, dropout rates have declined dramatically, achievement has improved, particularly in P-900 and rural schools, and spending on education has increased dramatically (Cox and Lemaitre 1999, 180; ECLAC 2009b, 121; OECD and Centre for Co-operation with Non-members 2004, 37, 59).

The OECD's external review of Chile's education system summarized the reforms by concluding that "for the past generation, Chile has acted systematically to improve student performance in school while greatly expanding access to secondary education. Since 1990, the principal strategies for achieving gains have been to focus on improving conditions in low-performing schools, to make high quality pedagogic materials available to all schools, to completely reform the K-12 curriculum, to raise teacher salaries substantially in order to make teaching a more desirable profession [that is] more attractive to 'better' secondary school graduates, and to move toward a longer school day for all children" (OECD and Centre for Co-operation with Non-members 2004, 265).

While the OECD (2004, 234) found that the reforms successfully eradicated some of the inequality that grew under Pinochet, yet there are still many sizable hurdles to overcome. Inequality remains a significant problem in the Chilean education system. Schools are highly stratified by income level across private and public school sectors. In addition to discrepancies in school quality, there are also large class-based differences in retention, completion, and attendance rates (OECD and Centre for Co-operation with Non-members 2004, 59). At the postsecondary level, even in cases when lower-income students are making academic headway and are potentially more qualified than their upper-income counterparts when they apply to university, they often do not enroll because the costs are prohibitive, in spite of government scholarships (OECD and Centre for Co-operation with Non-members 2004, 268).

While, in general, combating inequality has been a source of unification, recently many of the still marginalized have grown impatient. After the relatively stable 1990s, the mid-2000s saw growing dissatisfaction on the part of low- and middle-income students who argued that, despite efforts to increase access and equity, many of them were being shut out of top-quality universities because of tuition costs and unequal opportunities for preparation (Franklin 2006, 14). These students staged a protest in 2006 demanding financial support for university entrance-examination fees and tuition and for more input in indigenous instruction. President Bachelet's government responded by agreeing to spend US$60 million to help support students with testing, transportation, school repairs, and more food for poor schools (Xinhua News Agency 2006). Additionally, President Bachelet gave a televised address describing her support for education reforms and for the grassroots protest by students to advocate for their needs (Oppenheim 2007, 249–250; Rohter 2006, 3).

Despite President Bachelet's attempts to address student protests, their voices have grown louder under President Piñera. Student protests have become increasingly common in the Chilean political landscape once again.

Education is the source of the largest political protests since the ouster of Pinochet (BBC 2011, 1). Reforms promised to increase access for the less-affluent have not met the expectations of mobility and equal opportunity. Education continues to be highly stratified and both students and teachers want more reform (Wilson 2012, 1). As education is still seen as a primary policy lever to address mobility, and as a source of the county's inequality structure, it remains the most prominent site of tension. While some protests are peaceful, many have turned violent (Franklin 2011, 1). The nearly two-decades-long peace brokered with the help of education policy is at risk of coming undone.

Venezuela—Policies of Exclusion and Unrealized Reforms Contribute to Conflict

As in Chile, education in Venezuela was a source of political conflict and cooperation throughout the twentieth century. While not the only contributing factor, education policies and the debates surrounding them have been instrumental in preserving political power and undermining regime stability. During the economic prosperity and coordinated political harmony in Venezuela of the 1960s and the 1970s, broad education spending helped to promote cohesion. However, education reform was far from the political agenda, in contrast to the work that was done to improve education during the strong economic years of the *Concertación* government in Chile. As a result, the expansion and improvement of education were not on the ruling parties' agendas and, thus, education policy was largely neglected from the late 1960s to the 1980s, becoming a source of conflict as the economy faltered. Dissatisfaction with the distribution of education spending and inequality of access contributed to the political tensions that led to Chávez's ascension to power. In contrast to this period of neglect, education policy is a pillar of Chávez's Bolivarian regime. Despite the considerable attention and investment, education policy and the education-policy environment are not sources of political unity. Instead, exclusionary education policies currently contribute to political tensions that have, at times, led to violence and protest. While there have been notable efforts to expand education access, these moves are coupled with a deterioration of existing education structures, a lack of attention to larger organization and quality evaluation, and an increasingly ideologically motivated curriculum. These education policies contribute to the polarization of Venezuelan society along class and race lines and leave the country ripe for increased conflict.

Thus, Venezuela stands as a counterexample to Chile, as constructive education policy and policy climate never achieved a sufficient fit. While conflict was not present constantly, education was often implicated as conflicts arose. In times of relative calm, neglectful education policies that heightened inequality became a source of tension once the economic situation deteriorated. In other more hostile times, education was used as a tool of marginalization. In this case, the intentionality, the cooperation, and the development of mutually beneficial education policies seen in Chile have not been present in Venezuela. Even during the relative calm of the early Punto Fijo period, education policies perpetuated inequalities that would later spark the tension and conflict that ushered in Chávez. In Venezuela, education was used as a tool to either preserve inequality or increase the salience of class-based tensions. Rather than being used as a source of unity, it stood across time as a source of marginalization.

Historical Education Policies and Policy Context

Venezuela's burst of political modernization and push for a comprehensive national education plan came several decades after Chile's. Early after independence, education was mainly provided through private institutions affiliated with the Catholic Church, and was prohibitively expensive for most Venezuelans (Levine 1973, 32). The evolution of politics and education was closely tied to revenues provided by the growing global demand for oil, which expanded dramatically from the 1920s to the 1960s. Venezuela began a major campaign for education reform in the 1930s, which set the stage for a national power struggle over education. This pursuit of reform coincided with the rise to power of the *Acción Democrática* (AD), a party born out of the growing middle class, which held a strong commitment to expanding public education. Many of the party leaders were members of the Venezuelan Federation of Teachers and leaders in public education. These party members were committed to the idea of an *estado-docente* (educator-state), which held as one of its core tenets that education was an essential public function and should exclude religious content (Levine 1973, 32).

For the remainder of the 1930s, and into the 1940s, the AD aggressively pushed its commitment to the *estado-docente*, dramatically expanding public education spending and undermining the church's educational and political influence (Levine 1973, 70). Between 1945 and 1948 alone, the budget for education more than tripled (Levine 1973, 69), and the budget for secondary schools more than doubled (Levine 1973, 70).

The influence of the church in education experienced a resurgence during the dictatorship of Colonel Marcos Pérez Jiménez from 1948 to 1958, who came to power with heavy support from elites (Levine 1973, 94). His presidency came with widespread repression of the lower-income populations, creating a negative political climate. As a result of Pérez Jiménez's education policies, the expansion of public schools and funding for public education slowed significantly, allowing Catholic schools to regain lost ground relative to public schools. The populace grew disillusioned with Pérez Jiménez and his policies favoring the elites. In the face of violent repression from the Pérez Jiménez regime, the student groups joined with the major political parties, the AD, Comité de Organización Política Electoral Independiente (COPEI), the Unión Republicana Democrática (URD), and the Partido Comunista de Venezuela (PCV), to oust Pérez Jiménez (Levine 1973, 145–151).

Following Pérez Jiménez's dictatorship, Venezuela entered a time of relative political stability. The AD and COPEI created an enduring alliance, the pact of Punto Fijo, which ensured a peaceful, seemingly democratic political transition and lasted through the 1980s. The peace of a "pacted democracy" was strengthened by a burgeoning patronage system composed primarily of the upper and middle classes and benefited greatly from surging international oil prices (Ellner and Tinker-Salas 2007, 6). Despite their involvement in the ouster of Pérez Jiménez, the leftist parties, URD and PCV, were excluded from this agreement (Ellner and Tinker-Salas 2007, 9).

The one exception to the peace of the Punto Fijo period was a strong challenge from student groups in the 1960s. Leftist students, angered by the exclusion of the Left in the Punto Fijo agreement and influenced by the Cuban Revolution, clashed with AD president Rómulo Betancourt for much of the early and mid-1960s. After Betancourt began to curtail their civil liberties in response to their opposition, the students responded with violent protests. Betancourt responded with military intervention and universities and *liceos* (secondary schools) were closed. The school closures persisted until the next president, Raúl Leoni Otero, removed troops from university campuses in February of 1967. While some students pushed for a return to violence, others had become disinterested and student protests dissipated (Levine 1973, 204).

As the radicalization of student groups began to subside and tensions between political parties and the Catholic Church waned, Venezuela transitioned into a period of growth, development, and prosperity (Goodman, et al. 1995, 3–4). This economic boom was bolstered by increased corruption and the growing influence of the United States and its oil companies (Lander 2007, 21). During the 1970s, education policy and student activism no longer elicited a strong reaction in Venezuelan politics, and the country saw several democratic transitions among the different political parties. During the first years of democratic rule, access to public services, including education, expanded dramatically (Lander 2005, 25). Public and private school enrollments grew rapidly (Enright, Francés, and Saavedra 1996,

208). New schools opened around the country. Lower-income Venezuelans increasingly had access to primary and secondary education, while those in the middle class gained access to a university education, leading to increased social mobility (Lander 2005, 25).

Although oil money allowed for a vast expansion in education in the 1970s, true reform was lacking, and spending was disproportionately allocated to the politically connected. Growth and increasing oil prices were projected into the distant future, and the upper and middle classes saw no need to alter their desires for increased consumption to help support the lower classes because state income could finance increased services without relying on taxing the wealthy (Lander 2005, 25–26). As a result, political leaders did little to modify the structures of power and inequality that existed during the boom years (Lander 2007, 22). Despite the image of success and the reality of a vast expansion of education to serve a much larger percentage of the population, education quality remained unequal. While student access and funding grew, dropout rates surged, especially in schools serving low-income students. Poor teacher quality and high absenteeism led to inconsistent education in these new schools, and a significant portion of the education budget continued to be allocated to tertiary education, which was largely out of reach for lower-income students (Enright, Francés, and Saavedra 1996, 212).

The will for reform was nonexistent, and once oil income declined, the government's ability to spend broadly on education evaporated. The decrease in spending led to deteriorating quality for all but those with private funds to devote to education. As oil revenues declined in the 1980s, Venezuela faced a growing economic and political crisis. Within education, even as some called for reforms, the politically powerful resisted them (Albornoz 1993, 126).

In 1989, Carlos Andrés Pérez proposed education reforms and an antineoliberal platform during his campaign for a second term, which he claimed would restore the country to the heights of the 1970s. Once in office, he promptly changed course and undertook several neoliberal economic reforms, while ignoring education and other areas of need. In 1989, at the urging of the International Monetary Fund (IMF), Venezuela underwent "shock therapy," which significantly hurt the middle class and the poor (Burggraaff and Millett 1995, 59). As a result of the monetary reforms, many in the middle class usurped the social services previously designated for the poor while the government curtailed social spending (Del Bufalo 2005, 279–281), and the political environment grew tense.

In 1989, riots erupted in response to Carlos Andrés Pérez's IMF-styled austerity measures and rising transportation costs (Hurtig 2008, xiv). A series of extremely violent riots erupted from the poorest sectors of Caracas in February 1989 (the *Caracazo*) and shook the political structure. These riots shattered Venezuela's international image as a stable democracy (Ellner and Tinker-Salas 2007, 8). Public disapproval of Pérez was sizable and many felt that a military coup would occur if the situation did not improve (Grindle 2000, 74).

Due to receding government spending on education and other social services, the great majority of the population was excluded from access to benefits that they had expected to receive during the 1970s (Lander 2005, 27). While there were ample opportunities and resources to enact education policies that would further the expansion of the 1970s and improve education quality, no such policies were pursued. Instead, the increasingly limited state resources continued to be disproportionately allocated to the wealthy, and access to schooling contracted. During the 1990s, most other Latin American countries spent roughly half of what Venezuela did on tertiary education and at least four times what it spent on secondary education (Enright, Francés, and Saavedra 1996, 212). This pattern of funding greatly favored the wealthiest students to the point where, in the early 1990s, "a Venezuelan student who attend[ed] public schools from preschool through the end of the Diversified Cycle (high school) [would] end up receiving from the state less than half of the education subsidy received by a youth whose family paid for private schools and whose only participation in the public school system [was] five years at public university" (Enright, Francés, and Saavedra 1996, 212).

Lower- and middle-class frustration with the inequities of the education system became a source of tension during the 1990s. As the economic situation tightened, even those from the upper classes who attended universities began to feel the effect of cuts to education spending, which also caused political strife. There were regular student protests in several universities about cuts in education quality in early 1990s (Hurtig 2008, 85–86). Others around the country began to voice their opposition to the economic changes in the country. By 1992, tensions had reached a head. The military, led by Lt. Col. Hugo Chávez, staged a failed coup on February 4, 1992, followed by a November 27 uprising. Pérez was eventually forced out of power on charges of corruption in 1993.

After Pérez was removed from office, political power and resources were decentralized to the state and municipal level. While decentralization led to several innovations and improvements, education was not among the sectors that were reformed. President Rafael Caldera Rodríguez came to power in 1994, promising once again to end neoliberal reforms. Like Pérez, once in office, he also reversed course and embraced neoliberalism (Ellner and

Tinker-Salas 2007, 8). Caldera also sought to undo the decentralization of education begun by Pérez. However, he was unable to implement any reforms because support for the traditional political structure continued to fall, and the policy reversals he hoped to make were not realized. People felt that the government was still spending a substantial amount of money on education, but that it was careless in its spending and not at all effective in its delivery (Kelly 1995, 285). Specifically, education was seen as a sector that focused primarily on training professionals and the elite, neglecting the lower classes.

While economic crises shattered the economy, many began to question why government money continued to flow for the benefit of those who were already wealthy while the masses were suffering and experiencing a significant decline in service, quality, and coverage (Kelly 1995, 285). By the mid-1990s, Venezuela was characterized as "a country that should be rich, but is not; a country that has wealth that never gets to the people" (Kelly 1995, 285). Education policy was symptomatic of the more significant structural weaknesses plaguing the Venezuelan democracy, which pitted the classes against one another. Tensions between the upper and lower classes continued to build due to the perception that the wealthy were largely protected from the economic reforms, while middle- and lower-income Venezuelans bore the brunt of the adjustments. This, coupled with the inability of the existing political parties to enact reforms that truly reached all parts of the economic spectrum, contributed to widespread disenchantment with Venezuelan politics and an increasingly negative political climate in Venezuela.

Discontent with shrinking social spending and dwindling confidence in the existing political structure pervaded all levels of the social spectrum. The electorate had rejected the traditional political parties, and the electoral climate was ripe for dramatic change. In 1998, Hugo Chávez and his Movimiento Quinta República (MVR) won the presidential election with widespread support.

Venezuela's Current Education Policies and Policy Climate

Shortly after the election, Chávez began implementing several highly anticipated reforms. In December of 1999, he drafted a new constitution that was quickly approved, granting him widespread executive powers (Wilpert 2007, 19). Chávez was especially concerned with rectifying the quality of education for the poor, which had deteriorated in the 1980s and the 1990s; to do so, he increased education and social spending (ECLAC 2009a, 115–116). The government introduced a decree to improve educational standards at the end of 2000. Evaluators from the Ministry of Education inspected schools in order to improve these standards. This extended to the unregulated private school system, which had expanded as a result of declining public spending on education (Ellner and Hellinger 2003, 126).

After early reforms focused on school quality, Chávez redirected his attention to education policies targeting the underserved poor. However, rather than building consensus among political opponents and allies and improving the Ministry of Education, which was increasingly becoming a source of opposition, Chávez developed plans for a dramatic redesign of the education system, drawing heavily from his revolutionary ideology. His proposal was to create a new system of schools to quickly expand educational access outside of the existing public school system that would serve the poor and be guided by Bolivarian ideals. To fund this vast expansion of services, Chávez increased spending on education by funding his projects directly from state-owned enterprises, such as Petróleos de Venezuela, S.A. (PDVSA).

In 1999, the government began a trial run of the Bolivarian Schools. This trial later expanded to create a Bolivarian Schools system, starting first with primary and then moving to secondary schools. Its objectives were to raise the standards and variety of education, to mitigate the dropout problem, and to address malnutrition. The Bolivarian model emphasized cooperation and community in its curricula and universal access and egalitarianism in its organization. The goal of the Chávez government is to eventually convert all schools in Venezuela into Bolivarian Schools, including schools that were previously public schools under the Ministry of Education.

Despite the initial widespread support that Chávez enjoyed, it quickly became apparent that his reforms were much more drastic than anticipated and political tension increased (Wilpert 2007, 19, 22). The traditional elites and the middle class quickly aligned themselves in opposition to his policies, feeling that their interests were being threatened by his reforms (Wilpert 2007, 20–21). Many opposition members were concerned even early on with the changes the Chávez administration was making to the system, especially with the creation of the Bolivarian Schools. There were also growing political tensions about new laws in other sectors, but the discussions about reforms aimed at limiting the influence of private schools and the plans to eventually transform all schools into Bolivarian Schools were the primary sources of polarization of the political climate (Penfold-Becerra 2006, 15).

In early 2001, there were strikes and protests from concerned parents worried about indoctrination. Chávez confronted these parents and other opposition groups, including the Catholic Church and businesses. Strong opposition to Chávez's early education policies made education one of the key battlegrounds during the 2002 strike and lockouts (Cannon 2009, 136).

The *Economist* argued that concerns over changes to education policy were one of the primary causes of the 2002 attempted coup, saying that "the first time Hugo Chávez made a serious attempt to reshape the Venezuelan education system, the resulting political battle contributed to the coup that in 2002 briefly ousted him from the presidency" (*Economist* 2009, 3). As a result of the opposition, Chávez largely dropped his education agenda until he defeated the coup against him.

After the failed coup, Chávez became emboldened and, in addition to expanding resources on social policies in other areas, he devoted significant attention to education policy. However, rather than attempting to incorporate the views of the opposition, he worked strategically to dismantle their authority and influence (Wilpert 2007, 28). This era marked a change from a moderate period that was more focused on consolidating political support to a more radical time that became increasingly antineoliberal and was marked by confrontations with the opposition, which refused to recognize the legitimacy of the Chávez government (Cannon 2009, 79). A second strike in December of 2002 lasted for nearly two months and weakened the national economy. After the end of the strike, organizers next moved to create a referendum on the presidency. The process of organizing the referendum was slow, and in late 2003, following a general strike, Chávez created a plan to respond to the opposition (Penfold-Becerra 2006, 19).

The government responded to the opposition in several ways, including taking direct control over PDVSA and launching a new series of social spending programs that Chávez termed "Missions." The government launched seven missions in October 2003. While some of these programs were directed toward health and employment, four of the missions focused on an area of key importance to the opposition: education. With these missions, Chávez sought to create an education system parallel to the traditional private and public schools populated largely by the opposition. The stated aim of the missions in general, and the educational missions in particular, was to redistribute social services to low-income Venezuelans who were largely excluded from receiving services during the Punto Fijo government and to facilitate the Bolivarian transformation of the country. The big push for these programs began in 2003 when the state budget was increasing as the economy recovered from the oil workers' strike of late 2002 (Wilpert 2007, 121).

In addition to the stated goal of redistribution, the missions served several other political objectives. In targeting the poor with social spending, the missions fostered political support for Chávez. The missions also helped to marginalize the opposition, as some were prevented from receiving benefits. In addition, the missions aided in fostering the ideological mentality of the Bolivarian Revolution through the revolutionary education components of the programs (Hanoman and Hunn 2008, 88). Some argued that Chávez created the missions with the express purpose of educating people more sympathetic to the Bolivarian cause to staff the bureaucracies (Wilpert 2007, 121). As these educational projects took shape, Chávez increasingly described them as a key part of his socialist transformation of the country. Chávez called education one of the "five motors" of establishing twenty-first-century socialism.[2] Of the five, Chávez and his supporters most frequently highlighted education as their top priority (Wilpert 2007, 121).

Several of the missions focused on expansion of access. The first educational mission, Misión Robinson I, used the Cuban *Yo Sí Puedo* (Yes, I Can) method to teach basic literacy skills to Venezuelan adults and teens through an intensive seven-week course (Ortega and Rodríguez 2008, 6). Misión Robinson II was the successor to Misión Robinson I. Any graduates of the first program could automatically enroll to receive the equivalent of a primary school education through sixth grade in just two years. By 2004, the program had included more than 1.1 million people, nearly all those served by Misión Robinson I (Wilpert 2007, 121). Misión Ribas was launched with the goal of expanding secondary school access to the nearly five million Venezuelans who had dropped out of secondary school or had been previously excluded from attending due to economic conditions (Cannon 2009, 96). In addition to enrolling adults and teens who had previously attended traditional schools, Misión Ribas also targeted people who completed Misión Robinson II (Hanoman and Hunn 2008, 87).

To complement the primary and secondary missions, Chávez created the Bolivarian High Schools to address the dropout problem and prepare youth to be more effective upon entering the workforce. The emphasis in these schools was on relating the students' coursework to the real world through projects and participation in the community. The curriculum was based on more practical applications rather than a series of disciplinary-specific courses (Wilpert 2007, 126–127).

Three less well-known missions were also created to support students who had participated in either Misión Robinson or Misión Ribas with their transition into the workforce. Misión Robinson III was created to help students who had participated in other missions develop trade skills so they could find employment (Hanoman and Hunn 2008, 87). Misión Vuelvan Caras (Mission Turn Heads) was developed in 2004 to help graduates of the educational missions to find work (Cannon 2009, 94). Chávez also created a public preschool program known as Simoncito in 2005. One of main goals of this program was to provide universal preschool for all children. By 2004, about 1.38 million children (about one-third of the age group) were enrolled in public preschools as a result of this program (Wilpert 2007, 122).

Chávez's policies also targeted the tertiary education system. As part of Chávez's social investment campaign in 2003, he planned to open several Bolivarian Universities to help improve university admission rates for the poor, which were at only 19 percent in 1998. As with the other education missions and programs, two key goals of the Bolivarian Universities were to contribute to the political transformation of the Venezuelan state and to challenge the elitism of the traditional universities (Cannon 2009, 96; Griffiths 2009, 43).

Similar to the secondary school program from Misión Ribas, Misión Sucre was created to extend tertiary education to poor students who previously did not have access due to finances and admission requirements (Hanoman and Hunn 2008, 88). After a 2003 Ministry of Education census found that more than 500,000 Venezuelans met the requirements for university admission but were not admitted, this program sought to provide university access for these students. As part of the program, students were either entered in a university initiation program, in the Bolivarian University of Venezuela (UBV), in one of the regular public universities, or in a new "university village." By 2004, more than 90,000 students had joined the program and 40,000 of those were receiving scholarships (Penfold-Becerra 2006, 20).

Despite the expansion of access provided by several of the missions, many have been widely criticized for exaggerating their results and undermining instruction with ideology. The Misión Robinson programs were critiqued both for overstating their effects on literacy and their use as a political indoctrination tool (Ortega and Rodríguez 2008, 26–29). Critics of Misión Ribas argued that many of the facilitators were too inexperienced, were not certified teachers, and often did not know the material they were supposed to teach. The critics also cast doubt on the effectiveness of the program, which relied heavily on accompanying video material (Penfold-Becerra 2006, 19; Wilpert 2007, 127). Opponents argued that Misión Sucre expanded university enrollments beyond capacity because the government would not be able to accommodate 400,000 students who were to enter the university system as part of this mission (Wilpert 2007, 130–131). The nongovernmental organization Programa Venezolano de Educación-Acción en Derechos Humanos (PROVEA) argued that, like many other educational missions, Misión Sucre suffered from political patronage and from the creation of parallel state structures. In that vein, it often only benefited those who supported Chávez and expected the political and electoral support of its beneficiaries (Wilpert 2007, 131).

Recent education-policy efforts include moves to increase the ideological components of the curricular and school structures. In 2007, Chávez developed a new curriculum for all Venezuelan schools, public and private.

This curriculum focused on socialist ideology. Under these reforms, private schools were not outlawed, but had to adopt the new curriculum and could no longer have freedom over instructional content (*Economist* 2007, 4).

In 2009, Chávez again sought to add further changes to the education system. A new education law passed through Congress on the night of August 13, 2009, while opposition members and university rectors were teargassed as they approached parliament to try to oppose the law. This prompted some to argue that the law was passed too hastily without sufficient opportunity for debate (*Economist* 2009, 3). Under the new law, education was to be rooted in the Bolivarian ideals and supervised by communal councils. The central government seized control of all other aspects of the education system, including university admissions and membership in the teaching profession. The government said that the law would reverse centuries of exclusion, giving children of the poor equal access to education. On the other hand, critics argued that it would not address the key causes of inequality: low-quality teaching, buildings in disrepair, and widespread truancy in state schools. Opposition politicians, students, teachers, and parents hoped to gather signatures to repeal the law, while others argued that the law violated the constitution because it was signed too quickly. An opposition campaign grew, and although it remained mostly peaceful (*Economist* 2009, 3), some protests were met with police hostility (BBC 2009, 1).

Evaluation of Recent Education Policies and Reforms

The evidence that the education missions and the Bolivarian Schools improve education is mixed. In terms of improving access, the missions and Bolivarian Schools have helped to level enrollment across economic classes, in particular among the low income who were previously denied access. However, inequalities and systemic shortcomings persist. España (2008, 1) argues that the missions are not targeting the underlying systemic issues that caused the inequality in access to education, that they are merely a stopgap measure, and they are not as large and have not benefited as many people as claimed. Others find fault with overall quality, including employers who seem much less willing to employ those educated from the UBVs than those from the traditional universities (Gonzales and Oyelere 2009, 41).

Edwards (2010, 201) adopts a macro perspective to judge the success of Chávez's "Missions," concluding that while the missions aimed to improve the circumstances of the poor, they have not been effective. From a purely redistributive perspective, Edwards argues that social policies in several other Latin American countries, including Bolivia, Brazil, Costa Rica, Chile, El Salvador, Panama, and Paraguay, have been more successful at reducing poverty than Chávez's education and social policies in Venezuela. In each of these countries, redistribution policies account for more than half of the reduction in poverty in the 2002–2007 period, but in Venezuela, poverty has not been significantly reduced despite considerable government spending (Edwards 2010, 203).

While not necessarily successful at improving education outcomes, it is clear that the missions and other education programs succeeded in cementing political support for Chávez among the poor and have been used as a tool for marginalizing the opposition. Chávez gained political support against the 2004 referendum in part because of his massive expenditures on these projects (Edwards 2010, 198). Penfold-Becerra (2006, 26) argues that the timing of the launch of these projects was planned by Chávez to help him gain the support of the lower classes for the 2004 referendum. As Chávez has continued to expand his education agenda, he has selectively provided supporters with opportunities while further isolating opponents, often along economic lines (Kozameh 2008, 129–130).

While Chávez made numerous attempts to tightly control the education structure, tertiary education has been a source of conflict during his presidency, among both supporters and dissenters. Protests and conflicts emanated from both pro- and anti-Chávez student groups in the universities. Early on in Chávez's first term, there were multiple attempts to form a Bolivarian student movement, which consisted mainly of student takeovers of the rectors' offices at some of the state university campuses. In March 2001, a group of pro-Chávez students and employees took control of the meeting room of the University Council of the Central University of Venezuela, demanding the installation of a "university constituent assembly." The takeover lasted 34 days and was suspended once roundtable dialogues began in the different faculties (Norden 2003, 193). Students have also been active in opposing Chávez. In November 2007, in advance of the referendum to abolish term limits (allowing Chávez to stay in power) and overhaul the constitution, 80,000 university students marched in protest. These protesters were attacked by gunmen and the organizers received death threats for days after the march (Romero 2007, 3).

The future direction of the missions, the Bolivarian Schools, and Chávez's education policies remains uncertain. While the missions and Bolivarian Schools expanded quickly, growth slowed after the initial years (Wilpert 2007, 123). Funding remains tightly controlled by Chávez, but with the global economic crisis, budgets tightened, hurting all types of social spending, including education.

The situation remains tense, but highly uncertain as Chávez's health has deteriorated and as his second term comes to an end. As Venezuelans vote for a new president or six more years of Chávez, education remains a core policy platform. Many candidates have critiqued Chávez for prioritizing ideology over concrete improvements in access and quality (Radzischewski 2011, 13). Education policy will surely be relevant in the upcoming political conversation and possible transition.

Conclusions

Chile and Venezuela's historical and recent education policies demonstrate the prominent role that education plays in national policy agendas. Likewise, these cases demonstrate that somewhat similar policies can be met with vastly different responses when inserted into different policy climates. The contrasting historical and contemporary experiences underscore the myriad ways in which education functions as both a policy tool and a political climate setter.

Policy and context are both important in leading to peaceful, successful education outcomes, and both must work to support, rather than hinder, cooperation and improvement. The contrast of these cases underscores the need for policy-context fit. The examples drawn from both cases highlight the importance of this fit, but do so in different ways because of their dramatically different approaches to education policy as it relates to inequality and mobility, particularly in recent decades.

The Chilean case illustrates two important components of education policy that are relevant to reducing the likelihood of conflict. First, the historical Chilean case is instructive because of the multiple transformations of the education-policy climate over time and the drastic impact that each climate had on creating or preventing conflict. In the middle of the twentieth century, education-policy reform existed in a political climate that was receptive to change and thus the expansion and quality evaluations of Allesandri and Frei Montalva were met with little resistance. Even though Allende planned to pursue an agenda of expansion, the policy climate surrounding education soured due to fears over the ideological shift that Allende advocated, contributing to his violent removal. Likewise, after years of repression and exclusion under Pinochet, the policy environment continued to be hostile and protests from the lower classes ensued. In contrast to the tense political contexts during the Allende and Pinochet years, education policy under renewed democratic rule allowed education-policy reforms to be a source of unity rather than conflict. The mixed private-public school system forcefully orchestrated by Pinochet became a starting place for the *Concertación* government, which used compromise to build a stronger education system dedicated to redressing the inequities of Pinochet's system. The cooperative nature of the education-policy environment in Chile has been essential to the types of restorative education policies pursued in the past two decades. The ability of the government to draw in opposing political parties, teachers, families, and students to create a cooperative-policy context is every bit as important to preventing education-related conflict as the policies themselves.

Second, the recent Chilean education policies attempted to address conflict directly and to improve structural elements of the education system that were previously the source of conflict. Policies such as the high school social studies curriculum that addresses historical conflicts in the transitions from Allende to Pinochet to democracy serve as a tool for engaging with Chile's past while working toward reconciliation. Other policies such as the Mapuche bilingual program and the intercultural conflict-prevention program also target specific areas of ongoing disagreement with the goal of creating a peaceful resolution. Further, the aggressive way in which the Ministry of Education attempted to increase access to education at all levels, especially for the poor, has helped decrease the need for protests about the lack of educational opportunities, such as those that occurred at the end of Pinochet's presidency. Likewise, the intentional commitment to measuring progress and improving instructional quality has benefited poor and rich students alike, making education spending less of a zero-sum policy issue. These policies still fall short in many ways, but while education policies aimed to prevent conflict, decrease educational inequality, and improve educational quality for all Chilean children remained at the core of Chilean education policy, Chile moved away from conflict and toward reconciliation. In short, post-Pinochet, Chile succeeded in creating a fit between a constructive policy and the larger policy environment.

The Venezuelan conflicts provide multiple examples of why education policies and political contexts must fit together in order to mitigate conflict. The Punto Fijo period demonstrates that surface-level calm can mask the ways in which obstructive education policy, which increases inequality while appearing to support mobility, can set the stage for future conflict. The early Chávez years demonstrate that even policies that initially appear to support the goals of reducing inequality and expanding access, when implemented in a hostile context that has not gained widespread cooperation, can heighten tensions. Most notably, the years under Carlos Andrés Pérez and the later Chávez period demonstrate how ideologically driven, antagonistic education policies implemented in a contentious, suspicious climate are especially potent situations for promoting conflict. While the Chávez period never saw the levels of outright public violence that characterized Pérez's presidency, political conflict was strong, and random violence in Venezuela increased.

Both time periods are particularly emblematic of the conflicts that can arise when antagonistic education policies meet discordant political climates, also underscoring the need for policy-environment fit.

Both cases also offer suggestions about the ways in which the fit between the policy and the political climate will continue to be necessary to prevent future conflicts from arising. While it seemed that Chile was moving toward an evermore stable and peaceful political future, thanks in part to the use of education policy to tackle political and economic inequities and reshape the political environment, the calm did not last. Disappointment with unfulfilled expectations and persistent inequality are disrupting the previously cooperative political climate. Even as constructive policies of expansion and inclusion continue, many see them as inadequate and are increasingly demanding additional action. As Chile continues to struggle with this latest challenge, it will be important to draw from past experience. The key will be to redevelop a constructive-policy context by drawing the protesters into the political decision making and to develop ways for their objectives to be incorporated into the larger national discourse.

Venezuela is also entering a period of political uncertainty as a new presidential election nears. Many presidential hopefuls, along with the larger society, find that Chávez's educational policies were insufficient if not misguided. Whether or not Chávez is reelected, education will be an important issue moving forward, as many still view education as the primary vehicle for mobility and feel left behind in the current economic climate. What will determine whether education arises as an arena for future conflict is whether policy reforms are directed to widespread improvements, *and* a context that invites *Chavistas* and anti-*Chavistas* into a dialogue and convinces them of their mutual interest in pursuing such reforms.

The current education policies and policy contexts in Chile and Venezuela are a product of complicated histories. Both have had periods of constructive and obstructive education policies and policy climates. In both cases, education policy is but one of many causes and outcomes of elaborate political agendas. However, this comparison highlights why, for education to contribute to peace rather than conflict, policymakers must be conscious of the policies they pursue and those they neglect as well as the policy contexts, constantly striving for a fit while promoting mobility rather than inequality.

Notes

1. Chile's popular education movement also benefited heavily from the work of Brazilian Paolo Freire, educator and scholar between 1965 and 1969. He

contributed significantly to adult education programs and to the National Literacy Campaign, which worked to end illiteracy in the country, especially among the poor. His work and writings, most notably his 1968 *Pedagogy of the Oppressed*, inspired both domestic education policy and similar campaigns throughout the region (Austin 2003, 74).

2. The first motor was the "enabling" law that allowed Chávez to pass laws by decree for an 18-month period, the second was a constitutional reform, the third focused on "morals and enlightenment," and changed the educational system to promote socialist values, the fourth motor created a "the new geometry of power" and reconfigured state power, and the fifth motor expanded the role of communal councils in the participatory democracy system.

References

Albornoz, O. 1993. *Education and society in Latin America.* Pittsburgh: University of Pittsburgh Press.

Austin, R. 2003. *The state, literacy, and popular education in Chile, 1964–1990.* Lanham, MD: Lexington Books.

BBC News. 2009. Venezuelan clash over education. *BBC,* August 14, sec. Americas. http://news.bbc.co.uk/2/hi/8200828.stm.

BBC News. 2011. New clashes at Chile mass protest. October 19, sec. Latin America & Caribbean. http://www.bbc.co.uk/news/world-latin-america-15379672.

Burggraaff, W., and R. Millett. 1995. More than failed coups: The crisis in Venezuelan civil-military relations. In *Lessons of the Venezuelan experience,* edited by Louis W. Goodman, Johanna Mendelson-Forman, Moises Naim, and Joseph S. Tulchin, 54–78. Washington DC, Baltimore, and London: The Woodrow Wilson Center Press and The Johns Hopkins University Press.

Cannon, B. 2009. *Hugo Chávez and the Bolivarian revolution: Populism and democracy in a globalised age.* Manchester: Manchester University Press.

Cox, C., and M. J. Lemaitre. 1999. Market and state principles of reform in Chilean education: Policies and results. In *Chile: Recent policy lessons and emerging challenges,* edited by Danny M. Leipziger and Guillermo E. Perry, 149–188. Washington, DC: World Bank.

Davies, L. 2004. *Education and conflict: Complexity and chaos.* London and New York: Routledge Falmer.

Del Bufalo, E. 2005. Venezuela: From stability to turmoil. In *Political crises, social conflict and economic development: The political economy of the Andean Region,* edited by Andres Solimano, 263–321. Cheltenham, UK: Edward Elgar Publishers.

———. 2009a. *Social panorama of Latin America 2009.* Santiago, Chile: United Nations.

———. 2009b. *Statistical yearbook for Latin America and the Caribbean.* New York: United Nations.

Economist. 2007. Education in Venezuela: Fatherland, socialism or death, October 13.

———. 2009. Venezuela's education "reforms": Hugo Chavez seeks to catch them young, August 22.
Edholm, F. 1982. *Education and repression: Chile*. London: World University Service.
Edwards, S. 2010. *Left behind: Latin America and the false promise of populism*. Chicago: University of Chicago Press.
Ellner, S., and D. Hellinger. 2003. *Venezuelan politics in the Chavez era*. Boulder, CO: Lynne Rienner Publishers.
Ellner, S., and M. Tinker-Salas. 2007. The Venezuelan exceptionalism thesis: Separating myth from reality. In *Venezuela: Hugo Chávez and the decline of an "exceptional democracy,"* edited by E. Ellner and M. Tinker-Salas, 3–15. Lanham, MD: Rowman and Littlefield.
Enright, M. J., A. Francés, and E. S. Saavedra. 1996. *Venezuela, the challenge of competitiveness*. New York: Palgrave Macmillan.
España, L. P. 2008. The social policy of the Bolivarian revolution. *ReVista Harvard Review of Latin America*, Fall 2008. http://www.drclas.harvard.edu/revista/articles/view/1124.
Farrell, J. P. 1986. *The national unified school in Allende's Chile: The role of education in the destruction of a revolution*. Vancouver: University of British Columbia Press.
Fort, L., I. John-Abraham, M. B. Orlando, and C. Piras. 2007. *Chile: Reconciling the gender paradox*. en breve. World Bank, April. http://siteresources.worldbank.org/INTENBREVE/Newsletters/21455235/Apr07_105_GenderChile_EN.pdf.
Franklin, J. 2006. Protests paralyse Chile's education system. *The Guardian*, June 7, sec. Main.
———. 2011. Chile student protests explode into violence. *The Guardian*, August 5, sec. World news.
Freeburger, A. R., and C. C. Hauch. 1964. *Education in Chile*. Washington, DC: United States Department of Health, Education, and Welfare, Office of Education.
Glenn, C. L., and J. de Groof. 2005. *Balancing freedom, autonomy and accountability in education*. Nijmegen, The Netherlands: Wolf Legal Publishers.
Gonzales, N., and R. U. Oyelere. 2009. Are returns to education on the decline in Venezuela and does Missión Sucre have a role to play? IZA Discussion Papers.
Goodman, L. W., J. Mendelson-Forman, M. Naim, J. S. Tulchin, and G. Bland. 1995. *Lessons of the Venezuelan experience*. Washington DC: Woodrow Wilson Center Press.
Griffiths, T. G. 2009. Schooling for twenty-first-century socialism: Venezuela's Bolivarian project. *Compare: A Journal of Comparative and International Education* 1: 1–16.
Grindle, M. S. 2000. *Audacious reforms: Institutional invention and democracy in Latin America*. Baltimore: Johns Hopkins University Press.
Hanoman, J., and L. M. Hunn. 2008. The adult education social missions in Venezuela: An instrument for participatory democracy? Proceedings of the

Conference *Negotiating Cultural Values in a Learning Environment*, 86–91. Western Kentucky University, October 2. http://www.wku.edu/aded/MWR2P/MWR2P%20Proceedings2008.pdf.

Hurtig, J. 2008. *Coming of age in times of crisis: Youth, schooling, and patriarchy in a Venezuelan town*. New York: Palgrave Macmillan.

Kelly, J. 1995. The question of inefficiency and inequality: Social policy in Venezuela. In *Lessons of the Venezuelan experience*, edited by Louis W. Goodman, Johanna Mendelson-Forman, Moises Naim, and Joseph S. Tulchin, 283–310. Washington DC: Woodrow Wilson Center Press.

Kozameh, S. J. 2008. The misiones Bolivarianas: A study of participatory democracy in Venezuela. Masters thesis, University of California, San Diego.

Lander, E. 2005. Venezuelan social conflict in a global context. *Latin American Perspectives* 32(2): 20–38.

———. 2007. Venezuelan social conflict in a global context. In *Venezuela: Hugo Chavez and the decline of an "exceptional democracy,"* edited by E. Ellner and M. Tinker-Salas, 16–32. Lanham, MD: Rowman and Littlefield.

Leach, F., and M. Dunne. 2007. *Education, conflict and reconciliation: International perspectives*. Oxford: P. Lang.

Levine, D. H. 1973. *Conflict and political change in Venezuela*. Princeton, NJ: Princeton University Press.

Magendzo, A., and M. I. Toledo. 2009. Moral dilemmas in teaching recent history related to the violation of human rights in Chile. *Journal of Moral Education* 38(4): 445–465.

Minority Rights Group International. 2008. *World directory of minorities and indigenous peoples—Chile: Mapuche*. http://www.unhcr.org/refworld/country,,,,CHL,,49749d3e32,0.html.

Norden, D. 2003. Democracy in uniform: Chávez and the Venezuelan armed forces. In *Venezuelan politics in the Chávez era: Class, polarization & conflict*, edited by S. Ellner and D. Hellinger, 93–112. Boulder, CO: Lynne Rienner Publishers.

Oppenheim, L. H. 1998. *Politics in Chile: Democracy, authoritarianism, and the search for development*. Boulder, CO: Westview Press.

———. 2007. *Politics in Chile: Socialism, authoritarianism, and market democracy*. Boulder, CO: Westview Press.

Organization for Economic Co-Operation and Development (OECD), and Centre for Co-operation with Non-members. 2004. *Reviews of national policies for education: Chile*. Paris, France: Centre for Co-operation with Non-members.

Ortega, D., and F. Rodríguez. 2008. Freed from illiteracy? A closer look at Venezuela's Misión Robinson Literacy Campaign. *Economic Development and Cultural Change* 57: 1–30.

Penfold-Becerra, M. 2006. Clientelism and social funds: Empirical evidence from Chávez's "Misiones" programs in Venezuela. World Bank Conference on Inequality, Politics and Power. Washington DC: World Bank, June 5–6.

Radzischewski, A. 2011. Rap President on crime, jobs and education. *The Washington Times*, November 16, sec. World.

Roberts-Schweitzer, E., V. Greaney, and K. Duer. 2006. *Promoting social cohesion through education: Case studies and tools for using textbooks and curricula.* Washington DC: World Bank.
Rohter, Larry. 2006. Visit to U.U. isn't a first for Chile's first female president. *The New York Times,* June 8, sec. Foreign Desk.
Romero, Simon. 2007. Students emerge as leading force against Chavez. *The New York Times,* November 10, sec. Foreign Desk.
Ruiz, C., and M. Vergara. 2005. *Sistematización de la política Chilena: Programa liceo para todos y su línea planes de acción: Informe Final.* Santiago, Chile: MERCOSUR, June. http://www.porlainclusion.educ.ar/documentos/Chile.pdf.
Schiefelbein, E., and R. G. Davis. 1974. *Development of educational planning models and application in the Chilean school reform.* Lexington, MA: Lexington Books.
Spencer, D. E., and United States National Student Association. 1965. *Student politics in Latin America.* Philadelphia: United States National Student Association.
Tawil, S., and A. Harley. 2004. Education and identity-based conflict: Assessing curriculum policy for social and civic reconstruction. In *Education, conflict, and social cohesion,* edited by Sobhi Tawil and Alexandra Harley, 1–36. Geneva, Switzerland: UNESCO International Bureau of Education.
Vivallo Jara, R. 1978. Education in Chile under the Allende government. Dissertation, Philadelphia, PA: Temple University.
Wilpert, G. 2007. *Changing Venezuela by taking power: The history and policies of the Chavez government.* London: Verso Books.
Wilson, W. M. 2012. Student protests rile Chile. *The New York Times,* January 28, sec. Opinion / Sunday Review. http://www.nytimes.com/2012/01/29/opinion/sunday/student-protests-rile-chile.html.
Xinhua News Agency. 2006. Chile to spend 60 mln U.S. dollars to solve education conflict. *Xinhua,* June 3. http://findarticles.com/p/news-articles/xinhua-news-agency-ceis/mi_8007/is_20060603/chile-spend-60-mln-dollars/ai_n41628113/.

CHAPTER 8

Economic Exclusion and the Shifting Patterns of Violence in Argentina and Brazil

Peter Kingstone

As of 2012, the prospects for democracy[1] and peace in Latin America remain uncertain. Some countries suffer from serious political conflicts that threaten the integrity of the state and/or the regime. Mexico's vicious drug war, Ecuador and Bolivia's precarious balancing of procedural democratic forms with growing indigenous mobilization, Colombia's virtual civil war, and Venezuela's toxic polarization all stand as critical examples of the region's democratic frailties. By contrast, Argentina and Brazil stand out as relatively positive cases of democracy and political stability, despite appearing earlier as among the least likely to succeed in the third wave of democratization. Disastrous economic performance and incompetent governance into the early 1990s raised doubts about the longevity of their respective democratic experiments and the possibility of containing political violence. Yet, as of 2012, the two countries are among the more stable in the region, with Brazil tagged as a rising global power.

The relatively recent *comparative* good news, however, can distract attention away from the persistence of violence in both countries and their links to violent, unstable histories. This chapter considers the history and ongoing presence of violence by examining three contrasting patterns in the two countries. First, Argentina and Brazil present contrasting patterns of political violence in the twentieth century in the context of industrial development under import substitution industrialization (ISI). Both countries ended up under military rule for much of the period from the 1960s and the 1980s. Argentina's military rule came in the wake of what Guillermo O'Donnell referred to as an 'impossible game" in which the country witnessed repeated wild swings in politics within a deeply divided and mobilized polity (O'Donnell 1973). Ultimately, military rule in Argentina brought brutal levels of repression before its end in 1983. By contrast, Brazil's military coup in 1964 represented more of a break with the past. Politics in the period before the coup had its share of conflicts and episodes of violence, but did not seem inevitable in the way it had in Argentina (Stepan 1978). Similarly, Brazilian military rule was a much softer version than in most of the region, with more limited repression and important mechanisms of expression for opposition during much of the period leading up to the restoration of democracy in 1985. This first pattern raises the question of why violent politics emerged in both countries around the time of ISI as well as why authoritarian rule in Argentina proved much more violent than authoritarianism in Brazil.

The second pattern examines new patterns of social violence that emerged since redemocratization in the 1980s (1983 and 1985 respectively). Both countries have struggled with serious economic problems—notably inflation—and the challenge of implementing market-oriented policy reforms. In both countries, one important corollary of these reforms was a marked increase in violent crime. Violent crime has become one of the most salient and pressing priorities in all of Latin America (see the review by Bergman 2006). In Brazil in particular, the scale of violence has reached dramatic proportions and has been coupled with a pronounced sense of frustration about government unwillingness or inability to respond (Pereira 2008). The very week that Brazil celebrated winning its bid to hold the 2016 Olympic Games in Rio de Janeiro, criminal gangs went to war with the police, actually shooting down a police helicopter in the process. While crime rates are lower in Argentina, public concern is even higher—a national preoccupation with *inseguridad* (Seri 2012). And in both countries, rising crime has triggered police violence in response, backed by strong public tolerance of killings and beatings of "marginals' as well as judicial indifference to laws on the books against police brutality (Brinks 2006). Despite the decline of the threat of *political* violence, street crime represents a different kind of violence afflicting these countries. Thus, the second pattern raises the question of what has happened since the mid-1980s to provoke a rapid increase in the rate of violent crime.[2]

The final contrast is the difference in the rate of violent crime in the two countries, despite common levels of concern in the population. The actual level of violent crime has risen in Argentina, but in the aggregate still compares with countries like the United States. By contrast, Brazil's violent crime rate ranks among the highest in Latin America. Furthermore, while Brazil's violence is almost entirely *apolitical*, Argentina continues to suffer from episodes of politically motivated and organized violence. The second contrast refers to common changes in both countries in the period of neoliberalism and democratization, yet the third contrast points to very marked differences between them. Thus, the third pattern raises the question of why such different rates and types of violence occur despite a similar trajectory of rising violence in both countries.

In her chapter on Mexico, Judith Teichman notes the central role of inequality and exclusion in driving violence, citing Johan Galtung's notion of "structural violence" (Galtung 1969; see Teichman, this volume). Structural violence refers to a condition of physical and psychological harm that stems from the fundamental inequities and inequalities that arise from state policies, actions, and inactions—the set of state policies that limit humans living lives to their full potential. While Mexico's patterns of conflict exhibit important differences with Argentina and Brazil, the central underlying argument of this chapter is similar: at root, violence in both countries reflects the social inequities that stem from exclusionary models of development and the inability of the state to mediate the tensions that arise from them. In the earlier period, ISI gave rise to new social groups with demands for participation in both the political and economic benefits of society. Neither country was able to find a successful formula for mediating the resulting conflicts. In the contemporary period, the conflicts over economic policy direction have diminished greatly. But the shift to a more market-oriented economy has been accompanied by tremendous dislocation and weakening of support for the poor and vulnerable provided by the state. This has particularly hit young men hard, and criminality has risen in both countries in direct relation to the breakdown of economic opportunity and state-protection mechanisms. Ultimately, resolving the violence of the contemporary period will require a basket of policies that address the sources of deep, systematic inequities that stem from the structural violence of economic exclusion and state inadequacy.

A History of Violence

In both Argentina and Brazil, early periods of "democracy" displayed the forms of democratic procedure, but lacked any real substance. Thus, by the late nineteenth century, Argentina featured presidential elections and the beginnings of professional political parties along with a new integration of the country with the international economy. Yet in reality, Buenos Aires–based cattle oligarchs controlled politics and organized economic policy and development around their own commercial interests. Similarly, in Brazil, "empire" gave way to the "Republic of Coffee and Milk." But the forms of electoral democracy concealed the reality of a narrow coalition of oligarchs from the states of São Paulo (coffee), Rio Grande do Sul (milk), in addition to the state of Minas Gerais (Collier and Collier 1991). As in Argentina, the dominant landed classes followed economic policies designed to further their own export interests. In both countries, foreign capital was invited in to develop key areas of the infrastructure—particularly railroads and ports. Thus, in both countries, early development favored landed interests over urban ones, and only certain rural elites at that. The political system, in turn, was manipulated to maintain limited oligarchic control.

In both countries, this "republican" period ushered in rapid economic and population growth as success drew millions of immigrants. In turn, growth led to the emergence of larger urban sectors, including both an industrial working class and a diffuse middle class composed of a variety of activities including professionals, urban economic elites in commerce, finance and insurance, and small-scale domestic industrialists, as well as shopkeepers and artisans. The new sectors demanded increased political inclusion as well as a reorientation of economic policy in favor of the rising urban sector. In both countries, these challenges—what David and Ruth Collier refer to as the "Social Question"—forced the first tentative steps toward more substantive democracy (Collier and Collier 1991). Ultimately, the political "incorporation" of these emerging classes involved the creation of new political parties and the introduction of economic policies that fostered urban, industrial expansion. Despite some notable achievements, neither country was able to permanently settle the tensions between the emergent urban sectors and the landed elites, and both witnessed recurring struggles, violence, and ultimately the failure of democratic rule.

While the overall trend was similar in both countries, the two processes varied in ways that led to different experiences with authoritarianism. In Argentina, highly polarized politics led to ongoing regime instability as neither democratic nor authoritarian regimes could stabilize for even modest periods of time. Furthermore, the intensity of the polarization produced one of the most brutal and violent authoritarian episodes in Latin American history. By contrast, Brazil's democratic experiment lasted from 1945 to 1964 and the subsequent military dictatorship lasted until 1985. Moreover, the Brazilian experience was so much less violent that the military actually permitted quasi-competitive elections from the early 1970s on. In fact, defections in the electoral college in 1984 from members of the military party, ARENA (Aliança Renovadora Nacional—National Renewal Alliance Party), led to the election of a civilian candidate and as a result the somewhat unexpected and unplanned restoration of democracy. The following section reviews the key dynamics in the emergence of the "Social Question" to better understand both the common sources of conflict and violence as well as the very distinct differences between the two countries.[3]

Argentina

Competitive politics began in earnest in Argentina with the creation of the secret ballot in 1912 under President Roque Saenz Peña. The move was intended to induce middle-class cooperation with the leading oligarchs (dubbed the "Generation of 1880"), but instead, it backfired by opening political space for a rival political party, the Radical Civic Union (UCR). The Generation of 1880 oversaw a period of extraordinary economic expansion as the country overcame earlier postindependence conflicts over the status of Buenos Aires. By 1880, the issue was settled and cattle oligarchs had strong interests in strengthening the connection to the global economy. Beef exports fueled a rocketing pace of economic growth, with accompanying changes to society, including enormous increases in immigration that produced a roughly 800 percent increase in the population of Buenos Aires by 1914, with concomitant expansions of the urban middle and working classes (Collier and Collier 1991).

The political system was a contradiction, however. The forms of republican government coupled with a commitment to liberal European values of open expression and freedom of association stood in contrast to the controlled political process, electoral fraud, and overt repression the Generation of 1880 relied on to preserve their rule. The system faced a variety of political discontents. For one, it politically excluded some economically successful oligarchs in the provinces as well as others who suffered economically due to limited infrastructure investments and skewed internal transport pricing that made interior travel more expensive than overseas commerce. These rival oligarchs combined with rising working and middle classes presented a formidable challenge to the regime's manipulations.

In 1912, President Roque Saenz Peña of the ruling Partido Autonomista Nacional (National Autonomist Party) passed a secret ballot law in the hopes that they could co-opt the rising middle class against both oligarchic rivals and the increasingly radicalized working class (Smith 2005, 55–56). Instead, the new law undermined coercive tactics to control the vote and allowed the UCR to gain control of the presidency in the elections of 1916. But electoral victory simply presented new challenges for the regime. In short, the UCR's electoral coalition was skillfully stitched together by the charismatic leadership of its leader, President Hipólito Yrigoyen, but governing required him to find a balance among its diverse members. This included middle classes united in pushing for greater political rights with many also pushing for urban-oriented, industrializing policies[4]; an increasingly powerful industrial working class pushing for improved working conditions, wages, and collective bargaining rights; and "outsider" oligarchs looking to maintain the status quo, but with a seat at the table for themselves (Skidmore, Smith, and Green 2009, 81).

This dynamic left Argentine politics sharply polarized. On one hand, landed interests opposed both democratizing reforms that would grant greater voice to the middle class and especially workers, as well as economic policies that would promote urban industrial expansion over landed, free-trading interests. Although the Generation of 1880 policies sharply discriminated against "outsider" oligarchs, siding together against labor was a more palatable choice than combining with middle- and working-class challengers to the status quo (Collier and Collier 1991). On the other side, middle-class interests pushed for democratizing reforms—at least for themselves—and expanded government involvement in the economy. Finally, workers drew on European socialist, communist, and syndicalist ideas while demanding improvement on "bread and butter" issues as well as formal recognition of organizing and collective bargaining rights.

The intensity of the political conflicts increased as a result of the character of the economy and the related structural power of different groups in society. In particular, a critical source of intense political conflict flowed from the country's extraordinary dependence on beef exports. Beef production relied on cowboys, not peasants. Oligarchs were able to tolerate democracy in a number of Latin American countries by manipulating the peasant vote. But, the absence of a peasantry meant that democracy was singularly threatening to the country's economically powerful landed interests as it offered no meaningful political base to compete. Beef dependence further heightened the intensity of the conflict by exaggerating the structural power of labor. The concentration of labor in key areas, such as ports and even more notably railroads, made it possible for workers to exercise a stranglehold on the movement and processing of the country's most vital commodity. Labor protest, as a result, was deeply threatening politically and economically.

Between 1916 and 1945, successive Argentine leaders tried, without success, to navigate a course among these diverse and highly conflictive interests. The period was characterized by continuous outbreaks of violence: strikes and demonstrations, riots, violent counterdemonstrations and repression, as well as short-lived periods of direct military rule. In effect, no leader succeeded in finding a political formula or economic program that satisfied a large enough coalition to establish a stable rule. At the heart of the struggle was a seemingly intractable economic problem: urban interests largely preferred policies that promoted industrialization; increased government presence in the economy; and growing wages, benefits, and labor rights for both middle- and working-class groups. But, such policies depended on the export earnings of landed elites and their allied interests—all of whom resisted a growing role for government and urban-oriented economic policies. Thus, Argentine politics swung violently between democratizing steps and authoritarian regression, and on economic policy between free trade and domestic, urban industrializing policies.

The rise of General Juan Perón transformed Argentine politics, but ultimately did not alter its volatile and violent polarized pattern—indeed it exacerbated it. Perón, in concert with his wife Eva, forged an intense bond with the working class and the poor of Argentina. His efforts as labor minister from 1941 to 1945 helped unify the working class into a single labor central, the CGT (Confederación General del Trabajo—General Labor Confederation), and his party, the Partido Justicialista (PJ), established an electoral vehicle for working-class and poor voters. But the increasing organizational capacity, political mobilization, and labor and social rights sharpened conservative antagonism and forged an intense hatred of Perón and his party. Oddly enough, Perón was the only president of Argentina able to maintain the political support of the working class while implementing policies that favored exporters—something he did in 1949 in the face of rising inflation and balance of payment difficulties. Yet Perón's economic-policy reforms in favor of conservatives did not resolve the political opposition, and ultimately Perón was forced into exile in a coup in 1954.

From 1955 on, Argentina experienced the "Impossible Game" (O'Donnell 1973). On the one hand, no government was able to win office without the support of the working class. The working class, in turn, was not willing to offer support without the participation of the "Peronist" Party or some proxy. On the other hand, conservative interests and their allies in the military were not willing to permit Peronists or any obvious proxy for them to hold elected office or participate in elections. Governments that sought office through side-agreements with Peronists invited military intervention, even if economic policy was tailored to suit landed interests. Governments that sought to rule without the PJ faced aggressive labor protest, even in the face of policies designed to suit labor. For example, between 1967 and 1972, Argentina was rocked by roughly 70 major riots and demonstrations—double the number under the period of Peronist rule (Lewis 1990, 258). This fundamental tension played out through military rule from 1966 to

1973. Unable to see an alternative, the military permitted the return of the aged and feeble General Perón, who stood for election, won, and promptly passed away, leaving the presidency in the hands of his third wife, Isabel.

By 1976, polarization in Argentina had reached an extreme. The 1973 Organization of Petroleum Exporting Countries' oil shock profoundly shook the Argentine economy, with inflation rising rapidly and commodity exports falling at the same time. The PJ under Isabel lost the capacity to manage the organized working class and a violent left-wing movement, the Montoneros, emerged out of it. Middle-class support evaporated in the face of economic chaos, social violence, and increasingly obvious signs of Isabel's incompetence. The 1976 coup that brought the military back to power was a highly anticipated and widely welcomed event. What followed, however, was not.

The military in 1976 decided that it had to cure Argentine society of the ills in it that had produced decades of political turmoil and economic decay. As a result, they implemented an intense economic shock to force a rapid economic transformation and initiated a "Dirty War" on society to "save western Christian civilization" (Rock 1993, vxiii). Both had brutal consequences. The economic program—market-oriented policies that looked to remove government support and subsidy for domestic industry and the working class that benefited from it—decimated domestic industrialists, the middle class, and the organized working class, without producing new growth or eliminating inflation. The Dirty War attacked the Montoneros, but also reached into middle-class homes and into educated society. Ultimately, somewhere between 10,000 and 30,000 Argentines were killed by the military, and tens of thousands more were jailed and/or beaten and tortured in a brutal campaign between 1976 and 1983. Middle-class support for military rule disappeared in the face of this assault on Argentine society. When the military initiated and subsequently lost a war against England over the Malvinas/Falkland Islands in 1983, the last straw broke and the military junta resigned in disgrace. Democracy returned to Argentina, but with the country traumatized by the level of violence inflicted on its population in the name of order, and convinced that it was poorer than it had been in the 1920s.

Brazil

Like Argentina, Brazil made its tentative steps toward democracy in the early twentieth century as rapid economic change led to challenges to an essentially fraudulent republic. The Republic of Coffee and Milk, named for the two states that dominated it—São Paulo (coffee) and Rio Grande do Sul (milk) rested on a highly restricted franchise and elections that were tightly controlled by the various state oligarchies (Skidmore 1967). Like Argentina, Brazil's successful integration with the global economy brought prosperity and its attendant developments: immigration, urbanization, and the emergence of new classes making demands for political inclusion and economic reforms (Collier and Collier 1991). Finally, as in Argentina, rising new classes joined with politically excluded oligarchs to challenge the dominant states' hold on the political system. In Brazil, the onset of the Great Depression was the critical trigger for the final breakdown of the old system in favor of a new coalition led by Getulio Vargas, although violent conflict against an increasingly illegitimate regime had begun to emerge by the early twentieth century, including growing labor mobilization around wage and collective bargaining rights.

The Vargas presidency, beginning in 1930, was marked from the very beginning by increasingly violent tensions between the different segments of the highly diffuse coalition. Middle-class actors, rooted primarily in the city of São Paulo, pushed for the introduction of liberal political rules. Yet they faced resistance from more conservative elements, both in the military and among rural and urban elites, who promoted instead fascist models of political organization. Finally, segments of the military embraced communism, while the growing organized working class drew inspiration from a variety of leftist, anticapitalist ideologies including communism, socialism, and syndicalism.

Between 1930 and 1937, Vargas oversaw the implementation of a new liberal constitution that defined a set of rights to association and expression that ironically served primarily to protect increasing organization of highly illiberal groups (Skidmore 1967). These groups clashed with each other and with the state. Ultimately, the political violence of organized fascists and communists, coupled with repeated threats of uprisings from sympathetic segments within the military led to an *auto-golpe* (self-coup d'etat) in 1937. Getulio Vargas's *Estado Nôvo* (the New State) suspended the constitution, closed the Congress, and granted the president the authority to crush organized political activity in the country and remove disloyal military officials.

The political and economic model developed by Vargas consisted of three main components. First, Vargas introduced an extensive program of state-led ISI. Through a mix of subsidies, protection, and state production and supply of key inputs such as electricity and steel, Brazil produced the largest industrial sector in the developing world. The economic program generated benefits for the middle class, the working class, and the military. As in Argentina, Brazil depended on landed elites and their commodity exports for industrial investment capital. But, unlike in Argentina where a centralized government agency, Argentine Institute for Trade and Production (IAPI), directly taxed landed interests through a monopoly on trade (Lewis 1990, 159), successive Brazilian governments used primarily indirect means—notably multiple exchange rates—to tax exporters and subsidize industrial investment. The indirectness of the method helped minimize political resistance to the pro-urban program.[5]

The second component of Vargas's model was a program of centralization of the authority of the federal government that enhanced economic development capacity while protecting the concerns of landed elites. The Republic of Coffee and Milk was a highly decentralized system in which states maintained their own militias and pursued their own economic and even immigration policies. Vargas unified economic policymaking, especially in regard to revenue collection and state investment. To minimize political resistance, Vargas assured landed elites in two ways. First, he implemented administrative reforms that increased the technical capacity of the state, but also ensured regional oligarchs' access to patronage resources. Second, state investment promoted urban change, but left the countryside intact. Again, the contrast with Argentina is crucial. In Brazil, regional oligarchs maintained strong political and economic authority over a large peasantry. Leaving the rural sector unreformed and granting oligarchs access to federal patronage reinforced their clientelistic control over the countryside and reduced opposition to the pro-industrialization program (Skidmore 1967).

Finally, Vargas drew on fascist models of social control and developed the region's most extensive and most restrictive form of corporatist labor organization (Collier and Collier 1991). Although Brazil's industrial working class was larger in absolute terms than the one in Argentina, its power was diluted by the size of the country and diffusion of centers of activity. While the Argentine working class was able to exert influence by threatening key choke points in the economy, the Brazilian working class had far less structural power. The result was a highly organized, centralized, and mobilized working class in Argentina and a weak, decentralized working class contained and controlled by state agencies in Brazil.

Thus, overall, the Brazilian system promoted a similar program as in Argentina, but with power, influence, and access to resources diffused across a decentralized political system. The working class was organized, but in a way that enhanced state control over the movement. Many elites hated Vargas, and his presence in office inspired anti-Vargas political mobilization, the first of which led to his removal from office by the military in 1945 in favor of restored competitive elections; the second of which led to his suicide in the face of the threat of military removal in 1954. Yet, the basic program remained intact even after his removal on both occasions. In Argentina, ISI and labor mobilization led to extremes of political polarization and conflict and pitted a unified antagonistic working class against a highly unified and embittered coalition of economic elites. Hatred of Perón was not only personal, but also emblematic of the larger political struggle. Hatred of Vargas was largely personal and contained once he was no longer in office.

Nevertheless, Brazil's system grew increasingly tense and conflictual through the 1950s and into the 1960s, although much less violent than in Argentina. In both countries, the fundamental contradictions of the inward-looking ISI economic-development program fueled political struggles. By the 1960s, indirect taxation of exports weakened their competitiveness even as deepening industrialization produced a constantly growing need for new investment and for imports of more and more expensive capital goods (Baer 1995). State protection of domestic industry and support for middle-class and working-class wages pushed demand up against the limits of domestic supply. The two conditions generated constant struggles with balance of payments and inflation. These in turn produced conflicts as organized groups in society sought to protect their shares of the national wealth. In Argentina, this dynamic helped fuel the wild, pendular shifts in policy orientation. In Brazil, the overall policy orientation remained steady, but rising inflation led the previously controlled working class to mobilize more and more against producers. In addition, rural labor grew increasingly organized and radicalized, in part due to the influence and assistance of their urban labor counterparts (Welch 1999). This growing mobilization threatened both the urban middle classes and rural elites and led to shifting support for military intervention.

The military's renewed intervention finally came in 1964, but this time it lasted until 1985. They temporarily closed Congress and suspended all civil liberties. The labor movement was suppressed and its leadership jailed, exiled, or murdered (Skidmore 1988). The new military government aggressively squeezed the domestic economy to contain inflation, but by 1967 felt that it was sufficiently under control to allow renewed economic expansion (Fishlow 1973). Again, unlike in Argentina, the regime change did not result in a meaningful reorientation of Vargas's political and economic model. Brazil's military leaders promoted urban industrialization aggressively. The military was less focused on the agricultural sector, but did initiate programs promoting deepened commercialization of farming and concentration of ownership of land by large landholders and commercial agriculture corporations. They maintained centralized control of economic policy, but permitted the continued existence of extensive patronage networks that preserved a highly diffused and decentralized system of clientelistic relations (Hagopian 1996). Finally, they reasserted control over the labor movement organizationally, but renewed economic growth after 1967 delivered substantial improvements in living standards for the industrial working class.

In fact, economic performance was so strong from 1967 until the mid-1970s (the "Brazilian Miracle") that the military began to liberalize political control and even introduced a form of electoral competition that allowed civilian politicians to compete with an official military party (Skidmore 1988). The military retained control over an electoral college so that civilians could not win the presidency itself. But, the otherwise relatively competitive elections offered meaningful information about the popularity of the military government. The *abertura* (opening) of the 1970s permitted increased political freedoms, including those of the press and of organization. With the leadership of the labor movement removed, Brazilian society displayed little of the polarized politics in Argentina. The relative absence of violence and repression by the regime stands in stark contrast to the authoritarian experience in neighboring Argentina (or Chile).

Nevertheless, military rule in Brazil ultimately unraveled in the early 1980s in the face of some of the same economic pressures as in Argentina. The debt crisis,[6] slowing economic growth, and rising inflation—all direct products of the ISI-development model—eroded the military's claim to superior governing capability. The lower levels of violence protected the military from the kind of disgrace it experienced in Argentina, but economic failures pushed more and more elite groups into opposition. A revitalized labor movement, led by Luiz Inacio Lula da Silva, led the civil society opposition (Keck 1989) while middle class, business, and ultimately finance joined in the calls for the restoration of democracy (Frieden 1991). In 1984, the demoralized military party, ARENA, crossed the floor and voted for the civilian opponent, Tancredo Neves, in the electoral college and Brazil's long, stable period of military rule was over.

Comparing the Two Countries

At root, both countries experienced political conflict, violence, and ultimately repeated regime breakdowns that stemmed from the contradictions of the economic-development model both countries embraced. ISI presented extremely difficult policy challenges of balancing the competing needs of an export-oriented countryside with an inward-looking, capital-goods importing urban sector. The inefficiencies and limitations of a sheltered urban manufacturing economy did not generate the savings to finance investment or the dynamism to support high wages and widespread employment opportunities (Kuczynski 1988). Pro-ISI governments redirected export earnings to support policies for the urban sector, especially through overvalued exchange rates. Redirecting export earnings into the uncompetitive urban sector increased the vulnerability to exogenous financial shocks, such as capital flight and balance of payment crises. These policies also inspired political opposition and weakened agriculture economically, thereby undermining the source of financing necessary to support the needs of the urban economy. Inflation, balance of payments crises, and difficulties servicing the high external debts endemic to developing countries were unfortunate and politically explosive problems that emerged as a consequence. In general, the policies necessary to address these difficulties invariably adversely affected either urban or rural interests, or alternatively employer or employee interests. Politically, neither country was able to find a workable compromise.[7]

Nevertheless, Argentina was significantly less successful than Brazil, a fact reflected in both its much more unstable regime history and the economic consequences of instability. Between 1930 and 1983, Argentina experienced a regime change or internal coup on average once roughly every three years. By contrast, Brazil had one president from 1930 to 1945 (albeit democratically elected first and authoritarian in the latter half), one democratic regime from 1945 to 1964, and then a military dictatorship from 1964 until 1985. In economic terms, one measure of the consequences is the way the two countries fared relative to the "development gap" with the United States—a long-standing focus of comparison in the region (Halperin 2008). Over the mid-twentieth century, Argentina's relative wealth compared to the US economy shrank between 1950 and 2000 with per capita GDP falling from roughly half of that of the United States to only 30 percent of US GDP. Over the same period, Brazil's per capita GDP grew from 17 percent of US per capita GDP to 20 percent (Dominguez 2008, 73). Thus, Brazil made some progress in "catching up" while in relative terms Argentina's highly volatile pattern of economic growth led to relative decline.

The differences can be explained at least partially in the intensely political and centralized nature of conflict and violence in Argentina versus the diffused, decentralized, and considerably less polarized character in Brazil. In Argentina, a very well organized and socially cohesive rural elite as well as well-organized, albeit not unified, industrial elites competed directly and overtly with the region's best-organized, strongest labor movement. The CGT and the PJ had important internal divisions, but Argentine politics offered clear, invidious choices between elites and an autonomous, highly mobilized popular movement. Conflict centered on control of the presidency, which exercised singular control over resources and responsibility for managing societal conflicts—something that Luigi Manzetti has criticized as indicative of the failure of a broader set of representative institutions in the country (Manzetti 1993).

In Brazil, a much more diffuse economy with multiple sources of strength produced a diffusion of interests and organizations in agriculture, industry, and labor. Conflicts existed among and within sectors of the economy, but it took substantial economic crises to produce large-scale mobilization of labor versus employers, and even then the radicalism of the leadership exceeded that of the rank and file (Erickson 1977). Moreover, the ability of regional elites to maintain access to resources through political parties and Congress created mechanisms for satisfying demands outside of the office of the president. Patronage and clientelist networks in Congress and throughout the bureaucracy permitted a decentralized system of political influence and interest mediation that diluted larger political conflicts. Differences aside, in both cases, the inflation and debt-fueled crisis of the 1980s led to the withdrawal of the military. In both cases, the legacy the dictators left behind them did not augur well for the future.

The Surprising Successes of Argentina and Brazil

As of 2012, both Argentina and Brazil stand out among the more successful countries in Latin America by a variety of measures. Both countries have seen a string of successful, peaceful presidential transitions and have maintained democratic rule continuously since 1983 and 1985 respectively. Argentina experienced a severe economic crisis in 2001 and an accompanying political crisis, but even that was managed constitutionally and the resulting transitions among a series of interim presidents were orderly and nonviolent. Comparing the two countries on Freedom House's index of political and civil liberties, the two countries lag behind the region's leading countries, notably Chile, Costa Rica, and Uruguay, but ahead of almost all other Latin American cases (Freedom House 2011). On other measures of violence and protest, the story is somewhat more mixed. Homicide rates in Argentina are among the lowest in the region and lower in fact than in the United States, while in Brazil they are close to the regional average. Argentina has seen large numbers of protests—among the highest in the region, with over 27 percent of survey respondents reporting having participated in some form of protest. By contrast, only 5 percent of Brazilians reported such activity (Moseley and Moreno 2010). Protest, however, is not necessarily a sign of violence or instability, and in fact both countries compare favorably with the region on the World Bank's World Governance Indicators, particularly *Political Stability and the Absence of Political Violence* (World Bank 2011). Finally, economic performance for both countries since 2000 has exceeded the regional average, with Brazil's accelerating in pace since the global crisis of 2008. In general then, both countries seemed to have left behind the political conflicts that brought down regimes in decades past.

It is important not to overstate the degree of stability, especially in Argentina. The persistence of Peronist-organized political violence, the relative breakdown of the party system, the authoritarian inclinations of PJ presidents Néstor Kirchner and his wife and successor Cristina Fernandez, and the continuing institutional weaknesses of the country are all ongoing sources of concern about the quality of democracy in Argentina (Levitsky and Murillo 2005; McGuire 1997). Indeed, institutional weakness is one of the hypotheses offered to account for the level and frequency of protests in Argentina (Machado, Scartascini, and Tommasi 2009). Thus, the discussion of Argentina's success is relative both to a region experiencing a greater degree of violence and upheaval and to the country's past of much greater violence and polarization. Similarly, Brazil's successes can easily conceal ongoing weakness in the quality of political representation of the poor, as Janice Perlman's research in Rio de Janeiro's slums documents (Perlman 2008).

The relative success of the two countries is particularly noteworthy since neither democratic regime began auspiciously. Both countries began their new democracies facing dire economic circumstances with, unsurprisingly, intense political struggles. In both countries, a mixture of crippling external debt, slow or volatile GDP growth, and spiraling inflation seemed beyond the capacity of the political system to manage. In both, earlier patterns seemed ready to reproduce. In Argentina, the government of Raúl Alfonsín of the UCR struggled with the challenge of balancing competing demands from organized interests over how to address the crisis, and as in past periods, the office of the president served as virtually the only locus of bargaining and conflict mediation (Manzetti 1993). In Brazil, extensive, decentralized, and highly diffuse patronage networks were reflected in the party system where the liberalization of political rules led to a proliferation of political parties (19 represented in Congress by 1989). Diffuse interests undermined new president José Sarney's efforts to address sources of fiscal imbalance and inflation. In Brazil, public disenchantment with democratic rule and rumors of military unrest led some to suggest that Brazil was the region's leading candidate for a return to authoritarian rule (Linz and Stepan 1996). In Argentina, Alfonsín's efforts to prosecute the military for human rights abuses led to a series of revolts by junior officers (*carapintadas*) and Alfonsín's humiliating capitulation to military demands for an end to prosecutions. By the end of the decade, inflation was over 4,000 percent in Brazil and over 2,000 percent in Argentina.

Yet, by the early to mid-1990s, inflation had been tamed in both, economic growth had resumed, and the institutional deficiencies of the past seemed less of an obstacle. New presidents in both countries, Carlos Menem in Argentina and Fernando Collor and then Fernando Henrique Cardoso in Brazil, implemented neoliberal economic reforms to reduce the influence of the state and enhance the role of markets in the economy, and in both countries the reforms appeared to have overall positive effects (Corrales 2003). In both countries, events were not simple, and it is important not to overstate the ease of the transition to more democratic and more market-oriented societies. For example, in Brazil, Collor was impeached on corruption; and a run on the currency, the *real*, in 2000 presented significant economic challenges. In Argentina, the 2001 crisis, triggered by the collapse of the country's innovative, but excessively rigid "dollarization" plan (Starr 1997), had devastating economic effects, led to the resignation of the president, Fernando de la Rúa, and an uncertain period of interim rule until it was finally settled. Nevertheless, both countries recovered well politically and economically from their respective crises.

The comparative good news, both with respect to the past and with respect to the rest of the region, does not mean that violence has disappeared as an issue. Neither country is experiencing Colombia- or Mexico-style drug wars or Bolivian- or Venezuelan-style political polarization and conflict. Yet both countries face ongoing issues of violence. As noted earlier, although there is very little political violence in Brazil, crime rates have skyrocketed since the 1980s, with homicides doubling between the early 1980s and 1990 and rising steadily since then. In Argentina, crime rates have also doubled since the 1980s, though at much lower levels overall then Brazil. While crime rates are lower than in Brazil, public concerns about crime in Argentina are among the highest in Latin America. In both cases, a crucial consequence has been calls for "zero-tolerance" policing that in turn has led to high levels of police violence and impunity (Brinks 2006). Finally, Argentina has also seen a continuation of political violence, though in much more modest form from the sharply polarizing politics of the past. The PJ continues to be linked to organized forms of political protest and violence, even if it is no longer large labor unions pitted against employers. Instead, it is organized poor and unemployed who receive benefits in exchange for political gain (Levitsky 2003). In this regard, the politicized nature of violence in Argentina continues to pose a problem for the country.

At root, the spikes in violence in both countries are related to the economic crisis of the 1980s and the failure of the economic-reform process to generate opportunities for young males. Neoliberal economic reforms overall have yielded a number of important benefits, but their impact on the labor market has been mixed. Skilled workers have benefited greatly, but low-skilled workers have not. Young men suffer from a shortage of jobs while those that are available are likely to be low skill and low wage and in the informal sector (Saavedra 2003). Furthermore, economic pressures have pushed more women into the low-wage workforce, eroding some of the key community and household safeguards against violent behavior (Bergman 1999). Theories of criminal violence suggest that the combination of grievance/anger plus opportunity drives higher crime levels. Thus, the disappearance of decent work coupled with the weakening of community oversight of youth have helped drive up crime levels in both countries.

This type of crime may not be overtly political and is clearly not directed overtly at the state or at privileged groups within the society. In fact, as in the United States, the poor are the principal victims of crime, as well as police brutality. Nevertheless, criminality can be seen as political in both countries in that it reflects a weakness of the state or failures of the state to meet crucial needs. In both Argentina and Brazil, successive governments have begun to address these failures through a variety of social programs, most notably Argentina's *Jefes y Jefas de Hogar Desocupados* program and Brazil's *Bolsa Família*. Both programs have had some important benefits, but ultimately the solution rests in renewed economic opportunities, strengthening of the presence of the state in poor communities, and a strengthening of the rule of law.

Argentina

Politicized violence in Argentina has become increasingly uncommon since the restoration of democracy. In the 1980s, junior officers, dubbed *carapintadas*, led successive revolts against the administration of Raúl Alfonsín because of his efforts to investigate and prosecute officers for human rights abuses committed during the dictatorship. Senior officers declined to confront the revolting soldiers, and Alfonsín and his successor, Carlos Menem, offered a series of legal concessions that, in effect, granted the military immunity (Norden 1996). Nevertheless, Menem's concession—pardoning of leaders of the ruling junta—exchanged immunity for increased budgetary control, which in turn led to the eventual weakening of the increasingly defunded armed forces. As of 2012, the military is not a threatening institution, and in fact President Néstor Kirchner was able to void the earlier legal concessions and reopen the question of military accountability successfully.

Greater economic prosperity, substantially reduced union strength, and greater consensus over economic policy have led to sharp reductions in the polarized politics of the past. In particular, since the terrible shock of 2001,

Argentina's economy has grown on average over 7 percent per year, with modest inflation and declining unemployment. In the meantime, union participation and the capacity of worker mobilization declined through the economic crisis of the 1980s and the subsequent neoliberal adjustments of the 1990s, with union density falling almost in half (Smith 2005, 241). A major factor weakening labor mobilization has been sharp increases in open unemployment, roughly doubling between the 1980s to over 14 percent by 1995 (Murillo 2003, 106). In any event, the sharp choice between pro-urban and industrial policies and pro-commodity export policies has receded in all of Latin America. Neoliberal market-oriented policies did not prove as hegemonic as either its strongest champions or critics hoped. Yet, as of 2012, virtually all Latin American economies have found a greater balance between state and market orientations, and conflicts over economic policy have not been as sharp as in decades past.[8]

Nevertheless, there have been important periods of general social unrest, accompanied by violent protests and influenced by partisan political connections. The first came in 1989 in the context of hyperinflation and deepening economic crisis. Growing hunger led to food riots that ultimately accelerated the presidential transition from Raúl Alfonsín and the granting of extraordinary emergency decree powers to the incoming president Carlos Menem. In 2001, the calamitous currency crisis and its accompanying political upheaval also provoked angry demonstrations, rioting and looting, and occasionally violent attacks on those perceived as responsible (particularly bankers and politicians). As in 1989, violent upheaval led to the early resignation of the president. In both instances, a president of the UCR party was forced out in favor of a Peronist. In both periods of protest, Peronist leaders and networks were implicated in the organization and mobilization of violence. Hunger riots and looting incidents occurred continuously from 1989 through 2002, reaching a peak in December 2001 when press accounts reported on nearly 300 food riots in one week alone. Many of these incidents were simple reflections of the desperation of the moment—for example, spontaneous protests occurring in situations where promises of food aid turned out to be false or where supplies were exhausted. However, in at least 50 percent of these riots, neighborhood Peronist political brokers (*punteros*) were actively involved in the mobilization of local clientelistic networks, explicitly inviting neighborhood residents to participate in attacks on specific grocery stores. Furthermore, such actions occurred with explicit support/permission from higher placed authorities, such as mayors, and with explicit information about the presence or absence of police protection. Thus, Peronists' deep clientelistic roots in urban neighborhoods exploited economic circumstances to mobilize violence for partisan purposes (Auyero and Moran 2007).

Peronist links are also important in another area of sustained protest, punctuated by occasional violence. Social spending in Argentina prior to 1996 was relatively low and primarily universal in nature rather than assistance targeted to the poor. On average, social spending over the period 1990–1999 rose to only 8.6 percent of GDP from roughly 7.4 percent of GDP in the 1984–1989 period despite considerable increases in unemployment (Lodola 2005, 518). Urban unemployment in Argentina stood at 7.5 percent in 1990, but had risen steadily to 17.2 percent by 1996. In response, unemployed workers mobilized into a set of disparate protest movements called *piqueteros* (literally picketers—the term that emerged for protesters) for the purpose of demanding benefits to address the uncertainty of the labor market. The number of protests rose from roughly 50 in 1997 to over 2,000 by 2002. Angry protests in the 1990s led to the passage of Carlos Menem's *Plan Trabajar* in response (Lodola 2005). The plan introduced a new form of social assistance that broke with previous social policy by directing resources specifically to unemployed workers. But, it was not an entitlement or social right, or even a conditional form of assistance. Instead, resource limitations meant that it never affected more than 15 percent of all unemployed workers, and while disbursement did flow primarily to areas with higher unemployment, political considerations significantly shaped delivery to specific beneficiaries (Kostzer 2008). The funds came from the federal government, but were disbursed locally through political and NGO auspices.

One consequence of this mode of disbursement is that it strengthened the local clientelistic networks of the Peronist Party, allowing Peronist leaders to develop strong organizational ties with the various *piquetero* associations. In fact, Germán Lodola (2005) demonstrates that under both Peronist and UCR presidencies, monies flowed disproportionately to localities under Peronist control. Furthermore, the intensity of protests sharply increased after the transition to the de la Rúa presidency. As Aldo Ponce has argued, this reflects the deep partisan links that formed between competing Peronist leaders who in turn mobilized protest both against the UCR government and against each other in their efforts to gain ascendancy in the party. Thus, political violence in Argentina has also persisted through Peronists' ongoing mobilization of clientelistic networks for partisan political purposes (Ponce 2005).

Finally, the Peronist Party continues to protect violence through corrupt linkages with the police. Argentine police have been implicated both for their participation in criminal activities as well as their failure to investigate criminal activity. Police have been charged with involvement in the majority of kidnapping cases in the country, as well as participation in drug trafficking, prostitution, gambling, and auto-theft. In all these cases, police have been abetted by various political party—but especially Peronist—officials' protection from investigation or prosecution. In exchange for political cover, corrupt police officials have channeled resources from criminal activities to politicians for both private and political gain. This strong link between the police and Peronists has been one of the factors impeding police reform (Eaton 2008).

Another factor impeding reform is that growing concern about crime in Argentina has led to calls for "zero-tolerance" policing (Dammert and Malone 2006), which in turn has led to increased police violence, particularly against those perceived as *marginados* (marginals). As Daniel Brinks has noted, police killings of "marginals" in places like Buenos Aires are rarely investigated, let alone prosecuted or punished and killing of offenders perceived as violent are never convicted even if they are prosecuted (Brinks 2006). The call for harsh policing, in turn, reflects the sharp increase in concern about crime in Argentina. As of 2008, 92.7 percent of Argentines reported being very or somewhat concerned about crime—the fourth-highest level of concern in Latin America (Brinks 2012). Victimization self-reports indicate high levels of awareness of crimes committed against family or friends (Bergman 1999) and in fact suggest higher levels of crime, particularly property crime, than official statistics report. Unfortunately, a lack of trust in the police is another critical factor fueling fear of crime even though that leads to calls for harsher forms of policing and additional police violence (Dammert and Malone 2002). For example, police in Buenos Aires killed on average 160 people per year from 1990 to 2000—more than 3 times the rate of Los Angeles, the city with the worst police violence in the United States (Brinks 2006).

Argentine fears of crime are ironic to some extent, however. First, the actual crime rate in Argentina is considerably lower than almost all the rest of the region and in fact homicide rates are lower than in the United States. Violent crime rose throughout the 1990s, spiked around the economic crisis of 2001, and has fallen back since the economic recovery. Yet, even at its peak, there were only 9.5 homicides per 100,000 in Argentina as compared to 5.7 in the United States. By 2009, considerably improved economic conditions helped bring the homicide rate back down to 5.5 per 100,000 compared with a Latin American regional average of 22.9 per 100,000 (UN Office on Drugs and Crime 2011). Moreover, Argentines are not universally affected by violent crime, as 90 percent of the victims are young, male, poor, and overwhelmingly urban. High levels of fear tend to appear in more homogeneous communities where social network ties rapidly spread communication about crime and violence. Yet, the same elements of community and homogeneity also constitute stronger forms of supervision and protection against crime (Dammert and Malone 2006). Thus, ironically, the factors that generate high levels of awareness and fear may also work to keep crime rates lower than in other Latin American contexts.

Why the rise in crime? This remains a crucial but underexplained issue in Latin America. Theories of criminality identify a range of possible causes, but a leading contender in Latin America in general and the Argentine context specifically is the rise in labor market uncertainty over the course of the 1980s and the 1990s. The unemployment rate doubled overall from 1986 to 1996, but for males aged 18–25, the situation was markedly worse. In the same period, the unemployment rate quadrupled, reaching 25 percent while the high school–dropout rate tripled (Bergman 1999). This was at least partially a reflection of declining support for education and profound difficulties effecting education reforms (Corrales 2004). As Matt Singer has noted, surveys of Argentines indicated extraordinary levels of uncertainty about the availability of work. In 2002, over 85 percent of Argentines reported being concerned or very concerned (over 60 percent) with becoming unemployed within 12 months. Furthermore, younger workers reported higher levels of insecurity than older ones (in contrast to the typical dynamic in wealthier countries where older workers worry about being replaced by younger, inexpensive ones) (Singer 2007, 263). These data are not fully representative of the past two decades as the level of insecurity sharpened substantially after the crisis of 2001. After the currency shock and collapse of the peso, unemployment surged to over 21 percent while over 40 percent of Argentines fell below the poverty line. With the resumption of economic growth by 2003, conditions improved, yet even so unemployment remained around 10 percent by 2006, and 19 percent of Argentines lived below the poverty line (Kostzer 2008). Thus, economic uncertainty remained a critical factor affecting the lives of large numbers of Argentines.

To their credit, Argentine officials recognized the weakness of protection for the poor and the unemployed and in 2003 implemented an innovative social policy response, the *Plan de Jefes y Jefas de Hogar Desempleados* (Plan for Unemployed Heads of Households). Unlike the assistance program delivered to *piqueteros* through the *Plan Trabajar*, the Plan de Jefes y Jefas is a much more ambitious program designed to build human capital and drive renewed economic expansion. Limited social expenditure and weak and clientelistic influences on the *Plan Trabajar* meant that ultimately only about 350,000 people received benefits. By contrast, the new plan reached roughly 2 million people in its first two years. By 2005, it reached as much as 40 percent of all households in states with high levels of unemployment (Kostzer 2008, 20). The plan had several notable components. First, it was an *Employer of Last Resort* (ELR) plan—that is to say the government created work opportunities to offer employment to unemployed heads of households. The program had a range of expected benefits: it reduced the size of the informal sector and the greatly increased social, political, and economic vulnerabilities associated with informal employment; it addressed severe gaps in household needs that are associated with other human capital losses such as increased dropout rates or loss of health care; the ELR jobs focused on community development and infrastructure that supported larger neighborhood and economic improvements; and it increased domestic demand, helping to fuel consumption-driven growth and not just improved export performance. In addition, ELR salaries had the effect of establishing a wage floor and therefore driving up even informal-sector wages. Beneficiaries were required to work at least 20 hours per week in the program. Finally, the work commitment included such elements as on-the-job training and vocational education thereby helping to develop labor market skills (Kostzer 2008).

Ultimately, it is hard to measure the exact effects of the program per se, although both the aggregate economic and crime data both point to a general trend of improvement. Assessments of the program suggest that it helped alleviate the worst effects of the crisis, therefore succeeding as an assistance program. Furthermore, like virtually all targeted programs (as opposed to universal programs), it suffers from mismatches between estimated demand and actual demand (causing rationing in some cases and oversupply in others, both of which increase the risk of political/patronage manipulation), as well as challenges to verification of real household income. The *Plan de Jefes y Jefas de Hogar Desempleados* is a greatly improved social-policy response with important social benefits. But, it is less certain that it had real effects on either poverty or job creation (Módolo 2004; Alperin 2009). Ultimately, it is likely that structural sources of poverty need a more comprehensive set of complementary policies (such as education and health care) and sustained economic growth (Birdsall and Székely 2003).

Brazil

Political violence in Brazil has been even less common than in Argentina. The early years of the "New Republic" were hardly promising. Rapidly spiraling inflation, wildly volatile GDP growth rates and unemployment, and a progressive fragmentation of the party system left Brazilians skeptical about their new democracy and repeated efforts to address the economic crisis. The 1992 impeachment of Fernando Collor on corruption charges added to the sense that the new regime was incapable of delivering competent economic governance. Over that period of time, the military, which left office in much higher regard than its Argentine counterpart, was rumored to have expressed concern about the state of affairs. But, most critically, it was not inclined to return to power and nobody openly called for it to do so. Most importantly, an active civil society had emerged in the wake of the restoration of democracy and found a voice for communicating a broad set of concerns. Thus, the chaos was largely in the political arena—not in societal conflict. The success of the 1994 *Real* Plan in taming inflation significantly improved living standards for the poor, and established a firm base for an emergent consensus on economic policy. As of 2003, Brazil's economic growth grew at a faster and faster pace, with moderate inflation and strong fiscal balances. In short, the central *economic* conflicts that fueled past fights appeared to have been resolved.

In fact, there is arguably only one area of violent conflict that remains politicized in Brazil and that is over the distribution of land. While inequality has always been very high comparatively, land distribution is even more so in Brazil. Historically, the overall Gini coefficient has stayed in the range of 0.58–0.62—among the very highest in the world and the worst rate for middle-income countries or richer (World Bank 2004, 13). The inequality level declined modestly after 1995 and has declined again more significantly since 2003. But, the Gini coefficient for land was a shocking 0.86 as of 2000 (World Bank 2004, 22). In response, the *Movimento dos Sem Terra* (MST—the Landless Workers Movement) mobilized beginning in the 1980s for the purpose of protesting the conditions of rural poverty and forcing land distribution. Since its inception, it has remained committed to land invasions as a tactic, and through the 1990s and into the 2000s, there were multiple instances of violence against squatters perpetrated by armed attackers, notably state military police officers. The Catholic Church in Brazil estimated that there were almost 1,000 land-related murders between 1985 and 1998, including several highly visible and brutal massacres on land squatters by military police (Kay 2001). The election of Luiz Inacio Lula da Silva of the Workers' Party (PT) in 2002 led to a decrease in confrontation as a tactical decision on the part of the MST, although neither his government nor his predecessor have been able to redistribute land at a pace satisfactory to the movement. The failure to live up to the MST's expectations led to a resumption of invasions and other confrontational tactics, but the levels and intensity of violence are lower than in the past (Hochstetler 2008).

Rural violence over land inequality is not a new phenomenon in Brazil and dates back as early as the initial expansion into the frontier of the country 500 years ago (Simmons 2004). The contemporary situation of land conflict is marked by two features: it follows logically from explicit government development policy, even as both the Lula and Cardoso administrations simultaneously pursued land reforms; and it is organized more effectively today by the MST than at any previous point in Brazilian history. Beginning with the military coup in 1964, successive Brazilian governments (military and democratic) have sought to promote natural-resource development and exploitation for commercial purposes. Subsidies and tax incentives have encouraged land concentration and development of agriculture and natural resource extraction for exports at the expense of environmental concerns, indigenous settlement, or land inequities (Pereira 2003). In addition, successive governments have viewed the Amazon region as a strategic asset and have placed high priority on its development and integration into the national economy, again even at the expense of social justice and environmental considerations.[9] The result has been to systematically pit commercial and elite interests against the poor in the countryside. The Amazon regime, especially in states like Pará, has become the central battleground in this conflict.

The MST has emerged as the principal force organizing the poor in the countryside. The MST's origins lie in commercial agriculture modernization policies of the 1960s, particularly in the southern state of Rio Grande do Sul. Displacement by large landowners led to growing protests in the 1970s and the formal formation of the movement in 1984. By the 2000s, the MST boasted a membership of roughly 2 million people in every state in the country and hundreds of municipalities. It runs nearly 2,000 elementary schools teaching over 150,000 students as well as teaching literacy to thousands of adults and running a college. It runs hundreds of cooperative farms, offering assistance for marketing, credit and production, and technical capacity. In short, the MST has emerged as a virtual alternative governance structure for the landless and the rural poor. Through this development, it remains committed to collective decision making, rural autonomy, opposition to privatizing reforms in the countryside, and land occupation as the central and highest tactic (Welch 2006). In short, the potential for ongoing, albeit small-scale conflict in the countryside remains strong. Nevertheless, the level of rural conflict in Brazil remains low compared to high-conflict countries in the region and is about the only real source of overt political violence in the country.

Yet, low levels of violent political conflict stand in contrast with the exceptionally high levels of violent crime. Unlike Argentina, concern about crime is high (though lower than in Argentina) in response to very real issues. While 90.4 percent of Brazilians reported being concerned or very concerned about crime in 2008, the homicide rate stood at 22 per 100,000—or roughly four times the level in Argentina. As in Argentina, the homicide rate has declined along with the markedly improved economic performance since 2003. Homicide rates rose from 18.3 per 100,000 in 1990 to a peak of

29 by 2003 and have fallen steadily since then (United Nations Office on Drugs and Crime 2011). Even so, the homicide rate is among the highest in the region. Yet, the story is starkly different for young males.

As in Argentina, the victims of crime are overwhelming urban, young, male and poor. Brazilian males aged 15–24 are 15 times more likely to be killed than women, and Afro-Brazilians are two-thirds more likely to be killed than whites. Crime varies considerably by region, from a low of 10 per 100,000 in the northern state of Maranhão in 2002 to a high of 57 per 100,000 in Rio de Janeiro. Youth violence is particularly severe with over 50 percent of mortalities among 15–24 due to violence by 2002—a figure that has been rising steadily and dramatically since 1980. Rape and sexual assault and sex trafficking are significantly underreported, but surveys in the municipalities of São Paulo and Zona da Mata (Pernambuco) found that as many as 34 percent of women reported being physically assaulted by domestic partners and 14 percent raped (World Bank 2006, 12).

Argentina's homicide rate doubled between 1990 and 2000, but the difference in levels of violence between the two countries is dramatic. Three important differences stand out between the two countries. First, as noted above, income inequality is much higher in Brazil than in Argentina, as are absolute poverty levels and the absolute differences between the two countries help account for the sharp discrepancies. In particular, Brazil's urban shantytowns (*favelas*) are exceptionally violent zones in which the state is barely present (Perlman 2008; 2010; Scheper-Hughes 1993). To the extent that the state is present, it is typically in the form of brutal policing that residents fear as much as violent criminals (Perlman 2008).

Second, race is an important element that affects crime rates and institutional responses. Victims of crime are disproportionately black as are victims of police violence. Data on racial characteristics of crime are difficult to compare as they were not systematically reported or compiled until 2002 and even then suffer from incomplete reporting (Waiselfisz 2011). Nevertheless, the existing data tell a clear story: by 2008, the homicide rate for Afro-Brazilians was more than double the rate for whites—a ratio that has worsened since 2002 as the overall rate has fallen, but the rate for Afro-Brazilians has risen. In 2002, the homicide rate for whites was 18.9 per 100,000 compared to 26.9 for Afro-Brazilians. By 2008, the rate for whites had fallen to 14.7 while it had climbed to 32.3 for Afro-Brazilians (Waiselfisz 2011). Data on police killings further suggests the problem of discrimination. Police killings in Brazil are significantly more common than in Argentina, and as in Argentina, killing of *marginais* (marginal people) is rarely investigated or prosecuted and even more rarely results in a conviction. The racial profile, however, is clearly reflected in differences between the predominantly white city of São Paulo, with a police killing rate about 140 percent of Buenos Aires, and the predominantly Afro-Brazilian Salvador Bahia with a police killing rate more than three times higher than São Paulo and roughly five times more than Buenos Aires (Brinks 2006, 211). Furthermore, surveys reveal serious concerns about racial prejudice in the judicial system. For example, survey research in Rio de Janeiro found that 66 percent of respondents believed the justice system treated Afro-Brazilians more harshly than whites (Sussekind 1999).

Finally, the enormous growth of the drug trade, concentrated in Brazil's urban *favelas*, is a significant driver of violence. Various reports point to the virtual militarization of drug gangs and their prominence in favela life, including the dismantling and displacing of neighborhood associations and other mechanisms of favela self-governance. Drug gangs have repeatedly gone to war with the police, including most recently in the wake of Brazil winning the right to host the 2016 Olympics.

In Brazil, the central social policy response to conditions of poverty was an innovative social policy, alluded to above, called Bolsa Família.[10] Bolsa Família is a conditional cash-transfer program that pays a monthly stipend to female heads of households below a certain poverty threshold. All told, the program reaches roughly 45 million Brazilians. The key, however, is that families receive the stipend only if the household children meet certain requirements, most notably attend school on a regular basis. Therefore, like the Argentine Jefes y Jefas program, the intent is to build human capital and is very ambitious in its scope. The program has had substantial positive results, including nearly universal enrollment of school-age children up to the eighth grade. It has helped reduce poverty and inequality and increased household consumption of food. Indeed, it has rapidly become a politically untouchable program, with both leading candidates in the 2010 presidential elections promising to expand it.

Yet, it also has notable limitations. For one, dropout rates rise dramatically after the eighth grade. Only about 50 percent of children graduate from high school. Moreover, investments in schools have fallen since 2000 so that schools suffer from a host of poor conditions that mar the quality of education, including the absence of books, equipment, and even sufficient chairs and tables (Arends-Kuenning 2009). Poor schools suffer from serious infrastructure problems, such as broken windows and severe leaking. Teachers are poorly paid, poorly trained, and often unsupervised. Violence in schools is endemic and adequate counseling/psychological services are entirely absent in poor neighborhoods (Reiter 2009). In addition, the bleak job prospects for young people add to the set of disincentives for staying in school. For example, the program includes technical training to help facilitate the transition into the workforce. Unfortunately, that element has lagged far behind and is woefully inadequate. To illustrate, in 2009, the city of Belo Horizonte graduated its first set of recipients of technical training linking school to the job market, but the number was very small. Of 13 million eligible children across Brazil, a mere 460 received job-related training in one of the country's largest cities.

The end result is a bleak picture of astonishing levels of violence, especially among the young and the poor. While the homicide rate fell from 2003 to 2008, the youth homicide rate has actually risen from 1998 to 2008 from 30 per 100,000 to 52.9 per 100,000 by 2008 (Waiselfisz 2011). Data from the city of Rio de Janeiro illustrates both the general high levels as well as the disparity between middle/upper classes and the poor. The homicide rate for people between the ages of 15 and 34 ranged between 23 per 100,000 (Lagoas) and 56 per 100,000 (Copacabana) in higher-income neighborhoods. By contrast, the homicide rate in the slums of Rio Comprido and São Cristovão was an appalling 144 per 100,000 and 177 per 100,000 respectively. For boys between the ages of 5 and 19, the mortality rates also reflected these class differences. For example, Copacabana has a small number of *favelas* nearby. The mortality rate was 3.1 per 100,000 for non-favela boys and 8.6 per 100,000 for favela boys. In lower-income Madureira—a district with a large number of *favelas*, the mortality rates were 9.8 versus 19.6 for non-favela and favela, for young boys respectively (Briceño-León 1999). In short, violence in Brazil is not political and does not threaten the regime. But, its shocking level represents a significant social crisis.

As in Argentina, citizens have demanded improved security, including harsher forms of "zero-tolerance" policing. But, as in Argentina, the political system has not responded adequately to the demands (Pereira 2008). As in Argentina, Brazilian police are implicated in corruption and participation in crime. Brazilians report very low levels of trust in the police that compounds the problem of addressing crime. In short, the weakness of the state in the provision of key social services and protecting the rule of law have led to an epidemic of crime since the 1980s that disproportionately affects the young, the poor, and black Brazilians. Crime is not overtly political, but it reflects the political reality that the country's key institutions and economy work to protect a privileged subset of the population while functioning very poorly for the young and the poor.

Comparing the Two Countries

Both Argentina and Brazil appear to have resolved the deep, regime-destabilizing conflicts over economic policy and the respective challenges that repeatedly threatened political stability in the past: sharp polarization in Argentina, and paralyzing fragmentation in Brazil. The reasons for the diminished conflict and polarization in the context of neoliberal reforms are subject to considerable debate. One set of scholars argues that neoliberal is inherently destructive of social mobilization. For example, Marcus Kurtz argues that neoliberal reforms destroy the organizational capacity of social resistance, especially through its effects on labor (Kurtz 2004). Some argue that neoliberalism converts citizenship into a relatively hollow kind of consumerism, or what Phillip Oxhorn has called "neopluralism" (Oxhorn 2006). For Forrest Colburn, for example, this consumerism leads to the end of struggle over issues like social justice—the "end of politics" (Colburn 2002). Others suggest that neoliberal reforms coexist with a limited version of democracy in which meaningful societal change is off the table—in effect a bourgeois exchange of moderate prosperity or the chance of it at the cost of accepting a regime that does not pursue contentious social reform (Weyland 2004; Smith 2005). By contrast, others suggest that neoliberalism is not inherently demobilizing. James Petras, for example, argues the opposite: that the injustice of neoliberal reforms inherently drives mobilization of resistance (Petras 2000). Moisés Arce, for example, contends that the data do not support a view of a demobilized region (Arce 2010). In this view, neoliberal reforms are not a sufficient explanation for more limited conflict in the two cases in this study.

It is not possible to resolve the debate in this chapter, and therefore it is perhaps impossible to fully explain the apparent decline in sharp political conflict in the wake of neoliberal reforms. Four distinct observations, however, do help account for the decline in conflict. First, neoliberal reforms did play an explicit role in resolving profound economic crises in the 1980s and into the early 1990s in both countries. Given the success of market reforms in restoring growth and investment and taming inflation, there is no real model around which to mobilize. Thus, the second observation is that the polarizing conflicts of the past over market versus state or countryside versus urban simply aren't relevant in the current context. Oil-based populism, as in Venezuela, or indigenous identity-based mobilization, as in Bolivia or Ecuador, are not options in Argentina and Brazil. The argument in the 2000s is how to use state power to enhance development and promote social policy to support market society. Debates over the degree of state involvement are not major, competing ideological poles. Argentina has backed away from the "Washington Consensus" policies in the 2000s more than Brazil, but even there it has been mostly to reverse privatizations that fairly clearly failed (such as of water or pensions). A third element, as noted earlier, is that high unemployment, declining formal employment, and weakened labor unions (especially in Argentina) do weaken the capacity to organize and mobilize sustained, purposive resistance or political conflict. Finally, neoliberal reforms inherently weaken workers and the poor because they have diffuse effects, with some able to take advantage of new opportunities and others suffering the costs of the reforms (Graham and Pettinato 2003). In other words, neoliberal reforms have permitted a great deal of social mobility, both up and down, and that in turn has complicated the formation of political coalitions. In sum, neoliberalism has had some important successes overall. Those successes have weakened the resonance of alternative mobilizing agendas or ideologies. They have also led to organization weaknesses, not least because of their disparate effects within social classes. This may not provide a resolution to the larger debate over neoliberal reforms, but it does help understand the decrease in political conflict in Argentina and Brazil.

But, diminished polarized conflict over distinct development programs does not mean the end of violence. Politically motivated and mobilized violence persists in Argentina, albeit at a much lower scale and with lower stakes than in the past. Instead, both countries suffer from increases in violent crime, police brutality and impunity, and the paradoxical mixture of distrust of the police coupled with calls for harsher policing. Crime is not overtly political in either country. Yet, in both, it is hard not to see criminality as a reflection in important ways of the failure of the state. In that sense, it is political in that it calls into question the integrity and legitimacy of the state.

At root in both countries is a process of economic change that has weakened the opportunities for young, unskilled males even as it has generated new opportunities for considerable gains for skilled labor. Compounding this problem is the weakness of the educational system and the limitations on state support for young unemployed, undereducated men. Poverty and inequality are not causes of crime alone. But, poverty and especially inequality coupled with alienation, uncertainty, and pessimism about the prospects of employment are strong predictors of crime rates. The strong relation between crime rates and economic growth in both countries makes the point particularly clear.

Similarities aside, the much higher rate of crime in Brazil invites further comment. Brazil stands in sharp contrast with Argentina on four dimensions. First, crime in Brazil is clearly racialized, both in terms of its victims and the response of the judicial system, and arguably affects crime levels and police brutality. Second, the important presence of drugs in Brazil's shantytowns is a driver of exceptionally violent activity. Police responses to drug violence are themselves sources of violence and fear. Third, Brazil's much higher level of poverty and inequality is fertile ground for higher crime rates.

Finally, both Argentina and Brazil have developed innovative social policies to address their respective challenges. But, Brazil's much greater levels of poverty and inequality mean that its innovative response to the challenges facing older youth—after the age of 15—does not do enough to address the set of conditions that discourage young, unskilled men.

Conclusions: Policy Responses to Violence in the Contemporary Period

Argentina and Brazil experienced violent, unstable pasts reflecting apparently irreconcilable tensions around the problem of economic development. The challenges arising from an urban, industry-oriented society in conflict with landed elites is not unique to Latin America. This "Social Question" rocked Western Europe, the United States, and Canada and in many instances was only solved through violence and even war. In Latin America, very few countries found stable solutions to the problems of economic development. Argentina stands out for the wild instability of its politics. Both countries stand out for the emergence of highly institutionalized, bureaucratic-authoritarian dictatorships. Both countries also stand out for their apparent success in overcoming their respective struggles over economic development. As of 2011, Argentina and Brazil face democratic deficits, but neither country looks like a candidate for a return to widespread political violence or a return to authoritarianism.

The relative stability of the prevailing economic model—a kind of "pragmatic neoliberalism" in Brazil and a somewhat more statist version of the same model in Argentina—conceals the ongoing limits to development in both countries. Most importantly, market-oriented development has brought strong returns to skilled labor, but much less benefit and much less formal labor opportunity to unskilled labor. In particular, young undereducated males in both countries appear to be the biggest losers of the economic-reform process under way since the early mid-1980s. At the same time, the weakening of both community ties and state-support services over the same period of time have left in effect excluded significant segments of the population.

Galtung's notion of "structural violence"—that is, state policies that albeit unintentionally cause physical and psychological harm—points to the powerful effect of exclusion. In Argentina and Brazil, the young and the poor are not self-identified as a group, but the effects of this "structural violence" are no less systematic in their effects. Young men are unable to find work, satisfy their material needs in the home, or acquire educations that are sufficient to aid their life chances. In addition, they are the targets of brutal policing, called for by broader segments of society. While their violence is not overtly political, it can be seen as political in the sense that it reflects the failure of the state. Young men in both countries, but especially Brazil, in effect suffer from living life in a Hobbesian state of nature.

Ultimately, there is no straightforward, easy fix for the problem of this type of violence and a full review of the policy alternatives and efforts in the two countries is beyond the scope of this chapter. Although the causes and solutions to crime are still not fully and clearly understood, three crucial, interrelated issues stand out. First and foremost, young people need economic opportunity. The strong relation between economic performance and crime rates in both countries points clearly to the importance of a sufficient number of good jobs for reducing the grievances that lead young men into crime. Economic growth has to be sufficient to generate meaningful opportunities for unskilled labor so that the poor may raise themselves up—"bootstraps" rather than "band-aids" (Birdsall and Székely 2003). Second, both countries need to address inadequacies in educational institutions. Inadequacies of funding, training and supervision, and the weakness of the link between school and the job market have led to high dropout rates in both countries. This is doubly disconcerting in Argentina, which long enjoyed the distinction of the best education performance of any country in Latin America. By contrast, Brazilian policies such as Bolsa Família have helped fuel improvements in attendance, but overall quality continues to suffer. Finally, successive governments have pursued police reforms, but in both countries, it has met with little success. Most importantly, zero-tolerance policing has contributed to a climate of fear and pervasive violence. In effect, the state wages war against a population that suffers from its absence in the first place. A return to the past is unlikely in either country, but absent effective change in the three areas above, the young in both Argentina and especially Brazil will continue to face a Hobbesian world with an unacceptably high risk that life will be nasty, brutish, and short.

Notes

1. The focus of the chapter is on violence and stability, but as Adam Przeworski has observed, democracy entails a capacity to select leaders and to terminate disputes without bloodshed (Przeworski 1991; 1999). Under democracy, voters select and replace leaders, and all parties commit themselves to operating under a given set of rules that produce uncertain results. Actors then voluntarily commit to compliance with the outcomes and to seeking to reverse unfavorable outcomes only through the existing institutional rules. Thus, although this project is concerned with peace and stability, the level of democracy says something

meaningful about the possibility of social violence in a country and the capacity to "terminate" disputes without bloodshed even in a context of potentially sharp disagreements over policy, ideology, or identity.

2. In fact, crime has surged all across Latin America, constituting a regional problem as opposed to a problem of specific countries. Bergman reports that the average increase in homicides from 1985 to 2000 across 13 Latin American countries is 108 percent, while the increase for 15–24 year olds is 226 percent (although Guatemala's staggering increases drive both rates up, it is still 75 percent and 156 percent respectively excluding Guatemala's data). Despite the importance of the issue, Bergman points out that it has not yet generated a significant literature examining the problem (Bergman 2006, 50).

3. The discussion below draws substantially on the work of Ruth Berins Collier and David Collier for their deep analysis of the problem of "incorporation" of the working class. The Collier's work emphasizes the structural sources of oligarchic, middle-class, and working-class power and examines the bargaining dynamics that result. Ultimately, the argument turns on the institutional mechanisms that define labor's routinized, legalized integration into the polity—both in terms of labor regulations and political-party connections. Note that Argentina's highly organized and powerful labor movement was "incorporated" on highly favorable terms and linked to a radical political party. By contrast, Brazil's diffuse and much weaker labor movement was legally "incorporated" without political-party links and through a very extensive and repressive set of corporatist institutions—what the Colliers called "state incorporation" (Collier and Collier 1991).

4. Paul Lewis, however, notes that even the middle class was internally divided as leading industrialists split between agro-export-oriented industry and domestic manufacturers, each with rival business associations. This divide would continue to split industrialists through the twentieth century (Lewis 1990, 80).

5. Note however that both mechanisms contributed to a weakening of agricultural exports and growing balance of payment problems over time. The key difference is in the conflict produced by the overt political nature of IAPI versus the multiple exchange rate regime.

6. Debt is an inherent part of a developing countries' profile as capital scarcity forces governments to seek external savings to finance economic development. The debt crisis in Latin America was not an inevitable result of ISI. Rather, it grew out of conjunctural conditions, such as the OPEC oil shocks of 1973 and 1979, as well as Latin American governments' opportunistic and ultimately unwise heavy borrowing during the 1970s as recycled "petrodollars" were offered on very attractive terms. By 1980, Latin America's debt profile ran to several hundred billions, largely denominated in dollars and with floating interest rates. The second shock of 1979 was catastrophic as the US Federal Reserve sharply raised interest rates to contain US inflation. Nevertheless, ISI's imbalance between the constant financing needs of manufacturing and declining export competitiveness produced an inherent vulnerability to exogenous financial shocks.

7. Albert Hirschman (1968) points out that the failure of ISI was not inevitable—policy solutions that could help move Latin American countries from the "easy" phase of ISI to the more challenging phases necessary to promote development existed. The problem was a political one. Nevertheless, as James Mahon (1992) has demonstrated, the political problem, rooted both in the wage levels of the industrial working class and the profit levels of the domestic business community, was an enormously difficult one, and therefore it is not surprising that few Latin American countries were able to solve it.
8. There are of course a small number of exceptions. Economic policy in the more radical or populist left in contemporary Latin America is very controversial, and countries like Bolivia, Ecuador, or Venezuela have witnessed intense and often violent mobilizations over economic policy/program disputes. Much of the rest of the region has found something of a balance between market-oriented policies with some measure of state intervention, what Eduardo Silva dubbed "pragmatic neoliberalism" (Silva 1996). That does not mean that differences over policy have disappeared, but the conflicts tend to be more at the margins than fundamental, wholesale differences in philosophy (Tussie and Heidrich 2008).
9. Indeed, as of this writing, the Rousseff administration is aggressively pursuing the "Belo Monte" hydroelectric program initiated under the Lula government despite strong resistance from environmental and indigenous movements and the threat of displacement of 20,000 citizens.
10. Bolsa Família is actually an umbrella program that unified four already existing programs that had been developed in the 1990s at the municipal level. Success at the municipal level led electoral competitors from the two main competitors, the PT and the Brazilian Social Democratic Party (PSDB) to compete over who could claim credit for their introduction. Over the 1990s, this "competitive credit claiming" led to their introduction at higher and higher levels of government. Fernando Henrique Cardoso (PSDB) finally nationalized the programs, but his successor, Lula, succeeded in developing a single registry (*Cadastro Único*) and simplifying delivery of the benefits under the umbrella Bolsa Família. The four component programs were: *Bolsa Escola, Auxílio Gás, Bolsa Alimentação,* and the *Cartão Alimentação* (Melo 2008).

References

Alperin, María Noel Pi. 2009. The impact of Argentina's social assistance program Plan Jefes y Jefas de Hogar on structural poverty. *Estudios Económicos*, numéro extraordinario: 49–81.

Arce, Moisés. 2010. Parties and social protest in Latin America's neoliberal era. *Party politics*, published online before print. http://ppq.sagepub.com/content/early/2010/03/31/1354068809346005.abstract.

Arends-Kuenning, Mary. 2009. A report card for Lula: Progress in education. In *Brazil under Lula: Economy, politics, and society under the worker-president*, edited by Joseph Love and Werner Baer, 205–220. New York: Palgrave MacMillan.

Auyero, Javier, and Timothy Patrick Moran. 2007. The dynamics of collective violence: Dissecting food riots in contemporary Argentina. *Social Forces* 85(3): 1341–1367.

Baer, Werner. 1995. *The Brazilian economy: Growth and development*. New York: Praeger.

Bergman, Marcelo S. 1999. Conjectures about the new wave of Latin American violence. Paper presented at the Conference on Rising Violence and the Criminal Justice Response in Latin America: Towards an Agenda for Collaborative Research in the 21st Century. University of Texas at Austin, May 6–9, 1999. http://lanic.utexas.edu/project/etext/violence/memoria/session_1.html. Accessed March 15, 2011.

———. 2006. Crime and citizen security in Latin America: The challenges for new scholarship. *Latin American Research Review* 41(2): 213–227.

Birdsall, Nancy, and Miguel Székely. 2003. Bootstraps, not band-aids: Poverty, equity, and social policy. In *After the Washington Consensus: Restarting growth and reform in Latin America*, edited by John Williamson and Pedro Pablo Kuczynski, 49–73. Washington DC: Institute for International Economics.

Briceño-León, Roberto. 1999. Violence and the right to kill: Public perceptions from Latin America. Paper presented at the Conference on Rising Violence and the Criminal Justice Response in Latin America: Towards an Agenda for Collaborative Research in the 21st Century. University of Texas at Austin, May 6–9, 1999. http://lanic.utexas.edu/project/etext/violence/memoria/session_1.html. Accessed March 15, 2011.

Brinks, Daniel. 2006. The rule of (non)law: Prosecuting police killings in Brazil and Argentina. In *Informal institutions and democracy in Latin America*, edited by Gretchen Helmke and Steven Levitsky. Baltimore: Johns Hopkins University Press.

———. 2012. a tale of two cities. In *The handbook of Latin American politics*, edited by Peter Kingstone and Deborah Yashar. New York: Routledge Press.

Colburn, Forrest D. 2002. *Latin America at the end of politics*. Princeton, NJ: Princeton University Press.

Collier, Ruth Berins, and David Collier. 1991. *Shaping the political arena*. Princeton: Princeton University Press.

Corrales, Javier. 2003. Market reforms. In *Constructing democratic governance*, edited by Jorge Dominguez and Michael Shifter, 74–99. Baltimore: Johns Hopkins University Press.

———. 2004. Multiple preferences, variable strengths: The politics of education reform in Argentina. In *Crucial needs, weak incentives: Social sector reform, democratization, and globalization in Latin America*, edited by Robert Kaufman and Joan Nelson. Baltimore: Johns Hopkins University Press.

Dammert, Lucia, and Mary Fran T. Malone. 2002. Inseguridad y temor en la Argentina: El impacto de la confianza en la policía y la corrupción sobre la percepción ciudadana del crimen. *Desarrollo Económico* 42(166): 285–301

———. 2006. Does it take a village? Policing strategies and fear of crime in Latin America. *Latin American Politics and Society* 48(4): 27–51.

Dominguez, Jorge I. 2008. Explaining Latin America's lagging development in the second half of the twentieth century: Growth strategies, inequality, and economic crises. In *Falling behind: Explaining the development gap between Latin America and the United States*, edited by Francis Fukuyama, 72–98. New York: Oxford University Press.

Eaton, Kent. 2008. Paradoxes of police reform: Federalism, parties and civil society in Argentina's public security crisis. *Latin American Research Review* 43(3): 5–32.

Erickson, Kenneth Paul. 1977. *The Brazilian corporative state and working class politics*. Berkeley: University of California Press.

Fishlow, Albert. 1973. Some reflections on post-1964 Brazilian economic policy. In *Authoritarian Brazil: Origins, policies and future*, edited by Alfred Stepan. New Haven, CT: Yale University Press.

Freedom House. 2011. Freedom, in the world annual survey. 2011. http://www.freedomhouse.org. Accessed February 28, 2011.

Frieden, Jeffry. 1991. *Debt, development, and democracy: Modern political economy and Latin America, 1965–1985*. Princeton: Princeton University Press.

Galtung. Johan. 1969. Violence, peace and peace research. *Journal of Peace Research* 6(l): 167–191.

Graham, Carol, and Stefano Pettinato. 2003. Hardship and happiness: Social mobility and public perceptions during market reforms. In *Post-stabilization politics in Latin America: Competition, transition, collapse*, edited by Carol Wise and Riordan Roett, 56–87. Washington DC: Brookings Institution Press.

Hagopian, Frances. 1996. *Traditional politics and regime change in Brazil*. Cambridge: Cambridge University Press.

Halperin Donghi, Tulio. 2008. Two centuries of South American reflections on the development gap between the United States and Latin America. In *Falling behind: Explaining the development gap between Latin America and the United States*, edited by Francis Fukuyama, 11–47. New York: Oxford University Press.

Hirschman, Albert O. 1968. The political economy of import-substituting industrialization in Latin America. *Quarterly Journal of Economics* 82(1): 1–32.

Hochstetler, Kathryn. 2008. Organized civil society in Lula's Brazil. In *Democratic Brazil revisited*, edited by Peter Kingstone and Timothy Power, 33–55. Pittsburgh: University of Pittsburgh Press.

Kay, Cristóbal. 2001. Reflections on rural violence in Latin America. *Third World Quarterly* 22(5): 741–775.

Keck, Margaret E. 1989. The new unionism in the Brazilian transition. In *Democratizing Brazil: Problems of transition and consolidation*, edited by Alfred Stepan, 252–296. New York: Oxford University Press.

Kostzer, Daniel. 2008. Argentina: A case study on the Plan Jefes y Jefas de Hogar Desocupados, or the employment road to economic recovery. Working Paper No. 534. The Levy Economics Institute Working Paper Collection, Bard College.

Kuczynski, Pedro Pablo. 1988. *Latin America debt*. Baltimore: Johns Hopkins University Press.

Kurtz, Marcus. 2004. The dilemmas of democracy in the open economy: Lessons from Latin America. *World Politics* 56(2): 262–302.

Levitsky, Steven. 2003. *Transforming labor-based parties in Latin America: Argentine Peronism in comparative perspective.* New York: Cambridge University Press.

Levitsky, Steven, and Maria Victoria Murillo. 2005. *The politics of institutional weakness: Argentine democracy.* University Park: Penn State University Press.

Lewis, Paul H. 1990. *The crisis of Argentine capitalism.* Chapel Hill: University of North Carolina Press.

Linz, Juan J., and Alfred Stepan. 1996. *Problems of democratic transition and consolidation.* Baltimore: Johns Hopkins University Press.

Lodola, Germán. 2005. Protesta popular y redes clientelares en la Argentina: El reparto federal del Plan Trabajar (1996–2001). *Desarrollo Económico* 44(176): 515–536.

Machado, Fabiana, Carlos Scartascini, and Mariano Tommasi. 2009. Political institutions and street protest in Latin America. Washington DC: Interamerican Development Bank, IDB Working Paper Series, No. WP-110.

Mahon, James E. Jr. 1992. Was Latin America too rich to prosper? Structural and political obstacles to export-led growth. *Journal of Development Studies* 28(2): 241–263.

Manzetti, Luigi. 1993. *Institutions, parties and coalitions in Argentine politics.* Pittsburgh: University of Pittsburgh Press.

McGuire, James W. 1997. *Peronism without Perón: Unions, parties, and democracy in Argentina.* Stanford, CA: Stanford University Press.

Melo, Marcus André. 2008. Unexpected successes, unanticipated failures: Social policy from Cardoso to Lula. In *Democratic Brazil revisited*, edited by Peter Kingstone and Timothy Power, 161–184. Pittsburgh: University of Pittsburgh Press.

Módolo, Cristian. 2004. Los peligros institucionales del Plan Jefes y Jefas de Hogar. *Novenas Jornadas Investigaciones en la Facultad de Ciencias Económicas y Estadística*, November.

Moseley, Mason, and Daniel Moreno. 2010. The normalization of protest in Latin America. *Americas Barometer Insight* 42: 1–7.

Murillo, M. Victoria. 2003. Latin American labor. In *Constructing democratic governance*, edited by Jorge Dominguez and Michael Shifter, 100–117. Baltimore: Johns Hopkins University Press.

Norden, Deborah. 1996. *Military rebellion in Argentina: Between coups and consolidation.* Lincoln: University of Nebraska Press.

O'Donnell, Guillermo. 1973. *Modernization and bureaucratic-authoritarianism: Studies in South American politics.* Politics of Modernization Series no. 9, Berkeley: Institute of International Studies, University of California.

Oxhorn, Phillip. 2006. Neopluralism and the challenges for citizenship in Latin America. In *Citizenship in Latin America*, edited by Joseph S. Tulchin and Margaret Ruthenberg, 123–147. Boulder, CO: Lynne Rienner Publishers.

Pereira, Anthony. 2003. Brazil's agrarian reform: Democratic innovation or oligarchic exclusion redux? *Latin American Politics and Society* 45(2): 41–65.

———. 2008. Public security, private interests, and police reform in Brazil. In *Democratic Brazil revisited*, edited by Peter Kingstone and Timothy Power, 185–208. Pittsburgh: University of Pittsburgh Press.

Perlman, Janice. 2008. Redemocratization viewed from below: Urban poverty and politics in Rio de Janeiro, 1968–2005. In *Democratic Brazil revisited*, edited by Peter Kingstone and Timothy Power, 257–280. Pittsburgh: University of Pittsburgh Press.
———. 2010. *Favela: Four decades of living on the edge in Rio de Janeiro*. New York: Oxford University Press.
Petras, James. 2000. *The left strikes back: Class and conflict in the age of neoliberalism*. Boulder, CO: Westview Press.
Przeworski, Adam. 1991. *Democracy and the market*. New York: Cambridge University Press.
———. 1999. Minimalist definition of democracy: A defense. In *Democracy's value*, edited by Ian Shapiro and Casiano Hacker-Cordón, 23–55. New York: Cambridge University Press.
Ponce, Aldo. 2005. Unemployment and opportunism: The *Piqueteros* of Argentina. Paper presented at the Midwest Political Science Association, Chicago, April 7–10, 2005.
Reiter, Bernd. 2009. *Negotiating democracy in Brazil: The politics of exclusion*. Boulder, CO: Lynne Rienner Publishers.
Rock, David. 1993. *Authoritarian Argentina: The nationalist movement, its history, its impact*. Berkeley: University of California Press.
Saavedra, Jaime. 2003. Labor markets during the 1990s. In *After the Washington Consensus: Restarting growth and reform in Latin America*, edited by John Williamson and Pedro Pablo Kuczynski, 213–263. Washington DC: Institute for International Economics.
Scheper-Hughes, Nancy. 1993. *Death without weeping: The violence of everyday life in Brazil*. Berkeley: University of California Press.
Seri, Guillermina. 2012. *Seguridad: Crime, police power and democracy in Latin America*. New York: Continuum Press.
Silva, Eduardo. 1996. *The state and capital in Chile: Business elites, technocrats, and market economics*. Boulder, CO: Westview Press.
Simmons, Cynthia S. 2004. The political economy of land conflict in the eastern Brazilian Amazon. *Annals of the Association of American Geographers* 94(1): 183–206.
Singer, Matthew. 2007. The electoral politics of vulnerability and the incentive to cast an economic vote. PhD Dissertation, Duke University.
Skidmore, Thomas E. 1967. *Politics in Brazil, 1930–1964: An experiment in democracy*. New York: Oxford University Press.
———. 1988. *The politics of military rule in Brazil: 1964-1985*. Oxford: Oxford University Press.
Skidmore, Thomas E., Peter Smith, and James Green. 2009. *Modern Latin America*. New York: Oxford University Press.
Smith, Peter. 2005. *Democracy in Latin America: Political change in comparative perspective*. New York: Oxford University Press.
Starr, Pamela. 1997. Government coalitions and viability of currency boards: Argentina under the Cavallo Plan. *Journal of Interamerican Studies and World Affairs* 39: 83–133.

Stepan, Alfred. 1978. Political leadership and regime breakdown in Brazil. In *The breakdown of democratic regimes*, edited by Juan J. Linz and Alfred Stepan, 110–137. Baltimore: Johns Hopkins University Press.

Sussekind, Elizabeth. 1999. Justice and conflict in needy communities: The Balcão de Direitos Project. Paper presented at the Conference on Rising Violence and the Criminal Justice Response in Latin America: Towards an Agenda for Collaborative Research in the 21st Century. University of Texas at Austin, May 6–9, 1999. http://lanic.utexas.edu/project/etext/violence/memoria/session_6.html. Accessed on March 15, 2011.

Tussie, Diana, and Pablo Heidrich. 2008. A tale of ecumenicism and diversity: Economic and trade policies of the New Left. In *Leftovers: Tales of the Latin American Left*, edited by Jorge G. Castañeda and Marco A. Morales, 45–65. New York: Routledge Press.

UN Office on Drugs and Crime. 2011. International homicide statistics report. http://www.unodc.org/unodc/en/data-and-analysis/homicide.html. Accessed February 28, 2011.

Waiselfisz, Julio Jacobo. 2011. Mapa da violência: Os jovens do Brasil. Instituto Sangari, Ministério da Justiça, Brasília, Brazil.

Welch, Cliff. 1999. *The seed was planted: The São Paulo roots of Brazil's rural labor movement, 1924–1964*. University Park: Penn State University Press.

———. 2006. Movement histories: A preliminary historiography of the Brazil's Landless Laborers' Movement (MST). *Latin American Research Review* 41(1): 198–210.

Weyland, Kurt. 2004. Neoliberalism and democracy in Latin America: A mixed record. *Latin American Politics and Society* 46(1): 135–157.

World Bank. 2004. Inequality and economic development in Brazil. World Bank Country Study. Washington DC.

———. 2006. Crime, violence and economic development in Brazil: Elements of effective policy. World Bank Report 36525, Poverty Reduction and Economic Management Sector. Washington DC.

———. Governance Indicators. http://www.worldbank.org/governance. Accessed February 28, 2011.

Index

1988 Amparo incident (Venezuela): focus on external threat, 159; and legitimacy, 171; reparations, 159
1989 Caracazo, 169
1991 U.S. Andean Trade Preference Act, 16
1993 Agrarian Law (Colombia), 98
1999 Constitution (Venezuela), 167
2001 Land Reform Law (Venezuela), 165
2002 Andean Trade Promotion and Drug Eradication Act, 16

abertura, 224
Acción Democrática (AD) (Venezuela), 157–158, 160, 163, 194–195; commitment to expanding public education, 194; declining support, Venezuela, 160; Venezuela, 157
Acción Democrática Nacionalista (ADN), 138
Acemoglu, Daron, 76
ACNUR, 110, 159
Acuña Rodarte, Olivia, 53
AD. *see* Acción Democrática (AD)
ADN, 138
affirmative action, 5, 28
agrarian reform, 17; East Asia, 11; effect of mismanagement on, 13; Guatemala, 82; Latin America in contrast to East Asia, 11; Mexico, 45; Venezuela, 159, 165

Agrarian Reform (Venezuela), 165
agrarista vision, 45
agriculturalists: from eastern lowlands, support of violence escalation, Bolivia, 140–141; investment response to government pressure, Bolivia, 145; Santa Cruz, Bolivia, 144
agriculture, 8, 10, 12, 13, 14, 15, 19, 22, 28; absorbed by industrial expansion, 11; as basis for social peace, 12; in Bolivia, 128–131, 138, 140; in Brazil, 223, 226; collective farms, 11; in Colombia, 96–98, 105–106, 109–111, 114, 116, 119–120; commercial, 10, 97; commodities, 78; conversion to drug production, 56; in Costa Rica, 86; dependence on, 9; development of, 11, 78; in El Salvador, 84; exports, 14, 15, 28, 78, 79, 97, 131, 132; government neglect of, 11, 14, 236; in Mexico, 43–56, 60–61; plantations, 10, 74, 78, 85, 86, 95, 96, 109–114, 119; sharecropping, 10; state or collective farms, 11; subsistence, 53, 97, 129; transition from traditional to export-driven commodities, 97; in Venezuela, 158, 165; workers, restrictions on organization, 10

agro-industrialists, 137, 144–145; threatened by private land redistribution, Bolivia, 144–145
agro-industries: in Bolivia, 128, 131, 134, 139,145; capital-intensive, 131
Aguilar, Alberto Luís, 140
Aguilar, Alonso, 47
Alaimo, Verónica, 77
Albornoz, O., 196
Alfonsín, Raúl, 227, 230; efforts to prosecute the military for human rights abuses, Argentina, 227, 229; military demand for an end to human rights abuse prosecutions, Argentina, 227
Allende, Salvador, 183–186, 191, 205–206; resistance to constructive education policies, Chile, 184
Allesandri, Arturo, 185
Allesandri, Jorge, 205; review of Chilean education system, 185
Alperin, María Noel Pi, 234
altiplano, 79, 82
Amazon, Brazil: land control, 19; as strategic asset, 236
Amparo, Venezuela, 155
antigovernment violence: Bolivia, 139, 145, 146; Chuquisaca, Bolivia, 142; failure to mobilize, Bolivia, 143; by groups from old middle class, Bolivia, 141; mobilized by prefects, Bolivia, 142; Pando, Bolivia, 142; Santa Cruz, Bolivia, 142; Tarija, Bolivia, 142
antimedia violence: by government supporters, Bolivia, 137; by supporters of the Santa Cruz prefect, Bolivia, 141
antineoliberalism, Venezuela, 200
Antioquia, Colombia, 99
Arauca, Colombia, 100, 101, 103; peasant resistance, 100
Arbelaez, Maria Angelica, 96
Arbenz, Jacob, 82

Arce, Moisés, 240
Arcia, Gustavo, 16, 28, 29, 71–90
Arellano-Yanguas, Javier, 19
ARENA. *see* National Renewal Alliance Party (ARENA) (Brazil)
Arends-Kuenning, Mary, 238
Argentina, 4, 6, 8, 17, 21, 22, 23, 24, 26, 27, 31, 155, 213, 214, 217, 221, 228, 242; crime rates, 228; currency crisis, 230; decline as a result of centralization, 225; degree of violence and polarization, 227; dependence on beef exports, 218; dollarization plan and presidential resignation, 228; economic growth with modest inflation and declining unemployment, 229–230; economic performance, 226–227; elites *versus* labor, 225; GDP, 231; free trade and industrialization, 219; Impossible Game, 219; instability of politics, 242; lack of peasantry, democracy threat to landed interests, 218; nationalization, 17; ongoing issues of violence, 228; organized, centralized, mobilized working class, 222; patterns of conflict, 215; persisting political violence, 228; polarized politics and regime instability, 216, 222–223, 227, 239–240; political and civil liberties, 226; politically motivated and organized violence, 215; poor as principal victims of crime and police brutality, 229; public concern about crime, 228; reductions in polarized politics, 229–230; regime changes and internal coups, 225; swings between democracy and authoritarianism, 219; war with England over Malvinas/Falkland Islands, 220
Argentine Institute for Trade and Production (IAPI), 221; direct tax on landed interests, 222

Index • 253

armed forces, and societal discipline, 22
Arroyo, Viviana, 71, 87
Ascher, William, 22, 50, 170, 173, 174, 176
Aspra, Antonio, 46
Assembly of Civil Society (ASC) (Guatemala), 83
Austin, R., 185, 186, 188, 191
authoritarian government, 22; Argentina and Brazil, 214, 242; El Salvador, 84; Venezuela, 155; and violence, 88
authoritarianism, Argentina and Brazil, 216; risk for Brazil, 227
auto-golpe: Brazil, 221
autonomy, 171
Auyero, Javier, 230
Ayala, José, 48
Aymara, Bolivia, 128

Bachelet, Michelle, 17, 23, 190, 191, 192
Badel, M.E., 104
Baer, Werner, 223
bananas, 78, 96; in Colombia, 109; in Guatemala, 82
BANURAL, 45
Banzer, Hugo, 133, 139
Banzer-Quiroga administration, Bolivia, 139
Barndt, William, 16, 21, 29, 125
Bautista, Romeo, 9
BBC, 193, 203
Beall, Jo, 11
beef, 78, 218; dependence on exports, Argentina, 218; Colombia, 109
Beijing Consensus, 16
Belaunde, Fernando, 10
Belo Horizonte, Brazil, technical training in school, 239
Beni, Bolivia, 127
Bennett, Douglas, 44
Bergman, Marcelo, 214, 229, 232, 233
Betancourt, Rómulo (Venezuela), 195; assassination attempt on, 158

Bhavnani, Ravi, 120
Binswanger-Mkhize, Hans, 12
Birdsall, Nancy, 234
Boliburguesia (Venezuela), 170
Bolivarian High Schools (Venezuela), 201
Bolivarian ideals (Venezuela), 199; education and communal councils, 203
Bolivarian Missions (Venezuela), 164, 200–202; similarity to Cuban campaigns, 164
Bolivarian Revolution (Venezuela), 31, 155, 161, 163, 167; fostering of ideological mentality in education policy, 200; as government of the poor, 168
Bolivarian Schools (Venezuela), 199, 204
Bolivarian student movement (Venezuela), 204
Bolivarian University of Venezuela (UBV), 202
Bolivia, 4, 5, 6, 8, 9, 11, 14, 16, 17, 18, 20, 21, 23, 26, 28, 29, 125–147; Aymara in, 128; backsliding on policy reforms, 17; Bolivarian Revolution, 31, 155; Central Valleys, 127, 132, 145; coca-tolerance policy, 133; departments, 127; Eastern Lowlands, 127, 128, 132, 141, 143, 144, 145, 147; cultural divide, 127; indigenous populations, 127; fiscal recentralization, 137, 138; labor shedding, 16; martial law, 143; nationalization, 17; role of ethnicity in violence, 146; Western Highlands, 127, 128, 129, 132, 144, 145
Bolivian Cattleman's Bank *(Banco Ganadero),* 137
Bolsa Família (Brazil), 229, 238, 243; education requirements, 238; and human capital, 238; limitations of, 238

254 • Index

Boraz, Steven, 72, 86
Border Industrialization Program (Mexico), 47
Bourgois, Phillippe, 78
Bourguignon, Camille, 12
BP-Amoco, Colombia, 102
Brazil, 4, 5, 6, 7, 9, 11, 12, 15, 18, 31, 213, 220, 228, 234, 242; 2016 Olympics, 238; apolitical violence, 215, 239, 243; concealment of ongoing weakness in the quality of political representation, 227; crime and homicide rates, 228; decentralized, diffuse patronage networks and proliferation of political parties, 227; diffuse economy with multiple sources of strength, 226; economic performance, 226–227, 235; Gini coefficient, 235; Gini coefficient for land, 235; government inability to deliver competent economic governance, 234; indirect means to tax exporters and subsidize industrial development, 222; indirect taxation of exports weakens competitiveness, 223; industrial policy, 17, 18, 19, 20, 22, 23, 24, 26, 28; Corumbiara and Carajas massacres, 11; Landless Workers' Movement (MST), 14; lack of trust in police, 239; little polarization as result of removal of labor movement leadership, 224; lower violence and repression, 224; MST, 19; new classes join excluded oligarchs, challenge states' hold on political system, 221; paralyzing fragmentation and neoliberalism, 240; patronage network, 226; patterns of conflict, 215; policy centralized, patronage networks for decentralized clientelistic relations, 223; political and civil liberties, 226; poor as principal victims of crime and police brutality, 229; presidential impeachment, 228; progress due to decentralization, 225; protectionism and limits of domestic supply, 223; regime changes and internal coups, 225; as rising global power, 213; violent crime, 214; weak working class, 222
Brazilian Miracle, 224
Briceño-León, Roberto, 161, 239
Brink, Daniel, 12, 214, 228, 232, 238
British Petroleum, natural gas investment in Bolivia, 131
Bruneau, Thomas, 72, 86
Brunner Commission of 1994 (Chile), 189
Brysk, Alison, 130, 146
Buenos Aires, Argentina, 217, 232, 238
Burggraaff, W., 196
Byman, Daniel, 116

Cabañas, Lucio, 48, 55
Calado, Fernando, 109, 110
Caldas, Colombia, 105, 106, 108, 161; dependence on coffee, 105
Caldera Rodríguez, Rafael: embrace of neoliberalism, 197; promise to end neoliberal reforms in Venezuela, 197; unrealized reforms in Venezuela, 198
Calderón, Felipe, 25, 58, 59; election of, 58; platform for 2006 election, 58
Campesino Organization of the South Sierra (OCSS) (Mexico), 55
Canada, 4, 52
Cannon, Barry, 165, 166, 199, 200, 201, 202
Caño Limón oil field (Colombia), 101
canon minero, 19
canon petrolero, 19
CANTV. *see Compañía Anónima Nacional Teléfonos de Venezuela*
capital flight, 49; from Venezuela, 161, 177

Index • 255

capital-intensive industries, state promotion in Bolivia, 132–133
capitalization program, Bolivia, 131
Caquetá, Colombia, 111, 113; GDP, 111
Caracallo, Oruro (Bolivia), 137
Caracas, Venezuela, 167, 168, 197
Caracazo (Venezuela), 155, 160, 162, 169, 197
carapintadas, 227
Cárdenas, Cuauhtémoc (Mexico), 43, 60; and land redistribution, 50; presidential bid, 55
Cárdenas, Lázaro (Mexico), benefits to workers and peasants, 45; PRI establishment, 45; redistributive measures, 44
Cardenista reform, 45; peasant disillusionment with reversal, 47
Cardoso, Fernando Henrique (Brazil), 228, 235
Carlsen, Laura, 59
Carmona, Fernando, 47
Carmona, Pedro, 167
Carrillo Flórez, Fernando, 74, 77, 90
Carter, Michael, 97
Casanare, Colombia, 100, 101, 102, 110
cash-transfer programs, 7, 8, 18, 20, 24; *Bolsa Família* (Brazil), 238; direct transfers of oil and mining revenues to subnational governments, 18
Castellanos, J.M., 74
Catholic Church, 185, 194–195, 199, 235
cattle, in Casanare, Colombia, 103
Censo Nacional DANE (Colombia), 99, 101, 108, 113, 118
Central Obrera Boliviana (COB), 131
Central University of Venezuela, 204
Centre for Co-operation with Non-members, 189, 190, 191, 192; market incentives to stimulate private schools demand, 188
centrism, 23, 24

Centro de Investigación y Educación Popular (CINEP), 99; Base de Datos, 99
cero coca, 135
Cesar, Colombia, 110, 111, 113; GDP, 111
CGT. *see* General Labor Confederation (CGT) (Argentina)
Chalatenango, El Salvador, 84
Chapare region, Cochabamba, Bolivia, 127, 133, 134
Chávez, Hugo, (Venezuela), 6, 20, 23, 26, 30, 154, 155, 161, 169, 171, 172, 183, 194, 197, 202, 204, 206; alignment with darker and poorer sectors, 166; alliance strategy ms to buy international allies and challenge the United States, 163; appeal to the poor, 163; arrest of, 167; and class-based politics, 175; concentration of presidential power, 163; creation of hostility through education policy, 184; deepening of social cleavages, 163; dropped education agenda in response to opposition: Venezuela, 200; economic policies, 163; efforts to reclaim control of oil industry, 164; election of, 155, 163, 198; ethnicity, 168; exclusion former elites, 163; favoring the poor, antagonizing the wealthy, Venezuela, 170; health, 204; increasing salience of social differences, 163; oil wealth and renewed production, Venezuela, 168; opposition to, 200; petroleum royalties, 173; and political violence:, 176; redistributive aims, 163; rejection of neoliberalism, 163; rejection of old political elite, 163; restoration of power, 167; socialist political agenda, 155; strategy of education reform, 184, 193, 200, 203

Chavistas (Venezuela), 207
Chiapas, Mexico, 50, 51, 54; enduring grievances leading to unrest, 50; land invasions, 50
Chile, 4, 8, 9, 14, 18, 20, 22–26, 155, 206; disappearance of citizens, 188; education and policy, 30; free and compulsory education, 185; political and civil liberties, 226; public education, 185
Chile Crece Contigo, 190
Chocó, Colombia, 110, 111, 113, 116; GDP, 111
Chomsky, Noam, 72, 78
Christian Democratic Party (Chile), 186; and education, 185; resistance to Allende's education policies, 187
Chuquisaca, Bolivia, 127, 140
CIDOB. *see Confederación de Indígenas del Oriente, Chaco, y Amazonia de Bolivia*
CINEP. *see Centro de Investigación y Educación Popular*
citizenship: Costa Rica, 78, 85, 86; Limón, Costa Rica, 86; multicultural, 6
civic committees: Bolivia, 141–144.
civil conflict, 43; in Guatemala, 79
civil liberties, 81
civil war, 3, 182; in Bolivia, 134, 146–147; Colombia, 213; in El Salvador, 29, 84, 89; and gangs, 88; in Guatemala, 29, 79; Latin American, 1
clientelistic networks. *see* patronage networks
coca, 29, 96, 99; in Bolivia, 29, 125–127, 133–134, 145; in Colombia, 104, 114–117; eradication campaigns, 133; sectoral development, 95
cocaine. *see* coca
cocaleros, 134, 136, 141, 145–147; in Bolivia, 125, 134–135

Cochabamba, Bolivia, 127, 141
Cockcroft, James, 47
coffee, 21, 29, 78, 84, 85; 1992 market collapse, 10; in Colombia, 95–96, 104–106, 109; Mexican coffee marketing board, 53
Colburn, Forest, 240
Collier, David, 50, 51, 216, 217, 218, 221, 222
Collier, Ruth, 50, 216, 217, 218, 221, 222
Collor, Fernando (Brazil), 228, 234; impeachment on corruption charges, 228
Colombia, 4–6, 9, 10–12, 14–17, 19–20, 24, 26, 95–125; dismantling of drug cartels, 16; guerrilla groups, 19; state capacity, 104
Colombian Land Reform Law, 10, 98
colonization, 77, 80, 97; of Bolivia, 127; of Brazil, 11; of Colombia, 97–98; Iberian, 8
COMIBOL. *see* Corporación Minera de Bolivia
Comité de Organización Política Electoral Independiente (COPEI) (Venezuela), 157–158, 160, 163, 195
commodities, 28–29, 75, 78, 90, 95–100, 104–105, 116, 119–121, 218, 220–221, 230; association with violence, 119–120; Argentine, 220; Colombian, 104–105
Communism: and the Brazilians military, 221
Compañía Anónima Nacional Teléfonos de Venezuela (CANTV), privatization of, 161
Conaghan, Elizabeth, 130–132
Concertación para el No (Chile), 188
Concertación para la Democracia (Chile), 188–190, 193, 205
Concertación period, Chile, 183; education policy as part of the Pinochet recovery agenda, 183;

efforts to avoid conflict over education policy, 185; conflict resolution policies, 185
Conciencia de Patria (CONDEPA), 138
CONDEPA, 138
Confederación de Indígenas del Oriente, Chaco, y Amazonia de Bolivia (CIDOB), 135–136
Constituent Assembly: Bolivia, 138; debates over revenue redistribution, 140; Chuquisaca, Bolivia, 141; push for plenipotentiary powers, Bolivia, 142
constitution: Bolivia, 50, 140, 142; Brazil, 221; Chile, 187; Colombia, 50, 99; Guatemala, 83; Mexico, 52, 84; Venezuela, 163, 166, 167, 203, 204
Cook, Colleen, 56
cooperatives: agriculture, 22; industry, 22
Copacabana, Brazil, *favelas,* 239
COPEI. *see* Comité de Organización Política Electoral Independiente (COPEI) (Venezuela)
Corbacho, Ana, 53
Coronil, Fernando, 159, 161, 162, 171
Corporación Minera de Bolivia (COMIBOL), 132; labor shedding, 16
Corrales, Javier, 164, 176, 228, 233
corruption, 13, 75, 76, 81, 231–232; in Brazil, 234, 239; in Colombia, 101; effect on growth, 77; effect on violence, 76; judicial systems, 76; limiting the effectiveness of oil-related resources: in Mexico, 56–59; siphoning of international borrowed capital, 13; Transparency International's 2010 Corruption Perceptions Index, 176; in Venezuela, 161, 174, 176–177
Corumbiara, Brazil,11
Cossio, Mario, 143
Costa Rica, 4, 17, 26, 29, 71, 72, 74, 78, 85, 87; agriculture, 86; coffee export, 85; colonization, 72; crime prevention, 89; economic value of violence and crime, 74; ecotourism, 86; electronics, 86; immigrant labor, 85; investment in education and institutions, 79; political and civil liberties, 226; population diversity, 85; reported crime, 88; street crime, 89; self-image, 86; software industry, 86
Costas, Ruben, 141
coups d'état, 1, 82, 155, 158, 160, 162–163, 166–170,187, 191, 200, 214, 217, 219–221, 225, 236; Argentina, 219–220; Brazil, 214, 222, 236; Chile, 187; definition of military role, Guatemala, 82–83; implicit threat of force, 160; Venezuela, 154, 155, 158, 160, 162–163, 166–167, 197
Cox, C., 189–191
Creole social democracy, 18
crime, 81, 87–89; in Argentina, 214; in Brazil, 214; in Costa Rica 86–88; effect on investment, 77; effect on labor productivity, 77; effects of recession on, 87; in El Salvador, 78, 87; in Guatemala, 82, 87, 89; in Honduras, 87; reduction policies, 72; roots and policies, 87; in the United States, 215
criminal violence, 41–43, 52, 55, 72, 237; in Argentina, 214, 229, 232, 236–237, 240–241; in Brazil, 214, 229, 236–241; caused by rise in labor market uncertainty, 233; causes, Latin America, 233; as a corollary of market-oriented policy reforms, 214–215; correlation with economic growth, 241; correlation to inequality, 42; correlation to poverty and inequality, 241; in Costa Rica, 71; definition, 4; and drugs,238, 241; and income levels, 237; and lack

of jobs, 229; and market reforms, 214–215; in Mexico, 55, 61–62; and race, 237, 241; reflection of political legitimacy, 241; transformation from ideological-based to criminal, 31
criminalization of the peasant, Colombia, 97
criollo class, 43
Crisp, Brian, 14
Cristiani, Alfredo, peace negotiations, 84
crop-substitution plans: Bolivia, 133; Colombia, 104
Cruces, Guillermo, 25
Cruz, José, 3, 88
Cuba, 9, 22, 77–78
Cuban Revolution of 1959, 9, 77–78; as a model for local insurgencies, El Salvador, 84; as motive for persecution of leftist leaders, Guatemala, 82; idealism, Venezuela, 158
Cumberland, Charles, 43, 44
currency devaluation: Argentina, 228, 230, 233; Venezuela, 161
Curtin, Kevin, 96, 104, 110, 116

da Silva, Lula (Brazil), 23
Dabes, Cintia, 26
Dahl, Robert, 169
Damiani, Octavio, 97
Dammert, Lucia, 232, 233
DANE. *see* National Administrative Department of Statistics (DANE) (Colombia)
DATAGOB, 80, 81
Davies, L., 181
Davis, R.G., 5, 185
de Ferranti, David, 2, 9, 10, 11
de Janvry, Alain, 9
de la Madrid Hurtado, Miguel (Mexico),17; and market liberalizing reforms, 52
de la Rúa, Fernando (Argentina), 228, 231

de Navarette, Zander, 47
debt, 22; crisis during the 1980s, 13–14; and resource abundance, 172; Venezuelan, 161, 171–172
debt crisis, 13, 14; in Mexico, 51, 55, 60–61; structural adjustment responses to, 14, 15; in Venezuela, 161
debt negotiations, with international creditors, Bolivia, 130
decentralization, 20; of Chilean education, 189; Colombia, 98–99; of Venezuelan education, 197
deforestation, 19
deGroof, J., 189
Deininger, K., 78, 98
Del Bufalo, E., 196
democracy, 5, 18, 21–23, 74, 80, 169–170, 182–183, 189; alternative forms of justice, 3; in Argentina, 31, 213, 215–216, 218, 220, 226–227, 229, 242; in Bolivia, 145; in Brazil, 213–217, 220, 224, 227, 234–235, 242; in Chile, 182–183, 189, 191, 206; consolidation of, 21; in Costa Rica, 72, 79, 86; in El Salvador, 72, 84–85; and inflation, 169; link to social violence, 3; loss of legitimacy as contributing factor of decline, 170; in Mexico, 55, 58; outlook for Latin America, 213; in Venezuela, 30, 153–155, 158, 160, 172, 174, 182–183, 195, 197–198, 213
Democratic Security Policy (Colombia), 99
demographic change, Colombia, 102
Demoscopía, S.A., 87, 88
departmental revenues: as source of funding for jobs and aid, Bolivia, 136,140
Dermota, Ken, 56
development gap, 225
Di John, Jonathan, 171, 174
Díaz, Porfirio (Mexico), and structural violence, 43

Dirty War (Argentina), 220
disarmament, 90
discrimination: against people of African descent, 79; in Costa Rica, 86; government efforts to redress, 86; in Guatemala, 82
displacement: in Bolivia, 132–133, 139; in Brazil, 236; in Colombia,10, 96, 97, 109, 110, 112, 117; development-induced, 109–110; and paramilitary groups, 112; and ranching, 110
dollarzation plan (Argentina), 228
Dominguez, Jorge, 225
Dominican Republic, 9, 26
Doyle, Kate, 48
drug trade, 56; Colombia, 116; growth, concentration in Brazil's urban *favelas*, 238
drugs and drug-related violence, 1, 3, 15–16, 28, 41, 51, 71–72, 88, 134; in Argentina, 231; in Bolivia, 134; in Brazil, 238, 241; cartels, 16; in Colombia, 55–59, 98, 104, 110, 116, 228; drug lords as conflict entrepreneurs, 11, 15, 16, 24, 25; in El Salvador, 86; eradication programs, 16, 19, 28, 29; effect on peasant labor, 97; in Guatemala, 71, 82; and employment, 57; in Mexico, 56–61, 213, 228; and poverty, 57; and terrorism, 59
Dube, Oeindrila, 96, 100, 104
Duer, K., 181
Dulitzky, Ariel, 77
Dunne, M., 181
Durango, Mexico, land invasions, 48
Durnan, Michael, 116
Dussell Peters, Enrique, 54
Dutch disease, 49; in Bolivia, 145

East Asia, 13
Eaton, Kent, 131, 139, 141, 232
Echavarría, Juan José, 96

Echeverría, Luís, 60; concessions to rural dwellers, 48; social programs, 49
Echeverría, Luís, land reform, 50
ECLAC. *see* Economic Commission for Latin America and the Caribbean
Economic Commission for Latin America and the Caribbean (ECLAC), 5, 6, 54, 97, 191, 198
economic crisis, in Argentina, 214, 220, 226, 228, 230, 232–233; in Bolivia, 127; in Brazil, 214, 226, 228, 234; in Chile, 183; in Costa Rica, 85; in Mexico, 52, 54; in Venezuela, 155, 160, 166, 174, 183, 204
economic decline: and education as a source of tension, 194; and racist discourse, Venezuela, 166; roots of, Venezuela, 161; Venezuela, 154, 159, 160, 161, 166
economic development, 14, 15, 17, 23, 27, 215; in Argentina, 214, 224, 242–243; in Bolivia, 125–126, 130–132, 138, 145–146; in Brazil, 214, 221–222, 224, 242–243; in Chile, 188, 191; in Colombia, 96, 106,110, 116, 120; and conflict, 182; correlation to intergroup violence, 126, 157; in Costa Rica, 79–80; definition, 156; in El Salvador, 80; in Guatemala, 79–80; in Mexico, 47, 55, 60; neoliberal, 160; policies limiting human standard of living, 215; pro-urban and industrial policies *versus* pro-commodity export policies, 230; and resource abundance, 172; role in fomenting or deterring conflict, 155–156role of education in, 185; role of fairness and application of law in, 80; trailing of economic policies, 156; in Venezuela, 161, 171, 176, 195
economic policy, 154, 171–172, 218, 220, 239; in Argentina, 216, 218–220, 239, 241; in Brazil, 216,

223, 235; causes of weakened labor and education systems, Argentina and Brazil, 241; in Colombia, 97; and distribution of costs and benefits, 175; export-promotion, 76; industrial protection, 90; and political violence, 171; role in fomenting or deterring conflict, 155–156. *See also* import substitution industrialization: and social cleavages, 175; and social conflict, 171; social policy to support market society, 239; and subgroup identification, 175; in Venezuela, 156, 174–175, 177
Economist, 200, 203
Economist Intelligence Unit (EIU) (on Bolivia), 131, 133, 138, 141–145
ecotourism, Costa Rica, 86
Ecuador, 4, 8, 9, 16, 17, 18, 23, 25, 26
Edholm, F., 186, 187, 188
Education and education policy, 5, 7, 20, 24, 28, 29, 30, 31, 51, 75–78, 157, 171, 176, 181, 186; in Argentina, 233–234, 243; in Brazil, 236, 238, 243; in Chile,182–194, 203–208; in Colombia, 101, 112, 114, 118–119; in Costa Rica, 85; in El Salvador, 84; in Guatemala, 82; as a modernization tool, 185; as a policy and political tool, 205; and policy environment, 182; and political stability, 181; as a tool of marginalization, 194; in Venezuela, 30, 161, 181–184, 194–208
Edwards, S., 14, 204
EIU. *see* Economist Intelligence Unit (EIU)
ejidal agriculture, Mexico, 46
ejiditarios, 46
ejidos (Mexico), 44–48; elimination of, 52; elimination of bank credit to, 53; privatization, 52
El Bravo Pueblo Database, 159

El Salvador, 4, 9, 23, 26, 71–74, 78, 79, 84, 87, 88; authoritarian governments in, 84; Chalatenango, 84; civil war, 84, 89; compliance with peace accord, 85; consensus on causes of violent crime, 89; democratic restoration of economic growth and political tolerance, 84; Economic and Social Development Plan, 85; economic value of violence and crime, 74; exports, 84; human rights, 84; peace agreement, 84–86; presidential elections, 85; repressive policies, 89
elections, 23; in Argentina, 217, 219; in Brazil, 216–217, 221–222, 224; in Chile,186, 188; in Venezuela, 162, 184,198, 207, Chávez, Hugo, Venezuela, 198
electoral absenteeism, rural Mexico, 54
electoral fraud, Mexico, 55
electoral system, Bolivia, 138
Elhawary, Samir, 96, 100, 110
Elías Calles, Plutarco, new political party, 44
Ellner, Steve, 158, 161, 163, 164, 165, 167, 176, 195, 197, 199
ELN. *see* National Liberation Army (ELN) (Colombia)
ELR. *see* Employer of Last Resort (ELR) (Argentina)
Employer of Last Resort (ELR) (Argentina), 233, 234; estimated and actual demand, 234; program assessments, 234
employment, 5, 11, 14, 21, 24, 28, 76, 238–239, 241; in Argentina, 31, 223, 229, 231, 233–234; in Bolivia, 128–134, 145–146; in Brazil, 229; in Colombia, 96–97, 107; correlation to drug crimes among young males, 57; in El Salvador, 72, 84–85; factor in relative deprivation, 156; generation of, 7; in Mexico, 43, 46–47, 49,

53–54, 60–62; in Venezuela, 158–161
endogenous development, 23
Enright, M.J., 195, 196, 197
entrepreneurs, 28, 90; Bolivia, 132; Costa Rica, 77; El Salvador, 77; Guatemala, 77
ENU. *see* National Unified School (Escuela Nacional Unida) (ENU) (Chile)
EPR. *see* Popular Revolutionary Army (EPR) (Mexico)
Erickson, Kenneth Paul, 226
Escobar, Arturo, 96, 109
Eskridge, Chris, 57
España, L.P., 203
Espino, José, 48
Espinoza, Ana Nancy, 71, 87
Estado Nôvo (Brazil), 221
estado-docente (Venezuela), 194
Esteva, Gustavo, 46, 49
ethnic identification, 5; as social construct, 169; in Venezuela, 165, 168–169, 175
ethnic violence, political movements and ethnic-based claims, 147
Europe, 22, 90
exchange rates: in Argentina, 224–225; in Bolivia, 130, 145; in Brazil, 222, 224–225; in Venezuela, 161
exchange-rate devaluation, Bolivia, 130
Executive Decree 29322, Bolivia, 142
exports, 131; in Argentina, 217–218, 225; in Bolivia, 131, 133; in Brazil, 225; in Colombia, 96–97, 109; in Costa Rica, 85–86; dependence on exports to support urban sector policies, 224–225; in El Salvador, 84; in Mexico, 43, 47, 53; promotion of agro-exports, 10, 15; raw-material, 8
EZLN. *see* Zapatista Army of National Liberation

Fabre, Guihern, 57, 74
factories, confiscation of, 7
Faguet, Jean-Paul, 98–99
Fajnzlber, Pablo, 42
Falkland Islands, 220
FAM, 143
famine, in Mexico, 44
Fárber, Guillermo, 53
FARC. *see* Revolutionary Armed Forces of Colombia (FARC)
farm subsidies, Mexico, 55
Farmer's Direct Support Program (PROCAMPO) (Mexico), 53
Farrell, J.P., 185, 186, 187
fascism, Brazil, 222
favelas: Copacabana, Brazil, 239; Madureira, Brazil, 239
Fearon, James, 100
FEDECAMARAS. *see* Federación de Cámaras y Asociaciones de Comercio y Producción de Venezuela
FEDEPALMA, *see* Federación Nacional de Cultivadores de Palma de Aceite
Federación de Cámaras y Asociaciones de Comercio y Producción de Venezuela (FEDECAMARAS), 167
Federación Nacional de Cultivadores de Palma de Aceite (FEDEPALMA), 110
Felix, David, 47
Figueres, José (Costa Rica), 86
firearms: in Colombia, 110; correlation to street crime and family violence, 90; in El Salvador, 89; role in violence, 88
fiscal recentralization, Bolivia, 143
fiscal responsibility reform, 15
Fishlow, Albert, 223
Fitzgerald, E.V.K., 49
FMLN, *see* Frente Farabundo Martí para la Liberación
food, 51; exports and imports, Mexico, 49; land reform to increase self-

sufficiency in production, Venezuela, 165; riots, Argentina, 230; subsidies, Venezuela, 161
foreign investment: in Argentina, 216; in Bolivia, 130–131; in Brazil, 216; in Mexico, 43, 49
forest policy, 19
forestry, Bolivian, 128
Fort, L., 191
Fox, Vicente (Mexico), 25, 53, 54, 58, 59; agreement with Zapatistas, 59; Oportunidades cash-transfer program, 59
Francés, A., 195, 196, 197
Franklin, J., 192, 193
free-trade pacts, 16
Freeburger, A.R., 185
Freedom House, index of political and civil liberties, 226
Frei Montalva, Eduardo (Chile), 183, 185–187, 205
Frei Ruiz-Tagle, Eduardo (Chile), 189
Frente Farabundo Martí para la Liberación (FMLN), peace agreement with El Salvador, 84–85
Frieden, Jeffry, 224
Fundación Arias (Costa Rica), 74, 88
Funes, Mauricio, 23, 85
FUSADES, 72, 74, 89

Galli, Rosemary, 98
Galtung, John, 41, 42, 215
Gamarra, Eduardo, 130, 132, 133, 134, 139, 145, 146; Bolivia, 139
gangs, 1, 3, 16, 21, 73–74; in Brazil, 214, 238; causes of growth, 88; correlation to crime, 87; in Costa Rica, 87; and dysfunctional families, 88; in El Salvador, 72, 84, 86–88; in Guatemala, 71, 82, 87; in Haiti, 87; in Honduras, 86–88; in Los Angeles, 86; *maras*, 87, 89; in Nicaragua 87; nonideological, 25; number of members, 87; U.S.-originated, 29; as

vanguard of social mobilization, 5; as vehicle for crime, 87; warfare and crime, 72; and youth, 87
García Pérez, Leticia, 144
García, Haydée, 161
gas revenues, Bolivia, 143, 146
Gasparini, Leonardo, 25
Gaviria, Alejandro, 96
GDP (gross domestic product), 119
GDP/PC. *see* per capita gross domestic product (GDP/PC)
Geffray, Christian, 57
General Labor Confederation (CGT) (Argentina), 219, 225
General Union of Mexican Workers and Peasanta (UGOCM), 48
Generation of 1880 (Argentina), 217–218
Gil, Leslie, 139
Gilbert, Dennis, 47
Gill, Nathan, 26
Gini coefficient, 47, 157; Arauca, Colombia, 101; Brazil, 235; Casanare, Colombia, 101; Colombia, 107, 108, 113; for land, Brazil, 235; Guaviare, Colombia, 114, 119; Nariño, Colombia, 118; Putumayo, Colombia, 118; Venezuela, 161
Gini Index of Inequality, 25–27, 99
Glade, William, 47
Glenn, C.L., 189
Goebertus, J., 96
gold, 96
Gonzales, N., 203
González, Fernán, 97
Goodman, L.W., 195
government: capacity, Colombia, 99, 109; contracts, 28; distribution of resources, 171; expansion, 20; failure to fulfill obligations, 43; legitimacy, 22, 170, 171; power to enhance development, 240; trust in, 176
Graham, Carol, 8, 241
Grayson, Grayson, 57

Greaney, V., 181
Great Britain, and Jamaican slaves, 85
Great Depression, 44; catalyst for Brazilian regime change, 221
Green Revolution, 46
Green, James, 218
Grindle, M.S., 197
gross domestic product (GDP), 119; in Argentina, 225, 227, 231; in Bolivia, 17; in Brazil, 225; in Colombia, 80, 99, 101–102, 105–109, 111–114, 116, 118–119; in Costa Rica, 80; in El Salvador, 72–73, 80; in Guatemala, 80; in Latin America, 73–74; as a measure of overall wealth, 156; in Mexico, 46; and oil prices, 172; in Venezuela, 17, 156, 157, 172–173
Group of Friends, verification of El Salvador compliance with peace accord, 85
Guatemala, 4, 8, 9, 12, 15, 24, 26, 71, 74, 78, 79, 82, 87; *altiplano,* 79; civil war, 79, 83; class conflicts, 78; current peace, 83; economic value of violence and crime, 74; Human Rights Accord of 1994, 83; institutional neglect of indigenous populations, 79; Ministry of Education, 84; police repression, 89; population diversity conflicts, 83–84; state repression, 82; United Nations Verification Mission (MINUGUA), 83
Guatemalan National Revolutionary Unity (URNG), 83
Guaviare, Colombia, 116
Guerrero Baron, J., 73, 96
Guerrero, Mexico, 48, 54; dirty war, 48
guerrilla groups, 1, 3, 9–10, 16, 100, 110, 169; in Argentina, 24; in Brazil, 24; in Colombia, 24, 95–124; in El Salvador, 84–85; in Guatemala, 82; in Mexico, 41, 48, 51–52, 55, 57–59, 61; in Peru, 11, 19, 24;

154; recruitment by, 10, 170 : in Venezuela, 153–154, 158–159
Gulf Drug Cartel, 57
Gurr, Ted, 42, 156, 169
Guterman, Lisa, 98, 105, 109, 110
Gutiérrez de Piñeres, Sheila Amin, 10, 16, 20, 29, 95, 96, 104, 110, 116

Haber, Stephen, 43, 44
hacienda system, 8–9
Hagopian, Frances, 223
Haight, Libby, 53, 54
Hall, Gillette, 77, 79
Halperin Donghi, Tulio, 225
Hammond, J.L., 11
Hanoman, J., 201, 202
Hansen, Roger, 45, 48
Harley, A., 181
Harpelle, Ronald, 78, 79
Hart, John, 43, 44
Harvey, Neil, 50, 51, 52, 55
Hauch, C.C., 185
health, 7, 24, 51, 76, 77, 176; access to services: Colombia, 99; Costa Rica, 86; Guatemala, 82; maternal-infant program, Venezuela, 161; mental, programs to reinforce, Costa Rica, 89; Venezuela, 157
Hellinger, D., 199
Henriques, Gisele, 54
Hérnandez Navarro, Luís, 59
Hérnandez Pico, Juan, 78
Hérnandez, Sandra, 112
Herrera Salas, Jesús María, 166
Heshusius Rodríguez, K., 96
Hewitt de Alcántara, Cynthia, 45, 46, 47
High School for All *(Liceos para Todos)* (Chile), 190
Hirschman, Albert, 170
Hochstetler, Kathryn, 235
Holmes, Jennifer, 10, 16, 20, 29, 95, 96, 104, 110, 116

homicide rates, 3, 4, 87; in Argentina, 4, 73, 226, 232, 236–237, 241; in Belize, 72–73; in Bolivia, 4, 73; in Brazil, 4, 73, 226, 228, 236–237, 239, 241–242; in Canada, 4; in Chile, 4, 73; in Colombia, 4, 73, 99, 102–103, 109, 111, 114–116, 119; correlation with deprivation, 79; in Costa Rica, 4, 73, 87; in the Dominican Republic, 73; in Ecuador, 4, 73; in El Salvador, 4, 72, 73, 87; in Guatemala, 4, 72, 73, 83, 87; in Haiti, 72, 73; in Honduras, 4, 72, 73, 87; in Jamaica, 73; in Mexico, 4, 73; in Nicaragua, 4, 72, 73, 87; in Panama, 4, 73; in Paraguay, 73; in Peru, 4, 73; in the United States, 4, 226, 232; in Uruguay, 4, 73; in Venezuela, 4, 72–73

Honduras, 4, 8, 12, 19, 26, 87; economic value of violence and crime, 74; forest user rights, 19

Huber, Evelyne, 27

Hudson, Rex, 22

Huhn, Sebastian, 72, 86

Humala, Ollanta (Peru), 6, 23

human capital development, 7, 75, 77; *Bolsa Família*, Brazil, 238; Colombia, 120; costs of losses due to violence, 72; El Salvador, 73; Venezuela, 30, 176

Human Rights Accord of 1994, Guatemala, 83

human rights violations: in Argentina, 227; in Bolivia, 141; in Colombia, 99, 102–103, 106–107, 112, 114–115, 117, 119; in El Salvador, 84; in Guatemala, 83; in Mexico, 59

Humphreys, M., 120

Hunn, L.M., 201, 202

Huntington, Samuel, 171

Hurtig, J., 196, 197

hydrocarbons: in Bolivia, 128, 131, 140, 142, 145–146; and Dutch disease, 145; in Mexico, 50; in Venezuela, 164, 176

Hydrocarbons Law (Venezuela), 164, 176

hydroelectric power, Chiapas, Mexico, 50

IACHR. *see* Inter-American Court on Human Rights

IAPI. *see* Argentine Institute for Trade and Production (IAPI)

IDB. *see* Inter-American Development Bank (IDB)

identifications: in Argentina, 31; arising from education, 31; in Bolivia, 146–147; in Brazil, 31; collective, 4; effect of material deprivation, 42; ethnicity and race, 5, 27, 28, 30; formation of, 27; lack of self-identification, Argentina and Brazil, 31; race, 5

Ihlanfeldt, K., 57

illiberal economic policies, 14

Imbusch, Peter, 8

IMF. *see* International Monetary Fund

immigration: to Argentina, 216–217; to Brazil, 216, 221; from Colombia, 85; to Costa Rica: from Jamaica, 85; from Panama, 85

Immigration and Refugee Board of Canada, 78

import quotas, under NAFTA, 53

import-substitution industrialization (ISI), 2, 12, 13, 20, 31, 213–214, 215; in Argentina, 222–224; in Brazil, 224; and domestic focus, 12; failure of, 13; and financial backing, 13; in Mexico, 46; in Venezuela, 174

imports: end of licensing, Mexico, 53; obtaining hard currency for, 8; U.S., effect on Mexican prices, 53

Impossible Game (Argentina), 219

Incentive to Rural Capitalization (ICR) (Columbia), 98, 100

Independent Peasant Confederation
 (CCI), 48
Indicadores de coyuntura y
 económicos, DANE, 108, 113, 118
Indicadores de política social:
 Departamento Nacional de
 Planeación, 108, 113, 118
Indicadores Sociales Departamentales:
 Departamento Nacional de
 Planeación, 108, 118
Indigenous Congress, 51
indigenous populations, 18, 19, 28,
 42–43, 47, 51–55, 59, 71, 72, 77, 83,
 171; in Bolivia, 127–128, 135–136,
 143, 146–147, 213, 239; in Chile,
 191–192; in Ecuador, 213, 239; in
 Guatemala, 84; and land rights, 110;
 in Venezuela, 164–166
industrial development: in Brazil, 226;
 in Mexico, 46
industrialization, 12, 13, 28, 31;
 absorbing agricultural labor, 12; in
 Argentina, 219; bias toward, 12; in
 Brazil, 219, 221; draining wealth from
 agricultural sector, 12; elements of
 urban interests, Argentina, 219; failure
 of agriculture to fund, 13; in Mexico,
 60; reasons for Venezuela's difficulty,
 174; sequencing with agrarian reform,
 13; urban, aggressive promotion,
 Brazil, 223; in Venezuela, 174
infant mortality rates, 80; Mexico, 43
inflation, 12, 13, 22; in Argentina, 214,
 220, 225, 227–228; in Bolivia, 142;
 in Brazil, 214, 223, 225, 227–228,
 235; factor in relative deprivation,
 156; in Mexico, 49; in Venezuela, 161
information databases, on Central
 American violence, 90
INMECAFE, 53
Institutional Revolutionary Party (PRI)
 (Mexico), 25, 59, 61; corruption
 in, 56; creation of, 44; and drug
 violence, 58; link to paramilitaries,
 in Chiapas, 54, 57; as party of the
 Mexican Revolution, 45
Instituto Medicina Legal, 99
insurgencies, 8, 83; against
 economic liberalization, 129; in
 Argentina,228–229; in Bolivia,129,
 135; coalition of intellectuals and
 the poor, 78; in El Salvador, 84; in
 Venezuela, 153, 155, 159–160, 162
Insurgent People's Revolutionary Army
 (Mexico), 55
Integrated Rural Development
 Program (Colombia), 98
Inter-American Commission on
 Human Rights, 58–59
Inter-American Court on Human
 Rights (IACHR), 159
Inter-American Development Bank
 (IDB), 14, 90
interest rates, floating, Venezuela, 161
intergroup violence, 1, 74, 78,
 125–126, 147; correlation to
 economic development, 126; regional
 concentration in Bolivia, 125
International Coffee
 Agreement, 104
International Labor Organization
 (ILO), 97
International Monetary Fund (IMF),
 14, 49; agreement with Mexico, 49;
 and Venezuelan economic crises,
 160–161, 196.
International Trade Union
 Confederation, 97
intrafamily violence, 88
investment, 18, 75, 76, 77; effects of
 loss due to violence on, 73; public, 45
ISI. *see* import-substitution
 industrialization

Jaramillo, Rubén, 47, 97, 98
Jefes y Jefes de Hogar Desocupados
 (Argentina), 229; and human
 capital, 238

judicial reform: in Guatemala, 83
judicial system: in Brazil, 238; in
  Colombia, 99; confidence in, 81;
  El Salvador, 89; fairness of, 81;
  in Guatemala, 83; reform as high
  priority to address violence and
  conflict, 90; role in violence, 88; and
  violence, 88
JUNJI. *see* Junta Nacional de Jardines
Junta Nacional de Jardines (JUNJI)
  (Chile), 190
justice and security spending: in
  Colombia 106–109, 112–114,
  118–119

Karl, Terry, 157, 158, 172
Kaufman, Robert, 6
Kay, Cristóbal, 13, 235
Keck, Margaret E., 224
Kelly, Michael, 14, 198
Khan, Mahmood, 96
King, Timothy, 44, 46, 47
Kingstone, Peter, 21, 22, 24, 31, 213
Kirby, Peadar, 17
Kirchner, Cristina, 23, 227
Kirchner, Néstor, 23, 227; reopening
  of the question of military
  accountability, 229
Kostzer, Daniel, 231, 233, 234
Kozameh, S.J., 204
Kuczynski, Pedro Pablo, 224
Kurtz, Marcus, 22, 240
Kurtz-Phelan, Daniel, 133, 134

La Paz, Bolivia, 128, 129
La Prensa, 142, 143
labor, 12, 14–15, 22–24, 44, 97, 177;
  agricultural labor absorbed by
  industrialization, 12; in Argentina,
  218, 222, 228–231, 233–234, 242;
  in Bolivia, 130–132; in Brazil,
  221–224, 226, 228–229, 235, 242;
  in Chile, 188, 190; in Colombia,
  96–97, 100; and commercial
  agriculture, 10; in Costa Rica, 78,
  85; in Guatemala, 71; in Mexico,
  43, 45, 53, 60; productivity, 76,
  77; support of democracy, 18 : in
  Venezuela, 159, 163, 165, 167, 172,
  174, 199–200
Lacandon region of Mexico, land
  disputes in, 52
Lacruz, Tito, 161
Lagos, Richard, 17
Laitin, David, 100
Lambert, Jacques, 43
land, 51; access, 10–11; in Bolivia,
  130, 134, 136–138, 143; in Brazil,
  223, 235–236; in Colombia, 96–98,
  102, 104, 106, 109–110, 112, 120;
  colonization, 11; concentration,
  10, 47; confiscation of, 44; and
  conflict, 9; consolidation, 9, 10,
  28, 29; control in the Amazon, 19;
  in Costa Rica, 72, 78; democracy
  effect on, 12; distribution process,
  11; ejidal,28, 50; expropriation of
  indigenous community lands, 8;
  failure, 9; grants, 44; in Guatemala,
  71, 82; imposed by authoritarian
  governments, 8;omings in design, 9;
  invasions, 11, 50; in Mexico
  44–46, 48, 50–52, 60–61;
  ownership, 8, 9, 10, 19; peasant
  demand for redistribution, 48;
  power of state to grant access, 9;
  power of state to redefine rights,
  9;: redistribution, 10, 11, 12, 19;
  reform, 9–10, 11, 12, 21, 22, 29, 48;
  as result of revolutions, 8; reform
  as objective of rural policy, 49;
  reform by democratic governments,
  12; takeovers, 7; tax incentives, 78;
  unequal distribution as source of
  inequality: in Venezuela, 157–158,
  163, 165
Lander, Luís, 159, 160, 161, 174, 195,
  196, 197

Landless Rural Workers Movement
  (MST) (Brazil), 11, 14, 19, 235, 236;
  governance structure for landless,
  rural poor, 236; and schools,
  Brazil, 236
Lanzaro, Susana, 18
Lastarria-Cornhiel, Susana, 10, 15
latifundia system, 8, 11
latifundidos, 11
Latin American Newsletters, 144
Latinobarometro, 3, 25
Le Billon, Philippe, 116
Leach, F., 181
Ledebur, Kathryn, 134
Lederman, Daniel, 42
Left, 6, 11, 14, 15, 17, 22, 23, 24, 82,
  110, 170; in Argentina, 220; in
  Chile, 186; in Colombia, 96, 100,
  102–103, 106, 114–117, 119–120;
  in El Salvador: in Guatemala, 82; in
  Venezuela, 158, 168, 195
Lehoucq, Fabrice, 140–141
Lemaitre, M.J., 189, 190, 191
Leoni Otero, Raúl, 195
Léons, Madeline, 127
Levine, Daniel, 158, 194, 195
Levitsky, Steven, 6, 18, 22, 23, 227,
  228
Lewis, Paul, 219, 222
liberalization, 2, 14, 15, 17, 20, 21,
  22, 52; in Bolivia, 22, 29, 30;
  economic, 28; effect on low-income
  groups, 14–15; in Chile, 188; in
  Colombia, 98; in Mexico, 53.
  see also economy policy: import
  substitution industrialization: and
  state enterprises,16
Library of Congress (U.S.), 165
life expectancy, 80, 157; Mexico, 44
Limón, Costa Rica: citizenship, 86;
  and immigrant labor, 85
Lindert, Kathy, 24
Linz, Juan, 170, 227
Lipset, Seymour Martin, 169

literacy rate, 80
livestock, Putumayo, Colombia, 116
Loayza, Roman, 42; election as
  Secretary General, Bolivia, 134
Lodola, Germán, 231
Londoño, Juan, 73
López Gámez, Emilio, 53, 54
López Maya, Margarita, 155, 159, 160,
  161, 174
López Portillo, José (Mexico),
  predisposition to capital-intensive
  economic growth, 49–50
López, Ramón, 99
López-Calva, Luís, 7
Lora, Eduardo, 8, 15
Los Angeles, United States, 232
Los Tiempos, 142
lost decade, 13, 23
Lucero, José, 132, 134, 135, 136
Lula da Silva, Luiz Inácio (Brazil), 17,
  19, 224, 235
Lusinchi, Jaime (Venezuela), 161, 174
Lustig, Nora, 7, 53, 54

MacDonald, James, 56
Machado, Fabiana, 227
Madureira, Brazil, 239
Magdalena, Colombia, 110
Magendzo, A., 191
Mahler, Annegret, 159, 174
Mahon, James, 7
Malkin, Victoria, 56
Malloy, James, 130, 131, 132
Malone, Mary Fran T., 232, 233
Malvinas/Falklands Islands, military
  junta resignation, 220
manufacturing: collapse of output
  growth, Venezuela, 174;
  Mexico, 46
manufacturing industry, excess
  capacity, Mexico, 46
Manzetti, Luigi, 225, 227
Maranhão, Brazil, 237
maras. see gangs

marginal people: in Argentina, 232; in Brazil, 237
market regulation, 23, 24; and state power, 23; vulnerability to international fluctuations, 29
marketization. *see* liberalization
Martínez, Gabriel, 53
MAS. *see* Movimiento al Socialismo Party
Maule, Rodrigo, 12
MBR 200 (Venezuela), 163
McCoy, Jennifer, 161
McGuire, James W., 227
McIlwaine, Cathy, 11
McLean, P., 97
media, 8, 80–81, 171; in Bolivia, 136–138; freedom of the press, 8; role in creating "virtual reality," 8; role in political mobilization, 8; in Venezuela, 167;
Medrano, Diana, 109, 110
Menem, Carlos, 228, 229, 230, 231
Mesa, Carlos, 134
Mesbah, Dina, 97
mestizo population: in El Salvador, 72; in Mexico, 43
Meta, Colombia, 110, 111, 112, 113, 116; GDP, 111
Mexican Coffee Institute (INMECAFE), 53
Mexican Revolution, 42, 44, 45, 48, 50, 61; peasant aspirations, 52; resultant nationalistic economic model, 60
Mexico, 4, 5, 8, 9, 11, 12, 14–15, 24–26, 28, 41–70; absence of ethnic and religious conflict, Chiapas, 51; actions contributing to protests by rural dwellers, 50; cash transfers, 24; centralized authority, 43; composition of political elite, 43; copper production, 43; development trajectory, 41; failure to mitigate negative development factors, 41;
gang coexistence, 25; historical origins of violence, 43; international credit rating, 43; investment in infrastructure and oil production, 50; mafia, 25; patterns of conflict, 215; politicizing agents, role in violence, 41–42; reforms, 29; resource-based industrialization, 12; role of income equality in violence, 41; silver production, 43; social services, 14; state capacity, 18; state intervention, 14; state investment in oil, 50; state oil and mining companies, 18; state repression, 50, 54, 61; state response to societal grievances, 41; trade liberalization, 15; wars on drugs, 1; Zapatista Army of National Liberation (EZLN), 14
Mexico City, 60; student massacre in, 48
migration: in Bolivia, 127, 132–134; in El Salvador, 89; of low-income youth to the United States, 16, 132; of rural poor to cities, 28. *see also* immigration
military, 3, 10, 22, 23, 83; abolition of Costa Rican, 86; in Argentina, 219–220, 227, 229; in Bolivia, 134; in Brazil, 221, 223–224, 234–235; in Chile, 183, 187; in El Salvador, 8–85; in Guatemala, 82; in Mexico, 55–56; reincorporation of army soldiers into civilian life: in South America, 153; in Venezuela, 153, 155, 158, 160, 168, 171, 183, 195;
military rule: in Argentina, 214, 218–219; in Brazil, 214, 224; in Venezuela, 154
Miller, Michael, 43, 56
Millett, R., 196
Minas Gerais, Brazil, 216
Mingorance, Fidel, 110
Minimum Program of Government (Venezuela), 157

mining, 16; Bolivia, western highlands, 132; decentralization, 20; Mexico, 43; Oruro, Bolivia, 129; Potosi, Bolivia, 128
Ministry of Education (Chile), 185, 186, 191, 206; changing culture of teaching, 190; and the ENU, 186; improvement in effectiveness, rigor and equity for students, 190
Ministry of Education (Venezuela), 198, 199; and university access, 202
Ministry of Mines (Venezuela), oversight of PDVSA, 164
Minority Rights Group International, 191
MINUGUA. *see* United Nations Verification Mission
MIR. *See* Movement of the Revolutionary Left (MIR) (Venezuela)
miscegenation, Venezuela, 165
Misíon Ribas (Venezuela), 201, 202
Misíon Robinson (Venezuela), 201
Misíon Sucre (Venezuela), 202
Misíon Vuelvan Caras (Venezuela), 201
MNR, 139. *see* Movimiento Nacionalista Revolucionario
modernization, 43; of capital-intensive industrialization in Mexico, 60; of education in Chile, 185; of foreign investment in Mexico, 60; of infrastructure in Mexico, 60; political in Venezuela, 194; Venezuela, 164
modernization theory, 22
Módolo, Christian, 234
Monasterios family (Bolivia), 137
Mond, D., 96
monetary discipline, 23
monopolization, from efforts to address economic crisis, Venezuela, 161
monopoly concessions: Mexico, 43
Monterrey, Mexico, manufacturing sector, 43

Montoneros (Argentina), 220
Morales, Evo (Bolivia), 17, 21, 23, 30, 128–129, 134–138, 140, 142
Moran, Patrick, 230
Morelos, Mexico, 47
Moreno, Daniel, 226
Morgan, Jana, 160
Moseley, Mason, 226
Moser, Caroline, 11, 57
Movement of the Revolutionary Left (MIR) (Venezuela), 158
Movimiento al Socialismo Party (MAS) (Bolivia), 128, 140, 143–144
Movimiento Bolivariano Revolucionario 200 (MBR 200) (Venezuela), 163
Movimiento dos Sem Terra. *see* Landless Rural Workers Movement (MST) (Brazil)
Movimiento Izquierda Revolucionaria (MIR) (Venezuela), 158
Movimiento Nacionalista Revolucionario (MNR) (Bolivia), 138
Movimiento V (Quinta) República (MVR) (Venezuela), 163, 198
MST. *see* Landless Rural Workers Movement (MST) (Brazil)
multiparty government coalitions, Bolivia, 139
municipalities: in Bolivia, 142–143; and education, Chile, 188
Murillo, Maria Victoria, 227, 230

NAFTA. *see* North American Free Trade Agreement (NAFTA)
Nariño, Colombia, 110, 116
National Academy for the Mapuche Language (Chile), 191, 206
National Administrative Department of Statistics (DANE) (Colombia), 99, 101, 108, 113, 118
National Autonomist Party (Argentina), 217

National Bank of Rural Credit (BANRURAL) (Mexico), and support for *ejidos*, 45
National Capacity-Building for Intercultural Conflict Prevention and Management (Chile), 191
National Coffee Federation (Colombia), 104
National Development Plan (Colombia), 99
National Front, Colombia, 95
National Liberation Army (ELN) (Colombia), 5, 95, 102; recruitment, Arauca, Colombia, 100
National Literacy Campaign (Chile), 185
National Renewal Alliance Party (ARENA) (Brazil), 216–217, 224
National Revolutionary Civic Association (ACNR) (Mexico), 48
National Service for Customs and Tax Administration (SENIAT) (Venezuela), 176; oil dependency, 176
National Solidarity Program (PRONASOL) (Mexico), 53–54
National Transport Federation (Venezuela), 162
National Unified School (Escuela Nacional Unida) (ENU) (Chile), 186–187
nationalism, 6; Pinochet's policies in Chile, 188; in Venezuela, 166
nationalization, 17–18, 22; in Argentina, 17; in Bolivia, 17; in Ecuador, 17; in Venezuela, 17, 163, 165, 172, 173
natural gas. *see* hydrocarbons
natural resources, 18; in Bolivia, 138; in Brazil, 236; in Chile, 183; in Colombia, 120; in Mexico, 50–51, 60; price shocks, correlation to conflict, 96; regulation of, 19; in Venezuela, 173
Navarro, Zander, 12

neoliberalism, 6, 20–23, 31, 240–241; in Argentina, 31, 215, 228–230, 242; in Brazil, 31, 215, 228–229, 242; citizenship conversion to consumerism, 240; coexistence with democracy without pursuit of social reform, 240; and decline in conflict, 240; effects on workers and the poor, 241; in Latin America, 6, 21; in Mexico, 56, 59; and neopluralism, 240; statist version, 242; in Venezuela, 163, 197
Neves, Tancredo, 224
New Left, 22; political influence on economic agenda, 6
New Man, Chilean educational system goal, 186
New Republic (Brazil), 234
Nicaragua, 4, 5, 8, 9, 23, 26, 78; economic cost of violence and crime, 74
Norden, Deborah, 20, 23, 30, 155, 160, 204, 229
North America, 90
North American Free Trade Agreement (NAFTA), 52, 53; and Bolivia, 169; and Mexico, 53, 56, 60–61, 169; Security Prosperity and Partnership Agreement (SPP), 59

O'Donnell, Guillermo, 214, 219
Oaxaca, Mexico, 54
Observatory of Violence (OCAVI) (El Salvador), 88, 90
OCAVI. *see* Observatory of Violence (OCAVI) (El Salvador)
OCSS. *see* Campesino Organization of the South Sierra (OCSS) (Mexico)
OECD. *see* Organisation for Economic Co-operation and Development (OECD)
Oficina del Alto Comisionado de las Naciones Unidas para los Refugiados (ACNUR), 110, 159

oil, 12, 13, 18, 29, 96, 100; in Colombia, 100–102, 104, 116, 175; in Mexico, 49–50, 60; petro dollars, 13; sectoral development, 95; state oil and mining companies, 18; transport tax, Colombia, 100; underpricing for domestic industry, 12 : in Venezuela, 30, 156, 158–159, 162–164, 167, 171–175, 194–196
oil prices, 18, 173; and GDP, 172; impacts on Colombia, 96; impacts on Venezuela, 161, 172, 196; unpredictability of, 177
oligarchic control: in Argentina, 216–217, 222; in Brazil, 216, 221–222
Olson, Wayne, 47
OPEC. *see* Organization of Petroleum Exporting Countries
Oppenheim, L.H., 187, 188–189, 192
Organisation for Economic Co-operation and Development (OECD), 189, 190, 191, 192; educational system, Chile, 192; private school incentives, Chile, 188
Organization of the Petroleum Exporting Countries (OPEC), 156, 173; oil shock of 1973, 220
Orinco Belt, Venezuela, 17
Ortega, D., 202
Oruro, Bolivia, 128, 140
Oslender, Ulrich, 112
Ovallo Vaguera, Fredrico, 53, 54
Oxhorn, Phillip, 240
Oyelere, R.U., 203

P-900 school quality program (Chile), 190, 191
Padilla, Tanalís, 48
Painter, James, 127, 133
Palacios, Paola, 109, 110
palm: Colombia, 109; production, 110
PAN. *see* Popular Action Party (Mexico)
Pan American Health Organization, 4

Panama, 4, 26; economic value of violence and crime, 74
Pando, Bolivia, 127, 142
Pará, Brazil, 236
Paraguay, 4, 26
paramilitary groups, 110; in Colombia, 96–97, 99–100, 102–104, 106–107, 110–112, 114–115, 117, 119; and displacement, 112; in El Salvador, 84; in Guatemala, 83, 89; in Mexico, 57
pardo, Venezuela, 166
Parkes, Henry, 43, 44, 45
Partido Autonomista Nacional (Argentina), 217
Partido Justicialista (PJ) (Argentina), 219–220, 225, 227–228
Party of the Democratic Revolution (PRD) (Mexico), 58
Party of the Poor (Mexico), 48
Patel, Raj, 54
Patrinos, Harry, 77, 79
patronage networks, 102, 103, 132, 137, 176, 222–223, 230, 233; in Bolivia, 139–140, 143–145; of Peronist Partyin Argentina, 231
Paulson, Joshua, 55
Paz Estenssoro, Victor, 130
PCV. *see* Venezuelan Communist Party
PDVSA. *see* Petróleos de Venezuela
Peace Accords of 1996 (Guatemala), 82, 83
Pearce, Jenny, 100, 102
peasant organizations, 9, 14, 51, 54, 55
Peasant Wars of the Twentieth Century, 11
Peceny, Mark, 116
Peetz, Peetz, 89
PEMEX. *see* Petróleos Mexicanos
Penfold-Becerra, Michael, 164, 199, 200, 202, 204
Penner, Emily, 20, 30, 31, 181
pension plans, 18, 24; funded by hydrocarbon revenues, Bolivia, 142; reform, 15

PEP. *see* Plan to Confront Poverty (PEP) (Venezuela)
per capita gross domestic product (GDP/PC), 157; Venezuela, 173
Pereira, Anthony, 214, 236, 239
Peres, Wilson, 7, 17
Pérez Jiménez, Marcos (Venezuela), 158, 194–195
Pérez, Carlos Andrés, 196, 197–198, 206; antineoliberal education reforms, 196; public disapproval, 197
Pérez, Carlos Andrés (Venezuela), 155–156, 159–162, 166, 171, 183
Perlman, Janice, 227, 237
Perón, Eva (Argentina), 219
Perón, Isabel (Argentina), 220
Perón, Juan (Argentina), 219–220, 223
Peronist Party (Argentina), 219, 227, 230–232
Peru, 4, 5, 6, , 9, 10, 11, 15, 16, 17, 19, 20, 22, 23, 24, 26; canon petrolero and canon minero, 19; guerrilla groups, 19
peso crisis (Mexico), 52, 54
Petras, James, 240
Petrobras, natural gas investment in Bolivia, 131
petrochemicals, Mexico, 49
Petróleos de Venezuela (PDVSA), 163, 164, 172, 199, 200; capitalization for oil exploration and production, Venezuela, 173; financing of Bolivarian Missions (Venezuela), 164; oil management, 172; revenues dependent on world price of petroleum, 173; transfer of funds and investments outside Venezuela, 174
Petróleos Mexicanos (PEMEX), 50
Pettinato, Stefano, 241
Pickard, Miguel, 59
Piñera, Sebastián, and student protests, 192
Pinochet, Augusto, 183, 187, 189, 190, 191, 192, 193, 205, 206; disappearance of citizens, Chile, 188; education policy as a tool for exclusion, 184; liberalization and decentralization, Chile, 188; Seven Modernizations, 188
Pinstrup-Andersen, Per, 9
piqueteros, 231, 233
PJ. *see* Partido Justicialista (PJ) (Argentina)
Plan Bolivar 2000 (Venezuela), 164, 165
Plan de Jefes y Jefas de Hogar Desempleados (Argentina), 24, 233, 234
Plan Dignidad, 133, 139; disruption of equilibrium of liberal governance, 134
Plan Dignidad (Bolivia), 147
Plan to Confront Poverty (PEP) (Venezuela), 161
Plan Trabajar (Argentina), 231, 233, 234
plantations: in Colombia, 110, 117; in Costa Rica, 78, 85–86; sectoral development, 95
PNUD. *see* Programa de las Naciones Unidas para el Desarrollo (PNUD) (Guatemala)
Polaski, Sandra, 53
police, 3, 31, 80, 231–232; in Argentina, 228, 231–232, 237–239, 241–243; in Brazil, 214, 228, 232, 235, 237–239, 241–243; in Bolivia, 134; coexistence with gangs, 25; confidence in, 81; in Costa Rica, 86; in Guatemala, 83, 89; in Mexico, 57; and strong public tolerance, judicial indifference to brutality, Argentina and Brazil, 214; in Venezuela, 164
policy-environment fit, 182, 185, 205; in Chile, 183–184, 187, 206; in Venezuela, 183–184, 187, 206
political exclusion, 176; in Argentina, 217; in Mexico, 42; in Venezuela, 158, 168, 171,

Index • 273

political violence, 41, 43, 45, 71, 75, 81, 144, 170, 235, 243; in Argentina, 31, 213–214, 218, 223, 227–229, 231, 241; in Bolivia, 125–130, 133–134, 136–141, 143–144; in Brazil, 31, 213–214, 221, 234–235; in Colombia, 95, 106; as consequence of changed conditions or expectations, 169; contingence on perceptions of deprivation, 42; as distinct from conflict and instability, 168, 169; and economic policies, 171; effect on political trajectory, 135; and government loss of legitimacy, 170; and import-substitution industrialization, 214; in Mexico, 45, 61–62; root causes, 71, 125 : in Venezuela, 153, 155–156, 158, 166, 168, 170, 174, 177, 193
Ponce, Aldo, 231
Popular Action Party (PAN) (Mexico), 58; potential for agreement with Zapatistas, 59
Popular Revolutionary Army (EPR) (Mexico), 55
Popular Unity/Unidad Popular (Chile), 186; inner conflict, 187
population growth, 9, 80; in Argentina, 216–217; in Bolivia, 102, 132; in Brazil, 216; in Colombia, 100, 102, 109, 116, 118
populism, 6, 8, 21, 22, 23, 28, 30, 31; in Bolivia, 29; political, 90; in Venezuela, 163, 240
Porfirio Díaz, José (Mexico, 44, 46
Potosí, Bolivia, 128, 140
poverty, 2, 5, 6, 11, 13, 16, 24, 57, 80, 234; in Argentina,229, 233; in Brazil, 229, 238; in Colombia, 96, 99, 101, 108, 111, 113–114, 116, 118, 119; in Mexico, 47; structural sources and need for complementary policies, sustained economic growth, 234; in Venezuela, 160–161

poverty alleviation, 7, 10, 18, 157; in Colombia, 96, 100, 103, 107, 109, 114, 116; in El Salvador, 78, 85; in Mexico, 52, 60; in Nicaragua, 78; privatization and, 18 : in Venezuela, 157, 159, 161, 164, 204
pragmatism, in left-leaning governments, 17
PRD, see Party of the Democratic Revolution
prefects: in Bolivia, 140–141, 143–144
Prevot-Schapira, Marie, 50
PRI. see Institutional Revolutionary Party (Mexico)
pricing, 13, 18, 23, 24; in Bolivia, 130; coffee, 84, 104;: in Colombia, 96, 100, 104–106; commodities, 98, 172, 177; correlation to conflict, 96; in Costa Rica, 86; crude oil, 173; drop in corn and coffee, 55; effect of oil prices on wages, Colombia, 100; effects of adjustments on gasoline market rates, 173; farmgate, 15; gasoline, 173; meat, 111; in Mexico, 53, 60; oil, 156, 176; palm oil, 111; and sectoral development, 95; in Venezuela, 156, 161–162, 164, 171, 196;
privatization, 14–15, 17–18, 20–21, 52, 58, 240; in Brazil, 236; in Chile, 187–188; in Venezuela, 161
PROCAMPO, see Farmer's Direct Support Program (PROCAMPO) (Mexico)
product shortages, Venezuela, 161
product transformation, 76
productivity: in Brazil, 28; in Colombia, 96, 97, 99; crime as a constraint, 4; education as an input, 31; in El Salvador, 29; in Guatemala, 29; factor in relative deprivation, 156; income inequality and, 75; labor, 76–77; in Mexico, 45; in Venezuela, 154, 156, 161, 174

Programa de las Naciones Unidas para el Desarrollo (PNUD) (Guatemala), 82
Programa Venezolana de Educación-Acción en Derechos Humanos (PROVEA) (Venezuela), 166–167, 202
PRONASOL, *see* National Solidarity Program (PRONASOL) (Mexico)
protectionism, 11, 14, 31, 53, 215; in Colombia, 98; industrial, 28; in Mexico, 43, 60
protests: in Argentina, 219, 226–227, 230; in Bolivia, 129; in Brazil, 226, 236; in Chile, 181, 187–188, 191–193; by concerned parents, 199; in Colombia, 110; in Venezuela, 158, 164, 166–167, 171, 193–195, 197, 199, 203
PROVEA. *see* Programa Venezolana de Educación-Acción en Derechos Humanos (PROVEA) (Venezuela)
PT. see Workers' Party (PT) (Brazil)
public spending, 77, 90; in Bolivia, 131; in Colombia, 96, 99, 120; in El Salvador, 84; inability to deliver, 90; in Mexico, 48; patterns, Colombia, 120;: potential to diminish satisfaction from income equality, 157; in Venezuela, 159, 161, 196
public utilities, 18
punteros (Argentina), 230
Punto Fijo pact (Venezuela), 157, 195; challenge from PCV, 170
Punto Fijo period (Venezuela), 154, 157–161, 171, 194–195, 200, 206
Purcell, Trevor, 78
Putumayo, Colombia, 116

quality of life, 157
Quindio, Colombia, 105, 108
Quiroga, José, 134
Quispe, Felipe, 136, 147

race: Hugo Chávez identification, Venezuela, 166; Venezuela, 165
race consciousness, 5
racial democracy, 7, 28, 166, 175; Venezuela, 166
racism, 11
Radical Civic Union (UCR) (Argentina), 217–218, 227, 230–231
radical extremism, 90
radical movements and military governments, 29
radicalism, 6, 9; of student groups, Venezuela, 195
Radzischewski, A., 205
Rancheros (Mexico), 43
ranching, 10; association with paramilitary violence, in Bolivia, 128, 137; in Colombia, 96, 102, 104–106, 109–111, 114, 137; and displacement, 110
raw materials: promotion, 28; reliance on, 18; terms of trade, 12
Rawlings, Laura, 59
Real Plan (Brazil), 235
real wages, measuring overall wealth, 156
recentralization, 21
recession, 156; debt crisis in Mexico, 52; and effects on crime, 87
Redcliff, Michael, 98
redistribution. *see* income redistribution
rehabilitation: Costa Rica, 89
Reiter, Bernd, 238
relative deprivation, 42; and drugs, 56; in Mexico, 51, 61; and moral indignation, 170; and violence, 169
rent seeking, 75–76; in Colombia, 103–104; in Guatemala, 82
Repsol YPF, natural gas investment, Bolivia, 131
Republic of Coffee and Milk (Brazil), 216, 220, 222
resguardos (Colombia), 109–110

resource development: as cause of socioeconomic change in Mexico, 50
resource extraction, 5; revenue allocation, 19–20
resource management and reinforcement, 29
Rettberg, Angelika, 96, 104, 106, 107
revenue redistribution, in Bolivia, 141; to subnational governments, 18; transfers, 19
Revolutionary Armed Forces of Columbia (FARC), 5, 16, 95, 116
Reyes Villa, Manfred (Bolivia), 141
rhetoric, 6, 23; political, 6
Richani, N., 96, 104
Right, 14, 22; in El Salvador, 84
Rio de Janeiro, Brazil, 237, 238, 239; 2016 Olympic Games, 214; gang war with police, 214; slums, 227
Rio Grande do Sul, Brazil, 216, 220–221, 236
Rios Montt, Efraín (Guatemala), 82
Roberts, Kenneth, 6, 18, 22, 23, 160, 161, 163, 166
Roberts-Schweitzer, E., 181
Robinson, James, 76
Rochlin, James, 116
Rock, David, 220
Rodgers, Dennis, 3, 5, 11
Rodríguez, Victoria, 49, 96, 202
Rohter, Larry, 192
Romero, Simon, 204
Rosero, Luís, 72
Rousseff, Dilma, 23
Ruiz, Bishop Samuel, 51
Ruiz, C., 190
Russell, Philip, 55

Saavedra, Jaime, 195, 196, 197, 229
Sadoulet, Elizabeth, 8
Saenz Peña, Roque, 217
Salinas de Gotari, Carlos (Mexico), 52, 58

Salinas, de Gotari, Raúl (Mexio), money laundering, 58
Salomón, Leticia, 74, 88
Salvato, Sylvia, 161
San Salvador, El Salvador, 84, 89
Sanabria, Harry, 127, 133
Sánchez de Lozada, Gonzalo (Bolivia), 131, 139
Sánchez, David, 140
Sánchez, Steven, 98–99, 101, 108, 113, 118
Sanderson, Steven E., 48, 49
Sandoval, Luís, 140
Santa Cruz, Bolivia, 127, 128, 142, 147
Santander, Colombia, 110
São Paulo, Brazil, 216, 237, 238; center of middle-class citizens pushing for liberal political rules, 221; coffee, 220
Saragoza, Alex, 45
Sarney, José (Brazil), 227
Scartascini, Carlos, 227
Scheper-Hughes, 237
Schieflbein, E., 185
Schiray, Michel, 57
Schwartz, Jeremy, 53, 59
Sciacchitano, Katherine, 59
secret ballot law (Argentina), rising middle class against oligarchies, radical working class, 217
sectoral development: in Bolivia, 130; coca, 95; coffee, 95–96; and commodity prices, 95; and conflict, 95; and government policy, 95; oil, 95; and overall state presence, 95; plantation agriculture, 95; and provision of basic services, 95
SEDLAC (Venezuela), 161
Seguridad Social, 111, 112; in Colombia, 101, 107–109, 113, 118–111
SEHLAC Group, 5
Seligson, Mitchell, 72

Sendero Luminoso. see Shining Path guerrilla movement
SENIAT. *see* National Service for Customs and Tax Administration (SENIAT) (Venezuela)
Senior Angulo, Diana, 78
Seri, Guillermina, 214
Serrano, Monica, 57
Seven Modernizations (Chile), 188
Shapiro, Ian, 24
sharecropping. *see under* land
Sharpe, Kenneth, 44
Shining Path guerilla movement (Peru), 5, 11
Siderúrgica del Orinoco (SIDOR) (Venezuela), 161
SIDOR. *see* Siderúrgica del Orinoco (SIDOR) (Venezuela)
Silent Revolution, 16–18
Simmons, Cynthia S., 235
Simoncito (Venezuela), 201
Sinaloa, Mexico, land invasions, 48
Singer, Matt, 233
Skidmore, Thomas E., 218, 221, 222, 223, 224
Skoufias, Emmanuel, 24
Skurski, Julie, 159, 161, 162, 171
Sloan, John, 10
Smith, Peter, 44, 217, 218, 230, 239
Snyder, Richard, 116, 120
social democratization, 18
social inclusion, 17; Venezuela, 174
social mobility, 5, 11, 24, 175; education as a primary policy lever, 193, 207; in Venezuela, 196
social policies, 8; Bolivia, 203; Brazil, 203; Chile, 203; Costa Rica, 203; criticisms, Venezuela, 164; Cuban role, Venezuela, 164; El Salvador, 203; insufficient to address conditions that repress young, unskilled men, Brazil, 242; Panama, 203; Paraguay, 203; Venezuela, 164, 203, 204

Social Question, 216–217; in Argentina, 242; in Brazil, 242; in the United States, 242; in Western Europe, 242
social services, 17; in Brazil, 239; in Colombia, 104; neglect of, 10, 14; in Venezuela, 164, 196–197, 200;
social spending, 6; in Argentna, 231; and oil revenues, 172; in Venezuela, 27, 161, 163–164, 171, 176, 198, 200
social welfare: correlation between risk factors and economic variables, 75; manifestation of accumulation of negative policy consequences, 76
socialism, 23; in Brazil, 221; in Chile, 183, 186–187; in Venezuela, 163, 167–168, 183, 200
socioeconomic class: as social construct, 169; in Venezuela, 163, 168
socioeconomic exclusion, 5, 13, 28–29, 31, 41, 170, 213; in Argentina, 215, 242; in Brazil, 215, 242; in El Salvador, 29; in Guatemala, 29; in Mexico, 42–43, 45, 57; policies to reduce, 7; in Venezuela, 165
socioeconomic performance, 80; preconditions for, 79
Solís, Leopoldo, 46
Solt, Frederick, 7, 27
Sonora, Mexico, land invasions, 48
Soviet Union, 22
soybeans. *see* agro-industries
Spain: colonization of Colombia, 98; colonization of Costa Rica, 72; colonization of Guatemala, 79
Spanish, as a second language, Guatemala, 71
Sparovek, Gerd, 12
Spedding, Alison, 134
Spencer, D.E., 181
SPP. *see under* NAFTA
Stallings, Barbara, 6, 17
Starr, Pamela, 228

state capacity, Colombia, 109
state enterprises, and liberalization, impact on employment and dislocation, 16
state repression, 169, 171; in Argentina, 214, 217–218; in Chile, 188, 205; in Colombia, 97; in El Salvador, 84, 89; in Mexico, 42, 55; in Venezuela, 154–155, 166–167, 195
state revenues: Bolivia, 136, 139, 142
states-of-siege, Bolivia, 129
statist policy, 10, 23
Stepan, Alfred, 170, 214, 227
Stewart, Rigoberto, 86
Strategy of Strengthening Democracy and Social Development, Colombia, 99
street crime. *see* criminal violence
structural adjustment and reform: cause of hostile reactions, 15; in El Salvador, 78; first-generation, 15; hostile reactions, 15; indicators, 15; in Mexico, 60; in Nicaragua 78; second-generation, 15. *see also* macroeconomic policy reform: in Venezuela, 198
structural violence, 31, 41–43; in Argentina, 242; in Brazil, 242; central role of inequality and exclusion, 215; effect on crime rates, 42; link to rising criminal and political violence, 59; in Mexico, 59, 61; state inadequacy causing systematic inequities, 215
subnational revenues: Bolivia, 138, 143
subsidies, 10, 12, 18, 21, 24; in Bolivia, 132–134, 138; in Brazil, 221, 236; in Chile, 192; in Colombia, 98, 105, 110; in Mexico, 54; in Venezuela, 30, 157, 161, 197
Sucre, Bolivia, 128
sugar, 78
Sussekind, Elizabeth, 238

sustainability: failure of oil revenues to benefit Arauca, Colombia, 102; policy reforms, 154; Venezuela's economic development model, 174
symbolism, 23
syndicalism, inspiration for segments of Brazil's military, 221
Székley, Miguel, 49, 234

Tabasco, Mexico, 50
Tannenbaum, Frank, 44
tariffs: lowering, Venezuela, 161; reductions, 16; under NAFTA, 53
Tarija, Bolivia, 127, 143, 144
Tawil, S., 181
tax policies: and business interests, 176; Colombia, 109
taxes, avoidance, 76
technology, investment in, 76
Teichman, Judith, 15, 24, 25, 28, 49, 59, 215
terrorism, 169; correlation to coca production, 116
Themnér, Lotta, 5
timber, Bolivia, 128
Timmer, C. Peter, 9
Tinker-Salas, Miguel, 164, 174, 195, 197
Toledo, M.I., 191
Tolima, Colombia, 105, 106, 108
Tommasi, Mariano, 227
Tornarolli, Leopoldo, 25
Torres Rivas, Edelberto, 78
Torrico, José, 139
torture: in Chile, 187; by police, Mexico, 56
trade liberalization, 15, 16; Mexico, 52
Transparency International 2010 Corruption Perceptions Index, Venezuela's level of corruption, 176
Trinkunas, Harold, 158
Trujillo, E., 104

U.S. Andean Trade Preference Act, 16
U.S. Central Intelligence Agency (CIA), characterization of Chile's Popular Unity reforms, 186
U.S. Department of State, Bureau of Democracy, Human Rights and Labor, 56
U.S. Immigration Service, deportation of gang members, 87
UBV. *see* Bolivarian University of Venezuela (UBV)
UCR. *see* Radical Civic Union (UCR) (Argentina))
UCS. *see* Unidad Cívica Solidaridad (UCS)
UJC. *see* Unión Juvenil Cruceñista (UJC)
UNDOC. *see* United Nations Office on Drugs and Crime (UNDOC)
UNDP. *see* United Nations Development Programme (UNDP)
UNESCO. see United Nations Educational, Scientific and Cultural Organization (UNESCO)
Ungar, Mark, 159, 160, 161, 174
Unidad Cívica Solidaridad (UCS) (Bolivia), 138
Unión Juvenil Cruceñista (UJC) (Bolivia), 141–144
Unión Republicana Democrática (URD) (Venezuela), 157, 195;
unions, independent unionism, Mexico, 48
United Fruit Company, 78, 82, 85; and disenfranchised labor, 86
United Nations: El Salvador peace agreement, 84–85; Guatemala, 85
United Nations Development Programme (UNDP), 1, 2, 6, 7, 63, 74, 90, 157; Human Development Index, 157
United Nations Educational, Scientific and Cultural Organization (UNESCO), 191

United Nations Office on Drugs and Crime (UNDOC), 4, 73, 87, 99, 134, 232, 236–237
United Nations University World Institute for Development Economics Research, 6, 7
United Nations Verification Mission (MINUGUA), Guatemala, 83
United States, 4, 13, 52, 182, 225; Alliance for Progress, 22; and Hugo Chávez, 163; and its oil companies' influence on Venezuelan policy, 195; as market for exports, 16; opposition to Bolivian coca trade, 133; poor as principal victims of crime and police brutality, 229
United States Central Intelligence Agency (CIA), 48; role in Guatemalan military coup, 82
United States National Student Association, 181
Unitel, 137
UNU-WIDER (Venezuela), 7, 161
Uppsala Conflict Data Program, 5
urbanization, 11; in Argentina, 8; in Brazil 221, in Chile, 8; in El Salvador, 84; in Uruguay, 8; in Venezuela, 171
URD. *see* Unión Republicana Democrática (URD)
Uribe, Alvaro (Colombia), 6, 99
URNG. *see* Guatemalan National Revolutionary Unity (URNG)
Uruguay, 4, 8, 17, 18, 23, 26; political and civil liberties, 226
Uslar Pietri, Arturo, 174

Valdés, Alberto, 9
Valdez, José, 131
values, erosion of, El Salvador, 89
van Bronkhorst, Bernice, 57
Van Cott, Donna Lee, 136
Vargas, Getulio (Brazil), 221–223
Vargas, Juan, 72, 96, 100, 104

Index • 279

Vásquez, Genaro (Mexico), 48
Vázquez, Tabaré (Uruguay), 17, 23
Velasco Alvorado, Juan (Peru), 10, 11
Velasco, José Luís, 55, 56, 57
Venezolana Internacional de Aviación S.A. (VIASA), privatization, 161
Venezuela, 4,-6, 12, 17, 18, 20, 23–28, 30, 153, 155, 171, 175, 193–194, 206; access to public services, 195;: backsliding on policy reforms, 17; budget needs, 174; constitution, 198; corruption, 195; cultural expectations of the state's obligations, 170; democracy, 172; education and policy, 30; ethnicity, 168; GDP/PC, 173; failure to achieve education policy-environment fit, 193; nationalization, 17; nationalization of oil, 172; oil exports, 173; oil-based populism, 239; Orinco Belt, 17; political violence, 170; regional divisions, 168; resource-based industrialization, 12; socialist transformation, 200; socioeconomic class, 168
Venezuelan Communist Party (PCV), 158
Venezuelan Federation of Teachers, 194
Venezuelan Workers' Confederation (CTV), 167
Veracruz, Mexico, 50
Vergara, M., 190
VIASA. *see* Venezolana Internacional de Aviación S.A. (VIASA)
Villa, Pancho, 44
Villafuerte Solís, Daniel, 51
Virreira, Mario, 140
Vivallo Jara, R., 186

Wade, Robert, 42
wage freezes, Bolivia, 130
wage increases, 18
Waiselfisz, Julio Jacobo, 237, 239

Wallensteen, Peter, 5
War on Drugs and Terrorism, Mexico, 59
Washington Consensus, 23; impact in Argentin, 240; impact in Brazil, 240
Washington Consensus reforms, 15; Bolivia, 134
water and sewer access: in Colombia, 101, 107–109, 111, 113, 118–119; contribution to standard of living, 157
wealth: definition, 156–157; distribution in Venezuela, 198
Webber, Jeffrey, 164
Weinberg, Bill, 56
Weisbrot, Mark, 140
Welch, Cliff, 223, 236
Weyland, Kurt, 240
Wickham-Crowley, Timothy, 155
Wilkie, James, 54
Williams, Robert, 110
Wilpert, Gregory, 158, 159, 164, 165, 198, 199, 200, 201, 202, 204
Wilson, Peter, 173, 193
Wise, Timothy A., 130, 146
Wolf, Eric, 11
Wolford, Wendy, 8
Workers' Party (PT) (Brazil), 235
World Bank, 11, 14, 72–74, 79, 87–88, 90, 96–97, 235, 237
World Bank Commodity Price Data, 99
World Bank Enterprise Surveys, 4
World Bank Group, program on Urban Crime and Violence Prevention, 90
World Bank World Development Indicators, 173
World Bank World Governance Indicators, 226
World Bank's *Political Stability and the Absence of Political Violence*, 226

Xinhua News Agency, 192

Yacimientos Petrolíferos Fiscales Bolivianos (YPFB), 131
Yashar, Deborah, 130, 134, 146
Yo Sí Puedo (Yes, I Can), 201
youth, 5, 31; in Bolivia, 144; in Brazil, 237, 239; in Chile, 188; in El Salvador, 84; failure to protect and respect rights of, 88; in Guatemala, 83; job-related training, lack of investment in, 74; in Mexico, 88; in Nicaragua, 88; search for identity and self-protection, 87 : and social exclusion, 90; in the United States, 88; in Venezuela, 158

YPFB. *see* Yacimientos Petrolíferos Fiscales Bolivianos (YPFB)
Yrigoyen, Hipólito (Argentina), 218

Zapata, Emiliano (Mexico), 44, 47, 48, 55, 61
Zapatista Army of National Liberation (EZLN) (Mexico), 14, 41, 51–52, 54–55, 59
Zedillo, Ernesto (Mexico), 59
zero coca policy, Bolivia, 135
Zetas (Mexico), 57
Zona da Mata, Brazil, 237

CPSIA information can be obtained at www.ICGtesting.com
Printed in the USA
LVOW071342260113

317326LV00003B/32/P